THE
PLAYBOY
BOOK
OF
TRUE CRIME

THE
PLAYBOY
BOOK
OF
TRUE CRIME

PLAYBOY PRESS

𝐏𝐘𝐏

HANOVER, NEW HAMPSHIRE/NEW YORK, NEW YORK

The Playboy Book of True Crime
Copyright © 2007 by Playboy Enterprises International, Inc.
All rights reserved

For information about permission to reproduce selections
from this book, write to:
Playboy Press / Steerforth Press
25 Lebanon Street
Hanover, New Hampshire 03755

Jimmy Breslin, "The End of the Mob" © 2005 by Jimmy Breslin; reprinted by permission
of Sll/Sterling Lord Literistic, Inc. Murray Kempton, "Cosa Nostra" © 1970 by Murray
Kempton; reprinted with permission. Murray Kempton, "My Last Mugging" © 1971 by
Murray Kempton; reprinted with permission. Jerry Stanecki, "Playboy Interview Jimmy
Hoffa" © 1975 by Jerry Stanecki; reprinted with the permission of Jerry Stanecki (for a
CD of Jimmy Hoffa's last interview, send $14 to: Jerry Stanecki, PO Box 121, Bloomfield
Hills, MI 48301). Jerry Stanecki, "It Gets Dark at Night" © 1975 by Jerry Stanecki;
reprinted with the permission of Jerry Stanecki.

PHOTO CREDITS: Jimmy Hoffa (p. 20): Photography by Jerry Yulsman. Gary Gilmore
(p. 54): Photography by Lawrence Schiller. Lawrencia Bembenek (p. 156): Photo by
Taro Yamasaki/Time Life Pictures/Getty Images. Nicodemo Scarfo (p. 182): Image
© Bettmann/CORBIS. Lawrence Schiller (p. 276): Photography by Kathy Amerman.
Run-DMC (p. 308): Image © Lynn Goldsmith/CORBIS. Lucky Luciano: Photography by
Slim Aarons/Getty Images.

ACKNOWLEDGMENTS: Jason Broccardo,. Frederick Courtright, Kevin Craig, Kyle Kolbe,
Malina Lee, Mark Lee, Bradley Lincoln, Maria Mandis, Matt Steigbigel.

This volume has been catalogued by the Library of Congress.

ISBN 13: 978-1-58642-127-4
ISBN 10: 1-58642-127-1

FIRST EDITION

Contents

COSA NOSTRA *Murray Kempton*   1

MY LAST MUGGING *Murray Kempton*   17

JIMMY HOFFA INTERVIEW   21

IT GETS DARK EVERY NIGHT *Jerry Stanecki*   44

GARY GILMORE INTERVIEW   55

HIGH NOON IN SKIDMORE *Carl Navarre*   117

THE WISEGUY NEXT DOOR *Tom English*   143

THE BAMBI CHRONICLES *Mark Jannot*   157

COMRADES IN CRIME *Robert Cullen*   170

THE MOB'S LAST CIVIL WAR *George Anastasia*   183

DEATH OF A DECEIVER *Eric Konigsberg*   197

TOXIC TERROR *Michael Reynolds*   217

LAWRENCE SCHILLER INTERVIEW   227

VERSACE'S PARADISE *Pat Jordan*   255

DON'T WORRY, WE ONLY KILL EACH OTHER *Jamie Malanowski*   267

BIKER WARS *James R. Petersen*   276

L.A. HOOKERS, RUSSIAN GANGSTERS, SEX AND DEATH
    William Stadiem   295

THE LAST DAYS OF JAM MASTER JAY *Frank Owen*   309

STOLEN SCREAMS *Simon Cooper* 327

WHO KILLED JOEY GALLO? *Charles Brandt* 348

THE END OF THE MOB *Jimmy Breslin* 357

"The great thieves lead away the little thief."
—DIOGENES OF SINOPE

*"Most men only commit great crimes because
of their scruples about petty ones."*
—CARDINAL DE RETZ

Cosa Nostra

by **MURRAY KEMPTON**

December 1970

Crime does not pay when pretty much every sin comes for free. The grindings of this law explain the penury and even the desperation that afflict the affairs of the Mafia these days.

The Mafia has always existed to serve the personal habits that society outlaws as vices. But those make up a market continuously shrinking. Let any vice get itself popular enough and some state somewhere will license and tax it. The Mafia's pitiful efforts to penetrate legitimate business are only a tardy response to legitimacy's insistent incursion upon its hereditary domains. Organized crime was generally driven from the whiskey trade when Prohibition was repealed; the Mafia discovered Las Vegas and then had it stolen by its accountants, bit by bit. The lieutenant of Carlo Gambino who was caught selling dirty movies in his Staten Island meat market could hardly hope to compete with the capital and the imagination of Denmark. Nothing is safe from outsiders; the most admired pizza establishment in New York City turns out to be named Goldberg's.

The kingdom of the organized illicit has been reduced to street gambling and loan-sharking. We need no better witness to the uncertainties of such enterprises than Angelo "Ray" DeCarlo of Mountainside, New Jersey, who cannot afford to retire at the age of 68 after years of service crowned by the rank of a Mafia *capo* and a claim to pieces of at least two mayors and of so many policemen that it must be as hard for him to count as it seems to be to trust them.

One of his juniors asks him, "Ray, who's been winning all the money in the numbers business?"

"The detectives. The ice," DeCarlo answers.

We need no rebuttal more crushing for the notion that *mafiosi* do not pay taxes. The Jersey City Police Department's license fee for dice games reached a level so excessive that the FBI agents recording the conversations in DeCarlo's command center must have wondered about their status as a law-enforcement elite when they set down his complaints:

"DeCarlo said that everybody is trying to make a connection; and, as a result, you have to pay so much for it you can't make any money. [He] cited Hudson County as an example and said Bayonne Joe [Zicarelli] ruined Hudson County. Ray claimed that formerly, protection in the county cost $500 a month, until Zicarelli started paying everyone and now the price is $5,000 a month, which keeps you from making any money."

New York City, of course, is priced out of the market, demanding, as it does, the care and feeding of 7,000 policemen ("You'd have every sergeant in that precinct calling you up"); and even Jersey City ("the best department in the world") has become too expensive for middle-income Mafia families and has forced them to flee to the suburbs.

"Carteret [population 23,000] is the only town that's okay right now," Ray DeCarlo says. "Perth Amboy [population 40,000] is too big. You'd have 50 cops and all the detectives coming around to get on the payroll. You got to have a little town like Carteret, with about 10 or 15 cops. You put about ten of them on the payroll for a sawbuck a week, you can handle them."

Yet emigrations from urban blight are not often enough rewarded with the find of such a nest of simple folk; every country constable seems all too sophisticated about the going rate these days. A dice game is proposed for New Brunswick; Ray DeCarlo explodes when he hears the police department's service charge.

"Twenty-five hundred dollars a month, and you don't even know if you can get a crap game started down there. People who are handling these things are asking enormous prices, so you can't get no money at them. Who's going to open for them? Now, you know what you got to pay the state [troopers]? You got to pay the state at least $1,500 a month. You guys are crazy if you think you can't lose money at a crap game."

All in all, the New Jersey police seem never to have been better at enforcing the law than when their greed forced the price of their favors too high for the lawbreakers to meet. For Ray DeCarlo, the Sixties were a continuous confrontation with the agony and delusions of power: In 1962, he thought he had purchased a new state-police official; by 1963, the policeman was only a bitter thought:

DeCarlo: "Do you know what this [man] wants?"

Louis Percello, one of his branch managers: "He wants $1,000 [a month] for Long Branch and $1,000 for Asbury."

Carmine Persico, another of his branch managers: "For each town?"
DeCarlo: "Yeah. Each town. And for the whole county, he wants to make a different price. . . . He's no good. He knows every racket guy in the state. We'd have been better off with a dumb guy."

The police official whose perfidy was the subject of these moralizings left office with a reputation horridly spotted by the FBI's recordings of them; yet we owe him the compliment that an imagination too ambitious to conceive of any limit to extortion made him at least as effective a barrier to wrongdoing as the most passionate commitment to duty could have done.

The FBI has lately yielded up the records of its long eavesdropping on the business offices of Simone Rizzo "Sam the Plumber" DeCavalcante of Elizabeth, New Jersey, Angelo Bruno of Philadelphia and DeCarlo, three Mafia nobles who, if they are below the throne, are certainly closer to it than anyone whose name has been mentioned within the hearing of strangers. Thanks to these transcripts, we know more about their lives and have to believe less in their legend than we ever have before.

The FBI's transcripts of the DeCavalcante (2,220 pages, $95) and the DeCarlo (1,888 pages, $150) conversations have been photostated by Replica printers, of Elizabeth, New Jersey. Both are worth the price. Yet, the money market being tight, the thrifty may be forced to choose one or the other. Which you choose will depend on your taste. The DeCavalcante transcripts introduce us to a gentleman trying to maintain his standards in a bad profession; it thus deals largely with manners and will appeal to those to whom novels appeal. Ray DeCarlo, on the other hand, is an industrial manager contending with a trade recession; his discourses will be most useful to persons who enjoy market analysis, money and banking, economic history and other dismal sciences.

To recognize these conversations as an unprecedented resource is not, of course, to accept them as either unguarded or honestly intended. We can no more expect a businessman to be candid with partners, customers and employees than we can a policeman with a jury. But there are different kinds of lies: the constipated lie to, say, the Internal Revenue Service and the expansive lie to the companions of one's daily life. The second sort of lie is the only one useful to sober inquiry: There is a great deal to be learned about a man from the fantasies he tells his friends and even more from the fantasies he tells himself. These anxious boasts and diminishing illusions provide only the thinnest cover for the revelation of men too frequently near the ragged edge, with more to fear from the tax collector than to hope for from their own depredations, and more nearly victims than oppressors of honest people.

COSA NOSTRA

The lesson of the Mafia experience seems, in fact, to be that he who deals with respectable Americans walks on water. No matter how many cops you pay, there will always be one you overlook. The dice game on Staten Island is closed down by a police raid:

Ray DeCarlo: "[And we] were paying the borough and everybody else."

Monk Marrone (a lieutenant): "It's a new captain in there."

Jack Panels (another lieutenant): "He's been there three weeks. He came in from Harlem."

DeCarlo: "That's the end of that game. Close that game forever. No more crap games. . . . This is the last crap game we're going to have."

To go with the untrustworthy nature of the people you buy, there is the additional trouble of the untrustworthy nature of the *things* you buy. There is a persistent myth that, granted the cooperation of the police, any proprietor of a numbers bank might as well own the telephone company. The irony of this notion is suggested by one lament from Joe Ippolito, whose loyalty to Sam DeCavalcante, his Mafia boss, had been rewarded with the gift of a lottery franchise:

Ippolito [said] that he is making $700–$800 a week in his mason business. Ippolito claims that he is doing better at the mason business than with the numbers. . . . Ippolito claimed he lost $1,300 one day and $1,200 the next, paying off hits, and believes that his numbers business is on the decline. . . . He would give up his numbers in a minute if DeCavalcante would let him. Ippolito says he owes $50,000 to various people and DeCavalcante will not let him give up the numbers until he repays all the money he owes. Ippolito says he sweats out all day to six P.M., when he finds out what the day's number is.

Joe Ipp must have been flattered, if hardly gratified, when a federal grand jury indicted him last January as one of the paladins of what it called "a $20 million gambling ring."

The Mafia's clutch at legal enterprises may then be, more often than not, an effort less to disguise the profits than to conceal the losses from its illegal ones. DeCarlo's numbers bank in one New Jersey county did so poorly that he had to direct the harshest economies: He cut in half his payments to the police, and "Even the detective told us when we told him, 'We were wondering how you pay us that much.'" Sam DeCavalcante owns a plumbing-supply business and plainly cherishes it as insulation against the vicissitudes that are so much more frequent than the rewards of being a Mafia overlord.

4

"Bob, we're doing real good here," he tells his cousin. "I don't know how long it's going to last, but we're doing okay. If I can continue for two or three years, I will be able to show $40,000 or $50,000 *legitimately* and can walk out. Then my family situation will be resolved."

As long ago as 1961, when the FBI was still only a helpless eavesdropper upon his affairs, Ray DeCarlo, except for wistfully wondering where he could steal the azalea bushes to landscape his headquarters, was ready to abandon as profitless all crime except usury.

His friend Sammy Sinatra comes upon him saying goodbye to a customer. "We're getting away from all gambling," DeCarlo tells Sinatra and the FBI afterward. "The best racket in the world is the Shylock racket. This guy that just left [borrowed] $60,000. We get $200 for every $10,000 a week. That's $1,200 a week. At the end of a year, you got your money back and he still owes $60,000."

But if loan-sharking were that secure an enterprise, the Chase Manhattan Bank would certainly have thought of it; some legislature would docilely have approved five-percent-a-week-interest "high-risk emergency loans"; and Mafia collectors deputized by David Rockefeller would be working over garment manufacturers in every alley on Seventh Avenue. But the defect of loan-sharking is that its customers have no sense of honor; they either stiff the creditor or drive him to dangerous criminalities. Three years after consummating the arrangement that was supposed to ensure him $60,000 a year, perpetually renewable, Ray DeCarlo was heard to wail that the other party had stuck him for $150,000. It is impossible to withhold sympathy from those professional criminals who innocently enter into contract with persons as immoral as they are. The taint of debtors as a class is perfectly illuminated by the instance of Jimmy W., a brokerage clerk who borrowed $5,000 from Sonny Franzese and then, true to his white-collar heritage, defaulted on his pledge. He suggested that Franzese's collector take it up with his wife. ("I know she can get it, but she won't do it for me; maybe you can bust her head a little.") Franzese treated this proposal with the repugnance natural to any good family man and offered, instead, to let Jimmy W. depart in peace if he would fence a few stolen securities. Jimmy W. went at once to a district attorney and contrived the entrapment of his creditors, earning at once relief from his debts and the gratitude of honest men.

"You should never depend on a legitimate guy standing up to pressure," Ray DeCarlo often reminds his juniors. "A racketeer, no matter what a rat he is, will never squeal on anyone."

But that is a lesson his students or, for that matter, their teacher cannot afford to absorb. These are days when a *mafioso* can hardly depart one prison without, before he can hail a cab, being snatched at the curb by a police car and carried off to another. And the cause of these misfortunes, most of the time, is a dishonorable debtor. The Mafia credit department has to provide services exquisite beyond even the advertised solicitude of conventional bankers: When a saloonkeeper cannot afford to pay $30,000 owed him, Sam DeCavalcante has to hire the torch to burn down his debtor's restaurant on the promise he can collect something from the insurance. Antonio Corallo is stuck for a $40,000 loan to the New York City water commissioner; he has no way to collect except to find a contractor who will bribe his debtor, and he goes to prison for corrupting a public servant. The few resources of men who go to loan sharks do not include good faith; any collector accurately if indelicately describes the conditions essential to dealings with such persons when he tells the customer that his collateral is his eyeballs.

Such beginnings make inevitable the moment when the loan shark cries out, as Ray DeCarlo once did, "What the hell, are people supposed to take your money and just cheat you?" The creditor has no recourse then but mayhem. "Anything that keeps going all the time eventually you get grabbed," DeCarlo noticed once; and he became a proof of that axiom when loan-sharking at last brought him a 20-year sentence for laying violent hands upon the late Louis Saperstein, who had owed him $115,000. Saperstein had been a labor racketeer so brazen that he had even gone to prison for it; nonetheless, the prosecution in this case chastely called him an insurance broker, which amounts to describing Dick Turpin as a sportsman who enjoyed riding at night. But then, nothing launders a man faster than the process by which he is presented to jurors as the innocent victim of some mafioso he has cheated.

All in all, the desperation of the Mafia's search for legitimate investments must come from the knowledge that, without them, it will have to depend on those illicit ones that lead to penury. We ought, then, to understand the terror that besets Sam DeCavalcante when he learns that Lawrence Wolfson, his plumbing-supply partner, is using his fearsome reputation to persuade contractors that, if they buy from the firm, DeCavalcante will protect them from troubles with the building-trades unions, as the FBI recorded for us:

[DeCavalcante] criticized Lawrence Wolfson for his aggressiveness in "grabbing people" on union matters. Subject pointed out the danger of being charged with extortion if they continue this activity. He *noted that he feels very strongly about jeopardizing their legitimate business* . . . [and] has strictly forbidden Larry to start any more deals between contractors and labor officials.

He knew his priorities, after all.

• • •

The Sicilian spirit, faithfully preserved against every adulteration by exile, explains both the Mafia's survival in America so far and the blight that has fallen upon it now. Sicily is almost the last ornament of Western civilization whose inhabitants retain a character and a bearing that would not surprise those who described their ancestors centuries ago. The Palermo from which the late Joseph Profaci fled in the Twenties was a medieval city, and Profaci's ghost can hardly be blamed for having inhabited medieval personage.

Sicily's inhabitants have endured most of their history under foreign conquerors—up to and including the Italians. And any people whose past has been a succession of ravishments by invaders has an excuse for assuming that all property is theft, all government the imposition of larcenous aliens, and every native's proper habitat the burrow of the underground.

The Sicilian character has been exegeted down the ages most often by its oppressors; and those libels sound strikingly like what prosecuting attorneys say about mafiosi these days—or, for that matter, what members of the Society say about their brothers, too.

"Juan de Vega [their 16th Century Spanish viceroy] was fascinated to discover that some Sicilians genuinely preferred to use corruption and violence even where honest means would have attained the same end more cheaply," Denis Mack Smith tells us in *A History of Modern Sicily.*

That spirit still stirs in Ray DeCarlo, all of whose soldiers know that he can't resist a salesman who tells him the goods are stolen: "Someone said that DeCarlo would buy anything if it was swag, even if it was only worth 15 cents. Si Rega quoted Charlie Romano as saying that DeCarlo would buy a barrel of sand in the Sahara desert if the price was right."

Even the rich Sicilian assumed that there was never a good reason to pay any debt; the Palermo riots of 1647 were started by tradesmen indignant because the aristocracy would not pay its bills.

The Sicilian habit of never cooperating with the police was noticed by foreign governors as early as the 18th century, when an Austrian complained that for a Sicilian to be a witness for the prosecution "brought unspeakable disgrace even on the most abject member of society." Once, Sam DeCavalcante, then only a soldier, attempted to persuade Angelo Bruno, the Philadelphia family boss, to forgive another soldier who had for years carried the stain of having signed a confession to the police after they had seized numbers slips in his house. "No friend of ours is supposed to sign a statement with the police," Bruno goes on grimly insisting. DeCavalcante can only offer as extenuation the condition that the suspect's wife had been caught with the slips and that the raiding party threatened to arrest her unless he confessed himself solely responsible. "We're all married, Ange," DeCavalcante finally implores. "What man will let his wife go through an embarrassment standing alone with detectives, being questioned?" In his youth, Bruno coldly replies, the police had caught him and his wife in the same situation. "I gave them $700 to take me alone. But I didn't sign no statement."

The climactic act of every public uprising in Palermo's history has been to set fire to the police records. The cooperation—indeed, the competition—of policemen with criminals was always as sedulous as the citizens' resistance to policemen: The Duke of Osuna, a Spanish viceroy, introduced a series of unthinkably drastic civic reforms in 1611; but even he did not dare do more than suggest that persons with criminal records be barred from the police force. We can appreciate what an outrage to a lasting national tradition any such proposition was when we reflect that, when revolutionary Palermo ousted its Neapolitan oppressors in 1820, one of its first acts as a liberated city was to commission as people's policemen a number of convicted murderers. In 1849, having learned at least this lesson about the people's will, the restored Neapolitans installed a distinguished bandit as the chief law officer in the suburb of Misilmeri.

What Sicily's history produced was a society with no sense of the future and no concept of enterprise except to pillage the land or to drive its men, women and children as donkeys are driven. No one who witnessed the workday in the sulphur mines needed seek any farther to explain the Sicilian distaste for the appearance of hard labor. "Violence is the only prosperous industry," wrote Baron Franchetti, a Turin investigator, in 1876; he had summed up the history that is the tribal memory of the Mafia.

Violence was also the only prosperous industry of the Middle Ages. Reading about the Mafia brings continuous recollection of what we have been told about the passionate and dangerous world of 500 years ago. Scholars who exaggerate the perils to us of criminal and subversive groups have a tendency to move from there to overrating the dedication, the commitment and the honor of those who join them. The Mafia gets as much respect from its enemies as Ray DeCarlo wishes he would get from the policemen he pays to be his friends. Consider this summary of the Mafia code solemnly offered us by Dr. Donald Cressey of the University of California. What is all this except the code of chivalry in the Middle Ages?

The first article of the Mafia code, Dr. Cressey says, is "extreme loyalty to the organization and its governing elite." Or, as Roland said to Oliver, "Here we must hold for our king. A man should suffer for his Lord, endure heat and cold, though he lose his hide."

Dr. Cressey's second Mafia principle is "extreme honesty in relationships with members." In other words, as Parzival tells us, "False comradeship is fit for hell-fire."

The third article of the Mafia code is secrecy. As in what J. Huizinga, in *The Waning of the Middle Ages,* described as "the chain of Pierre de Lusignan's Sword-order [which] was made of gold S's which meant 'Silence.'"

Dr. Cressey's last Mafia rule expects "honorable behavior which sets members off as morally superior to outsiders." Or, as the old prince Gurnemanz said to Parzival: "You seem a mighty Lord. Mind you, take pity on those in need; be kind, generous and humble."

The rules of chivalry had, of course, very little relation to real life in the Middle Ages and not much more to their romances. We would have trouble imagining tricks dirtier than those Tristan and Isolde played on King Mark unless we remembered the tricks Lancelot and Guinevere played on King Arthur. The ideal suffers a similar violation by the real when we approach the intimacies of Mafia family life and hear Sam DeCavalcante talk about his sworn vassals: "Lou Lorasso is a cockroach. . . . Corky can't seem to settle down. He sent me a message saying he's going to start stealing again. . . . I have to keep Danny Noto in the family because he's a moneymaker." His troops turn out, in fact, to make no more faithful servants than the lives they have lived would lead us to expect; they make untrustworthy lieutenants, lethargic soldiers, wandering husbands; at the end of a day of trying to repair their delinquencies and stifle their scandals, DeCavalcante can only wearily decide; "In the end, the father of the family is left with the whole mess."

The Middle Ages, if seldom ethical, were continually violent in principle. To read their histories and be reminded of days where executions went on almost uninterrupted is to begin to suspect that the Mafia murder may have purposes as aesthetic as practical: "The cruel excitement and coarse compassion raised by an execution formed an important item in the spiritual food of the common people," Huizinga tells us. "They were spectacular plays with a moral. . . . During the Burgundian terror in Paris in 1411, one of the victims . . . being requested by the hangman, according to custom, to forgive him, is not only ready to do so with all his heart, but, begs the executioner to embrace him. 'There was a great multitude of people, who nearly all wept hot tears.'"

Some of the same mixture of sentiment and cruelty infuses the ritual of Mafia executions, whose amenities have been neglected of late but are still talked about with nostalgia and a certain bitterness toward coarsened modern habits. We can sense the proprieties of the good old customs in that decree of the Mafia's governing council, made necessary by the untidy disposal of Cadillac Charlie in Youngstown, which forbids the use of hand grenades in the future. Old men are proudest of those moments of chivalry when they acted upon the duty of punishing the sinner without embarrassing him:

Sam DeCavalcante: "Ray, you told me years ago about the guy where you said, 'Let me hit you clean.'"

DeCarlo: "That's right. And the guy went for it. There was me, Zip and Johnny Russell. So we took the guy to the woods. I said, 'Leave him alone, Zip.' I said, 'Look'—Itchie was the kid's name—I said, 'You gotta go, why not let me hit you right in the heart and you won't feel a thing?' He said, 'I'm innocent, Red, but if you got to do it. . . .' So I hit him in the heart and it went right through him."

The final echo of the Middle Ages sounds from that mingling of the superstitious with the cynical that the faithful bring to the contemplation of the Mafia's governing commission and which makes their conception of Brooklyn sound like what Rome must have been to the 15th century. Even from New Jersey this Holy Office is a distant mystery, its bulls reaching there as attenuated as Rome's must have to Flanders but, in this case as in that, no less sacred for being almost rumor.

Every provincial bishop approaches this college of cardinals to pray and seems, as happened in the Middle Ages, to remain to scoff. Joseph Bonanno, a Brooklyn family boss, is suddenly unfrocked by his fellow judges on the commission, and Sam DeCavalcante is drawn into the affair with vague credentials as a diplomat. At first, he approaches the sacred precinct with a reverence duly hyperbolic:

"When Joe defies the commission, he defies the whole world."

But then he watches and listens to those presences whose grandeur is the soul of the Mafia myth that is as respected in the editorial chambers of the *New York Times* as it is in any Jersey City candy store. Afterward, he can come home seeing only their warts:

You take Ange Bruno. What the hell does he know? He don't say two words. . . Jerry Catena wets his pants when they talk. . . . Now where's a guy even like Chicago [Samuel Giancana], where does he fit on the commission? You hear this guy talk and he's a nice guy. You can enjoy his company. But he's a jokester. "Hit him, hit him!"—that's all you hear from the guy. . . . Joe Columbo sits like a baby next to Carl [Gambino] all the time. He'll do anything Carl wants him to do.

Home from the pilgrimage, Sam DeCavalcante can only reflect to Frank Majuri, his underboss:
"You know, Frank, the more things you see, the more disillusioned you become. You know, honesty, honorability, all those things. . . ."
Historians tend to notice that the fundamental change in the medieval man began when he recognized that he no longer believed, in what had been the age of faith.

· · ·

The Mafia found its home in America because it had the luck to be accompanied here by an unchanged and unspoiled slice of Sicily. The first great influx of southern Italian immigrants found higher wages and steadier hours, but also indignities rather like those they had known in Sicily and Calabria. Here, as there, they were labor of the sort whose prime use is to be driven; and to drive them, Americans found other Italians, the ethnic identity of him who beats and him who is beaten being a principal of equality established in America with Emancipation; the driver, whom his victim would have called the *gabellotto* in Sicily, he called the labor boss here. The first successful American mafiosi—the Bufalinos in Scranton are one conspicuous family whose inheritance comes from that period—were these labor bosses; and their technique, the collection of small profits in perpetuity, remains at once the simplest and the most secure the Society has ever devised and the envy of those successors who were bemused by more distant and illusory horizons. "Do you know how they steal in Hoboken?" Ray DeCarlo asks. "Every man on the dock has to chip in a dollar a week. Eight hundred men— that's $800 week."
That was the Mafia the older Italo-Americans remember and not entirely without affection, since it reminded them of home—the Mafia that sold them their jobs, levied its tax on the artichoke market, governed the wheels at church festivals and would, no doubt, have kidnapped for ransom if its constituency had encompassed anyone who could pay up.

Its writ was not then conceived as running beyond the limits of our Italo-American enclaves; and the Mafia has clung closer to dependence on that original base than the persistent myth of its broader ambitions would suggest. When Vito Genovese, the defunct boss of bosses, was at the crest of his majesty, his estranged wife provided us with something unique in Mafia studies: a peek into his portfolio. By far the largest source of his income turned out to be from the New Jersey overseas branch of the Italian lottery, a business so ethnically unassimilated that its tickets were printed in Italian and the winning number drawn from the clearinghouse totals of banks in Bari and Naples. Just before the last World War, Joseph Profaci was reputed to be this country's largest importer of olive oil and a major processor of tomato paste. But, as Italo-Americans became less Italo and more American, Genovese's lottery lost more and more of its cultural appeal; and as the American diet became ever more Italianate and the pizza commenced displacing the hot dog, the major food packagers invaded Profaci's market and debased his products below the point where any man of Old World tastes could compete with them.

The Mafia's only successful foray into New World culture was during Prohibition, having begun as a response to the Italian community's traditional appreciation of wine as a diet staple and then widening its scope when all America awoke to discover its own appreciation of whiskey as a diet staple. Those few mafiosi with real property deserving the respect of their bankers built it up during Prohibition or, more precisely, upon its repeal, because they happened to have liquor stocks extensive and potable enough to be sold to legitimate distributors. Frank Costello, to take a rare case, is a certifiably wealthy man who has reached the eminence, alone in the Society, of being able to afford the care and feeding of uncountable and unproductive Irishmen. There is the legend that Costello was able to sell his bootleg stocks for $3 million. If he invested it half as well as the Rockefellers did their three billion dollars, his share of the national wealth would have outlived the New Deal's war on the rich, as large as it was in 1933.

His ownership of capital sets Costello apart from most of his brothers who, whatever their revenues, were debarred by the post-Depression tax structure from ever coming close to his property titles. The repeal of Prohibition was the first incursion of a rapacious Government on a Mafia enterprise; and it would never find one that could provide anything like the share of the gross national product that the whiskey business had. Every now and then, in a triumph of nostalgia over reality, an old mafioso gets arrested for bootlegging.

12

Repeal caught the Society in those labor-cost problems that have tormented it off and on ever since. Under Prohibition, it had acquired a work force toward whose welfare it has ever since demonstrated a sense of duty unusual in American enterprise. Ultimate though its system for breaking a man's contract may be, the Mafia never lays anyone off. It represents, in fact, the oldest welfare system in this country, antedating the New Deal and still offering unemployment benefits—$150 a week to the families of employees in jail, for example—considerably in advance of any standards yet achieved by our Social Security laws.

Scrabbling to find payrolls large enough to feed this hungry multitude at a fair labor standard has been an incessant struggle for the Mafia ever since repeal and it has carried on ever farther down the social scale. One result has been a detectable shift in the function of the Mafia-controlled labor unions, whose managers used to be able just to extort but have now been distracted by the new and pressing responsibility of providing jobs for soldiers inexperienced at even the imitation of an honest day's work. When you have persuaded a contractor to hire an unemployed *ziganette* dealer as a stonemason, you've left yourself a very small option for going back and shaking him down for cash thereafter.

Those scholars who have placed the imprint of the academies upon the notion of the Mafia's dominance of the economy would have a hard time explaining the pre-eminence in DeCavalcante's empire of Local 384 of the hod carriers' union. Local 384's position as a jewel in any Mafia boss's crown is indicated by the station of Joe Sferra, its business agent, as a *capo-regime* in the DeCavalcante family and by the anxiety with which Carl Gambino, that great prince, solicited DeCavalcante to open its hiring hall to some of the worthier of his own soldiers who were out of work. It is curious, faced with so much evidence of all this scheming to seize the high privilege of carrying brick, to be assured by Dr. Cressey that "the profits [of the Mafia] are huge enough that any given member is more likely to be a millionaire than not."

Sferra's management of Local 384 even produced a protocol dispute with John Riggi, another *caporegime* of DeCavalcante's. "Sam, I came to you yesterday," Riggi said, "because I felt that as an *amico nos* and a *caporegime*, I'm not getting the respect I deserve from Joe Sferra." The issue turned out to be Riggi's father, himself a loyal soldier, who had been groaning under the burden of the hod. Riggi had asked Sferra to find his father an easier assignment and had been refused. "I feel offended as an *amico nos*," Riggi explained, "that I can't go to my friend and get a favor for one of my soldiers. . . . I did what I did because of my father, who has lived a dog's life for three years." These are the problems of millionaires?

The shrinkage of the market and the expenses of its private welfare system quite a while ago impelled the Mafia's commission to close its books against the admission of new members. At that point, Albert Anastasia, a Brooklyn family boss, seems to have had an idea that might have saved the Society if it had not been inhibited by pride.

Anastasia began selling Mafia memberships for $40,000 apiece to young men beginning careers that they were deluded into thinking would be advanced by that credential. When the commission heard about this venture, it ordered Anastasia executed; and none of his survivors seems to have come up with a sound commercial idea since.

So the Society drifts downward, stubbornly enforcing its monopoly over goods and services that fewer and fewer people want to buy. Heroin is the only criminal staple to have lately enjoyed an increase in demand; even though we can hardly believe the disclaimers of the Mafia captains that they reject such traffic as immoral, there is every evidence that they think it too risky for indulgence in any except moments of acute fiscal desperation. They have made so little effort to organize the market that Michael Tabor, a former addict redeemed by the Black Panthers, can say that he has observed no instance of successful black capitalism except in portions of the heroin trade.

The Mafia must have been America's first conglomerate, and that contribution to our economic history may have been a factor in its ruin. An institution with too many businesses risks not having time for the proper management of any.

The Mafia, to be sure, goes on believing in the Mafia almost as stubbornly as do the journalists, the novelists and the academicians who constitute the industry of alarming us about it; the faith of witches and witch-hunters alike is proof enough of witchcraft. The talk in the Society's office is still about the great riches of its paladins, but the riches are always somewhere else. Every soldier in Chicago, we are informed—as we would be everywhere except, probably, in Chicago—makes $1,000 a week. "Listen," DeCavalcante tells an underboss, "if we don't join these big outfits and try to make a buck, we're dead."

But every now and then, reality breaks through, as in this *cri de coeur* from Anthony Russo, as he sits in his modest little duchy of Long Branch, New Jersey, and hears the crash of great kingdoms around him:

Sam, do you know how many guys are safecracking? What are they going to do? Half these guys are handling junk. Now, there's a [Mafia] law out that they can't touch it. They have no other way of making a living, so what can they do? All right, we're fortunate enough that . . . we didn't have to resort to that stuff. What are the other poor suckers going to do? Pretty soon, we'll have all the mob over here [in New Jersey]. Guys are coming over here, asking to be put on [work gambling games] and they're friends of ours, so I put them to work, because I can't let them starve to death. Sam, pretty soon I may have to say no to them, because I got to look out for myself.

The ragged actuality of this Grande Armée of the popular imagination may be the most plausible reason its soldiers seem lately so indifferent to the goal of a marshal's baton. The members of its governing commission are older on the average than sitting Justices of the United States Supreme Court: Buffalo's Stefano Magaddino is 80; Brooklyn's Carl Gambino, 68; and Detroit's Joseph Zerilli, in his 70s. Only Brooklyn's Joseph Columbo and Philadelphia's Angelo Bruno are younger than 60. None of them retire and the few who die do so peaceably.

Vacancies on this high bench have recently tended to remain unfilled; the full commission had nine members in the early Sixties; four have since departed and there is some evidence that their places are still empty. The command of the late Chief Justice Vito Genovese appears to have been diffused among Michael Miranda, Gerardo Catena and Thomas Eboli, all older than 65; Thomas Lucchese left no securely identifiable heir. Joseph Bonanno's family has been without a boss since he was deposed; the suspicion is that no one wants the job. Chicago's Sam Giancana, who, being in his 50s, represented what promise there was of a fresh generation on the court, tossed up the whole thing in 1966 and took off for the Argentine, leaving the management of his city-state to the vibrant youth of Paul Ricca, 72, and Anthony Accardo, 64.

This is largely an assemblage of personages who made their debuts in the police files of the early Twenties. If they were guarding any golden bough, some hungry junior ought successfully to have challenged one or another of them for its possession by now. Succession to Mafia command was regulated by the gun well into the Forties. But now it has been 13 years since a family boss has died anywhere but in bed. The last to get into difficulty with his comrades was Joe Bananas, who defied the whole world for two years and then settled in Tucson. The explanation of this anomaly in Mafia studies is that the Society governs itself more rationally and peacefully than it used to. It still kills people and in rather messy ways. But it kills for reasons of administration, as a management discharging unsatisfactory workmen; the difference is that no

COSA NOSTRA

one bothers to plot against the man above him on the ladder; and when the middle-level executive is that free of ambition, we ought to suspect that there isn't much left in the firm worth coveting.

Even so, we worry about the Mafia more now in its wither than we ever did in its flower. That is the normal progress of public agitation. The less we need the Mafia to serve our vices, the more essential it becomes to serve our sense of virtue. Our national history has continuously been that no improper conduct is to be noticed unless it is also exotic. For generations, the reform impulse was directed at whiskey and straight sex; but now alcoholism and adultery have become so general that virtue fixes its outrage on junkies and queers. No sinner need fear abuse once his sin becomes the sin of the majority.

We have also arrived at a time in our development when nearly every American cheats, lies or steals to some degree; there can't be many people left who could tell the whole truth to the Internal Revenue Service and not starve in the streets thereafter. The more pervasive the sin, the more intense the necessity to focus on criminals whose cultural difference from the rest of us makes it possible for us to go on thinking of crime as un-American. No American politician can run for office blaming the voters; he has to find an alien whose entire fault it all is.

Now we begin to run out of mafiosi, a resource we shall appreciate only when they are all gone, when the last of them has his elevation to boss of bosses announced in the papers and is thereupon seized and chained by the last prosecuting attorney lucky enough to attach such an ornament as train to his ascending chariot. The growth industry imperiled by the Mafia's ruin is not organized crime but organized-crime fighting. The cop who cooperates with the Mafia dies a retired cop; the district attorney who fights it can hope to die a governor emeritus. The good scores are made not by belonging to but by exposing the Mafia. Even Ray DeCarlo has come at last to understand that. In 1962, the radio brought him word that Charles Luciano was dead in Naples—Charley Lucky, the grand architect of the American Mafia's structure, the prime minister who has a place in its history like Cavour's in the forging of Italy United.

What was Ray DeCarlo's first reaction to this news?

"Ray bemoaned the fact that Charley had missed the opportunity to make $200,000 for his life story."

Ray DeCarlo and Charles Luciano both had to grow old before they suddenly understood where the money had been all along.

My Last Mugging

by **MURRAY KEMPTON**

December 1971

We are all addicts in various stages of degradation where I live on the Upper West Side, some to heroin, some to small dogs and some to *The New York Times*. The heroin is cut, the dogs are paranoid and the *Times* cheats by skimping on the West Coast ball scores. No matter; each of us goes upon the street solely in pursuit of his own particular curse.

I was plodding homeward with my *Times* at an hour no less decent than 11 on an evening in March when two figures, conspicuous through the dark for a condition of nerves frantic even for West 97th Street, came round the corner and converged upon me, one to the left and one to the right.

The one to the right was short and wore a porkpie hat of the kind one used to associate with the first account executive laid off in the agency's economy drive in the first Eisenhower recession. The one to the left was taller, sticklike, indeed, with those whitened cracks in the skin of his face that the winter of cities inflicts upon Negroes and that they call "the ashes"; and he held a knife at what I supposed to be my kidneys.

"Give us all your money," the little one stuttered. "Or we're going to cut you up right now."

"Now, be cool," the tall one said. "And just hand over your money. He means it."

Cops are said to go at criminal suspects in this fashion, in pairs, one short and mean, the other tall and protective. So here, then, were those two familiars of the station house, Jeff ravening on one side of the detainee and Mutt conciliating on the other. As jail seems to be the only institution left that can teach young black men to write, the back room of the precinct house is the last school for the techniques of negotiation. I was being accosted by ruffians who had learned their trade

17

by losing—laboratory animals who knew nothing of the science except what could be studied while being vivisected.

The knife was, to be sure, long enough and broad enough to establish itself as the one commanding presence in the assembly; still, it was a very old knife, with no sign of any recent impulse to clean it; the hand at my kidneys had, then, quite a while ago lost either the vanity that might have shined that knife or the hope that might have sharpened it.

The mind could grasp it only as an abstraction. Courage is the product of rehearsal, as cowardice is of recollection; neither comes on call upon occasions of surprise. Surprised, one merely stands and the head wanders down paths that prove how empty the event is, since they are not even literary, only sociological—a disgraceful knife, a failure of a knife, good only for my neighborhood, a knife a man would be embarrassed to carry in the East 60s, less a knife, indeed, than an artifact of urban decay. Where I live, we get the criminals and even the weapons of hopelessness we deserve.

"Gentlemen," I began, "I haven't got so much as a dollar. I do have some change and a subway token. But that's all I have. I'm sorry."

I took out my wallet and showed it to them with an anxiety to please that, at the moment, at least, had curiously less to do with the knife than with the recurrent sense of my own inadequacy on social occasions. I felt like a welsher. They had done their job; they had pulled a knife, such as it was, and quite enough for me; and I wasn't doing mine. Jeff had by now subsided into exhaustion from his bout of facsimile of active desperation; and poor Mutt was left to manage the affair to its end in disillusion.

"Let's get off the street," he said. "I gotta search you." And they pushed me unzestfully into the entranceway of a building I had never before known to be other than packed with inexplicably cheerful Latins, but empty now; and there, in the bright light that illuminated how much too old all of us were for such a scene, Mutt searched me, as the police must have trained him during his service in their laboratories, all the way to the crotch.

He came up empty and reproachful.

"You look like a workingman," he said. "What you doing out in the street with no money?"

It seemed entirely proper to apologize.

"Gentlemen," I said at last, "I feel like a shit."

"Don't you think we feel like shits?" Mutt answered. "We don't like to do this kind of thing. All we're looking for is a couple of bucks to get a shot of dope."

Where I live, we are rather stiff-necked about permitting someone else to claim the moral advantage. They turned and left the lobby, with Mutt trailing the knife slackly against his trouser leg, the whole night yet before him and without the will to recover from this first mischance.

I felt the 60 cents still in my hand and called after them, "Well, anyway, take the change."

And Mutt came back and took it, and we said good night, and I went home with no sense that I had made it up to them.

For a while afterward, I dined out on this event, and everyone I told it to seemed to find it a great relief from urban tensions. And yet the experience, whose telling seems to work to lessen the paranoia of other persons, has impossibly increased my own. Not just 97th Street but nearly every other in the city has become for me a swarm of horrible shadows. I have no way even of knowing when the fear will come over me; the other day a Negro teenager approached me in a subway station and just stood there. At last he asked for a dime and, sweating, I gave him all the change I had. He had intended nothing; and yet I was his victim; my flesh could not have crawled more shudderingly if he had pulled a gun. I have thought of buying a heavy cane. Yet if I went thus armed, I should suppose that I would bring my weapon down upon the head of whoever accosted me and then beat him passionately, if ineffectually, for mere rage at this city that has taught me that I am old and a coward. For these are scenes from which it is impossible to emerge unashamed. And I am thinking of moving away to some far place where a man can keep his mask and have no need to choose between wearing the face of the victim or the face of the beast.

Jimmy Hoffa

Jimmy Hoffa

the **PLAYBOY INTERVIEW**
December 1975

The bumper sticker read: WHERE'S JIMMY HOFFA? CALL 313-962-7297. It was on an old flatbed truck on the John C. Lodge Freeway in Detroit. Thousands of similar bumper stickers on cars and trucks across the country asked the question: What happened to the "little guy" who wheeled and dealed with money, words and clubs from the streets of Detroit to the huge white monument of a building known as Teamster International Headquarters in Washington?

Hoffa has been missing since July 30, 1975. His family last saw him when he reportedly left his home to attend a meeting with alleged mobster Anthony "Tony Jack" Giacalone, former Teamster vice-president Anthony "Tony Pro" Provenzano—a New Jersey man with alleged Mafia ties—and Leonard Schultz, a labor consultant and reputedly a key associate of Giacalone's. Supposedly, the meeting was arranged to mend fences after Hoffa and Tony Pro had a falling out while both were serving time at the Federal penitentiary in Lewisburg, Pennsylvania.

At 2:30 P.M., Jimmy called his wife, Josephine, and asked, "Has Tony Giacalone called?"

At 3:30 P.M., Hoffa called longtime friend Louis Linteau, who runs an airline-limousine service in Pontiac: "Tony Jack didn't show, goddamn it. I'm coming out there."

Two witnesses placed Hoffa in front of the Machus Red Fox restaurant in Bloomfield Township, Michigan, around the time of the call to Linteau.

Hoffa has not been heard from since.

James Riddle Hoffa devoted his life to the Teamsters Union; and if he is dead, as his family believes, it's likely that his hope to regain its presidency became his death warrant.

21

Hoffa first learned about power in the streets of Detroit in the Thirties, when being a union organizer often meant getting one's head busted—not once but many times. Hoffa stood 5'5½", had an eighth-grade education and had never read a book from cover to cover. But he understood labor contracts and how to get them.

He got his first contract by waiting for a giant load of fresh strawberries to arrive at a Kroger grocery dock, then calling a strike. Kroger got its strawberries and Hoffa got his contract—in record time.

He took charge of a 400-member union and a $400 pension fund. Within a few years, the membership was 5,000 and the fund was $50,000. Today, U. S. Teamsters number 2,200,000 and the fund is in the billions.

Tough and savvy, Hoffa whipsawed trucking companies like poker chips, playing one against another, until, by 1939, he had negotiated area-wide contracts, which were unheard of at the time. The Teamsters territory continued to grow until Hoffa controlled a series of interlocking "conferences" that spanned the country.

Then, in 1957, the Senate launched an investigation of racketeer influence and mismanagement in the Teamsters, and the McClellan Committee came down on the Teamsters with a vengeance. It charged that the Teamsters, allied with organized crime, ran their union with violence, fraud, sweetheart contracts and misuse of pension funds. Dave Beck went to jail and Jimmy Hoffa inherited the presidency of the International.

From the beginning, the confrontation between Hoffa and committee counsel Robert Kennedy was acrimonious. The hatred each man had for the other is supposed to have provoked a "get Hoffa" policy when Kennedy later became Attorney General. The bitterness did not change with time, for even recently, seven years after Kennedy's assassination, Hoffa described him simply as "that creep."

Whether or not there *was* a get-Hoffa campaign, the government *did* get Hoffa—not on the $1 million kickback indictment it returned in 1962 (which resulted in a mistrial) but for jury tampering. He was convicted in 1961 and four months later received additional convictions for mail and wire fraud and misuse of union pension funds.

Hoffa's 13-year sentence was commuted by President Nixon in 1971 after he had spent almost five years in Lewisburg prison. The commutation included a provision banning him from all union activities until 1980—a provision Hoffa claimed he did not know about (and would not have accepted) until after his release.

After getting out of jail, Hoffa was obsessed with a desire to return to union power. His suit before the U. S. District Court in 1974 failed to overturn the no-union provision of his commutation, but an appeal was still pending in the U.S. Court of Appeals. The appeal might well have been upheld by the court, and that probably would have returned Hoffa to power by 1976—unless something unexpected happened.

Before he went to prison, Hoffa named Frank E. Fitzsimmons, a 30-year friend and associate, to serve as acting president of the International. It was understood, Hoffa claimed, that he would be restored to power when he was released from prison, a release Fitzsimmons was pledged to expedite. After his release, Hoffa claimed that Fitzsimmons had double-crossed him, that he had made no effort to get him out of jail and, in fact, had decided that he liked his job as president of the International and intended to keep it.

Jerry Stanecki, an investigative reporter for WXYZ Radio in Detroit, owned by ABC, had had several long conversations with Hoffa by spring of this year. When PLAYBOY asked Stanecki to conduct a full-length interview, Hoffa told the reporter that he didn't want to be in a "magazine with tits on the back of my picture." He finally agreed, however. But because of the extraordinary circumstances surrounding this interview, not all of Hoffa's allegations could be verified through normal channels. The last conversations took place in June, a little over a month before the disappearance, and since events intervened, we were unable to send Stanecki back to Hoffa with the customary follow-up questions. Stanecki reports:

"I first met Jimmy about two years ago. His wife and son had been tossed out of their Teamster jobs—Jimmy Jr., a lawyer, as counsel, Jo as head of the women's political-action group. Newspapers were filled with speculation about a deepening Hoffa-Fitzsimmons rift. Most of the reports suggested that Hoffa himself had planted the speculation in the press. It was only after I called the manager of the condominium Jimmy owns in Florida and asked her to knock on his door with a request that he call me that I learned Hoffa hadn't talked with any reporters. 'I said no such a goddamn thing,' he told me.

"Apparently, he was impressed with the idea that I had gone to the trouble of finding him and getting his side of the story. From then on, Jimmy was available to me. He checked me out to see if I could be trusted, of course. And apparently I *could* be trusted. Often during the past two years I have gotten calls from Teamster officials, saying, 'Jimmy says you're okay. Here's what's going on.'

"I saw him many times and talked with him on the phone literally hundreds of times. Hoffa, a man who hated the press, seemed to consider me a friend.

"Jimmy lived in a modest lake-front home in Lake Orion, about 40 miles from Detroit. It sits on four acres of land that is neatly trimmed and decorated with statues of deer. He installed a teeter-totter and a merry-go-round for his grandchildren, to whom he was obviously devoted.

"When I arrived at his home to begin the *Playboy Interview,* Hoffa was dressed in work pants, blue shirt and chukka boots. He was feeling good. It was a warm, sunny May day. We walked first to the lake in front of his house, where he had been raking leaves and sticks from the swimming area. Back at the house, he offered me some coffee and we walked to his new kitchen. There we sat down and began to talk.

"It was said that Jimmy Hoffa's penetrating stare could make strong men wither, but he could also be a charmer. My wife, Carolyn, met Hoffa only under protest: As we drove onto his property, she said she really didn't feel comfortable and asked that we 'just stay 10 minutes.' As we walked to the door, I knew what she was thinking: Where are the walls, the bodyguards, the dogs? When we were sitting at a lawn table with Jimmy and Josephine, Carolyn asked him about security. Jimmy laughed. 'I don't have a bodyguard,' he said. 'If there's a problem, I can handle it.'

"Later, as we drove home, Carolyn said, 'Gee, he's a likable man, after all.' He is—or was—indeed. But it wasn't the only quality that took him to the top."

PLAYBOY: Let's start with your personality. You've been described as a man with a very big ego. Is that accurate?

HOFFA: Certainly, I got an ego! A man don't have an ego, he don't have any money and he don't have any ambition. Mine's big enough to do the job I wanna do. Actually, an ego is just imagination. And if you don't have any imagination, you'll be working for somebody for the rest of your life.

PLAYBOY: You don't like taking orders from anyone, then.

HOFFA: What the hell do you think, somebody's gonna push me? I don't get pushed. If somebody argues with me, I'll take him on; if somebody wants to rassle with me, well, I'll take him on, too.

PLAYBOY: You're 62 this year. Have you mellowed any?

HOFFA: Oh, I wouldn't say mellowed. I'd just say I got more common sense now than I had before. I used to take anybody on. Now I select who I take on.

PLAYBOY: How wealthy are you?

HOFFA: I think I'll be able to eat and live comfortable for the rest of my life. But so far as what I have . . . let it speak for itself. It's been in the press.

PLAYBOY: Are you a millionaire?

HOFFA: I would say.

PLAYBOY: We heard that you and Jimmy Jr., got into a discussion on money and you commented, "How many men can come up with two million cash immediately?"

HOFFA: I would say, exactly right. I'll put it to you this way: I just read an article the other day where they estimate that there's less than one half of one percent of people who can lay their hands on $50,000 liquid cash overnight.

PLAYBOY: So you're comfortable. What else are you living for?

HOFFA: For the sake of living. I enjoy every minute of it, good, bad or indifferent. I enjoy life every day—and I'm looking forward to spending that life as part of the labor movement.

PLAYBOY: Okay, let's get into that. By the terms of your release from prison, you've been banned from participating in the labor movement until 1980, and you're appealing that in the courts. If the courts ruled in your favor and you got your position back as president of the Teamsters, what would be your first priority?

HOFFA: Restructure the union back the way it was when I was there and reinstitute the trade divisions. Likewise, I'd reinstitute some additional organizers for the purpose of having master contracts. There's no other way unions can survive, except with master contracts—whether it's the building trades, retail clerks, meat cutters or anybody else. We need a common expiration date for the contracts of *all* unions.

PLAYBOY: That would virtually give you the power to bring the entire economy to a halt.

HOFFA: Well, corporations have it. The oil cartel, the lumber cartel, the steel cartel—they're all exactly the same.

PLAYBOY: But they're not united, the way you want the unions to be.

HOFFA: Of course they're united. There isn't a damned thing that happens in one of those industries that doesn't conform to what industry leaders decide together. The only thing they don't discuss collectively—at least openly—is prices. But as far as everything else goes, you'll find they have a master organization, a master contract. Put it to you this way: So far as power is concerned, does anybody believe the premiums of insurance companies are almost all uniform by accident? Is it an accident that if the price of gasoline goes up in one company, all the other prices go up the same rate in a matter of weeks?

THE PLAYBOY INTERVIEW

PLAYBOY: Still, giving one man control over union contracts with a common expiration date isn't something the Congress would look upon very favorably.

HOFFA: The Congress of the United States wants to be judge, jury and prosecutor over what's good for the American people. And they think anyone who has a bloc of votes is dangerous. Truth is, everything the Congress has touched has been a failure. Can't show me one progressive thing they've did that didn't turn out a failure.

PLAYBOY: What you want, however, would make Hoffa king, wouldn't it?

HOFFA: Not true.

PLAYBOY: Wouldn't it allow Hoffa to control the economy, to control politicians?

HOFFA: One of these days it will happen *without* Hoffa. And it's happening today. With inflation, unemployment, the states and cities going bankrupt, people will accept labor leaders in positions of power in the government, they'll want a voice in what's good for *them.* As far as being a king goes, well, I don't know if a king has that power today. There's damned few kings left. And there's gonna be a damned sight less before it's over with. But by birthright, by being an American, you're entitled to have a job. If the democratic system cannot supply you with a job, you have to change the system of government—whether it's Hoffa, politicians or whoever. Call it what you wanna call it.

PLAYBOY: How would you keep corruption out of government?

HOFFA: Isn't there corruption now? You sat through Watergate, didn't you? You see it going into the CIA, going into the FBI, going into state and city government. What is corruption? Is it corruption that you give a man a year's guarantee that he'll have a roof over his head, something to eat? Is it corruption that government should take over the utilities so people won't be deprived of the necessities of life? Take, for instance, Honduras. The banana people said they'd give over $2 million to the government there—is that corruption or survival? Would bananas go off the shelves of every supermarket in America if they hadn't paid? Of course they would. Now, what are you gonna do about it? What's corruption today is not corruption tomorrow.

PLAYBOY: Have the Teamsters gone to hell since you were forced out?

HOFFA: Well, they haven't advanced. There are no master contracts, other than the ones I left them. The organizing campaigns and the joint councils of the local unions have deteriorated. And the morale of the local officers, the organizers, is at an all-time low, from what I hear. Even the members feel uncomfortable they don't have someone steerin' the ship. The leaders are too busy on the golf course, flyin' around in

26

seven jet airplanes they own. Why the hell do they own *seven?* Most corporations don't own that many.

PLAYBOY: Do you blame the present head of the Teamsters, Frank Fitzsimmons?

HOFFA: Fitzsimmons has failed. He has failed in every promise he made to the union convention. He can't show one single thing that he said he would do that he did. Can't show one thing. Not one.

PLAYBOY: How did you and Fitzsimmons split?

HOFFA: Well, as far as I'm concerned, when I found out that Fitzsimmons, uh, lied when he said he'd been talking confidentially to John Mitchell about getting me out of prison.

PLAYBOY: Let's backtrack a bit. At first you thought Fitzsimmons was doing everything he could to get you out of prison?

HOFFA: During the whole time I was in prison, Fitzsimmons kept tellin' everybody—my son, my lawyers, all the union representatives—"Now, don't do anything, you'll rock the boat. I'm taking care of it with Mitchell." Well, when Mitchell later gave his deposition, he said the first time Fitzsimmons ever talked to him about me was in June 1971. I'd been in jail five years. It was when I'd already resigned and given Fitzsimmons the green light to become president. Then I found out that he'd fired Edward Bennett Williams as Teamsters' counsel and replaced him with Charles Colson. And when I found out there was a restriction on my parole until 1980, it didn't take a ton of bricks to fall on me to put two and two together—that he'd been lyin' all along.

PLAYBOY: You said Fitzsimmons kept saying he was going to work on Mitchell. Meaning what?

HOFFA: He claimed to all and any that he was responsible for getting me a rehearing on my parole and that Mitchell was going to take executive action to get me out of prison. As I said, when Mitchell gave his deposition later on, he said, "I talked to Fitzsimmons about Hoffa, among other things, in June 1971." Well, what a flat lie Fitzsimmons had been tellin' everyone in the union—for a period of almost five years!

PLAYBOY: How was Fitzsimmons going to persuade Mitchell?

HOFFA: I suppose by using his alleged influence with Nixon and by using his, uh, political arm to support the Republican Party.

PLAYBOY: With campaign contributions?

HOFFA: I don't know about that. I suppose he said that he'd give him $14,000 [a publicly disclosed campaign contribution], which is a lot of nonsense. But the truth of the matter is he never did anything. I also found out from Dean that he didn't even *know* Fitzsimmons and he was sitting right outside Nixon's door.

PLAYBOY: John Dean?

HOFFA: Yeah. And it'd be damned funny that anyone could go in and out of the White House without knowing John Dean. In any case, what Colson did was wait until the President was coming in or out of his office, then introduce him: "Mr. President, this is Frank Fitzsimmons." "Hello, how are ya?" Then Colson would take him up to have dinner in the Senate Building. Well, that's a hell of a big deal. Anybody must be out of their mind if they're head of the Teamsters Union and can be brushed off that way. In any case, John Dean testified that he and Colson had discussed the 1980 restriction and what with Colson already having the offer from the Teamsters to become general counsel, it all adds up to . . . it *leads* me to believe that Fitzsimmons deliberately double-crossed, uh, the membership, the convention, my lawyers and myself. And that's it. So I don't wanna do business with a double-crosser . . . or a liar.

PLAYBOY: If Fitzsimmons, Colson and Dean were working against you, how did you finally get a parole?

HOFFA: It came about because over 1,500,000 signatures were sent to the President of the United States. It came about by hundreds of thousands of letters going to the Attorney General and the President. Since Nixon was facing an election, in my opinion he didn't want to have to face all those people. So he met with Mitchell, according to Mitchell's affidavit, and they discussed the release of one James R. Hoffa. And it was agreed I would be released before Christmas 1971.

Immediately after that, when the recommendation was sent out, Dean intercepted it. Dean testified, or implied, that he and Mitchell talked about inserting the 1980 restriction into the recommendation at that time. Mitchell denies this.

PLAYBOY: So the original recommendation made by Mitchell and President Nixon did not have the 1980 restriction.

HOFFA: It did not. Furthermore, Dean called in Colson and [Presidential aide] Clark Mollenhoff and they decided on the restriction without talking to the Attorney General or the President and rewrote the recommendation, keeping it confidential even from everyone else at the White House—until 14 minutes after I was out of jail. They were convinced that it I knew the 1980 restriction was there. I wouldn't have accepted.

PLAYBOY: But the President *did* sign the order, didn't he?

HOFFA: Aw, sure. Along with 212 other ones. But I'm sure the President didn't think Mitchell had changed what they'd agreed upon. And I'm sure he didn't read through 212 commutations and pardons.

PLAYBOY: How about you? You read it, didn't you?

HOFFA: I *couldn't* read it! I wasn't there. Wasn't anything I signed.

PLAYBOY: And your attorneys?

HOFFA: *Nobody* knew! Fourteen minutes after I'd gotten out of jail, they announced the restriction to the warden, to my attorneys, to the public. I found out about it hours later on the news. When I went to see the head of the parole board after the holidays, *he* didn't know about it. Nobody had informed him. He had to call Washington to find out what they were talking about and it wasn't until January 14, 1972, that I received notification of the restriction in the mail. And I refused to sign it.

PLAYBOY: There was no hint, no suggestion before you left prison?

HOFFA: I had asked the warden specifically, was there any restriction other than the one banning me from union activity until March 1973 [when Hoffa would have been released anyway]? He called Washington and said, "No."

PLAYBOY: But you signed *something* to get out of Lewisburg, didn't you?

HOFFA: Commutation. Read every word of it. Being suspicious-minded as I am concerning public people, I asked the warden to call Washington and find out if that's all there was. He came back and said that was all there was to it.

PLAYBOY: So the letter you got on January 14 was the first you saw of the 1980 restriction?

HOFFA: That's right. And I never signed it to this day.

PLAYBOY: Your signature doesn't appear on any document that relates to the 1980 restriction?

HOFFA: Never will be on it.

PLAYBOY: And you blame whom?

HOFFA: In my opinion, Dean, Mollenhoff, Colson and Fitzsimmons.

PLAYBOY: So there was a conspiracy to keep Hoffa out of the union?

HOFFA: I would say, uh, there certainly was an understanding of, uh, everyone of 'em getting a piece of the pie they wanted. And they used Dean to get the pie.

PLAYBOY: What would Dean get out of it?

HOFFA: Oh, probably a favor to Colson. I don't know if he got any promises of the hereafter, when he'd be out of government. But it could have been a favor to Colson for whatever dealings they had together. If you read the Watergate deal, they had a lot of dealings together. Scratching each other's back, I suppose.

PLAYBOY: And Colson?

HOFFA: Colson would receive, first of all, the job of general counsel to the Teamsters.

29

PLAYBOY: How about Mollenhoff?

HOFFA: He'd have satisfied his own, uh, dislike for myself, to keep me out of the union.

PLAYBOY: Couldn't Fitzsimmons have gotten to Nixon directly through Colson?

HOFFA: Reading the White House transcripts, I don't think Colson was in much of a position to influence Nixon. I think he used Dean rather than the President to accomplish what he wanted.

PLAYBOY: Straight question: Was there any *financial* deal made with Nixon to get you out of prison?

HOFFA: Fitzsimmons says no. He says he only gave him $14,000.

PLAYBOY: So there was no offer of what might be called a bribe?

HOFFA: Absolutely not. Positively not. I did not.

[At this point, there was an interruption and Hoffa walked over to the window of his kitchen. The tape recorder was turned off, but, by mutual agreement, the conversation remained on the record. The interviewer asked: "Come on, Jimmy, was *any* money paid to Richard Nixon to get you out of prison?"

Hoffa turned from the window and said, "Yaaaaa."

The interviewer asked, "How much?"

The reply, deadly serious, came after a long pause: "You don't *wanna* know."

A week later, with the tape recorder turned on, the interviewer reminded Hoffa of this exchange. Hoffa denied saying "any such goddamned thing."]

PLAYBOY: But you had no one approach Nixon and say. "Look, $100,000 goes into your campaign . . ."?

HOFFA: I had nobody go there. If any body went there, it was without my knowledge—even though there is a statement floating around that Allen Dorfman [a special consultant to the Teamsters' largest health-and-welfare fund] said at his trial in New York that he had a receipt signed by Mitchell for a large sum of money—as a contribution.

PLAYBOY: How large was the sum supposed to be?

HOFFA: Now, that's never been proven. Mitchell denied it under oath. What the hell's the name of the other guy—Stans? Yeah, Stans. He denied it, too.

PLAYBOY: Is this Dorfman a friend of yours?

HOFFA: A hundred percent.

PLAYBOY: Isn't he the man you set up in business through your Chicago contacts back in the Fifties?

HOFFA: No. Nobody set him up in business at all. Allen Dorfman submitted a sealed bid for the insurance. And by unanimous vote of the trustees, he became the agent for the insurance company.

PLAYBOY: But didn't you control the trustees at the time?

HOFFA: I spoke my piece in favor of Dorfman. Of course I did.

PLAYBOY: All right. Besides Fitzsimmons it seems as if Colson were the one person who stood to gain most by the 1980 restriction. When did he go on the Teamsters' payroll?

HOFFA: Within months of the time I got out of prison. He certainly didn't command, by reputation, the retainer he got. Certainly didn't do that.

PLAYBOY: How much did he get from the Teamsters?

HOFFA: All told, probably in the neighborhood of $300,000 a year.

PLAYBOY: What qualifications did Colson have to be a Teamsters lawyer?

HOFFA: Well, he had a shingle.

PLAYBOY: So it was a deal?

HOFFA: In my opinion.

PLAYBOY: Jimmy, what *about* Frank Fitzsimmons?

HOFFA: Well, what the hell about him? I already said he's a double-crosser. And that's all there is to it.

PLAYBOY: You said——

HOFFA: A man I took off the truck! Made him an officer in the union, saw that he had more than one suit for the first time in his life, that he lived in a decent home, had an expense account! Kept raising him through the ranks of labor! And when I went to jail, he took over the presidency and then he became power-hungry. He accepted the belief that he was a great labor leader and came about doing what he did in the 1980 restriction. In my opinion.

PLAYBOY: Why did he come to believe he was a great labor leader?

HOFFA: How the hell do I know? Look at some of the Congressmen and Senators we got. They couldn't spell rat backward, they couldn't make a living! They get elected and for Chrissakes they're on TV, yakking around, telling you how to run the world, and they can't even run their own life! Same thing with him. People look in the mirror too often. They grow by inches—sideways and down—but they don't grow. Their heads get fatter but they don't get any more sense that they had before. I just think Fitzsimmons has gone completely power nuts, that's all. Someone took him up to the top of the mountain. Showed him the valley and he bought the valley. But he forgot the membership and he forgot the officers and forgot his responsibility to the oath he took for office.

PLAYBOY: Will Fitzsimmons be in office through 1980?

THE PLAYBOY INTERVIEW

HOFFA: I don't think Fitzsimmons will run in 1976.

PLAYBOY: Why?

HOFFA: Well, the best evidence is he's building a home at La Costa. With his golfing and parading around all over the country in his jet, I don't think he'll be a candidate.

PLAYBOY: You were the one who extended the first loan to develop La Costa, somewhere around $10 million, isn't that right?

HOFFA: Somewhere around there, yeah. Been a long time ago.

PLAYBOY: How did it start?

HOFFA: Well, Moe Dalitz was the major owner of the Desert Inn. We loaned him money, he paid it back. When he wanted to go into the La Costa enterprise, real estate was booming at the time. And it couldn't go wrong. *That* real estate's a good buy today!

PLAYBOY: Was Meyer Lansky part of that?

HOFFA: Meyer Lansky had no more to do with Moe Dalitz than you had, in my opinion.

PLAYBOY: Aren't you and Lansky good friends?

HOFFA: I know him.

PLAYBOY: Ever do business with him?

HOFFA: Nope. Never asked me to. My opinion, he's *another* victim of harassment!

PLAYBOY: Then you don't think he's a member of organized crime?

HOFFA: I don't believe there is any organized crime, period. Don't believe it. Never believed it. I've said it for the last 40 years. *Hoover* said it! Supposed to be the greatest law-enforcement man in America, with the means to find out. He said there was no Mafia, no so-called organized crime.

PLAYBOY: No Mafia?

HOFFA: That's what *he* said. That's what Hoover said.

PLAYBOY: But in 1958, during the McClellan hearings, it was said that you knew more dangerous criminals than Dave Beck.

HOFFA: Ah-ha! That's a different question! I don't deny the fact that I know, I think, what's going on in most of the big cities of the United States. And that means knowing the people, uh, who are in the big cities. I'm no different than the banks, no different than insurance companies, no different than the politicians. You're a damned fool not to be informed what makes a city run when you're tryin' to do business in the city.

PLAYBOY: What about people like Lansky and Frank Costello?

HOFFA: What about 'em?

PLAYBOY: The McClellan Committee said that they were organized-crime

members, members of the Mafia.

HOFFA: Yeah, yeah, sure. They said I was associated with the Mafia. They said Dorfman was part of the Mafia. And it's a complete, 100 percent lie. They know it. Everybody else knows it. So it's easy to say, "Well, he's a Mafia member, 'cause he got an Italian name." Once in a while they say, for a man like Lansky, who's a Jew, "Oh, well, he was accepted."

PLAYBOY: How about Paul "The Waiter" Ricca?

HOFFA: What about him? Jesus Christ Almighty! He was in Chicago for 99 years and a day and if they thought he was so much involved in organized crime, why the hell didn't they arrest him? Hell of a note that the FBI, and the Congress, and the newspapers and everybody else says So-and-So's part of the Mafia; So-and-So's doing this. . . . Why don't they arrest him? Why the hell don't they put him on trial? What the hell they doing? Keeping him alive, like a mummy, so they can keep writing about him?

PLAYBOY: So where is Ricca now?

HOFFA: Dead! [*Pause*] Dead! Why the hell—— What are you talking about all these people?

PLAYBOY: What about Johnny Dio?

HOFFA: Friend of mine. No question about that.

PLAYBOY: Member of organized crime?

HOFFA: Like *you* are.

PLAYBOY: Member of the Mafia?

HOFFA: Like *you* are.

PLAYBOY: Wasn't he convicted of extortion?

HOFFA: Ah-ha! That's a different question. I know Johnny's case. I know what Johnny's in jail for. Don't agree with it. Trying to help him get out. Should be out. Our association's trying to help him get out. And he's a victim of newspaper publicity, just like I was. [*Pause*] Damned funny, though! All these people are supposed to have millions and millions of dollars. Can't afford to hire lawyers. [*Pause*] Damned funny. I saw some of the biggest ones that there was supposed to be, in prison. And their wives were on welfare and they didn't have enough money to come down and visit 'em. And yet they keep talking about the millions they got.

PLAYBOY: Like who?

HOFFA: Well, I don't care to mention their names and embarrass them. But I seen 'em. They're there. [*Pause*] Damned funny. I know people in town *here*, right in Detroit, say they're part of the Mafia! Well, Christ! They ain't making a living! How come, if they're part of the Mafia, they're not making a living?

PLAYBOY: Care to be specific?

HOFFA: No, I don't want to . . . everybody knows who they are . . . the police department knows, the prosecutor's office knows, the media knows. . . .

PLAYBOY: What about Tony Giacalone?

HOFFA: Giacalone! Giacalone! Giacalone's a businessman!

PLAYBOY: Didn't he have dealings with La Costa?

HOFFA: La Costa! What the hell's *he* got to do with La Costa?

PLAYBOY: You mean he had no involvement at all?

HOFFA: Record speaks for itself. Got nothin' more to do with La Costa than *you* have. May have visited it—went to the spa or to one of the golf tournaments down there, 'cause he's a golfer. Why, he's got as much to do with La Costa as *you* have!

PLAYBOY: But Giacalone was named as a member of organized crime by a Senate committee back in——

HOFFA: What the hell has that got to do with it? I appeared in front of the same committee and they lied about me! They lied about Giacalone! They never proved it! And if they *had* such a charge, why in the hell didn't they charge everybody with conspiracy and go to court?

PLAYBOY: Conspiracy's hard to prove; it almost *impossible* to prove.

HOFFA: Like *hell*! The easiest crime in the world to prove. Anybody indicated for a conspiracy, a lawyer will tell you it's the easiest crime the Government can prove. And that's why they put it on the books as conspiracy. The mere fact that you meet with somebody, or the fact that circumstantial evidence is involved . . . What the hell're you talking about? It the easiest crime in the book to prove. That's why they use conspiracy.

PLAYBOY: As far as conspiracies go, you've always believed that the Government was out to "get Hoffa," haven't you?

HOFFA: Of course. First, Bobby Kennedy wanted to use the Teamsters as a vehicle to get the Kennedy name out front with something that was probably the greatest thriller that ever appeared on TV [the televised McClellan hearings]. And when he couldn't bull me, when he couldn't take over the Teamsters, why, it became a vendetta between he and I. And he used $12 million in government money to convict me. Who the hell ever heard of the Kennedys before the McClellan Committee? They were nobody. A bootlegger, the old man. Common, ordinary bootlegger.

PLAYBOY: Have you ever wiretapped anybody?

HOFFA: I've hired people to secure information for me where they could possibly secure it.

PLAYBOY: Did they secure it by wiretapping?

HOFFA: I didn't ask them. Not interested

PLAYBOY: Did you ever tap Bobby Kennedy?

HOFFA: If they did, I don't know. But I *received* information on Kennedy How they got it, none of my business. Wouldn't wanna know it.

PLAYBOY: Did you tap any FBI agents?

HOFFA: No. *I* didn't tap 'em. Somebody else . . . uh, Bernie Spindel [a freelance electronics expert] set up a monitoring system in Chattanooga and took information outta the air from three of the FBI radio channels. We found out the FBI was violating the law; they were surveilling my lawyers and my witnesses. We also proved they were attempting to get information which was tantamount to interfering with justice. And then we submitted the transcripts to the judge, Frank Wilson. He opened the envelope, then charged we had tricked him and he had a fit. The next batch we handed him, Wilson wouldn't open; I think it's because among the transcripts was one of him making a telephone communication to Bobby Kennedy—and that was in the middle of the trial.

PLAYBOY: So then you had issued orders to tap Wilson's phone?

HOFFA: No. It's not a question of tapping Wilson's phone.

PLAYBOY: Kennedy's phone, then?

HOFFA: No. Taken out of the air.

PLAYBOY: Bullshit! You can't just take phone conversations "out of the air."

HOFFA: Don't tell *me* it's bullshit! Don't tell me what they can do. I have the proof! Frank Wilson finally admitted he *did* talk to Bobby Kennedy during the trial, although he said he was talking about hiring clerks for overtime typing. But it took 45 minutes to do it! [Judge Wilson says that at no time did he communicate with Kennedy.]

As to taking out of the air, Bernie did it with about a ton of equipment he brought down with him. We gave him a suite and set it all up and, being the best expert in the United States, he just reached out with his communication system and took it out of the air. Right outta the air, everything that was going on. They knew it could be done. They do it every day in the week.

PLAYBOY: There's a story that you ordered Marilyn Monroe's phone tapped——

HOFFA: That's the silliest thing I ever read in my life.

PLAYBOY: And that the tapes are still supposed to be in existence.

HOFFA: Aw, that's a lotta crap! I never said no such thing. I read that stupid statement in that stupid book. And, uh, the "Mailer" who wrote that book, I think his name was——

PLAYBOY: Norman Mailer.

HOFFA: The stupidest thing I ever read in my life. He admitted he hardly interviewed anybody, that all he did was gather information other people had wrote and did a book on it. [It was not Mailer's *Marilyn* that contained the allegation Hoffa referred to, but *The Life and Curious Death of Marilyn Monroe*, by Robert F. Slatzer.] And I understand right now he's in the process of writing a book on me. When he does, I'm gonna sue him. Very simple.

PLAYBOY: What if Mailer called and asked to interview you?

HOFFA: Wouldn't talk to him, under no circumstances. I think he must be some kind of nut.

PLAYBOY: All right, what about the allegations about the Marilyn Monroe tapes?

HOFFA: Marilyn Monroe? I never knew she *existed* with Bobby Kennedy. If I did, I would've told him about it in open hearing. I already *had* a tape on Bobby Kennedy and Jack Kennedy, which was so filthy and so nasty—given to me by a girl—that even though my people encouraged me to do it, I wouldn't do it. I put it away and said the hell with it. Forget about it.

PLAYBOY: What was on the tape?

HOFFA: Oh, their association with this young lady and what they had did, and so forth. I got rid of the tape. I wouldn't put up with it. [*Pause*] Pure nonsense.

PLAYBOY: You didn't feel you had a way to get back at Bobby?

HOFFA: I would not embarrass his wife and family.

PLAYBOY: Well, you've mentioned it now.

HOFFA: Let it be at that. Let it stay that way. I'm not talkin' about what's dirty and nasty. Maybe some people wouldn't think it. I did.

PLAYBOY: Who was the girl?

HOFFA: I'm not sayin' that. [*Pause*] *I* know.

PLAYBOY: All right. Did you ever threaten to kill Bobby Kennedy?

HOFFA: Nope. Another lie.

PLAYBOY: What about killing people?

HOFFA: Self-preservation's a big word.

PLAYBOY: Have you ever exercised your need for self-preservation?

HOFFA: Never had to.

PLAYBOY: You've never killed anybody?

HOFFA: Never had to exercise the self-preservation. But I'm certainly not going to let someone kill *me*.

PLAYBOY: Have you ever *ordered* anybody to be killed?

HOFFA: [*Pause*] Mmm, nope.

PLAYBOY: Killing isn't the way to solve a problem?

HOFFA: No, I don't think it solves anything. It just creates a few more problems—the FBI, the local police, newspapers. [*Pause*] Kill 'em by propaganda. Kill 'em by votes. But not *physically* kill 'em.

PLAYBOY: How about busting heads?

HOFFA: Nothin' wrong with that, if they're in your way, uh, tryin' to break a strike or tryin' to destroy the union. Nothin' wrong with that, in my opinion.

PLAYBOY: You *do* have a reputation for busting heads that goes way back.

HOFFA: Survival of the fittest, my friend. What do you think industry does? What do you think the police do? Police broke our heads every day of the week in 1932. Ford Motors? They cracked heads all over the lot. Unless you were able to take care of yourself, they'd crack your head where it'd kill you. I survived.

PLAYBOY: Have you ever hired any bodyguards?

HOFFA: Never. Don't need 'em. Don't need 'em. They're in your way.

PLAYBOY: But not everybody loves Jimmy Hoffa.

HOFFA: I'm not interested in what everybody does. You got a bodyguard, you become careless, and if you look at all the gangsters that were *killed* with bodyguards, you'll know they went to sleep. I don't *care* to go to sleep.

PLAYBOY: What do you mean, gangsters?

HOFFA: People who allegedly were, uh, involved in bank robberies and other kind of illegal enterprises individually. They had bodyguards. How about the question of Roosevelt? He had all *kind* of bodyguards down in Florida, didn't he? Little guy pops up nobody ever heard of. He starts shooting. He killed the mayor [Anton Cermak of Chicago], didn't he? Well, what do you want? What do you want? Bodyguards make you go to sleep and I don't care to go to sleep. The only guy who needs a bodyguard is a liar, a cheat, a guy who betrays friendship. I don't do any of them. What the hell do you need a bodyguard for?

PLAYBOY: So you're not afraid of anything?

HOFFA: What the hell am I gonna be afraid of? I'm 62 years old. I should've been dead maybe 25 years ago. Lived three lives. Well, what am I gonna be afraid of? Never was afraid in my life and don't intend to start tomorrow. Who's gonna bother me? *They* do? Well, then I'll do somethin' about *that*.

PLAYBOY: You'll do what, exactly?

HOFFA: Whatever I have to do.

PLAYBOY: What do you mean?

HOFFA: Just whatever I have to do to eliminate somebody bothers me. . . . I'll do whatever I *have* to do.

PLAYBOY: Such as killing them?

HOFFA: Well, if they try to kill *me* and I'm in the position to take away their gun, or whatever the hell they're using against me. If they get shot, that's their trouble. It ain't mine. Hell, if I had people try to kill me, I survived it. Didn't have no bodyguard, but I survived the . . . the *threat* of being killed, the *attempt* to be killed. I'm still here. 'Cause I keep my eyes open—drive my own car, go where I wanna go, never need no bodyguard. I don't cheat nobody. I don't lie about nobody. I don't frame nobody. I don't talk bad about people. If I do, I tell 'em. So what the hell's people gonna try to kill *me* for?

PLAYBOY: To get you out of the way. If you win in your fight against the 1980 restriction, don't you think somebody will try to have you killed?

HOFFA: Hell, no. Hell, no. Go out and ask any 10 people you want—not union members—any 10 people in the United States, ask 'em whether or not I should have the right to get back in the union, and whether or not Fitzsimmons double-crossed me. You'll get your answer.

PLAYBOY: Do you think Fitzsimmons might go as far as trying to eliminate you?

HOFFA: Hasn't got the guts.

PLAYBOY: If he's gutless, then why did you bring him up through the ranks and give him the power he now has?

HOFFA: Very simple. We never asked Fitzsimmons to go on a picket line or get involved in violence. We never asked Fitzsimmons to go out and do anything that could get him bad publicity, because in every union you have to have somebody who the newspapers can't rap.

PLAYBOY: Let's return to the subject of organized crime.

HOFFA: Look, I never seen *a single person,* in the whole United States, even in front of the Senate committees, that under oath would say, "Jimmy Hoffa, Joe Doakes or Pete Wilkes is part of organized crime!"

PLAYBOY: Oh, come on. What about Frank Costello?

HOFFA: *They never said it!* They said that Frank Costello was a gambler, that he was an associate of organi—— Of, uh, of hoodlums. Never once did they say, *"He is a member of."*

PLAYBOY: Who's the guy who got shot in New York at Columbus Circle? Gambino?

HOFFA: No. Not Carlo. It was—well, I can't think of it offhand. [It was Joe Columbo.] But they never said Costello was part of organized crime, just that he was part of a *family* associated with organized crime.

PLAYBOY: Okay. The Mob. the family, the Mafia.

HOFFA: Well? Well? Well?

PLAYBOY: Well, doesn't it amount to the same thing?

HOFFA: Bullshit! Take me. I pick up the phone and call anywhere in the United States, I don't give a fuck what union it is, and I say, "Listen, this is Jimmy Hoffa." He says, "Hey, yeah, Jim! How are ya?" I say, "Listen, I want a favor." No questions asked. I tell him what I want. He says, "If I can do it, I'll call ya back." He gets busy, maybe calls six other guys. Now, is that an organized crime? Is that an organized Mafia or some fuckin' thing?

Guy in New York, Costello. Wants to call Joe Bommarito. He calls up, they go into dago. "Hey, whatcha do?" "What's goin' on?" "Hey, ya know So-and-So?" "Nah, I don't-a know him." "Well, find-a out who he is, then call me back." Blah-blah-blah-blah. Now, what is that? Organized crime? Or is that just like me calling you or you calling him, or what the hell is it? We know each other. We're maybe interrelated or some kind of a relative or some goddamn thing. What kind of bullshit's that? Take the guy who's supposed to be in charge of the Mafia—or whatever you wanna call it—in Chicago. Has anyone ever proved he was the head of it? He's said to 'em 49 times, "What the hell do you want from me? I'm in the *meat* business!" They never proved it, never indicted him. But they keep writing that he's head of the Mafia.

Some magazine said *I* control the Mafia. Now, I never heard a more goddamned ridiculous statement in the whole world than that goddamned magazine! They said my good friend Carlos Marcello called the Mob together and put up $1 million to get Hoffa outta jail. What kind of bullshit is this? Where'd they get those figures from? . . . So when I got out, Carlos called me and said, "Hey, you got that million?" He laughed! Yet the newspapers print it, the goddamned books write it. And it's a joke! *Mad* magazine, that cocksucker! They came out with a thing in there about Hoffa. Bullshit! *Esquire* magazine comes out with an article that says that Hoffa psyched out Sirhan Sirhan to kill, uh kill, uh——

PLAYBOY: Bobby Kennedy.

HOFFA: *I* psyched him out? Them cocksuckers! Like that roto system, I suppose. Shit.

PLAYBOY: What's the roto system?

HOFFA: Like movie actors have when they learn their lines. They put this recording on you; when you go to sleep, it's under your pillow. It's like hypnosis, they keep repeating certain things—boom, boom, boom—to instill in your mind what isn't the truth but what *will* be the truth when you repeat it. Like the Japanese did to our people during the war.

PLAYBOY: And you're supposed to have brainwashed Sirhan that way?

HOFFA: That's what they said in the fuckin' magazine! Why, I didn't even *know* the guy! The whole thing's so ridiculous, but my lawyer tells me you can't do nothing.

PLAYBOY: Why?

HOFFA: He says you gotta prove malice. Take Giacalone. This bullshit indictment he's got now. What is it? Five times now. Five times to bat, hopin' to break him—financially, physically, morally. And now when they can't do it, they come up with the "net worth" thing.

PLAYBOY: That's where they ask you to show how you can live so well on the income you file on your tax returns.

HOFFA: Right, it's the only thing in this country where you're guilty until proven innocent. They take you from the time you got outta school until now, ask people how much you've spent, add up your salary—and they just put it on you and the law says you have to disprove it. That's what Giacalone's gotta prove now. They put a net worth on him and now Giacalone's gotta restructure his whole life from the time he was born to show where he got his money. It's gonna be a hell of a thing to do.

PLAYBOY: Back in 1957, during the McClellan investigation, one of your safe-deposit boxes at your bank was opened.

HOFFA: Yeah, I laughed at the cocksuckers! The deed to my house is all they got.

PLAYBOY: Let's talk about your finances. How are you making money these days?

HOFFA: Real estate. Business. . . . Helping arrange business deals.

PLAYBOY: Do you want to talk specifically about any of the deals?

HOFFA: Nope. The very minute I would be connected publicly with any kind of enterprise, it would immediately frighten everybody concerned with the deal.

PLAYBOY: Okay. How's your private life? Do you get out much, to restaurants, that sort of thing?

HOFFA: Eh. Once in a while. Very seldom. Now, when we go out, arm and a leg. What the hell're you gonna do? Number one, I don't like the crowds. Number two, I don't like the prices. Number three, I don't like the service. So what the hell am I gonna go out for? Why should Josephine get dressed up for two hours? The hell with it. It's getting to the point where a guy with four kids, his old lady and himself has got to spend $70 a week for groceries.

PLAYBOY: What's the most important thing in your life right now?

HOFFA: Oh, my family. No question about that.

PLAYBOY: And what's more important to you, money or power?

HOFFA: Power. Power gives money. You got *both* if you got power. But you can have money without power.

PLAYBOY: For years you feuded with the Kennedys, one of the most powerful families in the country. What did you think, personally, of Bobby Kennedy?

HOFFA: He was a creep!

PLAYBOY: And John Kennedy?

HOFFA: Creep!

PLAYBOY: How about Teddy?

HOFFA: Well, I've known a hell of a lot of brothers in my life. Two, three, four to a family, the majority of 'em no good. And maybe one of 'em outta the lot, you couldn't *find* a better guy. Who the hell knows? Just because you're brothers, doesn't mean you're the same type. Don't mean that. Don't mean that at all.

Ted Kennedy I hardly know. But I know people who've known him since the day he was born. Our people in Boston've known him. And they say he's different from all two of the others. They say he likes a good time and that he would be the kind of guy who would gather around him a lot of people who wouldn't go to work for any other administration. I suppose they mean professors and what have you—I have no faith in 'em. So that's all I know about the guy. He never made any statement concerning me that I know of—even when it was fashionable. So I don't know a hell of a lot about him. Matter of fact if you talk to the guys in Washington goddamned few of 'em will say *anything* about Ted Kennedy. He apparently don't associate with other Congressmen and Senators. Of course, he can get in any time he wants it, he's got it.

PLAYBOY: You mean the presidency? You think he's going to run?

HOFFA: Oh, just as sure as you and I are here. Just as sure as you and I are here. It'll be a draft at the convention.

PLAYBOY: How much do you think Chappaquiddick will hurt him?

HOFFA: Aw, Christ! Fifty percent of the marriages are in divorces. And when you talk about morality, it went out the window. How the hell's that gonna hurt him? He's sure as hell gonna get the old people, the welfare people, the Puerto Ricans, blacks, Mexicans. He'll get the majority of those. No question of that in my mind. How the hell could he lose?

Unless—there's only one thing that could kill him and very well kill *all* Democrats. They got the House and the Senate now. If they keep fiddlin' around and not doing anything except quarreling with each other, very well, the American people could say, "Now, the hell with ya," and vote Republican. That's the way *I* see it. I don't see it no other way.

PLAYBOY: Why did Kennedy say he wouldn't run?

HOFFA: Get the heat off Chappaquiddick for 18 months. What the hell, they were banging him on the head with every kind of article, TV report, what have you. But you notice the very minute he said, "I'm not gonna run," it stopped. So he was smart.

PLAYBOY: Don't you think Chappaquiddick will have to be resolved at some point?

HOFFA: Phhht! He wasn't found guilty of no crime. What's he supposed to do? They didn't find him *guilty*.

PLAYBOY: If Teddy runs and gets elected do you think he'll be killed?

HOFFA: Naw. I don't think—— You just don't kill—— What the hell! I don think anybody's so cold-blooded that he shoots a guy because he's a Kennedy.

PLAYBOY: There was at least one publicized attempt on *your* life, wasn't there? In 1962, during your trial on charges of illegal kickbacks, a man walked into the courtroom and shot you from behind.

HOFFA: Yeah, don't know his goddamn name. I forgot it now. It's a matter of record. [It was Warren Swanson, a deranged drifter.] But everyone was searched that went in and out of the courtroom. How the hell did he get in with a gun? . . . I'm sure the marshal didn't overlook *him*. And he walked in with a gun, after everybody'd been searched! Like Martin Luther King. You're suspicious but you can't prove it.

PLAYBOY: The man had a pellet gun right?

HOFFA: Which would go through a two-by-four. Kill you just as sure as a .22.

PLAYBOY: What's your version of what happened?

HOFFA: Well, I looked and I *seen* him. I ducked down, come up, broke his jaw, took his gun away from him. The marshals were behind the file cabinets, same as the government lawyers, my lawyers, same as the judge. They all came pouring out after it was all over. I got the guy knocked out and this marshal comes out with a blackjack and hits the poor bastard! I said, "Ya dumb bastard! Get outta here! The guy's knocked out already!"

PLAYBOY: How about the attempt on George Wallace?

HOFFA: Who the hell *knows*? They got a file on every kook there is.

PLAYBOY: And John Kennedy? Why do you think he was killed?

HOFFA: Who the hell knows what deals he had? That he didn't keep? Who knows?

PLAYBOY: Do you think Oswald did it?

HOFFA: Aw, who the hell knows? I saw that simulation of the assassination on TV, which made more sense to me than the Warren Report did. I'll be goddamned. You tell me a guy can figure out how to be there at the right moment, right time, with a rifle—and hit a guy, you're a good man. I don't see how you do it. I see guys shooting at deer and I see *crack shots* shooting the deer. By God, *they* miss 'em. And a deer's about like a moving car. Ain't much difference.

PLAYBOY: Why did Jack Ruby kill Oswald, in your opinion?

HOFFA: That's the $64 question. Nobody'll ever figure that out. A fanatic, maybe. Who the hell knows?

PLAYBOY: What do you think of the conspiracy theories of that former district attorney in New Orleans, Jim Garrison? Is he just a kook?

HOFFA: No, sirree! Jim Garrison's a smart man. . . . Goddamned smart attorney. Anybody thinks *he's* a kook is a kook themselves.

PLAYBOY: All right, back to the Bobby Kennedy assassination. You don't think Nixon had anything to do with it, do you?

HOFFA: Hell, no. Hell, no. He ain't that kind of guy.

PLAYBOY: So it was Sirhan acting alone?

HOFFA: Well, I handled guns all of my life. Here's a kid that went out and got a gun. Not much practice with the damned gun. And I would question whether he was cold-blooded enough to be able to pop up and shoot the guy without someone . . . helping him. I just read about another guy, a ballistics guy, who said there was another type of bullet. Who the hell knows? *Who the hell knows?*

PLAYBOY: Do you think we'll ever know about all these killings?

HOFFA: Well, I watched the damned TV the other night, that *Police Story* and *S.W.A.T.* They killed more goddamm people than you got hair on your head. [*Pause*] Goddamned movies, TV! Kills 49 guys a night, for Chrissake—on Monday and Tuesday night! Forty-nine guys they kill! So who the hell knows what you can do? There was a nut on TV last night, just started *killing* people. Nobody knew why the goddamned fool killed people. Then they finally catch him . . . kill *him.* So he's dead. *He* can't tell why he killed 'em. People go off their rocker. Who can tell?

It Gets Dark
Every Night

by **JERRY STANECKI**
December 1975

The violence that had swirled around Teamster Local 299 in Detroit for the past year had preyed on Jimmy Hoffa's mind. It wasn't the violence per se, since Hoffa and violence were hardly strangers, it was the *why* behind the recent incidents and bombings that bothered him. First, a boat belonging to Dave Johnson, president of Local 299 and a loyal Hoffa supporter, had been blown out of the water. Then Ralph Proctor, an official of Local 299, had been severely beaten by two men. Finally, the parked car of Frank Fitzsimmons's son had been blown up near a Teamsters hangout.

"I can't understand the damn thing, Jerry," Hoffa said to me late last spring. "Dave Johnson's boat blown up—broad daylight. The Fitzsimmons kid's car—broad daylight. Ralph getting stumped by two guys—broad daylight. I just don't understand it."

"Why don't you understand it, Jimmy?"

"Well, because it gets dark every night."

• • •

Broad daylight. Wednesday, July 30, 1975, was going to be a scorcher. Hoffa's wife, Josephine, later told me that her husband seemed edgy and unsettled that morning—and it wasn't just the heat. "He didn't get up and start raking the yard as he usually did; he was upset. I'd never seen him like that."

The temperature was in the 80s by ten that morning, and Hoffa told his wife he was going to lie down on the picnic table and that she should

44

wake him at one P.M.; he had a meeting to attend. At five minutes past one, Josephine woke him. He showered, kissed her twice (which bothered her at the time, because it "wasn't like him" to kiss her *twice*), got into his car and left.

Hoffa drove to Pontiac, where he stopped at Airport Service Lines, a limousine firm owned by Louis "The Pope" Linteau, a longtime friend. Linteau wasn't there, but a couple of employees later said that Hoffa appeared very nervous. But he did go out of his way to mention the names of three men he was supposed to meet. When the employees were later questioned, they could not recall the names of the men. The Hoffa family hired a psychiatrist, however, and under hypnosis, the names emerged: Anthony "Tony Jack" Giacalone, Anthony "Tony Pro" Provenzano and Leonard Schultz.

At 2:30, the phone rang in the Hoffa home.

"Has Tony Giacalone called?" asked Hoffa.

"No," said Josephine.

"When he calls, tell him I'm waiting for him at the Red Fox restaurant on Telegraph."

(Josephine later told me, "I knew it was a message. He was telling me that if something happened, I'd know . . .")

While Hoffa waited outside the restaurant, two men recognized him and greeted him. They asked, "How's it going?" Hoffa replied, "Never felt better in my life."

At 3:30, Hoffa called Linteau from the restaurant. Linteau later said that Hoffa was angry. "Tony Jack didn't show, goddamn it," he said. "I'm coming out there."

The call was the last anybody heard from Hoffa.

• • •

Alibis. At the time the meeting at the Machus Red Fox restaurant was supposed to be taking place, Tony Giacalone was getting a haircut and a manicure at the Travelers Tower building in Southfield, a ten-minute drive from the restaurant. The building also houses the Southfield Athletic Club, a fancy exercise club run by Schultz's two sons and a favorite hangout of Giacalone's. Police sources told me that the activity that normally went on at the club was almost a routine: "Tony Jack walks in, sits down and starts doing business. One at a time, men approach him, talk quietly for a few minutes and walk away. It's like something out of *The Godfather*."

On that afternoon, Provenzano was on conspicuous display at a union hall in New Jersey. As for Schultz, he claims he was working in his garden.

"It's damn funny," Jimmy Hoffa Jr., said later. "Everybody involved in this damn thing was either getting his nails done or was someplace with 10,000 witnesses when Dad disappeared."

• • •

Four o'clock came and went. At home, Josephine was starting to worry. If Hoffa were going to be late, he would have called. Supper was generally served at four or shortly thereafter. The hour passed without word, and Linteau went to Hoffa's home to wait with Josephine. They waited all night. About seven Thursday morning, Linteau drove to the restaurant, where he found Hoffa's car. Linteau told me he knew there was trouble when he found that the door on the driver's side was unlocked; Hoffa was a stickler about keeping car doors locked. Linteau looked around and left his business card on the steering wheel. A few minutes later, he called Joe Bane, president of Teamster Local 614 in Pontiac, at his Southfield home. The line was busy, so Linteau had the operator interrupt with an emergency call. He told Bane that Hoffa was missing. Bane headed for the Hoffa home after calling a police friend and telling him to check out Hoffa's car. Jimmy Jr., flew in from Traverse City, where he was vacationing, about the same time.

The vigil, already tense, continued. Jimmy Jr., went to work and calls were made to any and everyone who would have any idea what was going down. Speculation ran wild. At the Hoffa home, the hope was that it might be "only" a kidnapping, but the fear of a "hit" was on everyone's mind. Hoffa's daughter, Barbara Crancer, was met at the airport about five P.M. Thursday by Bane. A little after six P.M.—27 hours after the disappearance—Jimmy Jr., notified the police. Hoffa was now officially missing. The FBI was notified but did not officially enter the case. (There was as yet no evidence of a Federal crime.)

Friday and Saturday passed with no word from Hoffa. Several times a day, I spoke with Jimmy Jr., and his sister. Barbara, as Hoffa once told me, "is a lot like me, while Jimmy Jr., is more like his mother." Barbara was now displaying her father's traits. She was on the phone constantly and she was making demands. By the time she got through to Edward Levi, U. S. Attorney General, and Clarence Kelley, FBI Director, she was shouting.

"You used 2,000 agents to put my father in jail," she said. "How about using a couple of agents to *find* him!"

A short time later, the Attorney General acted. On the basis of an anonymous threat—Kelley announced that extortion demands had been received by the Hoffa family—the FBI was entering the case. As a newscaster put it in a lead story on a Detroit station: "The FBI, which has yet to solve the Patricia Hearst case, has finally entered the Jimmy Hoffa case."

• • •

Josephine Hoffa is a friend of Jeane Dixon, the "seer" who became famous for having predicted the assassination of John Kennedy. Josephine told me that she had called Dixon just after the disappearance of her husband. Dixon told her, "Jimmy's alive—and he knows something very important." On Monday, the fifth day after the disappearance, Josephine said she woke up clutching her heart. "I knew then—and only then—that Jimmy was dead." Later that same morning, she received a call from Dixon. "I'm sorry," Josephine said Dixon told her, "but Jimmy's dead. He's in the water somewhere."

I'm not much of a believer in such things, but something that happened to me the next day, Tuesday, made me wonder. I had made a television appearance on Dennis Wholey's AM Detroit show to discuss the Hoffa case, and just after going off the air, I was told there was an urgent call for me from an unidentified woman. Her voice was trembling. She mentioned the name of a man and added, "He knows what happened to Jimmy Hoffa. He has a boat and they were both in the boat and they went to Harsens Island [an island in Lake Saint Clair]." She then hung up. I checked out the lead. The man she mentioned does own a boat, is very rich and has been linked to organized crime. The man has to remain anonymous for now, because the FBI is checking him out and the allegation may turn out to be spurious. But what unsettled me was the date the woman mentioned Hoffa had been in the boat: It was the fifth day after his disappearance. I told no one about the telephone call.

A week later, an elderly Detroit woman claiming to be a psychic appeared on a local television show and claimed she had had visions of Jimmy Hoffa. She said she could "see" him under water, shot twice in the head. He was naked, she said, with a strap around his chest. Hoffa's body could be found, she concluded, floating "near Harsens Island."

Then, in late September, there was new information, which police took more seriously. A Mob informant contacted the Senate Permanent Subcommittee on Investigations, then gearing up to probe the Hoffa affair under the chairmanship of Henry Jackson. He knew where Hoffa's body was buried, he said. It was not underwater but underground, somewhere in a field in Waterford Township, about 15 miles from the Machus Red Fox restaurant. Reports from the street had it that the Mob was holding one of the men involved in eliminating Hoffa and that the Mafia wanted the body found. That would place the murder under state jurisdiction and thus take federal pressure off the Mob—a result the Mafia badly wanted, since, as rumors had it, it was not directly involved in the hit. Police investigators, armed with shovels and bulldozers, plowed up the field but found nothing after three days. Officials vowed to continue digging.

• • •

Charles "Chuckie" O'Brien describes himself as Hoffa's "foster son," having been close to the Hoffa family since childhood, and is active in Detroit union politics. Today, the Hoffa family claims that O'Brien greatly exaggerated his ties to Hoffa. When O'Brien refused to be questioned in the days after Hoffa's disappearance, police officials said he was "missing" and began to leak their suspicions that O'Brien might somehow be involved.

"Missing, shit!" O'Brien told me later. "Who the hell started this bullshit?" He was unapologetic about his friendship with Giacalone and explained that he had had dinner with the Giacalone family on Friday, August 1, at a restaurant in Port Huron. On Saturday, he'd gone to the barber in the Southfield Travelers Tower building, where he'd seen Giacalone again. And on Sunday, he'd flown to West Memphis, Arkansas, to be with his new wife. "So where do they get all this 'missing' shit?" he asked. He got madder. "The fucking Feds are leaking this right and left, and if it keeps happening, I'm going to do some talking. Fuck the FBI!"

O'Brien and Hoffa had been close, but according to Jimmy Jr., and Linteau, they became estranged in November 1974. O'Brien had ambitions to take over the presidency of Detroit's Local 299, headed by Dave Johnson. At the time, Richard Fitzsimmons, son of Hoffa's archfoe Frank Fitzsimmons, was running against Johnson. O'Brien felt he could represent Hoffa's interests against Fitzsimmons better than Johnson could. So he made his pitch: "I tried to convince him that it'd be better if I were there [in the presidency] versus a guy 68 years old [Johnson]. With my youth, and using Jimmy's methods, I could get 299 back the way it was before he left. I really opened up to him, but Jimmy wouldn't give me his support. He's a compromiser and he was only looking for a deal to make everybody happy."

A week later, O'Brien denied he'd "pitched" Jimmy at all. When I reminded him that he'd told me about it and quoted the conversation verbatim, he just shook his head and said, "Hell, no! Hell, no! Hell, no!" It seemed to me that under the pressure, O'Brien was "spinning," trying to have it every which way.

O'Brien nonetheless insisted there had been no falling out between them. Still, there were rumors—and accusations—that he had switched sides, that he'd thrown his support behind Fitzsimmons. O'Brien denied it at every opportunity, but Jimmy Jr., took me aside and said, "Then why did Chuckie go visit Fitzsimmons in Washington on August 4—exactly five days after Dad disappeared?"

Jimmy Jr., made no bones about his suspicions regarding O'Brien's involvement. The confrontation between the two men came early Friday morning, August 1. O'Brien gave me his version: "Jimmy called and asked me to come out to the house. When I arrived, I could see he was frazzled. I said, 'Jimmy, you look exhausted. Why don't you go to bed and we'll talk in the morning?' Jimmy said no, he wanted to talk. And he immediately launched into me as if he was some kind of prosecutor. I told him to calm down, but he only got madder. 'You know more than you're talking about! I think you're involved!' I looked at Jimmy and said, 'I've had the guts taken out of me in my lifetime, but you just cut 'em out."

During that week, O'Brien came under increasing fire. He admitted to police that he was in the area of the Red Fox restaurant the day Hoffa disappeared. He admitted borrowing a car belonging to Tony Giacalone's son. When the FBI examined the car, bloodstains were found on one of the seats. "I was delivering a fish, a 40-pound salmon, to Bobby Holmes's house," O'Brien explained. "The fuckin' blood was from the fish." FBI analysis concluded that the blood was "not of human origin."

O'Brien continued to profess complete innocence. "It's tearing me up," he said. "Little Jimmy and Barbara are tearing my guts out demanding I take a lie-detector test! What the hell is wrong with them?"

O'Brien did not take a polygraph test. When subpoenaed before the grand jury convened to investigate Hoffa's disappearance, he took the Fifth Amendment.

• • •

IT GETS DARK EVERY NIGHT

Provenzano finally met with reporters on the front lawn of his Hallandale, Florida, home. "You're embarrassing me in front of everyone in the neighborhood," he said, wearing a white swimming suit. "You guys make me look like a mobster. I'm not. I'm just a truck driver."

Tony Pro denied he was in Detroit the day before Hoffa disappeared, as some reports had it, and claimed he hadn't been in Detroit for years. As to Jimmy's disappearance, just days before: "Jimmy was—or is—my friend." A slip of the tongue, perhaps, but reporters leaped on it. "You can put any verb you want!" Tony Pro barked, and he stalked into the house.

• • •

Tuesday evening, August 5, in a pouring rainstorm, Jimmy Jr., and Barbara walked to the white-metal picket fence that surrounds the Hoffa compound. "We are offering a $200,000 reward," Jimmy told waiting reporters, "for information about my father." There had been rumors from the underworld that a contract had been put out on Hoffa and that the price was $100,000. A reporter turned to a colleague and said, "Boy, I'll bet the hit man's pissed off. A hundred grand for the job—but he could have made two hundred by just reporting where Hoffa's body is." No one laughed.

I had been told by a source in Washington that the FBI was working on a theory that Joseph Zerilli, the reputed godfather of the Detroit Mafia, had been asked to go to the commission and get a contract. Zerilli allegedly is one of a dozen Mafia commissioners in the country. I mentioned this to Bane while we talked after the news conference and he looked at me and said, "If that's true, you can bet one thing—that ain't no three-two vote." A little later on, Bane said, "You know, Jerry, I don't think we'll ever see the little guy again."

Bane and I were both physically and mentally exhausted. It started raining harder, so we went to a nearby bar. Bane was clearly concerned about having gone to the Hoffa home. He looked at me and quietly said, "Jerry, they can't think bad of me for going to the aid of an old friend's family in time of need, can they?" I knew Bane was talking about rival Teamsters.

"No," I said, "I wouldn't think so, Joe."

• • •

A couple of days later and still no news—just more theories. Jimmy Jr., and I were talking. "The old man was a fool," he said. "I don't mean

a fool disrespectfully, I mean a fool because he'd take on anybody."
He was silent for a moment, then added, "I even gave him my Smitty
because he was concerned."

I knew it was unlikely that Hoffa had had the Smith & Wesson with
him on that Wednesday, because he hadn't carried a gun for years. But
as Jimmy Jr., said, Hoffa had to know whomever he met that day. "If
someone tried to take him in that parking lot," he said, "Dad would
have jumped him then and there. He had to *know* and he had to *trust*
whomever he got into the car with."

It was during this period, a week or so after the disappearance,
that one theory began to gain currency on the street: Tony Giacalone,
allegedly Detroit's most feared enforcer, had been given the contract.
Two weeks before Hoffa disappeared, he was visited at his home by
Giacalone and his brother, "Billy Jack." They proposed a meeting
that would include Provenzano, on the pretext of burying the hatchet
between Hoffa and Provenzano after a longstanding disagreement. I
was told by a close friend of Hoffa's that twice in recent weeks a meeting
had been scheduled—but Tony Jack had begged off.

With Giacalone's name out in the open, with O'Brien's movements
under question, I and the other reporters covering the case began
to dig into the motives of the supposed hit. In the months preceding
Hoffa's disappearance, the possibility that Hoffa might win his court
fight to end the ban against participating in union activity was becoming increasingly real. The court of appeals was going to rule in Hoffa's
favor, went one argument. Another theory involved a presidential
pardon. If Nixon could be pardoned, why not Hoffa? Or, more to the
point, Hoffa's old mentor, Dave Beck, had been pardoned earlier in
the year by President Ford. Many observers felt that might be a test
balloon: If there were no public outcry, it would be a clear signal that
Hoffa could safely be pardoned, too. There was no outcry. Finally, Hoffa
had expressed to me a feeling that Attorney General Levi was about
to recommend a presidential pardon. (Levi, however, later denied this
publicly.)

• • •

Subpoenas for the grand jury investigating Hoffa's disappearance
began to be issued on Monday, August 25. I had asked a source in the
FBI whom they expected to call to the stand. "It's simple," he told me.
"We're going to paper the country with subpoenas."

The parade to the fourth floor of the Federal Building in Detroit began the day after Labor Day. The first witnesses to testify were the employees of Linteau's limousine service who had recalled under hypnosis the names of the men Hoffa said he was meeting. The next day, September 3, it was Chuckie O'Brien's turn. He appeared with his attorney, James Burdick, and was decked out in an open-collared shirt and sports jacket. But despite his natty attire, he clearly showed fear—and, in my opinion, it was not the grand jury he was afraid of. He spent exactly six minutes inside the grand-jury room. Outside, O'Brien withheld comment and Burdick delivered an attack on the federal government and on the grand-jury system. Walking down the street, jostled by a crowd of reporters and cameramen, O'Brien said virtually nothing. I was still with him when he arrived at a nearby garage. I quietly asked, "Chuckie, did you take the Fifth?" O'Brien stared at me a moment and just as quietly said, "Yes. Numerous times." O'Brien got into Burdick's car and sped away for the airport, where he boarded a flight to Florida.

On Thursday, Leonard Schultz was called as a witness. Schultz was expected to take the Fifth but pulled a surprise. He talked for more than two hours. Several times, he came out of the jury room and conferred with his attorney.

The scene in the hall was like a carnival. Joe Bane Jr., had brought a lawn chair and got into a hassle with a U. S. marshal who demanded he remove the chair. After a loud argument, he did so. Linteau was tired of waiting, so he started pushing a mop down the corridor. Crowds of witnesses, marshals, attorneys and reporters milled about. Before testifying, Schultz got into a loud argument with a television reporter, calling him a whore. The reporter yelled back at him and the argument continued for about 30 minutes. And during all the commotion, a few feet behind the closed doors, the grand jury probed.

Joe Bane appeared to testify and was in and out after three minutes: He, too, took the Fifth. "You know, Jerry," he said to me, "those cocksuckers are after me. I've been told I'm going to be indicted on another union matter. You know I wanted to talk, to do anything to help Jimmy, but you can't trust the lousy motherfuckers. Sure as hell they'd throw me a curve." Joe Bane Jr., spent about the same amount of time before the grand jury and also admitted to taking the Fifth. Linteau spent several hours telling what he knew.

The morning of Monday, September 8, was unseasonably cool. Tony "Jack" Giacalone, dressed in a pearl-gray Western-cut suit, fought his way through the mob of reporters gathered in front of the Federal Building. He spoke not a word and walked directly to the elevators leading to the grand-jury floor. "My God," said a network artist who had sketched hundreds of courtroom faces, "he really is a mean-looking man."

There was a long wait, but at 12:15 Giacalone finally entered the grand-jury room. He was out three minutes later. The reporters swarmed around him again, but he refused to reply, giving them only an icy stare. On the elevator going down, one reporter made himself heard: "Can you just give us a correct age, Mr. Giacalone?" Not a muscle in his face moved. The reporter persisted: "We'll just say you're under 40." For the first time, Giacalone cracked a smile. The journalists followed him out onto the street. TV reporter Robert Bennett got into a revolving door behind Giacalone in a building down the street. Tony Jack looked back and, as he stepped out onto the sidewalk, jammed the door backward into the reporter's face. And with that gesture—as of this writing—the case of Jimmy Hoffa's disappearance was effectively slammed shut.

• • •

Did organized crime order James Riddle Hoffa executed? Police, the FBI and reporters close to the case think so. They also think Hoffa was murdered because of his public struggle to regain the presidency of the International Teamsters Union. As to the Mob figures involved, the Hoffa family, at least, thinks it knows who they are. On September 9, when Jimmy Hoffa Jr., said publicly that he thought his father had been assassinated, he was pressed for details. "The names have been publicized," he replied.

Hoffa's son also still considers Chuckie O'Brien a "prime suspect," an accusation O'Brien says he resents bitterly. "I loved the ground that man walked on," O'Brien told me. "I'd go myself first." And what of the Teamsters under Frank Fitzsimmons? If only because of the Mob ties that go back 20 years, it seems reasonable to assume there is some connection. If the Mob, with its lucrative trade in Teamsters business, feared that Hoffa would replace the easygoing Fitzsimmons, it is also reasonable to assume it would make a choice of one over the other. Fitzsimmons continues to deny any knowledge of the affair and will admit to no connection whatever with the Mob. (In fact, when I suggested as much to him over the telephone one day this past summer, he practically spat at me over the wire.) In any case, the driver of a car seen in Pennsylvania may be asking the most tantalizing question of all. The car had a bumper sticker on it. It read, FITZ—WHERE'S JIMMY?

Gary Gilmore

Gary Gilmore

the PLAYBOY INTERVIEW
April 1977

Why interview Gary Gilmore?
Why further glorify someone who cold-bloodedly killed two young men and became famous only because of a publicly expressed death wish?

Why give this criminal a posthumous format that might tempt others to try to "outcool" Gilmore's disdain for life—his own and that of others—and thus become celebrated by journalists and the public?

These questions, which might have been answered on purely journalistic grounds (by simply publishing a story nearly every other publication tried to get), were, in fact, especially difficult for us at PLAYBOY. The magazine for many years has strongly opposed the death penalty and the aberrations that follow in its wake. In Gilmore's case, we feared that an interview with him would be less a study in the effects of the death penalty than a less-justifiable look at a state-assisted suicide.

It was only when we'd embarked on the project, qualms and all, that we realized our interviewers were doing something else. As we looked over the early transcripts, it became clear that Gilmore posed even more puzzling questions about our society by the indications of his high intelligence, his articulateness and his brutal emotional detachment. Through the efforts of Lawrence Schiller, a Los Angeles journalist and agent who had bought the rights to Gilmore's story, and with the collaboration of writer Barry Farrell, a contributing editor to *Harper's* (who had written an article in *New West* on the "merchandising" of Gary Gilmore but was nonetheless intrigued by the story itself), Gilmore began to reveal himself over a period of two months. In looking over these conversations before deciding to publish them, we were struck by the likelihood that the street punk in Gilmore was responding to the craftiness of Schiller and the persistence of Farrell in a more honest, chilling way than if he'd talked to a battery of psychiatrists.

Many readers will find this a painful reading experience—and perhaps that is the point. Americans taught to believe that rehabilitation is the only logical alternative to locking up a criminal and throwing away the key—or, indeed, executing him—may be uncomfortable with the idea that a killer can be lucid, self-aware and quite prepared to go out and kill again if he's set free. As the project progressed, we became certain that the dialogue produced by Schiller and Farrell illuminated as rarely before a question more important than the ones we asked ourselves at the outset: Why do men kill? Farrell's report: "Gary Gilmore's real life lasted only 78 days, beginning last November first, when he told the judge who had presided at his murder trial that he was ready to see it end. Before that, Gilmore was known only to his victims, his keepers and the small, bewildered circle of his family and friends. When he died at the age of 36 on January 17, no one—not even the 100-odd men who had volunteered to serve on his firing squad—was more determined than Gilmore to obliterate a life so drenched in catastrophe and breakdown that only three of his last 22 years could be lived outside confinement.

"Had Gilmore not had the grim distinction of being the first man executed in the United States in nearly a decade, his wish to die would have attracted scarcely more attention than his crimes. He was, in his phrase, an eternal recidivist, locked into a hopeless cycle of attempts to conduct a normal life, attempts that invariably ended with his surrender to the shackles and bars that were his only restraints. The last attempt began with his release from prison on April 9, 1976, and ended three months later with his confession to the senseless, execution-style murders of Bennie Bushnell and Max Jensen, young Mormon husbands and fathers, in the town of Provo, Utah, on the nights of July 19 and 20, 1976. Gilmore's trial in October lasted only three days, and when he stood to be sentenced to death, fewer than 20 people were in the courtroom.

"The fame that came to him after November first was partly a reflection of the world's morbid fascination with a man who so urgently wished to surrender himself to its guns. But it was also due to the challenge he posed to the legal system, a passive challenge that asked only that it live up to the weight of its ultimate sanction and deliver its promise of death. An eye for an eye, Gilmore said, was a concise expression of logic—'true by virtue of its logical form.' The letters Gilmore wrote immediately after his trial show no trace of awareness that his acceptance of his fate would win him the world's attention.

"Any other man in his circumstance would likewise have been caught in the glare that always accompanies those who go first. But Gilmore managed to rise to the one occasion where every misery of his life acquired a surprising new meaning and every bitter turn began to count. The interview that follows is the first expression of his cornered intelligence, and its intensity casts a rare and revealing light on the dangerous confusions of a man who finally had to kill.

"Lawrence Schiller slipped through the screen around Gilmore on November 27, when the condemned man suddenly found himself the object of hotly competitive bidding for the rights to his story. It was the first of four clandestine meetings between the two. Schiller was there to compete for those rights, and after the first four-hour meeting with Gilmore and careful arrangements with his family and the heirs of his two victims, he acquired them. Soon after that meeting, a court battle ensued, in which the press petitioned for access to Gilmore. Schiller joined in that battle, which was lost before the Utah Supreme Court and, eventually, the U.S. Supreme Court. The Court's decision made note of the right of the press to communicate with Gilmore by only those methods prescribed by the prison authorities, including the right of relatives to visit, written correspondence and communications through Gilmore's attorneys. All these means were employed in producing this interview.

"In addition to Schiller's notes from his face-to-face meetings with Gilmore, the interview was compiled from 57 hours of tape-recorded conversations and approximately 10,000 words of Gilmore's written answers to our questions.

"Gilmore saw this interview as an escape from the familiar oblivion of his prison years, and he used all his craft and guile to devise ways in which the exchange could be completed in his final days. At odd hours, the telephone would ring in the motel room that Schiller and I made our office. It would be Gilmore calling—and his call would convey an urgency and a doomed wish to be understood that both chilled and inspired us."

(MID-DECEMBER 1976)

PLAYBOY: As far as we can tell from your prison record, you've been locked up almost continuously since you entered reform school, and that was 22 years ago. It's as if you never saw any choice but to live out a criminal destiny.

GILMORE: Yeah, that's kind of a way of putting it. In fact, that's very nicely put.

THE PLAYBOY INTERVIEW

PLAYBOY: What got you started thinking like a criminal?

GILMORE: Probably going to reform school.

PLAYBOY: But you must have done things to get yourself sent there.

GILMORE: Yeah, I was a-about 14 when I went to reform school and, ah, 13 when I started getting locked up.

PLAYBOY: What had you done to get locked up at 13?

GILMORE: Well, I started out stealing cars . . . but, ah, I guess my first felonies were probably burglaries, house burglaries. I used to burglarize houses on my paper route.

PLAYBOY:: Why? What were you after?

GILMORE: Why? Well, I wanted guns, mainly. A lot of people keep guns in their homes and, well . . . that's what I was primarily looking for.

PLAYBOY: How old were you then? Eleven? Twelve? Why did you want guns?

GILMORE: Well, see, in Portland, at that time, there was a gang, the Broadway gang. I don't know if you ever heard of it—probably not. But, man, I figured that, well, I would like to be in the Broadway gang. And I figured the best way to get in was to go down and hang around Broadway and sell 'em guns. I knew they wanted guns. I mean, I-I don't even know if the gang existed . . . it may have been a myth. But I heard about 'em, you know? So I thought I wanted to be a part of an outfit like that . . . the Broadway boys.

PLAYBOY: But instead you got caught and sent to reform school?

GILMORE: Yeah, the MacLaren School for Boys, in Woodburn, Oregon. You want me to be precise about the details?

PLAYBOY: Yes.

GILMORE: 'Cause I've got a thing about precision and detail, and if we're gonna do this, we better do it right. You guys sure you can handle it, the fact of me dyin'?

PLAYBOY: Not as well as you.

GILMORE: 'Cause that's an absolute condition. If you want me to talk, you can't talk to Nicole and you can't do anything, or use anything I might say, to butt in on my execution. I got lawyers workin' for me, and I can't even talk unless I got your promise you won't fuck around on this. Promise?

PLAYBOY: Promise.

GILMORE: Okay. Now, I can remember just about everything that ever happened to me, goin' back to an early age. Sometimes there's memories of places in my mind. I remember once, in Provo, I remember a bridge I walked across. I couldn't have been more than two or three. What sort of memories do you want?

58

PLAYBOY: Whatever comes to mind. [*Long pause*] You mentioned wanting guns when you were 11 or 12. What's your first memory of guns?

GILMORE: Well, the first time I can remember trying to shoot a gun—you hear that goddamn pounding?

PLAYBOY: Is that a prisoner doing that?

GILMORE: It's just some maniac. You hear shit like that all day and all night in here. Anyway, the first time I tried to shoot a gun, I was living with my grandparents in Provo. I was about three or four, I guess. Anyhow, my uncle had an old .22 rifle, and I couldn't figure out how to make the son of a bitch shoot. My grandpa told me, well, you gotta have powder. And my grandmother had these capsules she had to take for some kind of ailment, migraine headaches or some damn thing. And there was one of 'em lyin' on the table, and I just eased up casually and laid my hand over it and slipped it into my pocket and went out, took the capsule apart and dumped the powder that was inside down the barrel of the rifle. And the son of a bitch still wouldn't shoot. [*Laughs*]

PLAYBOY: Do you remember when you first shot a gun?

GILMORE: You're going to say it's strange, but I don't. I remember when I was about 13, I went to the movies downtown in Portland. I was always going to the flicks by myself. And this night, I was lookin' in the store windows, and there was a bunch of .22 rifles in there, and I picked out the one I wanted, a Winchester semiautomatic, just a beautiful gun, with a $125 price tag on it, way back in '53. I went across the street and got a brick and threw it through the window and got that gun and took it home.

PLAYBOY: Just took it home on the trolley?

GILMORE: No, I didn't wait for the trolley, 'cause it would have been an hour, and I'd cut my hand. So I dismantled the gun and wrapped it up in newspaper and just went and got the goddamn bus and had to walk the last mile home. I couldn't take it in the house or nothin' because my old man, I didn't want him to know I had it. So I took it down to Johnson Creek, where I used to go swimming and everything. And later I got a box of shells, and I'd go plinkin' with that .22.

PLAYBOY: All by yourself?

GILMORE: Well, I had these two friends, Charley and Jim, and after a while, I let them in on it. I was gettin' tired of the damn thing, tired of hidin' it. You know what I mean—if I can't have something the way I want it, I don't really want it. Charley and Jim—they really loved this gun, so I said, listen, if I throw this gun in the deepest part of the creek, where it's about eight feet or so, do you guys have the guts to jump in and dive for it? They said you're goddamn right, man, just as soon as you throw it in.

They thought I was bullshittin', then they heard a loud splash and they turned around and I didn't have the gun no more. There was a big old sharp rock stickin' up from the water about three or four feet from the bank, and I threw the gun just beyond it. So Jim jumped. He was gonna jump for that rock, but one foot slipped and he landed on his knee on that sharp rock and, boy, it hurt him bad. I laughed my ass off. Maybe that was the first gun I ever shot. I don't know.

PLAYBOY:: Are you good with guns? Do you handle them well?

GILMORE: I got 20-20 vision.

PLAYBOY: So you're a good shot?

GILMORE: Yeah. Why so much about guns?

PLAYBOY: Maybe just because it seems strange that a man of your age would commit his first two murders in the only state in the Union that has a firing squad.

GILMORE: [Laughs] How do you know they were the first?

PLAYBOY: There were others?

GILMORE: We'll talk about that later. I'm not sayin' anything that involves other people. But the firing squad had nothin' to do with it. I came here because I got paroled here.

PLAYBOY: You did choose the firing squad over the gallows.

GILMORE: Look, I only had two choices. Hangin' or shootin' was all they had to offer, and I'd prefer to be shot.

PLAYBOY:: Why?

GILMORE: Fuckers might not hang me right.

PLAYBOY: What if there were some other choice, like electrocution?

GILMORE: Fuckers might not electrocute me right.

PLAYBOY:: But doesn't the blood-and-guts aspect of a shooting appeal to you?

GILMORE: Shit, fuck you. Blood and guts, yeah, man, that really appeals to me. I'm gonna take a spoon.

PLAYBOY: Okay. You were talking about Jim and Charley—were they your best friends?

GILMORE: I'm probably closer to LeRoy Earp than anybody else. He's a white dude, LeRoy. [Laughs] Lotta spooks named LeRoy. We were always good friends as little kids, on the streets and in Woodburn, and then he came into the penitentiary about two years after I did. He's in Oregon State prison, far as I know, doing life for murder.

PLAYBOY: What do you like about LeRoy?

GILMORE: He's a real quiet guy. He never shows how he feels about anything. He's got a good sense of humor. He's pretty passive. He'll go two or three months without even speaking to friends sometimes—just hello, goodbye, I'll see ya. But that being LeRoy, I understand. We both always liked doing the same things—you know, nice cars, good clothes, lots of girlfriends. I shot him one time in the stomach, accidentally.

PLAYBOY: You shot him?

GILMORE: Yeah, with an automatic, when we were kids, just messin' around. He didn't make no big deal out of it and neither did I. His parents weren't too crazy about me, though. They always thought I was getting LeRoy into trouble. But he explained to them, he says, "Ma, I'm just going to get into trouble anyway, and Gary ain't nothin', he ain't influencin' me." LeRoy's sister really liked me a lot. She was a real beautiful girl. But I never messed around with her. I just didn't want to, you know. If I've got a real good friend, I don't mess with their sister.

PLAYBOY: Would it have offended LeRoy?

GILMORE: Oh, no, he tried to get me to take her out several times. But I had some other girlfriends I thought quite a bit about, and LeRoy's sister didn't really appeal to me. A real nice-looking girl, but she was a little too aggressive, too forward.

PLAYBOY: For someone locked up so much, you seem to have had no trouble finding girls.

GILMORE: I think the first time I felt any sort of love I was 13 and I was hung up on this little chick named Nancy Eve, who was also 13. She had a huge set of boobs that would have been big on a full-grown woman. On a beautiful 13-year-old girl they were alarming. We went together for a few months, but then I went to the reform school, and when I got out she had moved on to other interests.

PLAYBOY: Were women excited by the outlaw in you?

GILMORE: All ladies love outlaws, didn't you know that? [*Laughs*] It's true. I've seen things in girls' eyes where you can tell they're excited to know that you're a person who doesn't observe the normal limits.

PLAYBOY: Was that true of your girlfriend Nicole?

GILMORE: We aren't talking about Nicole, remember? Nicole is a part of me. She's the part that was missing for 35 years. And now those sleazy bastards have got her locked up where she can't reach me and I can't reach her. So Nicole isn't in it, okay? You can say any shit you want to about me, but I don't want her gettin' dragged in all the god-damn time.

PLAYBOY: Okay—don't get excited. Let's go back to your phrase "observe the normal limits." It's an interesting phrase. You make it sound as though you're fully aware of the limits and choose not to observe them.

GILMORE: Well, I always knew the law was silly as hell. But as far as limits between people go, that's something that gets shaped by the pattern of your life—you react in a certain way because your life is influenced by all the varieties of your experience. Does that make any sense?

PLAYBOY: It's hard to say. Give us an example.

GILMORE: Well, this is kind of a personal thing. It'll sound like a strange incident to you, but it had a lasting effect on me. I was about 11 years old and I was coming home from school, and I thought I'd take a short cut. I climbed down this hill, a drop of about 50 feet, and I got tangled in these briar bushes, and blackberry, and thornberry. Some of these bushes were 30 feet high, I guess, down in this wild, overgrown area in southeast Portland. I thought it would be a short cut, but there was no pass through there. Nobody had gone through there before. At one point, I could have turned around and gone back, but I chose to just go on and it took me about three hours to pick my way through there. All during that time, I never stopped for a rest and just kept going. I knew if I just kept going I'd get out, but I was also aware that I could get hopelessly stuck in there. I was a block or so from any houses, and if I screamed . . . well, I could have died in there. My screams would have gone unheard. So I just kept going. It was kind of a personal thing. I finally got home about three hours late and my mom said, well, you're late, and I said, yeah, I took a short cut. [*Laughs*]

PLAYBOY: What's the point of that story? Why did you stay in the brambles and struggle so hard when you could have turned around and walked right out?

GILMORE: I just did it, you know. And after I got about halfway, I w-was——

PLAYBOY: Past the point of no return?

GILMORE: Yeah, exactly. And it was kind of fun. It made me feel a little different about a lot of things.

PLAYBOY: What things?

GILMORE: Just being aware that I never did get afraid. I knew that if I just kept going, I'd get out. It left me with a distinct feeling, like a kind of overcoming of myself. It was just an incident that . . . well, I hope I relate it right.

PLAYBOY: Do you think that story applies to your situation now?

GILMORE: Well, it shows I'm capable of arriving at an end. [*Laughs*] I'm supposed to have a low frustration level.

PLAYBOY: But in fact you're perseverant, right? As the story shows.

GILMORE: Well, I've fought my way through every kind of delay and motion and waiver tryin' to get 'em to carry out this sentence, against every kind of asshole lawyer, goin' before senile judges all over the goddamn country . . . Jesus!

PLAYBOY: So going through the brambles taught you to keep trying until your situation was hopeless? [*Gilmore laughs*] Was that the point at which you just told yourself, from here on I'm in for trouble?

GILMORE: The point of no return! [*Laughs*] Ah, Jeez, I always felt like I was in for trouble. I seemed to have a talent, or rather a knack, for making adults look at me a little different, different from the way they looked at other kids, like maybe bewildered, or maybe repelled.

PLAYBOY: Repelled?

GILMORE: Just a different look, like adults aren't supposed to look at kids.

PLAYBOY: With hate in their eyes?

GILMORE: Beyond hate. Loathing, I'd say. I can remember one lady in Flagstaff, Arizona, a neighbor of my folks when I was three or four. She became so frustrated with rage at whatever shit I was doing that she attacked me physically with full intent of hurting me. My dad had to jump up and restrain her.

PLAYBOY: What could you have been doing to get her so mad?

GILMORE: Just the way I was talking to her and the way I was acting. I was never quite . . . a boy. My brother Frank can tell you about one evening in Portland, when I was about eight, we all went over to these people's house, and there were two or three adults there. I don't remember just what I did, giving everybody a lot of lip, fuckin' with everything in the house—I don't remember what all—but anyhow, this one lady finally flipped completely out. Screamed. Ranted. Raved. Threw me out of the house. And the other adults there supported her and all felt the feelings she felt. Apparently, shit like that didn't have much effect on me. I can remember just walking home, about three miles, whistling and singing to myself.

PLAYBOY: It sounds as though you were on the course you've always followed well before you went to reform school. Why did you say it was going to reform school that got you started——

GILMORE: You asked!

PLAYBOY: Yes, but your answer misled us. It sounds as though your life might have worked out about the same even if you hadn't been sent to Woodburn.

GILMORE: Look, reform schools disseminate certain esoteric knowledge. They sophisticate. A kid comes out of reform school and he's learned a few things he would otherwise have missed. And he identifies, usually, with the people who share that same esoteric knowledge, the criminal element, or whatever you want to call it. So going to Woodburn was not a small thing in my life.

THE PLAYBOY INTERVIEW

PLAYBOY: Was it bad at Woodburn?

GILMORE: Nothing really bad happened to me. It wasn't all that bad a thing. I was just locked up, deprived of my freedom.

PLAYBOY: That was the worst of it?

GILMORE: Yes. Jesus! Being deprived of your freedom when you're 10 or 14? A kid resents losing part of his life.

PLAYBOY: How did you fit in there?

GILMORE: Man, that place made me think that that was the only way to live. The guys in there that I looked up to, they were tough, they were hipsters—this was the Fifties—and they seemed to run everything there. The staff were local beer-drinkin' guys that put in their hours, and they didn't care if you did this or did that. They had a few psych doctors there, too. Psychoanalysis was a big thing then. They would come in and they would show you their ink-blot tests and they would ask you all kinds of questions, mostly related to sex. And look at ya funny and . . . things like that.

PLAYBOY: How long were you there?

GILMORE: Fifteen months. I escaped four times, and after that, I finally got hip that the way to really get out of that place was to show 'em that I was rehabilitated. And after four months of not getting into any trouble, they released me. That taught me that people like that are easily fooled.

PLAYBOY: Why did you want to fool them? Perhaps they were trying to help you.

GILMORE: The one way they could help you was by gettin' you released, and for them to do that, you had to fool 'em.

PLAYBOY: How did you feel when you were released from Woodburn?

GILMORE: I came out looking for trouble. Thought that's what you're supposed to do. I was anxious to do everything, like I couldn't burn up energy fast enough. I felt slightly superior to everybody else 'cause I'd been in reform school. I had a tough-guy complex, that sort of smart-aleck juvenile-delinquent attitude. *Juvenile delinquent*—remember that phrase? Sure dates me, don't it? Nobody could tell me anything. I had a ducktail haircut, I smoked, drank, shot heroin, smoked weed, took speed, got into fights, chased and caught pretty little broads. The Fifties were a hell of a time to be a juvenile delinquent. I stole and robbed and gambled and went to Fats Domino and Gene Vincent dances at the local halls.

PLAYBOY: What did you want to make of your life at that point?

GILMORE: I wanted to be a mobster.

PLAYBOY: What's your idea of a mobster? Like James Cagney with a piece?

GILMORE: No, man, a member of the Mob.

PLAYBOY: Which, in Portland, might have been a myth, like the Broadway gang.

GILMORE: Sure.

PLAYBOY: Didn't you think you had any other talents?

GILMORE: Well, yeah, I had talents. I've always been good at drawing. I've drawn since I was a child, and I remember a teacher in about the second grade telling my mom, "Your son's an artist," in a way that showed she really meant it. My mom used to tell me about my great-grandfather Kerby, who was a pretty well-known painter around Provo about a hundred years ago. And people in the family have always said, Gary's really lucky, he inherited all Grandpa Kerby's talent. I don't argue with that, but I don't agree. I think whatever talent I have is something I earned on my own.

PLAYBOY: How long was it before you were locked up again?

GILMORE: Four months.

PLAYBOY: Four months! We thought you said that reform schools educate. Couldn't you have used your esoteric knowledge to stay out of jail?

GILMORE: It was just the pattern of my life. Some guys are lucky all their lives. No matter what kind of trouble they get into, pretty soon they're back on the bricks. But some guys are unlucky. They fuck up once on the outside and it's the pattern of their lives to be drawn back to do a lot of time.

PLAYBOY: And you're one of the unlucky ones?

GILMORE: Yeah, "the eternal recidivist." We're creatures of habit, man.

PLAYBOY: What's the longest stretch of time you've been free since you first went to reform school?

GILMORE: Eight months was about the longest.

PLAYBOY: Your I.Q.'s supposedly about 130, and yet you've spent almost 19 of the past 22 years behind bars. Why were you never able to get away with anything?

GILMORE: I got away with a couple of things. I ain't a great thief. I'm impulsive. Don't plan, don't think. You don't have to be superintelligent to get away with shit, you just have to think. But I don't. I'm impatient. Not greedy enough. I could have gotten away with lots of things that I got caught for. I don't, ah, really understand it. Maybe I quit caring a long time ago.

PLAYBOY: But when you got out of prison last April, you'd just done 12 and a half straight years——

GILMORE: Except for a few weeks in '72 when I was on escape——

PLAYBOY: OK, but 12 and a half straight years, and here in Provo you had waiting for you all kinds of people who wanted to help you make it. Ida and Vern [Gilmore's aunt and uncle] gave you a room in their house and fixed you up with a job. You'd written 50 or more letters to Brenda [Gilmore's cousin, the daughter of Ida and Vern] telling her how desperately you wanted to make a decent life for yourself——

GILMORE: Just a minute—let me have a drink of this coffee.

PLAYBOY: Okay.

GILMORE: I didn't have any lunch, because the food was so goddamn cold. I know it seems like a small thing, man, but I let small things get to me. I always have, especially now, in here.

PLAYBOY: So were the letters to Brenda a con? She allowed us to read them, and they were very beautiful, convincing letters.

GILMORE: Thank you. The letters were sincere.

PLAYBOY: So when you came out in April, there was a period of time when you were confident of making it?

GILMORE: Making what?

PLAYBOY: Making good.

GILMORE: Ah, I don't know. The last two or three years, I've pretty well accepted the fact that I'd probably never be . . . free. I know I'm a little different from most people. Man, if, ah . . . I mean, I just. . . .

PLAYBOY:: Did you think last April when you were set free that you were bound to get into trouble?

GILMORE: I didn't know what the hell I was gonna do. I just . . . I didn't know what I was gonna do.

PLAYBOY: Brenda told us about picking you up at the airport in Salt Lake City after you were released. She said you were like a visitor from another planet. You'd never seen an automatic moneychanger. She took you to a mall to buy some clothes and you'd never seen a mall. You were so engrossed in looking at the girls that you fell into a fountain.

GILMORE: Brenda says a lot of things. She also said I looked like a scared rabbit. She told that to *Newsweek*. I never looked like a fuckin' scared rabbit. I weighed 190 pounds.

PLAYBOY: Maybe she was just moved by the sight of you. She hoped she could give you a break.

GILMORE: Brenda gave me nothing. You really misunderstand all of that, ole buddy. Look, my actions and what I said to Brenda in those letters may seem inconsistent. But I believe Brenda knows how I really feel about her. I've told her. She may not understand. But I don't want to feel those harsh, bum feelings. I ain't got time to hate. It ain't a matter of forgiving and it ain't a matter of forgetting.

PLAYBOY: But still, by the time you were home a month, you had a car, you had a job, and then you met Nicole. All of that was at least partly thanks to Brenda and Vern and others, wasn't it?

GILMORE: Well, as you say, I'd been locked up for 12 and a half years straight, and I wanted to have a little fun and drink a little bit of beer. I didn't need a lot of money, but I wanted to drive around and do a few things. Everybody seemed to think that I was . . . like, I should mellow out and settle down and do the things they were doing.

PLAYBOY: Isn't that what you tried with Nicole? With her two kids, you also had a ready-made family to enjoy before you were home a month.

GILMORE: But Nicole understood me. We're twin souls. We've known each other forever. But that was one of my arguments with Vern. He felt like I was drinkin' too much and going too fast, things like that, you know? Well, I told him he could think what he wants. I just felt like——

PLAYBOY: You had some catching up to do?

GILMORE: [*Sighs*] Yeah.

PLAYBOY: You think you might have been too impatient to make up for lost time?

GILMORE: Probably. Yeah, probably. I mean, you can go too fast and miss the small things, and seek too hard for pleasures and miss them when they come.

PLAYBOY: Well, yes, but what we're talking about is risking your freedom immediately by boosting things out of stores, cases of beer, water skis, hi-fis, stupid things like that. Did you think you could just keep getting away with things?

GILMORE: I did get caught a couple of times, but I just refused to be arrested. I wouldn't let the fuckers take me back in the store. I just told them to get fucked and I left. Told 'em I can't stand those long check-out lines. [*Laughs*] You don't always have to let some asshole arrest you, especially if he doesn't have a gun. Sucker ain't got a gun, how's he gonna arrest you?

PLAYBOY: But it went much further than that, didn't it? You broke into the store in Spanish Fork and stole eight or nine pistols. You took off for Idaho Falls and got arrested within 12 hours for beating someone half to death. Was that all part of the build-up to the murders?

GILMORE: No, that shit happened before I met Nicole.

PLAYBOY: And the murders came after.

GILMORE: After I lost her. Look, Nicole and I have known and loved each other for thousands of years. I know this. Nicole knows it. We parted. Through my stupidity, I hurt her and caused her to leave me on July 13, two months to the day after I met her again in this life. I was hurting bad. I've never felt so bad, and I've gone through some shit in my life you wouldn't believe. But I never felt so terrible as I did in that final week. I mean, I couldn't hardly walk, I couldn't sleep, I didn't hardly eat. Booze didn't even touch it. It got worse every day, a heavy hurt and loss. If this doesn't make sense, well, neither does the death of Jenkins and Bushnell.

PLAYBOY: Tell us what happened the night you killed Jensen.

GILMORE: That's right, Jensen. I call him Jenkins for some reason, but the name's Jensen, Max Jensen. Okay. Just a moment. [*Long pause*] Uh [*begins speaking in a rapid monotone*], I drove over to Nicole's mother's house and I had my new truck and Nicole's mother was there and, uh, she came out and we talked a little bit and I asked her if she would return a gun that I had given her earlier. She didn't want to, but she did. She asked me if I'd drive April down to the store to get her tennis racket strung or something, and I said okay. I really didn't have a thing about April. I was concerned about Nicole and thinkin' about Nicole and it was kind of nice having Nicole's little sister there. So April got in the truck and, man, she turned the radio on real loud and moved right over beside me and told me she didn't want to go home, and I told her, well, look, I'll keep you out all night, if you want. So I drove down to the place where I'd bought my truck and I talked to those guys about the financial arrangements. I had about four or five pistols left from that robbery and I left them with these guys as security for the truck. I kept one pistol with me, the loaded one, and I signed the papers and took ownership of the truck. I'm tryin' to remember this as I talk.

PLAYBOY: Okay.

GILMORE: So I signed some papers taking possession of the truck, and then I was drivin' around with April and we got out into Orem and I pulled around the corner to this service station and it looked fairly deserted. That's what I guess drew my attention to it. Just a moment [*takes an aspirin with cold coffee*]. . . . So I just drove around the corner and parked and told April to stay in the truck, I'd be back in a moment. And I went over to the gas station and told Jensen to give me the money, and he did, and I told him, well, come on in the bathroom and get down on the floor, and it was pretty quick. I didn't let him know it was coming or anything. It was just a .22, so I shot him twice in rapid succession, to make sure that he was not in any pain or that he wasn't left half alive or anything. And, and, I left there and I drove to, uh, I don't know just where that Sinclair station was, but I drove back to the main drag. State Street, I guess it is, and I went into Albertson's and bought some potato chips and different things to take to a movie and half a case of beer and some things that April wanted to eat, and I asked if she wanted to go to a drive-in and I took her to see *Cuckoo's Nest* and it kind of freaked her out. April's been in the nut house a time or two, you know.

PLAYBOY: Uh-huh.

GILMORE: So she didn't want to stay there, so we left and I drove over to Brenda's and stayed there for about an hour. Then we left there and I got lost, you know. I asked April if she wanted to go to a motel and she told me she still didn't want to go home. I don't know this area, you know, so I was drivin' around, and April was guiding me and, Jees, you couldn't have a worse guide. So I got lost a time or two and I ran out of gas and I ended up in Provo and I just walked to a drive-in and got a couple guys and I told them, "I'll give you five bucks if you take me to a gas station and get some gas." So they did and after I got my truck going again, I went to the Holiday Inn there in Provo and got a room, and then I went over to the restaurant and bought some food. I seen some kids I knew and I got a joint of weed from 'em and went back to the hotel room and smoked weed and that kind of flipped April out. She can't take things like that. It was pretty late then, probably two or three, so we just went on to sleep. It was twin beds and she slept in one bed and I slept in the other and the next morning I drove her home and she kissed me goodbye and we were still friends and everything. And I'm certain she had no knowledge of what happened at the gas station.

PLAYBOY: She didn't know about it at all?

GILMORE: I'm positive. She knew nothing about it.

PLAYBOY: You're sure she didn't hear the shots?

GILMORE: No, she didn't hear nothin'. She was in the truck. We were in the restroom. The door was closed. I'm pretty sure I closed the door. It was only a .22. April always kept the radio going, and I think I even turned it up louder than usual when I left. She always kept it loud, anyway. I'm certain she didn't hear the shots. She has no knowledge—she has no personal knowledge.

PLAYBOY: What was her mood when she left you?

GILMORE: Pretty good. April was in a pretty good mood all the time until she smoked that joint, and then it did somethin' to her and she just started getting real belligerent, bossy, you know, and April can get pretty rowdy. . . .

PLAYBOY: Were you able to sleep that night?

GILMORE: I think I slept for a couple of hours.

PLAYBOY: So you felt more or less all right?

GILMORE: I went to work the next day.

PLAYBOY: The day you killed Bushnell?

THE PLAYBOY INTERVIEW

GILMORE: Yeah.

PLAYBOY: But how could you explain to yourself what you'd done? Had Jensen said or done something to annoy you?

GILMORE: No, not at all.

PLAYBOY: Then what prompted you to take him back to the restroom?

GILMORE: I don't really know.

PLAYBOY: What do you mean, you don't know?

GILMORE: I mean, I don't really know. I said the place looked deserted. It just seemed appropriate.

PLAYBOY: Appropriate to kill a man?

GILMORE: Fuck!

PLAYBOY: Well, if this was your first murder, it seems curious that you'd describe it as "appropriate."

GILMORE: Are you guys listenin'? If you listen, and try to catch the nuances in what I say, you might not ask so many stupid questions. I'm trying to express myself clearly. I'm trying to be understood. If sometimes I use a little humor, or say something diabolical, you should goddamn sure take that into consideration.

PLAYBOY: Saying "appropriate" was meant to be funny?

GILMORE: [*Sighs*] No.

PLAYBOY: Well, tell us this: When you stopped at the gas station, was your intention to rob Jensen or kill him?

GILMORE: I had the intention of killing him.

PLAYBOY: How did that concept form in your mind?

GILMORE: I can't say. It had been building all week. Then that night, I knew I had to open a valve and let something out and I didn't know exactly what it would be and I wasn't thinking in words or terms of I'll do this or I'll do that, that'll make me feel better. I just knew something was happening in me and that I'd let some of the steam off and, uh, I guess all this sounds pretty vicious.

PLAYBOY: The steam was building up because of your breaking up with Nicole, is that right?

GILMORE: Because I couldn't rectify it, because I couldn't seem to get her back. It was so silly the way we broke up. She didn't want to any more than I did, and I knew that. But she was maybe a little stronger than I was. Maybe a little more stubborn. I'm the one that kicked her out of the car and told her I didn't want to see her anymore. I mean, you may think that she left me, but that's not really the case. But after I did that, I had immediate regrets and the next day I went and tried to get her back, but her pride had been hurt and she'd taken a firm stand against it. I guess I—I'm tellin' you these things and I don't think Nicole would mind. I'm telling you the facts as I know them. I think Nicole may have told you different things. Am I right?

PLAYBOY: We haven't talked that much.

GILMORE: I don't think she would mind if I told this exactly as it happened, which is exactly what I'm doin'. I'm not putting the blame on her and I'm not putting it on me. I'm just tellin' you what happened.

PLAYBOY: Sure.

GILMORE: And then the people who smoke pipes and make judgments can, uh, uh—neither one of you guys smoke a pipe, do you? [*Laughs*]

PLAYBOY: No.

GILMORE: Good. Let the pipe smokers make judgments. [*Laughs*]

PLAYBOY: When did you start thinking that your release might come by taking somebody's life?

GILMORE: [*Long pause*] I didn't w-want to kill Nicole and, and, uh, I had to either get her back and get it all straightened out or something was going to happen. There was no way on earth I could let it go. It wasn't a thing that I could just set aside.

PLAYBOY: Why?

GILMORE: Well, it just wasn't. Because I felt so strongly about Nicole and I knew she felt the same way about me and I felt that [*Sighs*] she may have just been avoiding me. She'd been hurt by guys before in her life and she didn't want that kind of thing anymore. Contrary to popular belief, I never really hurt Nicole physically. In fact, when we had arguments, I w-wouldn't . . . I'd let her win 'em.

PLAYBOY: We thought you said you were the one who threw her out.

GILMORE: I'm not trying to make myself look good. I would rather just give you the facts and then, if you've got the facts, I think you've got the whole thing.

PLAYBOY: Sure. [*Long pause*]

GILMORE: I thought that I'd lost her forever and I couldn't accept it. [*Long pause*] Ah, well, see, I thought I'd lost her forever and I couldn't accept that. I wasn't going to accept it, and. . . .

PLAYBOY: How did you feel that killing somebody would help you accept losing Nicole? Can you explain that?

GILMORE: I don't know. I didn't want to kill Nicole. Because I was thinking about killing her and if I had killed her, I would have killed myself. I wasn't thinkin', I was just doin'.

PLAYBOY: Is it possible that you were trying to end your life by doing these things, getting caught and winding up where you are now?

GILMORE: No, I was lookin' to get away with it.

PLAYBOY: Apparently, killing Jensen didn't do anything to take the pressure off. Why did you go out the next night and kill Bushnell?

GILMORE: I don't know, man. I'm impulsive. I don't think.

PLAYBOY: You killed him the same way you'd killed Jensen the night before—ordering him to lie down on the floor, then firing point-blank into his head. Did you think killing Bushnell would give you some kind of relief you didn't get with Jensen?

GILMORE: I told you, I wasn't thinkin'. What I do remember is an absence of thought. Just movements, actions. I shot Bushnell, and then the gun jammed—them fuckin' automatics! And I thought, man, this guy's not dead. I wanted to shoot him a second time, because I didn't want him to lie there half dead. I didn't want him in pain. I tried to jack the mechanism and get the gun workin' again, and shoot him again, but it was jammed, and I had to get my ass out of there. I jacked the gun into shape again but too late to do anything for Mr. Bushnell. I'm afraid he didn't die immediately. When I ordered him to lie down, I wanted it to be quick for him. There was no chance, no choice for him. That sounds cold. But you asked.

PLAYBOY: Did either Jensen or Bushnell show fear?

GILMORE: Jensen did not resist. Neither did Bushnell. Bushnell was huge. He looked like a college wrestler. I was struck by Jensen's friendly, smiling, kind face. I thought of these things at the time of the shootings.

PLAYBOY: You said that Jensen didn't say or do anything to annoy you. Did Bushnell?

GILMORE: I don't remember anything he said, except that he asked me to be quiet and not alert his wife. She was in the next room. He was anxious to comply. He was calm, even brave. I wasn't afraid of him.

PLAYBOY: Was there any difference in the way you approached the two killings?

GILMORE: No, not really. You could say it was a little more certain that Mr. Bushnell was going to die.

PLAYBOY: Why?

GILMORE: Because it was already a fact that Mr. Jensen had died, and so the next one was more certain.

PLAYBOY: Was the second killing easier than the first?

GILMORE: Neither one of 'em were hard or easy.

PLAYBOY: Had you ever had any dealings of any kind with either one of those men?

GILMORE: No.

PLAYBOY: Well, what led you to the City Center Motel, where Bushnell worked? If robbery was part of your motive, certainly there were better targets in Provo than that quiet, unpretentious motel.

GILMORE: Vern and Ida live right close by. I stopped by to see them. They weren't home. I just followed an impulse when I went in there. It wasn't anything I'd planned and schemed to do. Murder vents rage, and rage was what I was feeling.

PLAYBOY: Over Nicole?

GILMORE: Over Nicole.

PLAYBOY: Let's see if we understand: You left your truck in a service station where you were well known; you walked around with your pistol in your belt; Vern and Ida weren't home; so you just walked into this motel and shot the night manager, robbing him of about $125. Is that about it?

GILMORE: That's the whole story of Mr. Bushnell, right there.

PLAYBOY: But you said at your trial that you also stopped off at the apartment of a girl who wasn't home. Was she a girlfriend?

GILMORE: No, I just wanted some company. I wasn't planning anything, and I was walking around while they worked on my truck, and this girl was only a block and a half away, and she liked to drink beer, and she always had some beer. But she wasn't home.

PLAYBOY: But if she had been home, and if you'd wound up making love to her, would that have vented the rage you were talking about?

GILMORE: No, no, it's two different things. Just goin' for a fuck, makin' love, whatever man, I don't want to mess with questions like that. I think they're cheap.

PLAYBOY: We're just trying to understand the quality of this rage you speak of. It wasn't a rage that might have been vented in sex?

GILMORE: I don't want to bother with questions that pertain to sex.

PLAYBOY: But if, on the night you killed Bushnell, you had wound up with a friendly girl who could offer you beer and company and a relaxing time, wouldn't that have helped you feel better?

GILMORE: I don't want to answer that question.

PLAYBOY: You seem to find it easier talking about murder than sex.

GILMORE: That's your judgment.

PLAYBOY: If you hadn't been caught that night, do you think there would have been a third or fourth killing?

GILMORE: There would have been more than that, that night. [*Sighs*]

PLAYBOY: You would have just continued?

GILMORE: I was going to just continue.

PLAYBOY: How long?

GILMORE: Until I got caught or shot to death by the police or something like that. I wasn't thinkin', I wasn't plannin', I was just doin'. It was a damned shame for those two guys. But I've given some thought to the fact—well, I shouldn't use the word fact—to the *possibility* that maybe they were supposed to have been killed. How do I know they weren't meeting, at my hands, a karmic debt?

PLAYBOY: It must be very comforting for you to think in those terms.

GILMORE: It's just something I've pondered. There is so much similarity between Jenkins and Bushnell—both in their mid-20s, both family men, both Mormon missionaries. Perhaps the murders of these men were meant to occur.

PLAYBOY: At the hands of a man who lacked, and might have wanted, all the qualities you've just described?

GILMORE: I digress, I guess. I'm just saying that murder vents rage. Rage is not reason. The murders were without reason. Don't try to understand murder by using reason. Destruction, rage, futility, words like that—try them if you want to understand.

PLAYBOY: If you intended to go on killing that night, why did you throw your gun away?

GILMORE: I had other guns. I didn't want to keep that son of a bitch. It had just got through jammin'. I was taking precautions. I got rid of Jensen's money-changer. I don't think the Orem police ever did find that. And after the Bushnell murder, I thought I'd get rid of the gun. It was wiped pretty well—they never got any fingerprints off it or anything. I thought I was taking precautions. Of course, I wasn't thinking very coherently.

PLAYBOY: And in the course of getting rid of your gun, you shot yourself in the hand.

GILMORE: Well, automatics go off easy. They do. All you gotta do is press their triggers and the fuckers go off.

PLAYBOY: So it was an accident that could have happened to anybody.

GILMORE: Yeah, it's a touchy gun, man. I was pushing it into a bush and I guess I pushed it by the trigger and it shot me in the hand. I had thrown away the cash-box from the motel and I wrapped my hand in my jacket to keep from being noticed. But I was noticed by the kid back at the gas station where I'd left my truck. Sucker knew me. I tried calling Brenda and a-asked her to come and get me, and she said she would. But instead, she called the police and didn't give me any warning.

PLAYBOY: Just looking at the facts, it would seem that shooting yourself and calling Brenda demonstrated a wish to be caught.

GILMORE: No, no. I never thought Brenda would call the police. And shooting myself was a goddamn accident.

PLAYBOY: You don't think it was a subconscious desire to be caught?

GILMORE: I'm not gonna answer that question. Where you gettin' your info, from Brenda? You're about 35 degrees off course. Accidents can happen to psychopaths as easily as anybody else, man. That's what the psych doctors call me—a psychopath. They call you that when they don't get around to calling you a sociopath. You gotta be one or the other, you can't be neither or both.

PLAYBOY: You said before that you were planning on killing more people until you were caught or killed. So the goal would be getting caught or killed, right?

GILMORE: Whatever's fair.

PLAYBOY: Do you think some people might commit murders because they want to be killed themselves?

GILMORE: Some people might.

PLAYBOY: But not you?

GILMORE: Fuck, no.

PLAYBOY: Your murders couldn't have been encouraged or provoked by your knowledge that in Utah you'd die by a firing squad?

GILMORE: No, no. [*Sighs*]

PLAYBOY: Have you ever had a dream in which the image of the firing squad occurred?

GILMORE: No, just about every other goddamn kind of dream, morbid shit like that.

PLAYBOY: Like what?

GILMORE: Well, I used to dream that I was being led to this place, a place that had a wall with slots in it, like lockers, and they would open one of 'em, and it was all concrete and dirty, and they would slide you in there. I had that fuckin' dream about a dozen times.

PLAYBOY: Would you call it a nightmare?

GILMORE: Would you? [*Laughs*] No, no, I've only had one real nightmare.

PLAYBOY: What about?

GILMORE: About being beheaded.

PLAYBOY: Did you have it recurrently?

GILMORE: No, but it marked a conscious memory thing in my life. I was a kid then, but for years I was really afraid of losing part of my body. I thought being beheaded was the most horrible death imaginable.

PLAYBOY: More horrible than shooting?

GILMORE: Shootin's quick, man. It's over like that. You're dead before you hear the sound of the shot that kills you.

PLAYBOY: It's been said that the guillotine is actually the most humane form of execution.

GILMORE: For me, man, that is a morbid fuckin' image. That and the headsman's block, those two and the gallows. I've sounded people out on 'em, because they've stuck pretty deep with me. And most people agree that that's a pretty morbid bunch of images. But I don't think they hold the same effect for most people that they do for me. For me, they're like some kind of memory or some goddamn thing. It seems like, to tell you the truth, there's just something there I'm acquainted with in some way I don't understand.

PLAYBOY: Can you recall any film or newsreel or anything along that line in which you've seen men die before a firing squad?

GILMORE: Remember Goya's painting of a firing squad—*The Death Squad,* I think he called it? That may have stayed in my mind. And I've seen lots of cartoons about waving away the blindfold and taking a last puff on a cigarette. Then there was that movie, *The Execution of Private Slovik.*

PLAYBOY: When you saw the movie, could you imagine yourself in the condemned man's place?

GILMORE: Oh. I guess everybody that saw that movie probably imagined themselves in Eddie Slovik's place. I couldn't imagine myself saying all them Hail Marys, though. [*Laughs*] I thought Eisenhower was a real asshole to allow that execution to take place. Private Slovik should have been discharged from the Service. He was sentenced to die for cowardice, I guess, or dereliction of duty, or failing to be a good soldier, or some goddamn thing. If I'd a been in the war, I'd a fought, you know, I'd a been a soldier. But there was no goddamn excuse for killing the man, and Eisenhower is the son of a bitch that allowed it. Then the firing squad didn't kill him with the first round, and they were fumblin' and bumblin' and unable to reload, and Slovik had to suffer. It was an interesting movie, but I hated the actor who played Slovik, that Martin Sheen. Hail Marys! Jesus!

PLAYBOY: If some kind of morbid fascination with a firing-squad death wasn't part of the reason, what was it about you that made these murders happen?

GILMORE: I always knew I was capable of killing somebody.

PLAYBOY: How did you know that unless you'd done it?

GILMORE: It's just something you know.

PLAYBOY: Had you ever proved it before like you proved it with Jensen and Bushnell? You hinted earlier you had.

GILMORE: No.

PLAYBOY: Well, your record doesn't suggest you did. Up until the murders, your crimes were relatively tame.

GILMORE: Will you listen to that fool screaming for his goddamn cigarettes? This noisy motherfucker is some kind of rotten prison. It's like a second-class county jail in the South. Filthy motherfucker, too. The joint in Oregon is much more secure, and they keep that son of a bitch immaculate.

PLAYBOY: Yes, Gary, but this question is still with us: How did you always know you could kill somebody?

GILMORE: This may sound strange to you now, because I know I have developed a technique of making people like me. It's one of the things that I've overcome about myself. I think I have at least developed that: a way of making people like me. I can get along with people at least now. I—I always could, though, really, I guess. Nobody overtly disliked me. There was just the feeling that they'd rather not be around me if they had their druthers. I always kind of felt a victim of the "Fell" syndrome.

PLAYBOY: The what?

GILMORE: The "Fell" syndrome. It's from a 17th- or 18th-century quotation. It's anonymous. It goes simply:

I do not like thee, Dr. Fell,
The reason why I cannot tell;
But this I know, and know full well,
I do not like thee, Dr. Fell.

When I read that, I understood its meaning at once and applied it to myself. Nobody liked this guy, and they didn't know why, either.

PLAYBOY: We remember now reading that in a couple of your letters to Nicole. In fact, we remembered it all along. We just wanted to see if you'd tell it again the same, and you did, just about word for word.

GILMORE: It's a poem, man. A poem has a certain set of words.

PLAYBOY: Yes, but you also told the story of going down into the brambles in precisely the words you used when you wrote about it to Nicole——

GILMORE: Those letters are personal, man. . . .

PLAYBOY: Gary, be serious. The guards read them. The D.A. has a full set. So do Nicole's psychiatrists. Many of them have been printed in the newspapers. What we're saying is that these stories sound like recitations that you use in a calculating way. Maybe part of your "technique" of making people like you is to charm them with little stories.

GILMORE: I haven't learned to make people like me. I've learned how to like people. I should have never used the word technique. It's just a simple truth: Learn to like people and they'll like you. Ain't nothin' calculating about that. I got lonely. I like language, words, slang and rhymes and rhythms.

THE PLAYBOY INTERVIEW

PLAYBOY: The impression that you're running a con some of the time might come from the many voices you employ. Sometimes you talk like an East Texas drifter, sometimes like the mobster you wanted to be as a kid, sometimes, in fact, like a kid. It's as if you've learned half a dozen dialects and switch back and forth between them, depending on the listener and the subject at hand.

GILMORE: When I tell somebody something, I like to make myself clear. I like humor, too. I tell the truth. In jail you rap a lot, you know, to pass the time. Damn near every convict has his little collection of reminiscences, anecdotes and stories, and a person can get sort of practiced at recollecting. You probably got a few yarns you spin on occasion yourself. The fact that you tell something more than once to more than one person doesn't make it a lie. It doesn't make it calculating, either. And there's nothing wrong with tailoring your manner of speech to the listener. I mean, Jesus, what's wrong with that? I know I speak well. I'm not just a collection of stories.

PLAYBOY: This awkward way of communicating doesn't help. If we didn't have this glass between us or didn't have to write notes, if we could be face to face more often——

GILMORE: This is a bum way to talk, but we're tryin'! You probably noticed that when we talk personally, face to face, I don't put things quite as strong. See, I'm used to talkin' to somebody who I can't see. I lean on it a little bit to make goddamn certain I'm understood. Take this into account when you consider my fuckin' answers.

PLAYBOY: Of course.

GILMORE: Maybe I do try to entertain and charm. I do emphasize things. One reason, ah . . . or how I learned to do this, let's say, is perhaps because I've spent a lot of time in the hole. . . .

PLAYBOY: How much time altogether?

GILMORE: Maybe four years.

PLAYBOY: In isolation?

GILMORE: Well, sure, it's the hole. And when you're in the hole, you get used to carrying on a conversation with a guy you can't see. He's in the cell next door or down the line from you. And so, it, ah . . . just becomes [*Sighs*] necessary to kind of, ah . . . emphasize to make yourself clear and heard, because there might be other conversations going on and a lot of other goddamn noise, guards rattling keys, doors clanging shut, things like that. So think about that, and, you know, you're in the hole, you, and if you talk to somebody, you can't see 'em, yeah, and, well, when you get out, man, and you're talkin' to somebody face to face, it's something you have to get used to again.

78

PLAYBOY: Is there anything you'd like to add about the circumstances leading up to the murders?

GILMORE: The truth is the truth, and I'm telling you the truth not to pass blame, you know, to anybody. I'm telling it to you because it's true, and I think it's important. I thought about omitting it completely, and then I decided not to. I wanted to talk to Nicole first and get her permission, but the motherfuckers won't let me get through to her. Do you understand what I'm saying?

PLAYBOY: You'll have to say more.

GILMORE: Well, I've wanted to tell you this for weeks. I think it's time you should know.

PLAYBOY: Go ahead.

GILMORE: Okay. See, Jensen was killed on a Monday, Bushnell on a Tuesday. Sunday, I was really feeling down. I drove around the park out there in Springville for a while, and I was hopin' to just see Nicole or little Sunny and Jeremy Peabody [Nicole's children]. And, ah, I went to sleep up against a tree in the park for about an hour. And when I woke up, I really felt shitty. I drank a couple of beers and went over to Nicole's house, and I went in and I took a bath and, ah, then I heard the front door open and Nicole came in. I went over and I put my arms around her and she just stood there, you know. I could see that I couldn't communicate with her anymore. It really fucked me up. I only had a towel on, and the fuckin' towel fell off. She told me to get dressed and I got dressed and, ah, she . . . I kept tryin' to talk to her and she was being smart and rude, you know. So I grabbed her by the hand and I was going to pull her to me and she just started hollerin' at me and jerked free and said something like, "Can't you talk to me without touching me?" or s-somethin', and then she ran outside and I followed her. She was leaving, and when I went up to her car, she . . . just flipped out slightly, you know, and kept tryin' to get her kids in the car. She thought I was going to hurt her or something. I think I told her just don't go without taking the new Electrolux I bought for you, because the house would be empty and someone would rip it off. And I leaned up against her car and, ah, she pulled a gun on me and said, "Get away from my car, Gary Gilmore."

PLAYBOY: What kind of gun was it?

GILMORE: It was a magnum .22 Derringer. She had it pointed right at me. It was a gun I gave her, because she'd been hurt a couple times in her life by different guys, and I told her, man, if anybody ever fucks with you, slaps you around, gives you a hard time, just don't take it, you know. I didn't think it was loaded, and I was thinking about taking it away from her, but I didn't want her to start screaming. We were outside, and all the neighbors would hear and . . . and . . . she might start runnin'. So I just stood there and leaned against her car and told her, "I don't think your fuckin' gun is loaded, Nicole, so go get your vacuum cleaner, put it in your car and leave. If that's what you want. I mean, if you want to go, then I want you to." I don't remember all the words. I didn't say a whole lot. I didn't give a shit about getting shot, you know. In fact, I think I told her, hey, if you're going to shoot me, do it. And, ah, she wavered on that one a little bit, and I think she put the gun away and I didn't advance on her. I just left. I felt real bad. And I saw everything . . . well, it just seemed like a final ending to me right there.

PLAYBOY: You say you left? Or did Nicole drive off?

GILMORE: Well, I finally just moved away from her car and let her get in, and she got in real quick and rolled up all the windows and locked the doors. I don't know if that little story is as dramatic as it seems. . . .

PLAYBOY: Go on.

GILMORE: I wanted to tell it to you because there were some things that may not have made sense. I told you that I didn't want to kill. . . . I told you that I killed Jensen because I didn't want to kill Nicole. And Nicole told me later that the gun *was* loaded and that if she had shot me, man, she would have shot herself immediately afterward. So she didn't hate me at the time. It's just things happenin' to us—a little bit too much for both of us, I think. I don't know. Let me see if I can get a cup of coffee and rest for a while.

PLAYBOY: Sure, that's fine. [*Gilmore is escorted away by a guard. Five minutes later, he returns.*]

GILMORE: Always feel better after a hit 'n' miss. That's Cockney rhyming slang for a piss.

PLAYBOY: You were saying before there were some things that didn't make sense. Certainly one of them has to be how losing Nicole explains killing Bushnell and Jensen. Your girlfriend leaves you, so you go out and kill two guys.

GILMORE: God, hmmmm, well . . . I mean, ah, it makes sense to me. I mean, I don't say it makes sense that those guys are dead. I don't want to say it makes sense, because that'll make it seem acceptable, and it's not. It's a damn shame that it had to happen. But, ah, ask that again. Let me give it a little thought.

PLAYBOY: Ask now?

GILMORE: No, later.

PLAYBOY: Your former cellmate, Richard Gibbs, says you told him that you killed two men in prison. Brenda says the same thing. Even Vern says you told him about two killings.

GILMORE: No, they're mistaken. These stories, they involved near killings. Gibbs will say it did involve a killing, two killings, but neither guy died.

PLAYBOY: One involved a black homosexual in the Oregon prison?

GILMORE: Just a moment, please. Jesus fuckin' [*pauses*] it's so goddamn *noisy* in here today I can't think. Goddamn guards kept me up all night with their bullshittin', playin' cards, shufflin', shit like that all night. I think I deserve a little fuckin' serenity at least.

PLAYBOY: You always say you're willing to accept your sentence. Perhaps the noise is part of the sentence.

GILMORE: You don't have to listen to the motherfucker 24 hours a day. [*Pauses. Loud noises in background.*] Well, okay [*Sighs deeply*], this kid comes to me in the joint in Oregon and asks if he could talk to me, go out in the yard with me, walk around with me, you know? And I asked him, "What's wrong?" and he said that this, ah, nigger was tryin' to fuck him. And the kid was going to check himself into the building, you know, isolation, just turn himself in and go to the hole and be locked up to get away from it. He didn't know how to handle it. What do you want me to do? I asked him, and he says, well, I'll be your kid if you protect me. And I tell him, I don't want a kid. I don't like punks, and I don't want you to be a punk, anyway. I told him, well, let me . . . let me think about it. So I just went and got another guy and I told him about it, and he said let's kill the motherfucker. So we just caught the guy comin' up the stairs and we both had pieces of pipe in our hand, and we beat him half to death and drug him down to another nigger's cell and drug him in and put him on the bunk and slammed the door and left. He was unconscious. We hit him so fast and so hard . . . he was a boxer, we didn't give him no chance. We was goin' to kill him, but we decided not to. And, uh, I mean, if we'd beat him to death, that woulda been okay, too, but we didn't.

PLAYBOY: Okay, tell us about your nickname, Hammersmith.

GILMORE: Well, just a minute. Where did you hear that?

PLAYBOY: Gibbs, Brenda, your letters to Nicole.

GILMORE: Yeah, well, this friend of mine, LeRoy, the guy I shot in the stomach when we were kids, he came to the penitentiary two years after I did, and he had a life sentence. He liked dope a lot, you know, and he was always gettin' fucked up and he'd stay fucked up for months. He had a Valium habit and he was just stayin' so fucked up, he didn't know whether he was comin' or goin' and he got in debt with this guy named Bill who was a big rowdy, a bully-type guy who had a lot of money and was dealing in dope and pushing people around and fucking with people. Once they busted him for being drunk and they took him to the hole. And he sent word to me from the hole that this Bill, this dealer, had come into his cell earlier that day and robbed him and beat him up, kicked him, put the boots to him while he had him on the floor and then took his outfit, you know his syringe and needle, and took his money and everything that he had. I knew LeRoy was awful drunk and I know that Valium will make you hallucinate a little bit and I wasn't certain whether the story was true. But LeRoy asked me if I'd fuck Bill up, you know, and so this other guy—the same guy that helped me with that nigger—he was going to the hole and I talked it over with him and he said, well, listen, I'm going to the hole tomorrow and I'll go down and talk to LeRoy and then I'll tell you whether it's true or not. So he went to the hole, stayed seven days—'cause in those days, you only stayed in the hole seven days for minor shit; now you spend months, you know—and when he came out, he told me, he says, it's true, LeRoy says go ahead, he wants you to stab Bill or pipe him or something.

And he asks me, you want me to help you? I told him no, I'll do it myself, LeRoy is my personal friend, he's been my friend for years, and I'll do this one myself. So I worked on the wreck crew, and we were doing some construction out in the yard, and I just went over, stole a hammer, and that night I caught Bill sitting down watching a football game and I just planted the hammer in his head, turned around and walked off.

PLAYBOY: How bad did you hurt him?

GILMORE: How bad did I hurt him! [*Laughs*] I felt the hammer go into his skull. About four days later, they busted me for it. They had two or three snitchers that said they seen me do it, but they weren't willing enough to reveal themselves, so they just kept me in the hole for four months and took Bill up to Portland for brain surgery. But Bill was pretty fucked up anyhow. So, to answer your question, this guy nicknamed me Hammersmith over that. He gave me a little toy hammer to wear on a chain, you know.

PLAYBOY: You're certain that both these men lived?

GILMORE: Yeah, they lived. [*Sighs*] Kind of altered their lives, though.

PLAYBOY: Well, why did you go around telling everybody that you'd killed them? Were you bragging or confessing?

GILMORE: [*Laughing*] More bragging, probably, to tell you the truth.

PLAYBOY: Were you trying to frighten people, put them on the alert?

82

GILMORE: I didn't tell those stories to *everybody*. Just selected audiences. That'll probably get garbled, so I'll repeat: selected audiences. But having to be brutally frank, yes, it's true, I guess I must have been bragging.

PLAYBOY: It sounds like the kind of bragging a person might do if he didn't believe he could kill——

GILMORE: I *told* you that was something I always knew. You must think I'm pretty goddamn shallow or forgetful.

PLAYBOY: Well, why not tell us how you knew? Did you torture or kill pets when you were a kid? Did people see a mean streak in you?

GILMORE: Yeah, there was some talk of it.

PLAYBOY: Arising from what kind of thing?

GILMORE: Once, when I was about 13, I got into a fight with a kid named Jim. I got angry and beat him half to death—choked him. Jim's dad was a rough-and-tumble fucker, and he just lifted me off Jim and picked Jim up and Jim was gasping for breath and chokin' and hurtin' and bleedin' a little. Jim's dad asked him if he wanted to go out in the yard and finish it, and Jim backed down in front of his dad, you know. He was beat, physically and mentally. Jim's dad didn't like the fact that his son wouldn't fight anymore. So he just turned on me and told me, "Don't ever come around here again, and leave right now, and I don't ever want to see you again."

PLAYBOY: Did that make you feel bad about the fight?

GILMORE: I just went out and got on my bike. I didn't say anything. I just got on my bike and left. But Jim's dad looked at me in a way that, a way, well . . . a grownup shouldn't look at a kid.

PLAYBOY: Was a fight like that rare or common for you when you were a kid?

GILMORE: That was the most vicious fight I was ever in as a kid.

PLAYBOY: Did it scare you that you could lose control of yourself?

GILMORE: Scare me? Is that a serious question? It didn't scare me—it scared Jim.

PLAYBOY: Was that fight what made you aware that you were capable of killing?

GILMORE: Well, yeah, I think so. I don't know.

PLAYBOY: It was just one of those things you did without thinking?

GILMORE: Maybe I didn't . . . the feeling I got . . . I-I remember . . . it was the way Jim's dad looked at me and told me never to come around.

PLAYBOY: That's what stays in your mind most about that event?

GILMORE: That and the way that Charley looked at me the next day.

PLAYBOY: How did Charley look at you?

THE PLAYBOY INTERVIEW

GILMORE: Like he was feeling things he didn't understand.

PLAYBOY: How did your parents react when you got into scrapes like that?

GILMORE: My dad wasn't around that much. I guess he was kind of a fugitive. I didn't know that until I was about 21, but I guess he'd done a little time on the chain gang, and then in San Quentin in the Twenties, and sometimes even after I was born, he was runnin' from the law.

PLAYBOY: Taking the family with him?

GILMORE: Sometimes. He was a rounder, you know? He'd been a circus acrobat, at one time a tightrope walker, and then sometimes he'd just disappear. My mom would tell us, well, he just walked out. The fact was, as I found out later, that he was in jail here and there for things lots of times. So up until the time I was eight, it was all knockabout, and we slept in a lot of train and bus depots.

PLAYBOY: How did your mother take the trouble you were getting into?

GILMORE: She never liked it. She resented it. She tried to understand the best s-she could.

PLAYBOY: Even after you started getting into serious trouble?

GILMORE: Her love was always strong, constant and consistent.

PLAYBOY:: Three strange and unsentimental words to describe a mother's love.

GILMORE: I don't think they're strange at all. My mom isn't all that doting and sweet. Maybe, ah, some people's mothers are. Mine, my mother's pretty practical. We're not a real tight sort of emotional family. We don't write to each other all that much. But she was always there. We always had something to eat; we was always well taken care of.

PLAYBOY: Do you think it upset you in your early life to be dragged around the country by a woman in love with a man who was on the lam?

GILMORE: She stayed with my dad because she loved him.

PLAYBOY: Loved him more than the kids?

GILMORE: No, goddamn it. She kept the family together. Doesn't that count for something?

PLAYBOY: How about your father—did he love you, too?

GILMORE: God. I don't know. He was kind of a strange man. He was nearly 50 when I was born—I think that's too goddamn old to be starting a family.

PLAYBOY: But there were two more sons after you?

GILMORE: Yeah, but I just don't think he liked me. I think he felt this thing. I don't know. I'm not sure. But sometimes I felt that he particularly disliked me. My brother Frank, Dad had a sort of an admiration and respect for. Frank wouldn't cry when he got spanked, so he'd let

84

him alone. And Mike he really loved. My brother Gaylen, I don't know how he felt about Gaylen. But I can say, just about say, that he didn't like me at all.

PLAYBOY: Did he beat or whip you?

GILMORE: Yeah. . . . I used to get whippin's with a razor strop a lot. He always . . . yeah, he favored things like that.

PLAYBOY: You mentioned that Frank wouldn't cry. Were you quick to cry when the strop came out?

GILMORE: Yeah . . . ah, man, it seemed like the thing you were supposed to do. Like start smokin' when you're about 12 or 13, because it seems like you're supposed to do that. And I thought, well, I was supposed to cry. I thought maybe that would get me out of the whoopin', but, man, it never did. Finally, I took a cue from Frank and, an . . . learned to take it. That way, pretty soon, the whole thing dies down better.

PLAYBOY: What was your relationship with your father at the time of his death?

GILMORE: Oh, just strained. We argued. It was '62 when he died, in case you want to get that fact down.

PLAYBOY: Where were you at the time?

GILMORE: I was in jail, the Rocky Butte Jail, and I was doing two weeks in the hole, I forget what the hell for—fightin' over some goddamn thing. Anyhow, I was in the hole, and this Lieutenant Cunningham came down, and he said, did you know your dad had cancer? I said, yeah. He said, well, he just died up in Seattle. And I said, all right. And he turned around and walked off. And about a day later, he came down and told me I was going to get to go to the funeral. He took me up to C Tank and I borrowed a razor and some shit from friends and got all cleaned up, and my mom came out with a suit, and then the judge who had me in there refused to sign the order granting permission for me to go. He figured I was an escape risk.

PLAYBOY: So you didn't get to go.

GILMORE: No, they took me down to the hole and left me there for another eight days or so. I was doing two years on traffic violations.

PLAYBOY: Two years on traffic violations!

GILMORE: Well, part of 'em was state and part was city. Driving without a license, utterly refusing to get a license, running red lights, all kinds of tickets stacked up that I wouldn't pay.

PLAYBOY: Actually, according to your record, you were picked up in Vancouver.

GILMORE: No, I was in jail.

PLAYBOY: Weren't you really on the road to see your father on his deathbed when you were arrested for drunk driving and contributing to the delinquency of a minor?

GILMORE: Oh, yeah, right! In Vancouver. Yeah. . . .

PLAYBOY: You keep referring to your killings, and even your own execution, as strokes of fate—"maybe it was meant to be." Does a lapse or failure like not getting to your father's bedside make you feel bad, or do you think you just weren't meant to get there?

GILMORE: Shit. I got busted for a faulty taillight. Goin' through Vancouver. They impounded my car and all that shit. And, yeah, I felt bad, I would've like to saw him. . . .

PLAYBOY: How did your mother take your father's death?

GILMORE: She's strong. But my dad didn't have any insurance or anything. She didn't have any money. She lost a lot of things she loved.

PLAYBOY: Did it hurt you that she lost them because of your dad, or because you were in jail and couldn't help her?

GILMORE: My dad should have provided better.

PLAYBOY: How about you as a father? If you could escape and disappear, do you think you could live peacefully with Nicole and her kids?

GILMORE: I think so, now. Yeah, I love Peabody and Sunny.

PLAYBOY: Can you picture yourself as a good father?

GILMORE: Yeah, I can.

PLAYBOY: Then how could you encourage Nicole to join you in suicide?

GILMORE: Oh, fuck you.

PLAYBOY: Well, Gary, it's pretty obvious from your letters and from the fact that you both attempted suicide on the same day in November, that she was trying to comply with your urgings that she meet you on the other side.

GILMORE: I never said any of that shit. That's the *National Enquirer* version you've been readin'.

PLAYBOY: Don't forget what you said to her in the letters—"Come along, kid," and other lines like that. You don't actually tell her to kill herself, but you sure don't let the subject drop.

GILMORE: Yeah, like her mother thinks I'm "Mansonesque," that I got a hold on Nicole like Manson had on his family or some goddamn thing. She's forgetting one big difference between me and Charley Manson: I do my own killing. . . .

PLAYBOY: But we're talking about Nicole killing herself. After writing her so many encouraging words about suicide, why did you get so angry with her for attempting to kill herself before you got around to it?

GILMORE: I wanted to be there first to catch her. Why should she commit suicide before I die? Listen, I wanted to go first, that's all, because

I think I'm a little stronger, and she might get lost out there. I know I ain't. I know I can go where I want. Some things you know. I wanted to be there to catch her when she came through the rye.

PLAYBOY: You think it's easier to go first or last?

GILMORE: Dead's dead.

PLAYBOY: Well, if she's going to die to be with you, don't you want her to do it on her own terms, wherever or however she can manage?

GILMORE: Dead's dead.

PLAYBOY: It doesn't matter?

GILMORE: Well, yeah, I'd like it to be a gentle, soft thing for her.

PLAYBOY: Have you arranged a way?

GILMORE: No. In fact, I-I . . . if I talk to her before I'm executed, I'm not going to ask her to do any particular thing. I may even encourage her to go on living and raise her kids. Ah, but, well, I don't want anyb-body else to be able to have her, and that's a big concern to me.

PLAYBOY: So you're on the horns of a dilemma. . . .

GILMORE: You might say that it's giving me a little pause.

PLAYBOY: She does have a responsibility to her children.

GILMORE: Aw, no more responsibility than anybody has for their kids. Listen, your kids come through you, but they're not really *of* you. Nicole knew that before I ever met her. I mean . . . everybody is an individual little soul. . . .

PLAYBOY: Do you think her kids could get along as well without her?

GILMORE: Them kids are famous, or . . . semifamous, and there's money, and, ah, there wasn't before, but, w-well, I guess this sounds like a cold-blooded thing, but I'm not really overconcerned about them kids. They're not going to starve to death. [*Sighs*] I'm concerned about Nicole and myself.

PLAYBOY: Do you think there might be an element of cruelty in your love for Nicole?

GILMORE: Oh, there might be. There might be an element of tenderness in there, too, if you look close enough.

PLAYBOY: But if you wished her well, and wished well for her children, wouldn't it be kinder to tell her to forget you, get over you, and find a man who could do good for herself and her children?

GILMORE: I'm not even going to answer that.

PLAYBOY: Is it possible that you're trying to make Nicole do to her kids what your mother did to you? Your relatives say there was a time when you were small when your mother went through a phase of being very cruel to you.

GILMORE: No, that's not true. Absolutely not.

THE PLAYBOY INTERVIEW

PLAYBOY: You think your mother was always loving and always did all she could for you?

GILMORE: I think so.

PLAYBOY: Even when she was on the run with your dad, making you kids move so often.

GILMORE: [*Long pause*] I think so.

PLAYBOY: Did she ever consider giving you up?

GILMORE: No, never. She never did, she never . . . I'm sure she wouldn't have considered that.

PLAYBOY: Yet that's what you're asking of Nicole.

GILMORE: I'm not asking anything of Nicole. I just don't want her to be with anyone else. I want to be back with her.

PLAYBOY: But Nicole still has a chance. She's only 20. She's got a good lawyer to help her get straightened out when she comes out of the hospital.

GILMORE: What's he like?

PLAYBOY: The lawyer? He's not too old, kind of bashful . . .

GILMORE: He better not make no passes at Nicole.

PLAYBOY: No, he wouldn't do that. He's a straight arrow.

GILMORE: I'm worried about her. She's probably getting as much mail as I am. You know, I accidently got one of her letters. It was addressed to Nicole Barrett, Utah State Prison, and they gave it to me. And some goddamn son of a bitch in New York was writin' to ask her for $1,200 and he wanted to marry her and . . .

PLAYBOY: What is Nicole to you, anyhow? You hear that she's got a good lawyer and your only concern is that he might make a pass at her. You're getting thousands of letters from lovesick, lunatic girls, and you're furious that she should get one from some nitwit in New York. You fight with her and drive her away when you're free to love her, but as soon as you're in jail, she's your angel, your elf, and all the other things you call her.

GILMORE: Well, King Solomon said, "Vanity, vanity, all is vanity," and I used to believe that until I met Nicole. From her I found out there was more to life than fucking vanity. There's love and duty. Period, stop, as they say in Mailgrams.

PLAYBOY: So you don't want to answer?

GILMORE: Try me next week.

PLAYBOY: Okay, but just answer this: You must have written her more than 2,000 pages since you were arrested in July, and your letters are filled with sayings, quoted poems, little lessons, cute drawings, observations— all your stories, wishes, lies and dreams; but where in all those pages is there one word that indicates a sense of "love and duty" in your feelings for her? Where do you thank her for her love or indicate that she ever did anything for you?

GILMORE: Well, she did: She got me re-interested in art, for one thing. At one time, I almost quit drawing. I'd become pretty disinterested and decided there were too many pictures already in the world, and if you painted or drew more, you'd just have to put up more walls to hang 'em on. But Nicole got me interested again. If I'd stayed out, I'd a mellowed out eventually. I would have done some more paintings.

PLAYBOY: Once again, you define Nicole strictly in terms of Gary. Maybe she's just not real to you.

GILMORE: Nicole's an intelligent girl. She's sensitive. When you're with her, she understands you. I think she's the only person who's ever understood me.

PLAYBOY: Not counting your mother.

GILMORE: Yeah, that's right.

PLAYBOY: Has it struck you as the least bit odd that you keep praising your mother for keeping your family together, and then, in the next breath, you're persuading Nicole to abandon her children to a "gentle, soft death" with you?

GILMORE: I'm just trying to get the truth out. If it sounds cold or whatever, let other people make the judgments.

PLAYBOY: It does sound a little cold, but maybe you're just steeling yourself against the fact that it's Christmas.

GILMORE: Maybe.

PLAYBOY: When was the last time you were out of jail at Christmas?

GILMORE: Nineteen-sixty-one.

PLAYBOY: A long time ago.

GILMORE: Yeah. It's like what W. C. Fields said: "All things being equal, I'd rather not spend Christmas in prison." [*Laughs*] W. C. Fields said a lot of cool shit.

(EARLY JANUARY)

GILMORE: Listen to this shit: [*reading from a newspaper*] "Attorneys opposing the scheduled execution of Gary Gilmore"—blah-blah-blah—"will meet to determine which strategy"—blah-blah, okay, listen: "The attorneys represent the ACLU, the NAACP and other death-row inmates." It goes on, let's see, blah-blah, okay, now: "The ACLU attorney said there may still be a chance that Mr. Gilmore will flip-flop and change his mind." Okay, now you know that term flip-flop, man, it has a certain jailhouse connotation that this idiot ACLU lawyer has got to know, what with all the clients he must have doin' time. It means a guy who's a punk, a guy who sucks dicks and things like that. That's what flip-flop means in jailhouse jargon, and you never hear it anywhere else.

So when my lawyers come today, I'm giving them an open letter to release. I've just got to answer some of the bullshit I keep readin' in the papers. And I'm going to say that as far as flip-flop goes, the ACLU is tops. They take one stand on abortions, which are actually executions of innocent souls—they're all for that—and then they take an opposite stand on capital punishment. And the NAACP, ain't nothin' you can say to discourage that Uncle Tom outfit. I told 'em before, in my last letter, "NAACP, look, boy, I am a white man! Get that through your Brillo-pad heads, boy!" But nothin' discourages 'em, I guess. Do any of these people have any true convictions, or have they just let their thing about me develop into a personal matter?

PLAYBOY: Aren't you the one who's taking it personally?

GILMORE: It's my life, goddamn it. It's my case. It's my sentence.

PLAYBOY: But all the others on death row have lives and cases, too. Aren't you at all concerned about the effect your execution might have on them—almost 400 people?

GILMORE: If I thought my death would cause the death of these other guys on death row, yes, I would probably back up on it. In fact, I made two valid, not bullshit, suicide attempts, and part of my thinking there was not only to speed it up and get it over with but also to do it in a way so these other guys would be left with their same arguments and me dyin' wouldn't cause what they call this snowball effect. But it's still my case. It's not their goddamn case. They can appeal their cases. I accept mine. They got theirselves in trouble. It's their business.

PLAYBOY: But you've called them sniveling cowards.

GILMORE: Yeah, well I put that a little strongly to offend them. I don't know if they're physical cowards or moral cowards, or what they are. Apparently, they're just desperately afraid of me being executed. Goddamn it, my execution ain't gonna affect them, because they'll stay alive on the merits of their own fucking cases. I don't really, I-I just don't understand those sons a bitches. . . .

PLAYBOY: Or care about them?

GILMORE: No. I don't give a shit. I'm going to say that, man. Goddamn it, I'd pull up on my case if I thought it would affect them guys. But because I get executed, they're not going to get executed. They're going to meet whatever fate awaits them. I attempted suicide twice. How much do I owe 'em?

PLAYBOY: If you had the other condemned men in mind when you

attempted suicide, that's very noble. But don't you think you've com-
promised your wish to die "with dignity and grace" by trying to sneak
out softly on drugs?

GILMORE: That's a possibility. But also, I was anxious to get it over. You
know I'm an impatient guy. I'm impatient about this, too. I don't like
layin' around in here till the 17th, and I thought that if I did commit suicide, then all these other death-row guys that are cryin' about,
screamin' about, them bein' killed because I'm bein' killed, they wouldn't
have anything to talk about.

PLAYBOY: Haven't you made your executioners feel they're just collaborating in your suicide?

GILMORE: I don't really care what they feel. I haven't made them feel
anything. They can feel what they want. When they get done, they can
go drink some beer and talk about it.

PLAYBOY: You don't give a shit.

GILMORE: Man, how could I? They can drink beer and talk about it and
then go deer hunting next season and shoot something else.

PLAYBOY: So you do feel there's a big distinction between you and the
other condemned men.

GILMORE: It's pretty obvious, isn't it? I accept the sentence. I figure if a
sucker don't wanna get hisself capital punished, he shouldn't get the
death penalty put on him. I mean, any damn fool that's stupid enough
to get sentenced to death, what the hell's he got to snivel about afterward? I'd like to put out this open letter and maybe plan some kind of
legal counterattack against these assholes.

PLAYBOY: Why are they assholes just because they want to stay alive and
beat the cases against them?

GILMORE: Because they're buttin' in on my life. I mean, I did kill those
two guys, and what the hell, was anybody bein' unfair to me, the judge,
society or anybody else? No. And now the people that're tryin' to stop it
are buttin' in on my life, and they have no right to do that. I think it's a
sin to butt in on somebody's life.

PLAYBOY: Coming from you, that's an odd statement. Didn't you butt in
on Jensen and Bushnell?

GILMORE: Yes.

PLAYBOY: You say you accept your sentence, but you seem to deny that
it's just, maybe because you refuse to show contrition. In all your statements and remarks, we detect no hint of remorse that you took two
men's lives away from them and their families. Why?

GILMORE: Because it's a private and personal thing. I'm not saying I don't
feel bad about it, but I ain't gonna tell you how bad I feel about it, and

I ain't gonna ask you to forgive me, and I ain't gonna ask the priest, either. It's something I'm willing to give my life for, and I'm willing to meet whatever consequences or whatever is coming to me for it.

PLAYBOY: By that answer, you indicate that there really is remorse.

GILMORE: Man, I know what I did and I know it was wrong and unreasonable and totally senseless.

PLAYBOY: You're sorry—but it's personal. Is refusing to say you're sorry in public some kind of point of pride?

GILMORE: No. It's a personal thing, goddamn it.

PLAYBOY: You're saying now that the killings were wrong, unreasonable, senseless. But not long ago, you said, "If you kill somebody and get away with it, that's cool." Did you mean that?

GILMORE: Yeah.

PLAYBOY: Well, if you hadn't shot yourself in the hand and been caught for those killings, do you think they would have stayed cool in your mind?

GILMORE: I don't know.

PLAYBOY: Wouldn't it have bothered you to realize what you'd done?

GILMORE: It did bother me. But I could've, ah, well, I w-wouldn't have turned myself in or anything.

PLAYBOY: Maybe we don't understand what you mean by cool.

GILMORE: Lookit, if you do something wrong, you're supposed to try to get away with it. And if you do get away with it, that's cool.

PLAYBOY: What's cool? You just finished saying that the killings bothered you.

GILMORE: Ahhh, man, Jees, I don't mean that you've done something real cool by murdering somebody. I don't mean cool like Fonzie's cool. But if you do it, man, try to get away with it. I think in any frame of reference, if you do something wrong I think you, ah, you know, expect y-yourself to try to get away with it.

PLAYBOY: Somehow we get the feeling that your last thought before the bullets strike will be, "I got away with it!" Maybe capital punishment for you is the ultimate escape. The eternal recidivist won't be going back to jail.

GILMORE: Yeah, that's one way of lookin' at it.

PLAYBOY: If you'd merely robbed Jensen and Bushnell, instead of killing them, you'd be looking at another 10 or 20 years. That's a fate worse than death in your terms, isn't it?

GILMORE: Lookit, man, I told you that robbing them didn't have anything to do with it. We're creatures of habit, and my habit was to do things like that. I don't like what I did. I thought about it, I-I, I've realized that eventually somehow it'd come back to me, maybe not in this life but sometime. You always meet yourself. And I figured, well, when the time comes, I'll just accept it.

PLAYBOY: Accept what? Meeting Jensen and Bushnell in the next life?

GILMORE: If that happens, I'll just—well, they got a right to be mad. I'm not gonna, ah, run from them. I'm . . . they got a right to be goddamn mad. I mean, you can't escape from some things. You can't escape from anything, really.

PLAYBOY: At your trial, the prosecutor said you had learned one lesson from your last armed-robbery conviction in Oregon: Don't leave any witnesses.

GILMORE: That's his thing for the jury. That's his words to the jury. That's the way he tries to impress them.

PLAYBOY: Was getting rid of the witnesses part of the motive?

GILMORE: Man, they didn't know me. They would've been able to give a description of me, but I've robbed people before and got away with it.

PLAYBOY: Oh? When?

GILMORE: When I was out on escape in '72, I did a couple of things.

PLAYBOY: Not big enough to travel very far on, apparently.

GILMORE: Well, I got $18,000 from a Safeway store once, when I was 18.

PLAYBOY: Have you scored anywhere near that since?

GILMORE: No.

PLAYBOY: So you were a better robber as a kid than you have been as a man.

GILMORE: Yeah, I was a more successful thief then.

PLAYBOY: So the prosecutor was off course, as you'd say.

GILMORE: Completely.

PLAYBOY: Gibbs says you told him that the idea of killing Jensen came to you because you were with April, and by involving her in a murder, you'd have something to hold over Nicole.

GILMORE: Gibbs said that?

PLAYBOY: Yes.

GILMORE: He's lying. That sorry son of a bitch just made that up.

PLAYBOY: It's an imaginative lie.

GILMORE: Give the fucker credit, then. He's got imagination.

PLAYBOY: You never told him anything like that?

GILMORE: No.

PLAYBOY: You told us that April knew nothing about your killing Jensen. But Brenda says she was scared to death when you stopped by her house after you left *Cuckoo's Nest*. She says April was almost incoherent with fear and sat staring into the corner of the room, babbling. . . .

THE PLAYBOY INTERVIEW

GILMORE: Brenda's a dramatic woman.

PLAYBOY: Okay, but she also says that April told her, "Gary really scares me." And when Brenda challenged you about it, you said, "April, tell Brenda that I didn't try to rape you or molest you or anything," and that April then said, "Oh, no, you know I didn't mean that, but it really scares me when you do that stuff, I really get afraid of you." And when Brenda asked her what stuff, she said she couldn't say.

GILMORE: Ah shit. You got any more like that? I told you enough times already: April didn't know a goddamn thing. She wasn't involved. She was just shook up from seein' *Cuckoo's Nest*.

PLAYBOY: How about later, when you and April went to the motel? Didn't you try to get her into bed with you?

GILMORE: I'm not going to dignify that with an answer.

PLAYBOY: You wouldn't do that?

GILMORE: What do you think? [*In September, April, by then a patient at Timpanogos Community Mental Health Center, told doctors that Gilmore had "busted the side of my panties" trying to undress her.*]

PLAYBOY: Your code of conduct seems very strict when it comes to sex. You even seem a little prudish.

GILMORE: Yeah, probably. Compared to today's standards. I've been locked up, see, while the sexual revolution revolted, or whatever, and I'm not exactly a youngster, not a spring chicken anymore. I'm 36, and I think I'm kind of oriented in the Fifties. Because the Fifties, that's the last time I really made any move of any kind, you know. Man, I was just about like any other kid growin' up in the Fifties. You found out what you could on your own and passed it on to your friends. You'd talk about broads, and exaggerate and lie, and embroider the fucking truth. If you copped a feel, man, you'd really done somethin', and if you swore around a broad, she acted shocked.

PLAYBOY: And you still respect those limits?

GILMORE: Well, one time when I was in about the seventh grade, this girl was standing on top of a table, decorating the room for some fuckin' holiday, and I just stuck my hand up under her dress and took a good shot at her ass, and she went fuckin' insane, enraged, man. Nowadays, a girl would be flattered if you did that to her, I guess.

PLAYBOY: It still involves the use of force, though.

GILMORE: Yeah, maybe, if you want to look at it that way.

PLAYBOY: You find the use of force in sex objectionable?

GILMORE: Yeah, I do.

PLAYBOY: What other sexual behavior strikes you as objectionable?

GILMORE: Well, when you start bringin' in the wild animals. [*Laughs*] And

I find them closet queens objectionable, because they don't have the courage of their convictions, and, ah, them real blatant, simperin', whimperin' sissies, well, they're bitter, lonely frustrated people. There's some pathos there. I don't know if objectionable is the word. I find that sad.

PLAYBOY: In prison, though, don't men who aren't homosexuals sometimes resort to each other for sex?

GILMORE: I don't think so, not by and large. If a guy's a faggot, he's a faggot. And if he's in the joint, it's gonna come out, and if he's on the street, it's gonna come out. Take these goddamn questions down to some gay bar. I don't know that much about it.

PLAYBOY: Call you tell us about your sexual encounters in prison?

GILMORE: I haven't had any.

PLAYBOY: Not in 19 years?

GILMORE: Not in 19 years.

PLAYBOY: This whole conversation upsets you. You are prudish.

GILMORE: Shit. Fuck. Guess I'm just a goddamn prude. Maybe it's because I'm Irish and kind of puritanistic.

PLAYBOY: You'd rather think about killing than sex.

GILMORE: Yeah, that's my Irishness. You know us Irish are crazy killers. Go to Northern Ireland and you'll see what I mean. You can't buy no PLAYBOYS up there, but you can goddamn sure get killed.

PLAYBOY: You're a man who could take two people's lives, attempt suicide, sink a hammer in a man's skull—yet when it comes to sex, you say there are all sorts of things you could never do, right down to dating a buddy's sister. What are some other things you could never do?

GILMORE: Oh, I couldn't snitch on anybody. I couldn't rat on anybody. I don't think I could torture anybody.

PLAYBOY: Isn't forcing somebody to lie down on the floor and shooting him in the back of the head torture?

GILMORE: I'd say it was a very short torture.

PLAYBOY: But how could any crime be worse than taking a person's life?

GILMORE: Well, you could alter somebody's life so that the quality of it wouldn't be what it could've been. I mean, you could torture 'em, you could blind 'em, you could maim 'em, you could cripple 'em, you could fuck 'em up so badly that their life would be a misery for the rest of it. And for me, that's worse than killing somebody. Like, if you kill somebody, it's over for them. I-I believe in karma and reincarnation and shit like that, and if you kill somebody, it could be that you just assume their karmic debts. If you kill them, t-t-ther-thereby you might be relieving them of a debt. But I think to make somebody go on living in a lessened state of existence, I think that could be worse than killin' 'em.

Another thing, I think some forms of behavior modification, the irreversible forms, like lobotomies, and, ah, Prolixin, a drug that can have real damaging effects on a person—in fact, there may be people around who have been fucked up by it, badly, man—well, I won't say doin' that shit to a person is worse than murder, but you gotta give it some thought.

PLAYBOY: Did you have to take much Prolixin?

GILMORE: Man, they really fucked me over with that shit. A normal dose, as I understand it, is not to exceed two cc's a month. They were giving me 16 cc's a month. They damn near killed me with that shit.

PLAYBOY: How long did they give it to you?

GILMORE: About three months. *Listen* to that goddamn son of a bitch down there poundin'. How would you like to listen to that half the night?

PLAYBOY: Couldn't stand it.

GILMORE: Motherfuckers! Anyway, those prison psychiatrists will pull any shit to get those drugs into you. A lot of guys, they'd go to the shrinks and try to get some Seconal or yellow jackets so they could sleep or whatever. And the shrinks would trick 'em into tryin' this dangerous experimental shit they always had ready. "Hey, man, let me lay this new trip on ya!" The bastards. I didn't get it that way. I got it forcibly. I was handcuffed to a bed and they shot me with the shit.

PLAYBOY: They'd just come in and shoot it into you?

GILMORE: Yeah, twice a week. They were fuckin' me up bad with it. My mother came to see me and she couldn't stand it. She started cryin'. My little brother Gaylen—and he was dyin' at the time, he only lived a few months longer—he came down and raised all kinds of shit with the warden, and we got lawyers, and finally it stopped.

PLAYBOY: How long were you chained to your rack?

GILMORE: Well, I was chained down on four or five separate occasions. The longest was for two weeks. It wasn't chains. It was handcuffs, one on each hand, and leg cuffs, one on each ankle, with rings going over the bed, and you there spread-eagle. The last couple of times I got chained down, I made 'em beat me up first. I just decided I'd fight instead of just takin' it. So I just started swingin' at 'em. I lost them fights, but I felt a little better. The first or second time, they were knockin' me out with some goddamn thing, and I'd wake up and be so pissed off that I'd start screamin', and they'd come in and knock me out with the needle again. Finally, the fuckin' doctor comes in, and I said, man, I'll play this cool. And I asked him, how 'bout lettin' me up, doc? And I said, when I was raisin' hell the other day, I wasn't myself. And he says, if you weren't yourself, who were you? So I says, come here a second, doc, and he kind of creeps over a step or two, and I coughed up a lunger and spit it right in his face.

PLAYBOY: What happened then?

GILMORE: Well, the two guards that were there punched me out. One of 'em choked me. He reached down with his thumb and forefinger and dug into my esophagus and pulled the pillow out from under my head and pushed it down tight over my nose and mouth. I thought the goddamn fool was gonna kill me. His lip was twitchin', man, and he had a real sadistic look on his face. He said, "I just don't like you, Gilmore," only he said it a lot meaner.

PLAYBOY: Sounds like the old Dr. Fell syndrome.

GILMORE: Well, man, they had reason to dislike me. I gave 'em plenty reason.

PLAYBOY: And they expressed their dislike with Prolixin, with beatings and chokings? Or were they trying to cope with someone who was becoming unmanageable?

GILMORE: I can't answer that properly, because my thoughts are ahead of my verbal ability at the moment. They've just brought me some cold food on a goddamn paper plate. I mean, I think I'm entitled to a goddamn tray. They say that they don't take anything away from you until you've abused the privilege. Last night they gave me a tray. This morning they gave me a tray. Now at noon they tell me I have to eat off paper plates. And I've never done anything with the trays. It's that inconsistent policy that gets to you. Fuck! Excuse me a minute. [*Falls silent for several minutes*] Okay. Let's go.

PLAYBOY: Okay, what else was done to you by the psychiatrists—because you couldn't be handled, because they didn't like you—for whatever reason? Were you given electric-shock treatments?

GILMORE: Yeah, a series of six. I'll tell you why I received them: I got drunk and tore up a cell while I was in the hole.

PLAYBOY: Did any prison doctor ever discuss psychosurgery?

GILMORE: No. I'm hip to all the behavior-modification techniques. There are all kinds, and I'm just naturally adverse to anything like that. But I never was threatened with psychosurgery.

PLAYBOY: Why was none of this brought out at your trial?

GILMORE: 'Cause my attorneys said it was no defense.

PLAYBOY: But with the kind of heavy therapy you were given in Oregon, there must be some reason to believe that you were out of control. . . .

GILMORE: Aw, man . . . there was just no defense. I killed those guys.

PLAYBOY: At your trial, though, you expressed your shock and amazement that the defense rested without calling a single witness. You seemed surprised. . . .

GILMORE: Surprised, yes, because the two lawyers defending me didn't let me know there would be nothing, not even a meager defense. I went into the trial thinking I had a good insanity defense, but the doctors didn't concur. The bastards would only talk to me under conditions that were impossible and, well, adverse to me. They'd talk to me with a posse of about 40 patients sitting in the room, like group therapy, man, and I wouldn't talk to 'em under those conditions, and I just blew my whole defense away. It wasn't fair to me, but, fuck—I accept it.

PLAYBOY: There was no psychiatrist who might have helped you?

GILMORE: Not according to my lawyers.

PLAYBOY: Have you ever been seen by a psychiatrist who seemed to be trying to help you?

GILMORE: I don't know. There's one here . . . but he seems a little too enthusiastic for me. I talked to him before my trial, and, you know, he's one of the ones who start calling you Gary right away, and . . . you know, man, kind of seems like a backslapper or something.

PLAYBOY: So you don't trust him?

GILMORE: Trust him? You serious?

PLAYBOY: You've had shock. You've had Prolixin. You've spent four years in the hole. Guards and cops have kicked out all but two of your teeth. And even with all this, they couldn't handle you in Oregon and had to send you to the heaviest prison in the country, Marion—the new Alcatraz. Was that because you always chose to do your time the hard way? Or are there aspects of your behavior that are beyond your control?

GILMORE: [*Laughing*] I gotta pick A or B, huh? Multiple choice? [*Laughs*] Ah, man, I'm just a fuck-up. I just get in trouble. Damn. I guess it's just my habit to wind up in the worst kind of shit. Lookit, man, they got so many rules in these goddamn places . . . it's s-so damn easy to . . . Look, I just can't abide by all these goddamned rules, man. Once I-I went for so long as a year without even gettin' one write-up in Oregon, completely stayin' out of trouble. I guess I can do it if I want to, but you know, after you get known as a troublemaker, ah, it's so easy to keep gettin' in trouble, 'cause all them guards, man, like, they put your picture on the hot list up in the fuckin' guards' lounge, and it's "watch this guy," and "suspected of doing this and that," all the time, man. And some guards take a personal dislike to you, and you can feel it, you can see it in the way they look at you, how they antagonize you in little ways that'll make you blow up, you know, and you can get a lot of write-ups that way. You get frustrated because you're in a s-situation where you're always wrong . . . and never right. Because you're the prisoner. And they got the hammer.

PLAYBOY: Then why not keep your head down and not call attention to yourself?

GILMORE: Because once you get a lot of write-ups, there's no way you can be inconspicuous, and in Oregon, I must have had at least 70. They get after your case, man, and out of that 70, at least four or five must have been bum beefs.

PLAYBOY: Did we hear you right, four or five out of 70? Isn't that about as much justice as anyone can expect, inside jail or out of it?

GILMORE: *They're* charged with being honest, I'm not. It's their duty to be honest and fair. They aren't supposed to bum-rap me. It's my prerogative to fuck up if I want, 'cause I'm the crook.

PLAYBOY: Is that the same philosophy you subscribed to when you went home to Provo?

GILMORE: Fuck you.

PLAYBOY: No, seriously, think about it. The whole country has heard you say that you want to accept your death sentence with dignity and grace. So why couldn't you muster a little dignity and grace when you went back to Provo, where there were people who loved you, instead of frightening them by doing everything you could to show that you were a confirmed, habitual, highly dangerous criminal who was going to get himself and probably everybody else in bad trouble as soon as he could?

GILMORE: You're tryin' to bring me a little bit of anger, right? A little bit of anger here so you can X-ray me better, and maybe get me to react a little more spontaneously, perhaps. That it?

PLAYBOY: Here's just one example: Brenda introduces you to a girl, and the girl goes out with you, and the next night she's busy, so you smash the windshield of her car.

GILMORE: All right. I broke the girl's windshield. It was a chickenshit thing to do. I had no real reason. I felt bad about it and still do. She was a nice chick. I guess I just wasn't her type.

PLAYBOY: Another example, then: You're hardly home when you decide to take off for Idaho Falls. Vern pleads—he doesn't want you to lose your parole. But you take off anyway, and hitchhike, and wind up in a car with a "fruiter," as you would say, and he makes some kind of move toward you, or says the wrong thing, and you come close to killing the man. Why couldn't you restrain yourself just a little? Wasn't that a completely inappropriate response to what was, after all, merely an annoying sexual gesture?

GILMORE: I don't really think that was an inappropriately strong reaction to that kind of shit. But, okay, here's your answer. I didn't hitchhike. I stole a car down the street from Vern's. I never told anybody about that. I left the car in Idaho Falls, because I was gettin' leery about drivin' it any longer, afraid of gettin' stopped. So this guy in a bar offered me a ride. And when he started that shit, I just unloaded on him. Apparently, he was pretty well known to the cops. Because when they stopped us, when I was tryin' to get him to the hospital, hopin' I could just leave him there and walk away, the cops just held me overnight and the next day let me go. So I figured they knew what was happenin'.

PLAYBOY: We're trying to understand your capacity to control yourself. . . .

GILMORE: I can control myself pretty well. . . .

PLAYBOY: Pretty well?

GILMORE: Well, you try and live under these fuckin' situations. Let's see you put up with it for three fuckin' days. Can you hear that loud, fuckin' goddamn noise? Jesus!

PLAYBOY: But there were situations on the outside in which you could have controlled yourself.

GILMORE: I wasn't used to livin' on the fuckin' outside, man. You're locked up for 12 and a half years and, ah . . . go out and, ah . . . expect to im-immediately adjust to the shit. You're thinkin', Jeez, there's a subconscious thing that, ah . . . governs the way you act, and you know you shouldn't. [*Long pause*]

PLAYBOY: But did you have the capacity——

GILMORE: Look, man, I mean, I'm not wrong over every goddamn thing, you know. Every fuckin' thing that comes up. Sometimes things are other people's faults. What are you arguing with me about it for?

PLAYBOY: We'd just like to know——

GILMORE: You think I have the answers for everything? You ask me a question and then you're not satisfied with my fuckin' answer, man. I'm not the goddamn almanac, you know.

PLAYBOY: Let's go at it a different way. You told us the story of how Nicole pulled a gun on you the day before you killed Jensen. And you told how the loss of her resulted in a seething rage that you could release only through killing two strangers. Another way of looking at it might be that it wasn't rage at all—it was just humiliation. You couldn't stand the idea that a little 20-year-old girl could back down Gary Gilmore with a tiny .22.

GILMORE: It was a magnum, motherfucker. [*Laughs*] You get shot with a .22 magnum and it'll put a hole in you like a .45. I told you that I didn't think the gun was loaded. As a matter of fact, man, I just stood there for about three or four minutes and told her to go ahead and shoot me if she wanted to. She told me to get away from her car. I wasn't gonna get away from it until I felt like it. I didn't think the goddamn gun was loaded. Fuck!

PLAYBOY: Do you think Nicole would have had the nerve to pull it if it wasn't?

GILMORE: Goddamn right she would've. If she wanted to. She finally put it in her purse, and I didn't go over and do anything to her then, either.

PLAYBOY: Well, if you could restrain yourself then, why take it out on two innocent——

GILMORE: I don't know, man. I don't know. Just the habit of violence, maybe.

PLAYBOY: You always speak of "habit" when we get around to talking of your crimes. Could this be a sly way of saying you're a junkie, a trouble junkie? Could it be that the impulsiveness of your behavior is not an impulse toward crime but an impulse toward punishment?

GILMORE: I've thought of that. Maybe it's true. There's a term, institutionalized. Nobody wants to admit, n-nobody admits to being institutionalized. It means being so used to prison that no other way of life is possible anymore. It's a terrible thing to believe about yourself. But lock a motherfucker up for half his life and, well . . . it would have to breed some kind of habit. Perhaps a habit of return.

PLAYBOY: Which might explain why you shot yourself in the hand. . . .

GILMORE: That was a goddamn accident! Nobody believes that, huh?

PLAYBOY: It's like something out of *Macbeth* to shoot the murderous hand.

GILMORE: I told you I took precautions not to get caught.

PLAYBOY: Like calling Brenda. . . .

GILMORE: I didn't know Brenda was going to betray me.

PLAYBOY: No? What else could she do? You had everybody who knew you terrified.

GILMORE: Okay, think what you want, say what you want, print what you want after I'm dead. I just ain't gonna go for this psychological bullshit.

PLAYBOY: Why not, if it's based on the wish to understand?

GILMORE: I'll answer that after I have a little coffee. [*Silence*] Shit.

PLAYBOY: You okay?

GILMORE: Yeah.

PLAYBOY: How do you explain the fact that the first thing on your mind after you were arrested for the Bushnell murder was getting through to Brenda and telling her, "Be sure and tell Mom"?

GILMORE: I'm gonna answer that right now. It was Brenda's idea. I agreed, reluctantly. She insisted. She seemed eager.

PLAYBOY: Whether it's "psychological bullshit" or not, it's difficult to believe the murders didn't have something to do with how you were treated as a child.

GILMORE: I swear to God that I cannot recall—and I have a terrific memory—I cannot recall my mom ever hitting me, or even spanking me. She always loved and believed in me. Fuck what everybody in the family says. I have a beautiful mother. [*Louder*] I have a beautiful mother. I repeated that because of all the goddamn noise in the background.

PLAYBOY: Then why not make things easier for your mother by at least expressing some remorse, or fighting for your life. . . .

GILMORE: Aw, man, join the writ club. You can appeal a thing like this for years, and you'll still go down in the end. Even if I got the goddamn case thrown out, they'd just convict me on the other and I'd be right back in this miserable son of a bitch again. Look, man, I'm not dumb. I know I could have taken a stance of utter remorse, and started readin' the Bible, and started preachin', and with the money I had there for a while, the publicity I was gettin', I could've hired Clarence Darrow, if he were around [*laughs*], or Melvin Belli . . . but I'm just sick and tired. I'm leadin' a bad life this time around and, ah, if I did get out, I-I would probably get back in trouble even right now. I'm the same goddamn person. What I'm saying is, well, man, I just don't want to go through it all again. I don't want to mess with the law anymore.

(EVENING, JANUARY 14)

GILMORE: What are the ethics involved if I reneged on the donation of my eyes to the Lions Club? I mean, they get eyes all the time, don't they? Christ! I got a letter last night from a man, he's 90 years old and he wants my eyes. I hate to refuse somebody a thing like that, but I think it would be better to give them to somebody younger. A man 90 years old ain't gonna live a hell of a lot longer, and there are young blind people in the world. You think my ethics are okay here?

PLAYBOY: Absolutely.

GILMORE: The Lions Club Eye Bank is a good institution, I guess, but I'd just rather give 'em to an individual, maybe a young person. And then I got this letter from a doctor, and inside was a newspaper clipping, says, "EFFORT BEGINS TO GET CORNEA FOR OGDENITE." And this guy's only 20. I don't want to be harsh about it, but it seems better to give 'em to the young guy. I think I'll just get the lawyers to call that doctor and, ah, just tell him simply: "You got 'em! Gary Gilmore." Or maybe we can give him one eye and give one to another. I don't know.

PLAYBOY: It sounds like you've been giving these matters lots of thought.

GILMORE: Whatever's fair, man. I mean, why not? Maybe there's something else somebody could use. I don't think the heart will be usable. [*Laughs*]

PLAYBOY: Your attitude is pretty amazing. You've got only 72 hours to live.

GILMORE: You get right down to it, don't you? [*Laughs*] But, see, the one big advantage I got is that I know when I'm gonna die. That way, I can take care of everything beforehand. So I've made all the arrangements to have this and that taken care of. The pituitary's goin' to a cousin—they can't transplant it, but they'll use it in their research and give you credit. And I was just told today that the liver and kidney are easily salvageable. And I was truly and really deeply glad to hear about that, man. I mean, what the fuck, I'm in good shape, I haven't wasted my body with smokin' and drinkin', I ain't even messed with that many women. Now, if I could just have a little serenity to answer my mail.

PLAYBOY: You're getting lots of mail?

GILMORE: It fell off to 50 or 75 letters a day for a while, but now it's up to 1,000 a day. [*Laughs*] I guess I've got about 7,000 letters so far. [At the time of his death, Gilmore had received more than 40,000 letters at Utah State Prison.] One rural oaf in Georgia even sent me a hunk of rope. There's a god-awful lotta mail from Christians. Did you know that every person in Texas is a stomp-down, knuckles-to-the-ground Bible back? Well, that's okay—everybody in New York is nuts, too. It balances out. Lots of this mail is from young tomatoes. I'll read a sample: "Dearest Gary, I admire you very much. I think you are a very brave man to want to die. I adore, love and respect and worship you very much. . . . I hate to see such a very handsome man die. . . . You're so manly, very masculine, sexy, very appealing. [*Laughs*] Good luck in the other world."

PLAYBOY: How about mail from people you've known?

GILMORE: There's a lot from people who think they knew me. Two different guys asked me are you the Gary Gilmore I was in the Marines with? And one guy says, if you're the Gary Gilmore I know, you won't go through with it. And if they televise it, I'm kicking the tube out. I wrote to him and said, don't kick the tube out on my account. Then I got a letter from a woman who said her son's name is Gary Gilmore, and he's an evangelist. I've never run across a Gary Gilmore. I was hopin' I was the only one.

PLAYBOY: Are there many who keep writing?

GILMORE: This one chick keeps writin', and she's in love, and I thought about her a lot, but I figured I have enough problems. She writes: "How's my wild pony with those wild eyes?" [*Laughs*] I got three letters from her today. Christ, oh, ah, man—it's a good thing I'm not in California. These kids'd wear me out. [*Laughs*]

PLAYBOY: Do young kids appeal to you, particularly?

GILMORE: Why you ask that?

PLAYBOY: Because of the story you told Nicole in one of your letters about the young boy you were in love with . . .

GILMORE: Where'd you get that? That letter wasn't in the bunch the goddamn D.A. had. That wasn't in the ones the newspaper published.

PLAYBOY: No, it got delivered to Nicole's mother by mistake.

GILMORE: Holy shit. Nothin's sacred, huh?

PLAYBOY: When you write letters that pass through censors, Gary, you can't assume they're sacred.

GILMORE: So all them bastards probably read that, too, huh?

PLAYBOY: It's a good idea to assume they did.

GILMORE: Well, shit, there wasn't anything to it, except I did love that boy. I was in the state hospital in Oregon trying to beat an armed-robbery beef and this 13-year-old boy came in, 'cause he couldn't get along at home. He was really pretty, like a girl, but I never gave him much thought until it became apparent that he really liked me. I was 23 then. I'd be sittin' down and he would come up and sit beside me and put his arm around me. It was just natural to him, a show of friendship. He didn't have a dad, there was just him, his mother and a younger brother in the family. One time he came up to me in the locker room and asked if he could read this PLAYBOY I had. I said sure, for a kiss. Man, he was dumbfounded! His eyes got big as silver dollars and his mouth dropped wide open. He said, *"No!"* and it was really pretty, and I fell in love on the spot. He thought it over then and decided he wanted to read that magazine pretty bad, 'cause he gave me, or rather let me take, a very tender little kiss on the lips. I used to watch him down at the swimming pool. He was one of the most beautiful people I've ever seen, and I don't think I've ever seen a prettier butt. Anyhow, I-I used to kiss him now and then, and we got to be pretty good friends. I was just struck by his youth, beauty and naivete.

PLAYBOY: And then one of you was sent elsewhere?

GILMORE: Then one of us was sent elsewhere.

PLAYBOY: After the life you've led, what do you think explains the country's fascination with you?

GILMORE: Jeez, I don't know. I guess it's that I'm going first. I think that's the heart of it. Then there's the romantic thing . . .

PLAYBOY: Between you and Nicole?

GILMORE: Right. And then I'm sorta young, I guess. It is amazing, though. A black guard here who tells me shit says they're makin' lots a dough on Gary Gilmore T-shirts in California, with the *Newsweek* cover on 'em, you know, sayin' DEATH WISH. Did you see that picture of me in *Time,* near one of Mr. Ford? Is that his name—Gerald Ford? [*Laughs*] It's weird getting used to seein' your picture all over the place. That picture in the Provo paper ruined me. I don't look good when I look up. I look better when I look down a little bit. I'm not really a very photogenic person.

PLAYBOY: Does it bother you at all to be attracting such attention? Maybe you saw that old movie—*Angels with Dirty Faces.* Jimmy Cagney is on death row, and the padre comes by and tells him, if you go out like a man, the kids are going to be inspired by it and do all kinds of stupid things to show the world they're as tough as you are. But if you go out like a sniveling rat, it will turn them away from a life of crime. Cagney, of course, does the right thing and goes out like a sniveling rat.

GILMORE: Hang on a minute, my chow's here. [*Silence*] Okay, I'm back. In answer to your question: Sick minds will find encouragement, no matter what. If I start wondering and worrying about things like that, then I'm gonna have to start wonderin' and worryin' about every goddamn thing. I mean, I just can't be responsible for every son of a bitch in the world. I think we taught ourselves things that we've earned and deserved. From past lives. Just by being what we are. And, man, if you go around worrying about other people, and how you're gonna affect them, well, then, you're interfering in their lives. I mean, what the fuck, man, I don't have the right to even start thinking that way.

PLAYBOY: Then why do you bother to stay up all night answering letters from obviously weird and unhealthy people who are attracted to you simply because you want to die?

GILMORE: Not all of 'em, man. I get letters from people who understand all this in a beautiful way. Very concisely. They read all the shit that gets into the newspapers and they take out just the truth. Some of 'em really understand. They don't want publicity, like that surgeon who wants the eyes. Transplanting eyes, man—that's an act of genius. It takes a genius to do it. And this doctor, he don't want no attention. He just wants eyes.

PLAYBOY: Why do you think so many people write to you?

THE PLAYBOY INTERVIEW

GILMORE: Well, at first I was amazed. I mean, nobody came to my trial, you know? Couldn't have been more than 20 people there the day I was sentenced. And when I first started seeing things in the paper, I wasn't surprised—a little bit, you know, but after a while, it dawned on me, man, that my name was known around the world. And that really did surprise the shit out of me. I told Nicole, I said, listen, man, things like money can go to a person's head. So can fame. You gotta keep everything in perspective. But I didn't need to tell her that; it was something she already knew.

PLAYBOY: It's a strange kind of fame, though, isn't it? It's important to remember that if you'd only robbed those men, and been sent back to prison for life, or if you'd fought your sentence and appealed, you'd be a nobody.

GILMORE: You think I'm concerned about the publicity, man? I try my best not to let it have any effect, and it doesn't really have any goddamn effect. It doesn't do that much for me to read my goddamn name in the paper. I mean, Jesus, I'm just in here for murder—what the hell is there to feel so good about?

(MORNING, JANUARY 15)

GILMORE: [*Left alone for a moment in the maximum-security superintendent's office, Gilmore whips open every desk drawer, browses the shelves, pockets two pens, some paper clips, a pair of shoelaces.*] My greatest caper to date is these goddamn shoelaces. They're really somethin', man. [*Laughs*] You should see these babies—I mean, they're both black, and maybe a little plastic's worn off on the ends, but I don't think they're gonna break that easily. I know I am proud of these shoelaces. For a man in my circumstances they're handy to have.

PLAYBOY: Your ability to swim through the prison, to smuggle in pills, to make two serious suicide attempts, to snatch a radio for a while, to shake down the superintendent's office—these talents in prison take all the years you've spent in prison to acquire.

GILMORE: You just do things, you know. You don't wait to sneak around and be furtive. You just seize the moment. You take your own shoelaces out and put 'em in the drawer, and then you put the new ones on. New shoelaces—it ain't a bad feeling.

PLAYBOY:: You've said before that you can defeat fear by banishing its symptoms. It's getting close now—48 hours. What are the symptoms?

GILMORE: Symptoms? Well, some people, the symptom of fear might be that their minds kind of stop. Some people, it might be an overabundance of adrenaline, like if you were runnin' from something, and the more you ran, man, the more it would feed the fear. It might be the hair rising on the nape of your neck. Knees knock, teeth chatter. I don't know.

PLAYBOY: What symptoms do you feel?

GILMORE: I didn't say I was scared, did I?

PLAYBOY: No. But are you feeling fear?

GILMORE: Fear's negative. Why feel it? You could damn near call it a sin if you let it run your life.

PLAYBOY: Obviously, you're not acting out of fear now, but do you *feel* it?

GILMORE: I guess I'm lucky. It hasn't come in. I don't think it will come in Monday morning—I haven't felt it yet. You know, a true man, a true b-brave man, a true man, ah . . . a truly brave man is somebody who feels fear and goes out and does what he's supposed in do in spite of that. I don't feel that fear, see, so you couldn't really say I'm that fuckin' brave. I ain't fightin' against fear and, ah, overcomin' it. I don't know about Monday mornin'.

PLAYBOY: Most people, under the circumstances, would count not feeling fear as bravery.

GILMORE: I don't. I don't. I don't . . . say I'm courageous or brave. I'm, well, not even sure I understand the meaning of those words.

PLAYBOY: You can control your mind, perhaps. But doesn't a body that knows it's going to die protest in some way?

GILMORE: I eat good. [*Laughs*]

PLAYBOY: Seriously?

GILMORE: Yeah. I also sleep good,

PLAYBOY: How about your nerves?

GILMORE: How about 'em? They're relaying all messages to my brain. Aren't the nerves the ones that do that? [*Laughs*]

PLAYBOY: Well, one thing that is observable is that things do upset you pretty easily. Your moods change.

GILMORE: I've always been moody.

PLAYBOY: Is there anything about your life that feels undone and makes you want to hang on?

GILMORE: I'd like to have another go at that miserable bastard of a dentist who fucked me up in Oregon. [*Laughs*]

PLAYBOY: You really wouldn't want to give life another try?

GILMORE: Oh, I'd love it. I wish they'd let me go right now. I'd go get a gun and get Nicole out of that, ah . . . hospital. Then I'd pistol-whip these idiot ACLU lawyers. . . .

PLAYBOY: Same old Dr. Fell.

GILMORE: Well, you asked. And, yeah! Yeah, of course. Why not? If I went up there to the hospital and just asked for her, and got insistent, well, shit—you asked. I got carried away here. I forget what the hell. . . .

PLAYBOY: We were talking about hanging on to life.

GILMORE: Or accepting fate. Man, we all gotta accept our fate. You think you can evade yours? Does anybody? Sooner or later, you're gonna meet yourself.

PLAYBOY: But when you talk about getting a gun and rescuing Nicole. . . .

GILMORE: Man, they got her in a new ward where they got the men and women sleeping together. And I don't like that at all, man, because they got nuts in there. They got unlocked rooms, and one dude that sits out there in the corridor, and he could fall asleep any time. And they got goddamn nuts in there who could rape you. I want Nicole out of there. I want her out of that goddamn place. And I know there ain't nothin' I can do. The Salt Lake police have got all kinds of our letters. The fuckin' shrinks have got all kinds of our letters. The words we've meant for us alone are the property of newspapers that take copyrights out on 'em. The warden won't let Nicole come to the execution, or else some goddamn psycho doctor won't. And now they tell me today I can't even record a cassette to send her. I ain't askin' 'em for another goddamn thing. I just want it to get over.

PLAYBOY: The frustration you're feeling isn't yours alone.

GILMORE: I don't understand that.

PLAYBOY: Take Ida and Vern, for instance. They don't want to see you shot.

GILMORE: I'm not crazy about the idea myself.

PLAYBOY: Yes, of course, but you're willing to accept it. They're not. Now that the uncertainty is over, it's just going to be a painful time for everyone.

GILMORE: Man, ah . . . I-I'm not in pain.

PLAYBOY: Yes, but others are.

GILMORE: It's no big deal.

PLAYBOY: All right, whatever you say.

GILMORE: I don't want anything. I'd like to see Nicole. I'd like to stand. I don't want the goddamn hood. I just want a little quiet. I don't think I'll even come out tomorrow night. I don't want the papers to say, well, we really treated him great on his last night. He got to see his uncle and his lawyers.

PLAYBOY: You've still got 48 hours to live—why not live them?

GILMORE: I just see the fuckin' futility in asking for anything. It makes 'em happy when you ask for somethin', 'cause then they can say, "Well, let me get back to you on that one." And they never get back. And there ain't no time left anymore. Cocksuckers! They've put two of them fools out there guarding me, and all they do is talk to each other and play cards . . .

PLAYBOY: When you get an execution date, you get a death watch. That's what you're undergoing right now.

GILMORE: Well, okay, then. Okay, man. But, man, it's so fuckin' noisy. If I could have some quiet during these last hours. I stayed up till three last night answering letters, you know. Fuck! People are decent enough to write you a fuckin' letter, least you can do . . . I answer about 50 of 'em a day. I've been givin' away autographed Bibles, too. Is that blasphemous? [*Laughs*]

PLAYBOY: From the way your mail's running, you could probably sell them.

GILMORE: Oh, hey, man, I've got somethin' that'll make a mint. Listen to this: Get aholda John Cameron Swayze right now, and get a Timex wristwatch here. And have John Cameron Swayze come runnin' out there after I fall over, he can be wearin' a stethoscope, he can put it on my heart and say, "Well, that stopped," and then he can put the stethoscope on the Timex [*Laughs*] and say, "She's still runnin', folks."

(EVENING, JANUARY 15)

PLAYBOY: You seem depressed.

GILMORE: Ah, man, I think sitting down and wearing a hood is a morbid, macabre thing. I never wore a hood before. Why should I start wearing one now?

PLAYBOY: You think it's more manly to do it your way?

GILMORE: No. I just want to look them fuckers in the eye when they shoot me.

PLAYBOY: Maybe the warden is worried that you'd move or flinch at the last minute.

GILMORE: I won't budge. I would assume those marksmen they got would prefer a moving target. But I'm not gonna satisfy the bastards.

PLAYBOY: Can't blame you for that.

GILMORE: I asked the fucker, are you going to ask me if I have anything to say, any last words, like? And, ah, yeah, he looked like he hadn't thought about that one. And I said, well, are you gonna do it before or after you put the fuckin' hood on me? And he says, well-l-l-l, and you know, that fucker had never given it any thought. [*Laughs*] So I told him, well, look, no use thinkin' on it there, warden, 'cause I'm tellin' ya: Don't ask me any questions after you put that hood on me, 'cause I ain't answerin' 'em. I told him I can't help what you impose on me, bein' seated and hooded, but I need to keep dignity, no matter what.

THE PLAYBOY INTERVIEW

PLAYBOY: Did he say what the hood would be like?

GILMORE: Fuck, I didn't ask him. A hood's a hood. Listen to them miserable sons a bitches back there. [*Loud noises in background*] They're tryin' to get the door closed, is what they're tryin' to do. Jesus!

PLAYBOY: Have you always been this sensitive to noise?

GILMORE: Man, noises bother everybody. Almost everybody in here's got earphones, big things that cover your whole ears. They can put 'em on and listen to the radios, tune out on this shit. But where I'm at, there isn't anything . . . I have to listen to this shit, ah . . . an awful lot of noises, man. I can put up with it. I've put up with it for 19 years. But right now, particularly, I would like some serenity, some quiet, and I think I'm entitled to that fuckin' much.

PLAYBOY: Are you getting any sleep?

GILMORE: I do about 1,000 jumping jacks at night and, man, I do sit-ups, I do 50 push-ups, I chin myself, I run up and down this little four-cell corridor where they got me, and it's still a motherfucker to sleep with the lights on all the time and these two fools starin' in on me, and bullshittin', and carryin' on all night.

PLAYBOY: You don't like your guards? You sort of liked the last ones.

GILMORE: Ah, shit, they're pretty cool. I mean, they're men. If I gave 'em some shit, they would react. Some guys, you know, whether they're prison guards or not, they're still men.

PLAYBOY: Something still seems to be bothering you. We thought you'd be glad that the wait was almost over.

GILMORE: Of course.

PLAYBOY: Something else, then?

GILMORE: Ah, well, the warden came and talked to me while my brother Mike was here, and he told me he's not gonna allow you [interviewer Schiller] in the last night. And I told him, listen, man, you're doin' this personally, you're not being objective, you're bein' subjective because of the way I've talked around here and acted around here, and I said, now that's what you're doin' to Larry, he came in here, and he tricked you, and now you're punishing me for that. And now this is exactly what he said, he said, "Who else can I punish?"

PLAYBOY: He actually said that?

GILMORE: Those were his exact words.

(MORNING, JANUARY 16)

PLAYBOY: Has the warden made up his mind about the hood?

GILMORE: I believe he's concerned that my standin' there and lookin' at the firing squad will unnerve 'em. He's worried about them guys gettin'

110

nervous. But listen, he did say this—emphatically. He said they usually come to your cell, put a hood on you there, and you wear the hood from the time you leave your cell 'til you're dead. He said he wouldn't put the hood on me until after I'm in the chair. I want the son of a bitch to keep his word on that much, at least.

PLAYBOY: With only 24 hours to go, it's unlikely he'll change his mind.

GILMORE: Man, you don't know wardens.

(NOON, JANUARY 16)

GILMORE: The father just came in and said a Mass. Gave me a sip of the weakest wine I ever drank in my life. Then they told me I couldn't have a cassette to say goodbye to Nicole. They said, hey, there's still a chance you'll get your phone call. Shit! Lieutenant Fagan says, "My hands are tied," and I says, "Well, how does it feel to walk around with your hands tied? Why don't you change? Have you ever thought about feeling like a man, instead of a sleazy son of a bitch?" Then I find out that there's still some kind of goddamn appeal being heard in federal court here by some fumblin', bumblin' judge who wants to get famous off me. I'm afraid he'll decide to *ponder* it for a day, and that'll mean another 30-day wait for me.

PLAYBOY: You're pretty much alone in your wish to see it happen tomorrow morning, you know.

GILMORE: Well, I'll just hang myself tonight if they stay it.

PLAYBOY: The shoelaces!

GILMORE: You guessed it. They're gonna have to watch me constantly, continuously. 'Cause I'm not gonna fuck around with them anymore.

PLAYBOY: How are you feeling, now that the time is drawing short?

GILMORE: I tell you, I don't feel any different now than ever. Maybe I will in the morning. But I've talked to people who know more than I do, and people who know less, and I listen to all of 'em. And the only fuckin' thing I know about death, the only real feeling I have about it is that it'll be familiar. I don't think it'll be a harsh, unkind thing, because I think things that are harsh and unkind are here on earth, and they're temporary—all this passes.

PLAYBOY: Are they treating you all right? Are they loosening up at all?

GILMORE: Ah, yesterday I blew up and cussed out one of 'em, and today again the same. I like to cuss 'em out, you know. And I put it to 'em on a personal basis, too. You know, if you're gonna fight with somebody or say something to 'em or call 'em names, make it personal. Take it a step further than just a frivolous insult. I don't just do it on a whim to amuse myself or something.

THE PLAYBOY INTERVIEW

PLAYBOY: When we spoke yesterday on the phone, you said you were planning to do some writing.

GILMORE: No, man, it's too goddamn noisy, and these assholes are starin' in on me, so I just write thank-you notes to the people who've sent me letters.

PLAYBOY: Doing any reading?

GILMORE: No, ah . . . I don't read anymore. Shit. [*Sighs*] I've read all I'm gonna read.

PLAYBOY: Do you draw anymore?

GILMORE: No.

PLAYBOY: You said you were going to draw a self-portrait.

GILMORE: No. Don't have a mirror.

PLAYBOY: I guess you don't have much of anything in there.

GILMORE: I've got myself.

PLAYBOY: You're certainly . . . well, remarkably composed. [*Pause*]

GILMORE: Hey, lookit, man, am I missing something here? I mean, have I-I, am I bein' kinda rude? You guys are a little upset about this, I guess. Goddamn. That's what bothers me. That's just the one thing that bothers me, when I see somebody . . . like when my brother Mike came by, and I seen his eyes get red. And, shit . . . I'm not . . . I wasn't unaware of that. I'm not, well, quite that egocentric. I mean, I'm capable of discerning somebody else's feelings. I understand that other people might have thoughts for me . . . and . . . I hope you don't think I'm tryin' to be rude. The fact is, well, I know your thoughts. I shouldn't say that. How can you know another person's thoughts? But I can sense some of your feelings, even through this wall, these windows, this fuckin' situation. I wish I could dissuade you from any troubling thoughts. Actually, I'm very fortunate. I'm dying and I know when. I've been given time to make arrangements for different things. Some people can't . . . they leave things undone. Think of Jensen and Bushnell.

(1:02 A.M., JANUARY 17)

[*Gilmore telephoned from the office of Lieutenant Fagan, the maximum-security chief. He had spent the evening hours dancing, singing and talking with a few relatives and other visitors, and he had drunk a little whiskey they smuggled in to him. His last request for a pizza and a six-pack of beer was denied by the prison authorities, so he hadn't eaten since morning. His mood was cheerful as he clowned around, wearing Fagan's hat, and his voice was a little slurred.*]

GILMORE: I just heard on the radio that it's all over. That appeal they were arguin' before Judge Ritter—I guess they lost out. So now there's no way anybody can butt in.

PLAYBOY: We may not be talking again. Is there anything you'd like to add to all we've said?

GILMORE: Like what?

PLAYBOY: Like the one question you never quite answer: Have you ever killed anyone other than Jensen and Bushnell?

GILMORE: No.

PLAYBOY: No, for sure?

GILMORE: Nobody else.

PLAYBOY: We're still left with the feeling that something has to explain why suddenly you would choose to——

GILMORE: I was always capable of murder. There's a side of me that I don't like. I can become totally empty of feelings for others, unemotional——

VOICE: Hello?

GILMORE: Hello.

VOICE: Is this Mr. Pagan?

GILMORE: Who's this?

VOICE: This is the warden.

GILMORE: This is Mr. Gilmore, I'm makin' a phone call.

VOICE: Okay. Thank you. Pardon me.

PLAYBOY: You there?

GILMORE: [*Sigh*] Yeah.

PLAYBOY: We still don't understand what goes on in a person's mind who decides to kill——

GILMORE: Hey, look. Listen. One time I was drivin' down the street in Portland. I was just fuckin' around, about half high, and I seen two guys walk out of a bar. I was just a youngster, man, 19, 20, something like that, and one of these dudes is a young chicano about my age and the other's about 40, an older dude. So I said, hey, you guys want to see some girls? Get in. And they got in the back.

I had a '49 Chevrolet, two-door, you know, fastback? And they got in. And I drove out to Clackamas County, a very dark . . . now I'm tellin' you the truth, I ain't makin' this up, I'm not dramatizin', I'm going to be blasted out of my fuckin' boots in a few minutes, and I've already told you the goddamn truth, even if you don't believe me, and if it sounds like I'm tryin' to make up a story. . . .

PLAYBOY: No, there's no feeling of that. . . .

GILMORE: Goddamn. I swear to Jesus Christ on everything that's holy that I'm tellin' you the truth ver-fuckin'-batim. This is a strange story.

PLAYBOY: Go ahead.

GILMORE: So they got back there and I got to tellin' them about these

113

broads, I was just embroiderin', how they had big tits and liked to fuck and had a party goin', and how I left the party to get some guys to bring out there because they were short on dudes, and these two were about half drunk when we drove out there. I drove out to a pitch-black road, and I stopped, and I had a bar about 16 inches long . . . just a minute. [*Pause*] Lieutenant Fagan walked in. He told me to take his hat off. Okay. [*Deep sigh*] Jesus fuckin' Christ. Okay. So-o-o-o, I got these guys in the car, and drove 'em down this pitch-black fuckin' road, it had gravel on it, you know, not a rough road, black, smooth, flat, chipped fuckin' concrete, that's how I remember it, and I reached down under the seat—I always kept a baseball bat or a pipe, you know . . . and I reached down under the seat . . . just a minute! . . . [*Silence*] Ritter just issued a stay.

PLAYBOY: What?

GILMORE: Ritter . . . just . . . issued . . . a . . . stay.

PLAYBOY: For how long?

GILMORE: [*Off phone*] For how long? For what reason? [Back on phone] Ritter issued a stay because of a taxpayers' lawsuit saying it's illegal to use taxpayers' money to shoot me. [*Silence*] Foul cocksuckers! That Ritter! I knew! A taxpayers' suit! I'll pay for it myself. I'll buy the bullets, rifles and pay the riflemen! Jesus fuckin' goddamn Christ. Man, I want it to be *over*!

PLAYBOY: There's a lot of thinking you've got to do before you make your next move. Maybe there's something worth saving. We've done a lot of talking. We've done——

GILMORE: I don't care about that!

PLAYBOY: I know, but maybe you should think about it.

GILMORE: Shit. I gotta listen to all this goddamn noise in this motherfucker . . .

PLAYBOY: Maybe you're not meant to die. Maybe what you're going through now is a greater atonement. . .

GILMORE: Goddamn, they gave me a sentence, and I'm willin' . . .

PLAYBOY: You're not listening, are you?

GILMORE: Huh? I'm listenin'.

PLAYBOY: Let's just spend the next hour talking and see if . . .

GILMORE: Aw, shit. Piss. Fagan wants to use the phone. I can't stay on here. I'll try and call back.

PLAYBOY: Okay. We'll be here. Goodbye.

GILMORE: Goodbye.

[Gilmore did not call back.]

(JANUARY 17, PREDAWN HOURS)

[*Gilmore stayed up the night, believing, and profoundly bitter over, the news that his execution had been stayed. He was determined to end his own life if the state refused to do it, so the death watch over him did not slacken or abate.*]

PLAYBOY: This close to death, is there anything you feel you still must hide?

GILMORE: I'm gettin' pissed off at that kind of question. I've been honest with you.

PLAYBOY: What about——

GILMORE: Goddamn! I don't give a damn what anybody else says, I ain't bein' defensive about my mother. My mother is a hell of a woman. She did the very goddamn best she could and, man, she was always there, we always had somethin' to eat, we always had somebody to tuck us in. I ain't bein' defensive about her. I know she'd be here if she could, and if she was here, I could make her feel a lot better. She's got rheumatoid arthritis real bad, she's had it about four years, and she never says a word about it, never bitches about it at all. Up until she got sick, she worked as a busboy. A buswoman. Not a waitress, like *Time* or *Newsweek* or some-goddamn-body said. And she worked in that café until the boss finally told her, I'm gonna have to let you go. My dad was dead by then. He didn't take out any insurance or anything—and my mom, she didn't have any money. My brother Frank had to help out as best he could, tryin' to hold on to that beautiful house we had, with a nice swing-around driveway, where you drive up and it makes a circle . . . she wanted that. She wanted some things and she lost 'em. She tried to hang on, she tried to keep it together, but she lost 'em. And she never said nothin'. My dad should have taken out some insurance. He should have provided better. But she never bitched about it at all. I keep bein' asked if I love her, if she loves me, if she loved me when I was a baby. Yeah, goddamn it! Yes! I don't want to hear any more fuckin' bullshit that she was mean to me. She never hit me. She loved me and believed in me!

[*Shortly after 7:42 A.M., six guards arrived at Gilmore's cell and informed him that his time was up: The Tenth Circuit Court in Denver had met in a special predawn session and overturned Judge Ritter's stay. He was ushered out of his cell and escorted to a waiting van that drove him and the execution party to the prison cannery, where the firing squad awaited. The witnesses Gilmore had invited came forward and exchanged parting words with him. Then the warden, standing a few feet from Gilmore's chair, read the execution order and asked the condemned man if he had anything to say. Gilmore looked past the warden to stare deep into the dark-gray-fabric curtain that concealed the five riflemen. He rolled his head back for a long moment and looked up at the ceiling. Then he leveled his gaze, looked back at the warden and spoke his last words:*]

GILMORE: Let's do it.

High Noon in Skidmore

by CARL NAVARRE
July 1982

Indian Summer—and in the café across the street from the court-house, the flies that have been roused by the sudden heat bounce against the window, hoping for one more spin in the sunshine before winter deals its trump. The place is Savannah, Missouri, a one-elevator corn-and-bean town 75 miles upriver from Kansas City. The time is October 1981. The subject is murder; specifically, the public killing of an illiterate, unemployed drifter named Ken Rex McElroy in an even smaller town called Skidmore, about 20 miles away.

Murder, of course, is a rather common crime, even in the Bible-thumping Missouri hinterlands; yet what distinguishes McElroy's death from the 20,000 or so homicides reported in America each year is that a majority of Skidmore's citizens claim that it wasn't murder at all: that McElroy—unarmed and shot in the back by at least two gunmen while a crowd of local farmers watched approvingly—represented a threat to their community so dire and uncontrollable that killing him was a case of justifiable homicide.

Alden Lance, a former county prosecutor whom I have come to the café to meet, agrees with them.

"What else could they do to protect themselves?" asks Lance, who served as prosecutor here in Savannah from 1956 until 1976, a tour of duty that has made him an expert on crime in northwest Missouri. "McElroy was a vicious criminal. During the past ten years, he shot at least two men and openly supported himself by stealing livestock and farm equipment from his neighbors. In 1971, I had him arrested eight separate times for felony theft, but I had to drop the case when my witnesses decided not to testify against him. That was the pattern with McElroy: You'd work hard to build a good case and then you'd have to drop it because the witnesses were scared to testify. McElroy wasn't the kind of criminal you could get rid of with conventional methods. Look at his record: dozens of arrests for everything from arson, theft and rape to assault with intent to kill. And not a single conviction. The man never spent a night in prison in his life.

"People have a right to protect their lives and their property. McElroy stole from those people for years and terrorized them and they were sick of it. When people lose confidence in the courts and the police, they'll protect themselves any way they can. The law was no help to the people in Skidmore. They had to get rid of McElroy themselves and they knew it."

Lance pauses and our eyes lock.

"If you want to know the truth, I expected this to happen sooner than it did. There's an old saying I believe in: 'The will of the people is the law of the land.' Although technically a crime was committed in Skidmore, the will of the people was served."

Lance tilts his chin for the last drop of coffee and rises to leave. "You know," he says suddenly, turning back to the table and lingering as though he's had a revelation, "what happened in Skidmore is just like this John Lennon thing. The Beatles' music ruined a whole generation of our young people, but you couldn't stop them, because the Constitution guarantees everyone—good and bad—the right to free expression. Obviously, killing John Lennon was against the law, even though the guy who did it did us all a big favor. It was the same thing up in Skidmore. The means were bad, but the net result was good." He glances at his wristwatch. "Hey, I really got to run. Nice talking to you." We shake hands and he disappears.

A few minutes later, a doughy teenager with frizzy hair slinks into the café and buys a pack of cigarettes. Above his Levis he wears a white T-shirt with blue lettering that neatly expresses the prevailing local sentiment about Ken Rex McElroy's murder.

WHO SHOT K.R.? the shirt says on the front. WHO GIVES A DAMN? says the back.

• • •

The town appears abruptly as you crest a hill: SKIDMORE, POPULATION 447, the sign announces, and beyond it, a narrow ribbon of closely spaced white houses cuts an arrow-straight swath through fields of corn and soybeans that press right up against the edges of mowed lawns. This is serious farm country: From St. Joe, the road to Skidmore winds over a roller coaster of hills that from April to November are blanketed by a patchwork quilt of cultivated grain. The farmhouses, most of which are set far apart, are plain clapboard affairs with rusting machinery scattered in the yards and, near many of them, a fenced rectangle of bare earth containing hogs. Every few miles, you pass through a little town identifiable chiefly by its grain elevator: Savannah, Maitland, Graham and, finally, Skidmore. If you acknowledge the fact that the 40th parallel roughly divides America laterally and that the 95th meridian halves the country longitudinally, then Skidmore, which happens to be where they intersect, is the geographic center of America.

At first glance, Skidmore seems surprisingly small—much smaller even than you'd expect of a town with fewer than 500 inhabitants. After following the row of houses for maybe a quarter mile, you arrive suddenly at the business section, which would fit comfortably within the boundaries of a football field. At one end of town looms the requisite grain elevator and feed store; at the other, where Missouri 113 makes an abrupt turn east, are a pair of old-fashioned gas stations, a bank, a grocery, a beauty salon (open by appointment only) and a hardware store. Between those goal lines are a small brick building that houses Inez Boyer's café and the squat, steel-sided honky-tonk called the D & G Tavern. Across the street is the Skidmore post office, the only sign of life in a block of abandoned concrete buildings that record a prosperity now faded. On the whole, Skidmore has the look—exhausted, anachronistic—of a town that's being wasted by a cancer. In this case, the cancer is the Nodaway County seat of Maryville, 12 miles northeast, whose three factories, shopping malls and neon-lit saloons are so attractive to the rural population that Skidmore can no longer compete.

It was the tail end of summer, just before harvest, when I arrived in Skidmore to study the failure of the American legal system as represented by McElroy's killing. Everything seemed so clear back then: McElroy, I'd been told, was a sadistic bully who had terrorized the town for decades; the citizens of Skidmore were law-abiding folk who had begged the sheriff and the prosecutor to protect them and who resorted to murder only when there appeared to be no alternative.

But after a month in northwest Missouri, nothing appeared quite so clear as it had from the distance. First, the fabled monolith of opinion about the righteousness of the murder shattered with the slightest probing. Next, I was unable to find any substantial evidence that McElroy had been the extraordinary criminal people said he was. I checked the court records in six counties; I questioned state and local policemen; and I discovered that while McElroy had frequently been accused of crimes and had stood trial, his record was clean enough for him to have run for public office.

Likewise, McElroy's contravention of justice through terrorism proved difficult to locate. I couldn't find a prosecutor or a policeman in northwest Missouri who could remember a single witness who'd formally requested protection from McElroy. Even Lance's claims that McElroy had intimidated witnesses were suspect. When questioned, those witnesses said they were arrested without charges and held without bail until they agreed to testify. Soon after they were released, they refuted their testimony and Lance, who could have charged them with wrongful oath, dropped the case.

Even so, it didn't take long to hear plenty of horror stories about McElroy—tales of rape, torture, child molesting and murder so gruesome they made my skin crawl. But I heard some chilling stories about the respectable, God-fearing families who killed him, too: stories about how Hangman's Bridge (which crosses the Nodaway River west of Skidmore) was so named because of the rustlers who were introduced to justice while swinging from its stout oak frame; about an itinerant hired man named Razco, who was lynched north of Skidmore after a farmer's wife accused him of raping her; about Raymond Gun, a young black man who was burned to death by a mob in Maryville; and about Chester Leggans, a so-called thief and troublemaker, who was murdered six years ago in the presence of witnesses who all swore they hadn't seen a thing.

Like Alden Lance, a lot of people could make a brutal public execution sound reasonable and justified, right up to the point where they compared it with the murder of John Lennon.

• • •

The first person I met in town was Harry Sumy, a rail-thin elderly gentleman with stubbled cheeks, who owns the service station about 30 yards from the spot where McElroy was killed. While Sumy filled my tank, we chatted about the weather, which was hot and dry, perfect for the harvest. When I asked about the killing, the crow's-feet around his eyes wrinkled and all traces of spontaneity vanished. After that, he spoke in a careful, practiced tone, as though he were reciting a speech from memory. It was an act I was to encounter often in Skidmore; justified or not, a murder had been committed and nearly everyone seemed aware that loose talk about it could send someone to death row.

"You can look all you want, but you won't find any vigilantes around here," Sumy told me earnestly. He wore oil-stained work boots and clean overalls that were faded nearly white. He certainly didn't look to me like a man who would take part in an organized killing, though I later heard that he'd been standing nearby when McElroy was killed and, like the rest of his friends who had witnessed the murder, had told the police that he hadn't seen the shooting.

"If you want my honest opinion," Sumy said, "I think that whoever killed McElroy wasn't even from around these parts. Probably it was a professional killer from Kansas City. You know, a man like McElroy had a lot of enemies and not all of 'em lived around here. I hear he was involved with the Mafia down there and they sent someone up here to get him."

It didn't seem worth the effort to ask why a professional killer would snuff a man with a crowd of people watching when it would have been considerably less troublesome to fulfill his contract when McElroy was alone. Perhaps Sumy thought that professional killers, as a rule, were sportsmen. I thanked him for the information and parked across the street, in front of the Sam R. Albright American Legion Hall, where, only minutes before the murder, a town meeting had been held, the subject of which was McElroy and what to do about him.

Several people who were present say that about 60 men had attended that meeting. Most of them were farmers, who in Missouri are characteristically strong, stout and independent. There's no doubt that most of those present believed McElroy was a master thief and a vicious bully whose continued freedom was a threat to their lives and their property. Judging from subsequent events, at least two of them believed that the law was incapable of protecting them and that in order to ensure their own safety, they would have to get rid of McElroy themselves.

Fundamentally, Skidmore's case against McElroy—and the legal system—was based on three recent incidents, as well as a deep-seated prejudice that McElroy aggravated by his refusal to conform to prevailing standards of morality and behavior.

In 1976, a prominent Skidmore farmer named Romaine Henry accused McElroy of shooting him in the stomach. According to Henry, McElroy had been standing in the road near Henry's house with a shotgun, and when Henry stopped to ask what he was doing, McElroy gave him both barrels. Arrested for assault with intent to kill, McElroy was brought to trial. Henry testified that McElroy had shot him; McElroy, supported by two witnesses, claimed he had been at home at the time

Henry said the shooting occurred. The jury believed McElroy. "We all sympathized with the man who'd been shot," juror William Groomer says of that case, "but there just wasn't no evidence that McElroy had shot him. The prosecutor didn't have no case at all. I don't think it should have ever come to trial."

In Skidmore, where Henry is generally liked and McElroy was not, people were angered by what they considered the impotence of the courts.

Four years later, McElroy was again charged with assault with intent to kill. This time, his alleged victim was a 70-year-old Skidmore grocer named Ernest Bowenkamp, who, like Henry, claimed that McElroy had shot him without provocation. At the trial, held 60 miles away in Harrison County on June 26, 1981, McElroy admitted to shooting Bowenkamp but said he'd done so in self-defense when the grocer attacked him with a butcher's knife. The verdict was a compromise: McElroy was found guilty—but only of second-degree assault; the jury recommended a sentence of two years instead of the 15 the prosecution had requested. As required by Missouri law, the judge gave McElroy 25 days to file a motion for a new trial and released him on bond. Again, the citizens of Skidmore were outraged, both by what they considered a meager sentence and by McElroy's continued freedom, which they viewed as a dangerous opportunity for him to strike back at those who'd testified against him.

Five days later, a wave of hysteria swept through town. In statements submitted to the Nodaway County prosecutor, four Skidmore men claimed McElroy had swaggered into the D & G with a loaded M-1 carbine and threatened to kill Bowenkamp and anyone else who tried to send him to prison. The conditions of his bond prohibited him from carrying firearms; when the prosecutor filed a motion to have the bond revoked, word spread quickly that McElroy had repeated his threats. The four men who'd signed the statements appealed to the rest of the town for help, and on the morning of July 10, the meeting was convened at the American Legion hall. When someone brought the news that McElroy had stopped at the Skidmore honky-tonk—even as they were debating how to get rid of him—60 determined men headed for the bar for a showdown.

McElroy, who stood 5'8" and weighed more than 250 pounds, betrayed no emotion when confronted by the hostile crowd. He was wearing brown-suede cowboy boots, brown sports pants and a brown shirt that revealed the numerous tattoos on his ham-sized arms. He struck up a conversation with one reluctant farmer, finished his beer with a steady hand, ordered a six-pack of Bud and a tube of Rolaids and left. About half the crowd followed him outside. They glared from the weed-cracked sidewalk as he calmly started his pickup. Meanwhile, at least two gunmen assumed position across the street, directly under the stars and stripes of Old Glory that hangs in front of the Skidmore P.O. According to Trena McElroy, who was in the truck with her husband, one of the gunmen raised a lever-action .30-30 and pointed it at Ken, who was unarmed. Outside the air-conditioned pickup, it was nearly 100 degrees. Everyone was sweating but McElroy, who nonchalantly put a Camel between his lips and prepared to light it.

The first shot—the one from the .30-30—shattered the rear window of the truck and struck McElroy an inch below his right ear lobe. Traveling at approximately three times the speed of sound, the steel-jacketed bullet incised a shaggy groove through both sides of his lower jaw and tongue and fractured his left axilla and upper palate, all of which clogged his throat with so much blood and fleshy debris that he would have suffocated if a second shot hadn't blow the back of his head off. As he died, McElroy's foot jerked reflexively against the throttle pedal, jamming it to the floor board so that the engine raced until it eventually seized and burned. The shot that killed him—the second one—was fired from a .22 magnum. His unlighted cigarette, flecked with what appeared to be bits of rust, was later found on the dashboard.

After those first shots, a lull ensued; then more shots were fired from those and perhaps other guns. The shots were staggered, deliberate, evenly spaced, several of them directed in apparent jealous rage upon the vehicle itself, which was a nearly new four-wheel-drive Chevy, an object held in high esteem by Missouri farmers. As the shooting ceased, Trena was pulled from the truck and led into the bank nearby, and the crowd that had witnessed the execution gradually dispersed. At the D & G Tavern, beer was served on the house for the first time in memory.

Despite a phone on the wall just inside the door, no one bothered to call an ambulance or the police. Consequently, more than half an hour passed before the first law-enforcement officers arrived to investigate. What they found was like a scene out of *The Twilight Zone*: respectable, churchgoing men, women and children conducting their business as usual, carefully ignoring the smoldering pickup and the bloody man within, who was slumped forward peacefully, as though asleep.

A few hours later, events took another strange turn when Trena McElroy gave a statement to the highway patrol in nearby St. Joe.

HIGH NOON IN SKIDMORE

Trena swore that the man behind the .30-30 was Del Clement, 27, the scion of Skidmore's wealthiest farming family. Normally, the Nodaway County Sheriff's Department would have responded to such eyewitness testimony by arresting and charging the suspect. But because of the unusual social implications of the killing and the certain unpopularity of arresting anyone named Clement, the case was shunted from the sheriff to the county prosecutor and the Northwest Missouri Major Investigation Squad (NMMIS), an ad hoc committee of lawmen responsible for investigating crimes deemed too complicated for local authorities to handle alone.

Two months later, when I arrived in Skidmore, no arrests had been made, no charges filed and McElroy's killers were still at large—a singularly sobering fact of life for anyone walking around town asking questions about the shooting.

• • •

Lois and Ernest Bowenkamp, who own the B & B Grocery, are proof that opposites attract: Lois is short, heavy, quick-tempered and outspoken; Ernest is tall, thin and phlegmatic. The Bowenkamps' trouble with McElroy had started in April 1980, when, after an argument, Mrs. Bowenkamp had told McElroy to leave her store and never come back. Three months later, McElroy shot Mr. Bowenkamp in the neck. As they awaited the trial for the next 11 months, the Bowenkamps lived in fear that McElroy, who was free on bond, would return to finish the job.

"This was not a vigilante action," Lois says categorically about McElroy's murder. "This was an eruption of fear and frustration, and it never would have happened if the law had worked. The police would arrest him and the courts would let him go. That's what made everybody so mad. After he was found guilty of shooting Bo, he was right back here in town, free as can be, telling everybody how he'd never go to prison and bragging about it. The Bible says there should be an eye for an eye. Those who live by the sword die by the sword. Well, Ken McElroy lived by the gun and that's the way he died. Justice has been served."

The Bowenkamps aren't the only Skidmoreans who had reasons to want McElroy dead.

"My only regret about what happened to Ken McElroy," says Tim Warren, pastor of the Skidmore Christian Church, "is that somebody didn't kill him sooner."

Obviously, those are harsh words for a man of God. Yet Warren, who is 28, believes that his sentiments are justified by the horror that was inflicted upon him.

About a year before McElroy was killed, Warren claims to have received the first of numerous anonymous phone calls from a man who threatened to torture and kill him, his wife and their two children. According to the preacher, the caller was McElroy—who went to such lengths to harass and terrorize him for the absurd offense of having visited Bowenkamp in the hospital after he was shot.

"McElroy must have had the hospital staked out," Warren says, "because when I got home from visiting Bo, the phone calls started. 'Mind your business or else,' the first one said. When I didn't back down, they got worse."

Instead of minding his own business or calling the police, Warren loaded his guns—a .22, a 12-gauge shotgun and a snub-nosed .38 special that he carried on his person. The threats intensified: The caller threatened to castrate Warren, to kidnap and maim his children, to rape and mutilate his wife and send him her breasts in a manila envelope. Twice, claims Warren, he had armed confrontations with McElroy, who backed down both times. And although the phone calls stopped about six months before McElroy's death, Warren says that it was impossible for him to feel safe as long as McElroy was alive. "You can't believe what it was like here," Warren says. "As far as I'm concerned, McElroy got exactly what he deserved."

Like Warren, David Dunbar, 25, is a relative newcomer to Skidmore who says he was happy when McElroy was killed. Oddly, Dunbar, who served for five months as Skidmore's marshal (a part-time job with little actual authority), says that he and McElroy were friends—until McElroy threatened, without provocation, to kill him.

"It happened up at the D & G Tavern," Dunbar says. "I got a call that there was a fight going on, so I went to break it up. Well, there wasn't no fight, but McElroy was there, so I drank a couple of beers with him. When I left, he was leaning against his pickup outside. I started over toward him and he reached in the pickup and pulled out a rifle, but I grabbed the barrel before he could point it at me and held on real tight. We stood like that a while, then, finally, he backed down. After that, even though I tried to stay away from him, I figured it was just a matter of time before he got me. I decided then that if he tried to harass me like he harassed the Bowenkamps I'd kill him. That's the way most people felt. To be honest with you, my only regret about the way Ken died is that I didn't pull the trigger myself."

Then there is Romaine Henry, the barrel-chested farmer who accused

HIGH NOON IN SKIDMORE

McElroy of shooting him in 1976. Henry, whose 1,000-acre farm is only a mile from McElroy's house, says that after he was shot, McElroy would park outside his house at night and shine a spotlight on the windows, and that once, while he was plowing a field, McElroy shot at him with a high-powered rifle.

"I've got no idea why he was after me," says Henry, an extremely courteous, soft-spoken man of 47. "I really never had any involvement with Ken and there was no reason for him to be after me, but he was, and you'll just have to believe that, despite what the jury said."

Although Henry, Dunbar, Warren and the Bowenkamps were the only Skidmoreans who told me they'd actually been threatened by McElroy, nearly everyone with whom I talked knew at least one hair-curling story about him. At Inez Boyer's café, where farmers gather every morning to gossip over weak cups of coffee, one man told me that McElroy had worked for the Mafia as an arsonist and had made $10,000 for each building he burned.

Another man, a farmer, said he had been the biggest rustler in the state. "McElroy stole everything that wasn't tied down," he said. "Last year, this county had six times as many hogs and cattle stolen as any other county in the state. Everybody knew McElroy was doing it, but the law we got around here, they never could catch him at it. Last winter, it got so bad with livestock disappearing, I'm surprised somebody didn't take McElroy out and lynch him then."

Up at the D & G, a dim barroom with two pool tables and pictures of rodeo cowboys on the wall, I heard that McElroy had had $40,000 in cash on him when he was killed; that there had been a grocery sack full of dope in his truck; that one of his close relatives was a homosexual who starred in porno films in St. Joe; and that yet another had thrown gasoline on his wife's first husband and burned him to death. Everybody explained McElroy's irrational behavior—shooting Henry and Bowenkamp for no reason—by recalling that he'd been run over by a tractor when he was a boy and that the doctors had put a steel plate in his head. Since that accident, they said, he'd been like Dr. Jekyll and Mr. Hyde. One day, he'd be as nice as the next guy; the next day, he'd come right out of the blue and shoot you.

Outside the Skidmore bank, an attractive matron with a blonde bouffant told me that McElroy had cut Trena's breast off with a knife, a story I was to hear many times. "Dr. Humphrey from Mound City said it was the worst thing he ever saw," she said. "Of course, I'm sure you know that before they were married, McElroy was arrested for raping Trena and then for burning her parents' house when she tried to leave him.

He just walked over with a can of gasoline and set the house on fire with the whole family watching. He would've gone to prison for that, except he married Trena so she couldn't testify against him. What else could she do? He would've killed her if she hadn't married him. Everybody knows he drowned his wife, Sharon Mae, when she wouldn't give him a divorce. They found her floating in the river down by St. Joe, but he was never even charged for it. Let me tell you, there were plenty of people around here who figured Trena would be overjoyed if someone killed Ken. With him dead, she'd be free from him, just like she always wanted."

• • •

The voice is shaky, sliding uncertainly over the short sentences. Trena McElroy sucks air rapidly, fighting for control. Her eyes are red and watery, the pupils slightly dilated.

"When I knew what happened, I opened my door. They was still shootin' and I was beggin' them to stop. I tried to get out, but this guy told me to stay where I was. He said they was gonna shoot me, too. Then Jack Clement [Del's father] pulled me out real hard and put me in the bank with all these women. All the men that was on the street came up and stood around in a circle, lookin' in the windows. I thought they had me set up. I wanted to get out, but they wouldn't let me leave. I went over to the women who was standin' there talkin'. 'You didn't have to do him like that,' I told them. Then this lady said to me, 'Honey, we just didn't have no choice. . . .'"

The voice breaks and she sniffs hard, pawing at her nose with a wadded Kleenex.

"I sat down, still thinkin' they was gonna kill me, too, when Del and Royce Clement came into the bank. They didn't say nothin' to me but went to the back to talk to the manager. After a while, Timmy [McElroy's brother] came and got me. He wanted to check on Ken, but I told him it weren't no use, that Ken was. . . ."

The voice gets away from her again and she ducks her head, waiting for it to return.

"I was still afraid of what they might do to me. So I told Timmy just to drive on by the truck. We didn't even stop. As soon as we got home, I got in touch with Gene [McElroy's lawyer] and he tried to get ahold of somebody to get the law out there. When he finally got ahold of someone, they didn't know nothin' about it, because nobody even bothered to call in . . ."

HIGH NOON IN SKIDMORE

Her voice escapes into a high keening whine, and this time she just lets it go and weeps. This is where all the smug avowals of vigilante justice begin to sound thin and a little weak. This is where you come face to face with the reality that what got shot in Skidmore on July 10 was a man with a wife and children who loved him and not merely some psychotic redneck, the fabricated villain of a tabloid story.

McElroy was born in 1934, one of 13 children of a dirt-poor itinerant farm hand who drifted to Skidmore during the Depression. Ken quit school before he could read or write and hitchhiked to Colorado, where he worked for several years at construction. He returned to Skidmore around 1953, the same year his brother Bobbie Dick was sent to prison for stealing a truckload of corn from a neighbor's bin. For the next 20 years, McElroy drifted from one rural town to another, supporting the children from his three marriages by trading livestock and second-hand furniture that he bought and sold at country auctions. By the time he settled down with Trena on his mother's hard-scrabble 60 acres near Skidmore, he had devoted himself to the single abiding passion of his life: raising and training coon hounds.

Now, eight years later, at the age of 24, Trena has a thick mane of blonde curls and baby-pink cheeks. At 14, when her romance with McElroy started, she must have been a stunner: soft, ample and shy. In Skidmore, people point to the rape, child-molesting and arson charges Trena brought against McElroy in 1973 as proof of his depravity. Trena emphatically disagrees. She says she told the prosecutor that McElroy had raped her and burned her parents' house because she wanted to force him to marry her.

Their affair had begun in the autumn of 1972, when McElroy was 38. Because he was a friend of her stepfather, Ronnie McNeely, Trena had known Ken since she was a baby. When she was 12, she developed a crush on him; two years later, after considerable flirting, Ken invited her to spend the day with him in St. Joe. She accepted. Ken took her shopping and bought her some clothes. They danced at a honky-tonk and finished the date at a motel named for Jesse James, who was shot in the back in St. Joe. She returned to the Jesse James with McElroy at least seven more times that fall, and by Christmas she was pregnant.

Trena desperately wanted to marry McElroy—not only to give her baby a father but because she loved him—but he was already married. When the baby was born, prematurely, in May, she was resentful and deeply depressed. Poor, unwed, without any hope of supporting herself and her child, Trena went to the county welfare department for help. As in all such cases, the welfare officer required that she identify the baby's father. Since sexual intercourse with a female under 16 was at that time punishable in Missouri by life in prison (whether or not the sexual act was consensual), soon after she had named McElroy as her baby's father, the county prosecutor paid Trena a visit. It didn't take long to convince her that the best way to force McElroy's hand in marriage was to agree to testify against him. On the day after McElroy was charged with rape and child molesting, McNeely's house burned down and a charge of arson was tacked on to the indictment. The next day, when Trena's uncle claimed that McElroy had threatened to shoot him, a charge of flourishing a weapon in a rude and angry manner was also added.

Almost immediately after the alleged weapons incident, Trena was hospitalized for nervous exhaustion. After three months in a state mental hospital, she was moved to a foster home in Maryville; then, because the prosecutor was afraid McElroy might try to harm her, she was secretly transferred to Whiteman Air Force Base. Soon after she arrived at Whiteman, she contacted McElroy, who by then was divorced and who asked Trena to marry him. Six months later when he received a copy of the marriage certificate, the prosecutor dropped all but the weapons charge; and although Trena's uncle testified against him, McElroy was acquitted. As to the fire at her parents' house, Trena says it was caused by faulty wiring.

"The police harassed my husband constantly," she explains. "They hated him because they were always trying to pin something on him that Ken never did and Ken would make a fool of them every time. They were always challenging him, and my husband, he wouldn't back down for anybody.

"People were just always talking bad about Ken, and that's how the trouble started. They were just going on what they'd heard, not what they'd seen. There were plenty of lies told and plenty believed. Like that day in the tavern, just before he was killed, when they said he had a loaded gun. Ken never touched the gun. He told some guy he'd just bought this antique Army gun and the guy said he'd like to see it. So Ken told me to go out to the truck and get it, and I did. It wasn't loaded or anything, and Ken never touched it. After we left, they said he'd threatened them with it but it wasn't like that at all."

Still scared and still under police protection two months after her husband was killed, Trena had yet to return to Skidmore. After she named Del Clement one of the assassins, several of her relatives were advised by anonymous telephone callers that Trena ought to change her story and shut her mouth, or the people who murdered her husband would get rid of her, too.

• • •

Nearly everyone you talk with about McElroy eventually mentions his devotion to coon hounds. At the time of death, he owned about 20 dogs, some worth as much as $3,000. Trena says that McElroy trained his dogs daily and on weekends took them to the field trials held in the rural towns of Missouri, Iowa and Kansas.

Soon after I arrived in Skidmore, I went to one of those field trials in Fillmore, Missouri, with a couple of farmers named David and Lionel.

"Ken pretty much raised the best dogs in this part of the state," David said as we headed for the meet in his pickup. It was a brilliant day in late September and the fields of soybeans along the road had turned from green to yellow to a fine, rich chocolate brown. "Ken had this one walker named Rugged, had a voice on him prettier than Kenny Rogers's. I don't believe I ever saw Rugged lose a treeing contest."

The Fillmore Saddle Club, where the meet was held, was a three-acre clearing circled by an immense field of soy beans and milo. Pickups were parked for about 100 yards on either side of the road. Hitched to some of them were elaborate dog trailers with the name of the owner stenciled on the side. (PO BOY'S TREEING WALKERS, one said.) Up by an enormous maple, the treeing competition was just starting. In a treeing contest, each hound barks at a caged raccoon for 30 seconds; the dog that barks the most is the winner. As we edged through the circle of men in overalls who were standing under the maple, I could see that a raccoon in a steel cage was being lowered by a rope from a branch. At the foot of the tree were about 20 men holding lunging hounds on leashes. This was the warm-up. As the cage was lowered and the raccoon walked nervously from one end to the other, the hounds barked and leaped and snapped. It was a hot day and a ring of foam formed around the raccoon's mouth. The animal was clearly distraught beyond any comprehensible notion of fear.

"Once, I was over in Bethany at a dog meet," Lionel said, "and as they was raisin' and lowerin' the coon, the rope broke. When it hit the ground, that old cage split open and the coon jumped out right under the nose of a fool redbone. That hound looked at that coon and that coon looked at that hound—and then, quick as a snake, that coon laid that hound's throat open from ear to ear. They got claws and teeth like razors, you know. They can cut anything. Then the coon took off and he like to make it across a soybean field to the timber before the other dogs caught him and tore him to pieces. That redbone bled to death before they could carry him to the truck."

Lionel's story haunted me long after the field trial was over. At the time, it seemed to be the perfect metaphor for the McElroy killing, with the citizens of Skidmore cast as the distraught raccoon tormented by the hound. But the longer I stayed in Missouri, the more evidence I found suggesting that it might have been the other way around.

• • •

Not long after the murder, Lester Doss, an unemployed farm hand who had been one of McElroy's closest friends, received the following letter:

> This is the only warning you will get. Our bellys [sic] are full of your kind. Ken did not pay attention to leave the county when told to. Get out of this territory while you can. You have been warned. We don't want any thieves or rustlers or troublemakers.

Another friend of McElroy's, a man with a reputation for cattle rustling, was abducted at gunpoint, driven into the country and hanged from an oak branch. This man, who wears a brown necklace of rope burn to support his tale, was told that if he didn't leave the area within a week, he would be hanged again—and the next time would be final. He didn't even bother to notify the police.

A week after McElroy was murdered, Alice Woods, his former common-law wife, who lives outside St. Joe, was threatened while returning from a visit to McElroy's mother, in Skidmore. On the blacktop road south of Graham, a car passed her and pulled sideways across the road so she had to stop. Four strangers approached her.

"Don't you know it's dangerous to be driving around this county in one of McElroy's trucks?" one of them said.

Woods, who'd already heard of the other threats, had a sawed-off 12-gauge ready. Although she was scared senseless and isn't handy with firearms, she poked the gun out the window and the four men scattered. A few weeks later, a black jeep stopped in front of her house while her three children played in the yard, and shots were fired over their heads. Then the phone began to ring in the middle of the night, "If you know what's good for you, you'll take this warning and stop stirring up trouble," an anonymous caller said. Despite the threats, Woods still lives in the same cramped six-room clapboard house. Random garbage—hubcaps, derelict tires, a half-chewed possum with its entrails strung out in the dust—decorates the weeds on her lawn.

HIGH NOON IN SKIDMORE

"You know, everybody up around Skidmore hassled Ken all the time," she told me. "They were jealous of him and they had reason to be. They worked hard out in those fields every day and Ken never worked like that at all. Ken had a knack for making money by being smart, not by being strong. They didn't like the idea that a man could support himself without sweating all day like they did. So they claimed he stole their livestock, but there was never any proof that he did. They were always after him, them and the law. They just wouldn't let him alone."

We were sitting in the living room where a picture of the Last Supper that she'd torn from a magazine is taped to the wall. "Let me ask you this," Woods said. "If Del Clement's wife said Ken McElroy shot her husband, how long do you think it would've been before they'd had Ken in jail?"

She let the question hang there for a moment before she continued. "The law says that murder, no matter who does it, is murder. Well, Ken McElroy got murdered and 30 people seen who did it. Lester Doss got a letter saying they'd kill him, too. I've been threatened and my children have been shot at, but nobody's been arrested or charged for any of it."

Yet McElroy's friends and family aren't the only people around Skidmore who have reason to be afraid. Many Skidmoreans—especially those who watched the killing and lied to the police to protect the killers—are afraid of one another. In Skidmore, everyone is aware of the extreme fragility of the web of lies that has thus far prevented an indictment; if only one witness cracked and went to the police with the truth, perhaps 30 others could be charged with conspiracy to commit murder. And every month, the fear that someone will crack gets worse.

Still, there are people in town who aren't afraid to say they don't think McElroy deserved to be killed. Ronnie Charles, a 19-year-old Marine whom I met when he was home on leave, was among them. Charles was one of the state's key witnesses against McElroy at the Bowenkamp trial. Charles's testimony—that he had seen McElroy park behind the grocery store only minutes before Bowenkamp was shot—prevented McElroy from claiming he wasn't there at all and forced his plea of self-defense. Many people in Skidmore say that McElroy consistently evaded prison by intimidating witnesses, yet Charles told me that McElroy never tried to influence him. In fact, he considered McElroy his friend.

"I never heard of Ken hurting anybody who wasn't messing with him," Charles said. "People who had never met him were always gossiping about him and running him down. Most of them deserved to have their asses kicked. You know, if those people hadn't talked about McElroy so much, they never would have had to shoot him."

Although Romaine Henry does not recall it, Charles says he was walking down Main Street in Maryville one night last July when Henry stopped him and said there would be a meeting about McElroy the next morning in Skidmore. They were going to get rid of him, Henry said—burn him out and run his women off. Henry asked Charles if he wanted to help, but Ronnie didn't want any part of it. The next day, McElroy was killed.

Like Charles, Inez Boyer, who was born and raised in Skidmore and who owns the café that is the social center of the community, doesn't think McElroy's execution was just. I had known Inez for nearly a month and had talked with her daily before she said anything about the killing. It happened without any prompting. One day, she simply stared at me and said, "You know, I never felt so sick in my life as the day they shot Ken McElroy. I was right here in the café when it happened and I knew there was a meeting about him, but I didn't know they were going to kill him until I heard the shots. There was a lot of them. It sounded like a war. When it got quiet, I went over to a window to look out. 'Well, they've shot McElroy,' I said to myself. Right then, I knew that nothing around here would ever be the same."

By the time Inez unburdened herself to me, most of the tight and gruesome little tales I'd heard about McElroy had already come unraveled. According to James Rhoades of the highway patrol in St. Joe, who had known him for 25 years, McElroy had no connection to the Mafia and was never known to sell drugs.

"I hear these stories that McElroy was a big-time drug dealer and a rustler and I just laugh at them," says Rhoades, a member of the highway patrol since 1949 and the most experienced lawman in northwest Missouri. "McElroy was a punk, a petty thief. He was like a crow: He stole whatever people were careless enough to leave lying around. Sure, he stole some hogs, but compared with big rustlers, what McElroy stole wasn't even noticeable." Rhoades, who was a member of NMMIS and investigated McElroy's death, says there was no dope in McElroy's truck when he was killed, nor $40,000 in a paper sack. The coroner's report states that there was no steel plate in his head. And his first wife, Sharon Mae—the one I was told he had drowned—is alive and well in Helena, Missouri, and when I asked her about him, she said she'd loved him a lot.

Likewise, the most brutal story I'd heard about McElroy—that he'd cut off Trena's breast—proved false. Dr. James Humphrey, who delivered Trena's first baby, said he had never treated her for a breast wound, nor did she show scars of such.

But if, as Rhoades maintains, McElroy wasn't an extraordinary criminal; and if, as Charles and many Skidmoreans believe, McElroy had been more the coon than the hound, why had 60 farmers sacrificed a morning's work to discuss getting rid of him? And why had at least two of those men risked prison to blow him away?

• • •

There are three kinds of soil in Nodaway County: sand, loam and gumbo, the last of which is as black as oil and, for those who own it, considerably more valuable. The 1981 harvest set a record for farmers in Skidmore. While prices for crops were generally low and the costs of planting and harvesting higher than ever, the average profit per acre of farmland was about $100, while the value of the land itself (conservatively estimated at $1,500 an acre) appreciated by 15 percent. Big farmers, such as the Clement-Patterson clan—who together farm about 15,000 acres—may have realized an income of $1.5 million from an asset base worth $22 million.

All this surprises many visitors to rural Missouri, who expect anyone with that kind of income and assets to wear Brooks Brothers suits, own elaborate houses and drive flashy automobiles. In fact, it takes a trained eye to distinguish between the Haves and the Have-Nots of Nodaway County, because most the Haves are frugal folk with the same simple tastes as the Have-Nots. In Skidmore, a man who owns a piece of ground worth $1 million (and machinery worth half as much again) is likely to wear the same frayed overalls and torn flannel shirt as his hired man, who doesn't have a nickel.

Like everywhere else, however, Skidmore has its own symbolism of class and wealth, and within the community those distinctions are closely monitored.

The most common indication of affluence is the pickup truck. Four-wheel drive is a must in any status machine; so is a special 50-gallon gas tank behind the cab, which implies that the farmer who owns the truck also owns other machinery—such as tractors and combines—that must be refueled in the field.

Other, more subtle, marks of affluence in Nodaway County are cowboy boots (men who work in the mud wear lace-ups), fine rifles and registered livestock. Because pigs smell bad, nobody fools with them unless he has to. Anyone who can still afford to raise cattle in quantity (the cattle market has been ruinously bad the past few years) or who owns more than a dozen saddle horses can be considered pretty well off. A house should be judged not by the quality or the beauty of the structure itself but by the quality and the size of the trees in the yard, which, besides offering shade, imply ancestry.

Yet the clearest distinction between the Haves and the Have-Nots is the nature of their employment. Even if they dress and live alike, the Haves all work for themselves on land they own, and the Have-Nots—unless they punch in on one of the shifts at the Union Carbide plant in Maryville or support themselves dishonestly—all work on farms for the Haves.

During the past 50 years, the nature of farming has changed radically. Today, on land that once required the labor of 20 men, a single farmer can work alone, planting aboard a $50,000 tractor and harvesting with a $100,000 combine. But while the technology of farming has changed, certain time-honored values persist, and self-reliance is chief among them. In order to succeed today, a farmer must be an agronomist, a mechanic, a veterinarian, a chemist, a meteorologist, a businessman and a commodities speculator. Last, but certainly not least, he must be able to protect what he owns.

A modern farm is like a store with no doors and no guards. Virtually anyone with a mind to can drive up to a farmer's gas tank—in which he stores fuel for his tractors—and steal 30 gallons. Or thieves can back a pickup against his grain bin (which may hold $50,000 worth of corn), knock a hole in the side with an ax and drive away with a cargo that can be sold for cash at any elevator. They can hop aboard his combine, which he often leaves in the field at night (one key fits all), drive it to a waiting tractor-trailer and have it unloaded and sold in another state before he notices it's missing in the morning. Because hogs are so easily and frequently stolen, many farmers don't even bother to report their loss to the police.

How, then, does a farmer protect himself from thieves? The country is too big and too empty for the police to help him until after something has been stolen. Besides, a farmer distrusts policemen the way he distrusts anyone who charges to do a job he prides himself on being able to do alone. Yet, short of sitting up every night with a shotgun, what alternative does he have?

"There's only one way to keep people from messing with you out here," one farmer told me. "You've got to let them know that if they try to hurt you, you're not going to get mad, you're going to get even. And you've got to have the kind of personal credibility to back it up.

People don't steal from a man who they know won't back down from anything."

Although it might not be recognized in the court in Maryville, this code is as fundamental to life in rural Missouri as seed corn. And because it has functioned effectively since the land was settled, it is something that every farmer who doesn't want to be bled dry by thieves lets it be known he subscribes to. The ways that a farmer can advertise his compliance vary: He may carry a rifle in his pickup, or he may spend some time bragging in taverns how he'll shoot the eyes out of any son of a bitch he sees sneaking around his farm. But by far the easiest way to demonstrate his belief in the code is to join up with a few of his friends and kill a suspected thief. And after the law in Maryville has tacitly approved that method—by failing to even slap him on the wrist—he's likely to believe that what he did was justified by the demonstrated inefficiency of the courts and the police.

Had McElroy been chosen and sacrificed as a scapegoat, in accordance with this code? Two farmers I met in Maryville at a bar called the Shady Lady persuaded me that he had been. I'd seen one of them, a man named Pete, at the D & G in Skidmore a few days before. The other, whose name was Kriss, had forearms like Popeye's and a chest the size of a 50-gallon drum. When I asked if they'd known McElroy, Kriss became visibly nervous, tugging at his hair and looking quickly around the bar to see if anyone were watching. Since McElroy's killing, paranoia had spread to every level of social intercourse around Skidmore. Strangers like myself were automatically considered reporters, and most reporters were thought to be FBI agents or private investigators working for Trena McElroy's attorney, trying to pick up evidence for an indictment. Kriss asked for identification and I showed him some.

"This doesn't mean anything," he said to Pete. "Anybody could carry this stuff. Let's take him out to my office."

They each gripped one of my arms and escorted me to the rear of a Chevy van. Kriss unlocked it and we climbed inside.

"Okay, buddy," he said. "Who are you really working for?"

I told him again, but he didn't appear to believe me.

"We might look like hayseeds," Kriss said, "but lemme tell you something: If you're lying to us, you're in bad trouble. We've got a saying around here. We say 'The payback's a motherfucker.' You know what that means? It means that if you try to hurt me, I don't just get even for it, I hurt you at least twice as bad. Let's say I know you stole a tire from me. Well, for that, I'd steal your car and set it on fire. The payback's a motherfucker. That's the way it works 'round here. That's how you keep people from fucking with you."

I'd gotten in the van with considerable apprehension; after listening to Kriss, I wished I were somewhere else. Clearly, I was in a place where men were ready to fight—even kill—over any perceived insult or injury, where the veneer with which we hide our basest instincts was beginning to wear thin. This was life reduced to fundamentals: *Don't back down. The payback's a motherfucker.*

Kriss and Pete were staring at me. I could see their faces only in silhouette. Again I told them who I was, adding as many details as I could to convince them that they had nothing to fear from me. When I finished, the van was quiet for a very long minute.

"You want to know about McElroy," Kriss said suddenly. "Well, let me tell you about him. He was a tough son of a bitch and everybody around here was scared of him. I don't know if you've noticed, but a lot of people around here think they're pretty tough and don't like to think they're scared of anything. Well, I used to think I was pretty tough, too. One night, I was at the bar in Skidmore with Ken and I was a little loaded, so I said, 'Ken. if you're such a great sportsman, how'd you miss old Bowenkamp, since he was standing right next to you? And how'd you miss Romaine? You must be the worst goddamn shot since Don Knotts.' Ken laughed and said, 'Come on outside, I got something to show you.' We went out to his truck and he reached in and pulled this rifle out real slowly. Let me tell you, he backed me right down, buddy. I thought I was tough—I'm real good with my fists—but I found out that if you put a gun on me, I'll back down every time. Do you know how hard it is for me to say that? You ask anybody who lives around here: What's the best thing you can say about any man? They'll tell you 'He never backed down.' You got that? *He never backed down!* That's what it means to be a man around here. Well, Ken McElroy backed me right down, just like he did everyone else. Until they got so ashamed of themselves they had to kill him."

• • •

The office is at what used to be the epicenter of the meat-packing industry: North Kansas City, the corner of Armour and Swift. The business card of a 24-hour bail bondsman is taped to the frame of the door. The paneling is fake walnut. The rug is a piss-yellow shag. The man behind the desk is short, fat and neckless. He wears a three-piece suit made from material so shiny you expect to see your reflection in his vest. Diamond rings gleam from the third finger of each hand. His name is Richard Eugene McFadin and he used to be McElroy's lawyer. Now he represents Trena McElroy, who has instructed him to do everything in his power to see that McElroy's killers are caught and punished.

In Skidmore—where the hatred expressed at the mention of the name McFadin is only slightly less intense than the hatred that was felt for Ken McElroy—most people consider him a sleazy opportunist who is using McElroy's widow to attract a fortune from Hollywood. McFadin denies this vociferously; even so, he would hardly be the only person connected to the murder who is trying to turn a buck. In Skidmore, people offered to sell me everything from bits of bone, bloody hair and teeth scavenged from McElroy's pickup to snapshots of the murder scene. And there are rumors that the Bowenkamps, Warren and Henry have signed exclusive contracts for their stories.

"I'm doing this gratuitously" is the way McFadin puts it. "I don't stand to make a dime. But this vigilante stuff bothers me and I'm interested in seeing justice done. Despite what they say in Skidmore, this is a classic example of vigilante-type activity. Why do I say that? Look at the evidence. A whole community watches this murder. The prosecutor has the murderer identified by an eyewitness. But no charges are filed. Now, what does that say about the American legal system?"

On McFadin's desk are three copies of the issue of *People* that carried a story portraying McElroy as a redneck sociopath who terrorized a community for a decade. In one of his file cabinets, McFadin has a manila folder three inches thick stuffed with press clippings about the murder. "The Beast of Nodaway County" is what one reporter called McElroy, though McFadin's description of his former client is strikingly different. Instead of the brooding sadist and master thief depicted by most people in Skidmore, McFadin describes McElroy as a quiet man, a loner, who, though unable to read or write, had a remarkable talent for trading livestock and for buying and selling old furniture.

"If McElroy had lived 100 years ago, none of this would have happened," McFadin told me. "He would have fit in back then, but he didn't fit in with those farmers in Skidmore at all. You know, you don't have to be a criminal for people to dislike you. Some people are hostile toward anyone who's different. McElroy didn't live like the other people in Skidmore. Instead of working all day in a field, he was able to support himself with his wits, and they resented that. And sometimes he lived with two or three women at the same time, and people up there thought that was immoral. But McElroy was proud

138

of who he was, and he was absolutely without fear. Right or wrong, he wouldn't back down from anyone or anything. If anybody told him he couldn't do something—like, 'Don't come into our town'—he'd take it as a challenge and they'd have to keep him out. He knew they were talking about getting rid of him, and he told me about it."

Because McFadin doubts that Del Clement will ever be indicted in Nodaway County, much less be convicted by a jury of his peers, he has written to U.S. Attorney General William French Smith, urging the Justice Department to prosecute Clement in federal court for conspiracy to deprive Ken Rex McElroy of his civil rights.

"Listen, I'm no fool," McFadin said. "I know the law's not perfect. I know there's no such thing as real equality, that the law favors some people—rich people, mostly—and hurts others. But as imperfect as the law is, it's all we've got standing between us and chaos."

• • •

The Nodaway County courthouse in Maryville is an elaborate brick building recognizable for miles around by its spirelike clock tower, which rises a full 100 feet over the rest of the town. During the autumn of 1981, the front steps of the courthouse were blocked by a cordon of rope and a sign: COURTHOUSE UNDER REPAIR. PLEASE USE REAR ENTRANCE. A little more than 50 years earlier, on January 9, 1931, a mob of 3,000 enraged citizens had gathered before those same steps to abduct a 27-year-old black man named Raymond Gunn, who had been accused of raping and killing a popular young schoolteacher. Although the evidence against Gunn was at best circumstantial and the National Guard had been called to maintain order until his trial, the size and the mood of the mob convinced the sheriff to relinquish his prisoner. Gunn was then marched three miles to the schoolhouse where the crime had been committed, chained to a crossbeam, doused with gasoline and burned. According to the account of the killing in the *Maryville Daily Forum*, the mob chanted "To hell with the law" as Gunn was set on fire. No one was ever charged with the murder. When asked about it today, the few people I talked with who had witnessed that killing said it was best to forget it had ever happened.

David Baird, the Nodaway County prosecutor, is 28. The son of a local feed-store owner, Baird returned to Maryville after law school and, with less than three years experience as a Legal Aid attorney, was appointed to his current job when the elected prosecutor unexpectedly resigned. Baird has soft brown hair and a chinless, cherubic face and wears tortoise-shell aviator glasses. He is intelligent, articulate and ambitious.

Despite his youth and his inexperience, Baird managed to distinguish himself with his first major trial as prosecutor: case number CR 880-2027, *State of Missouri* vs. *Ken Rex McElroy*. According to those who saw the trial, Baird handled himself competently, and although the verdict was a compromise and the sentence much lighter than the 15 years he had requested, Baird was widely commended for his performance. In fact, he was something of a local hero. For four days. Then the trouble started again.

On the night of June 30, the sheriff called Baird to report that McElroy, armed with a rifle, had threatened four men in the tavern at Skidmore. Although Baird filed a motion to have his bond revoked, McElroy remained at large. Ten days later, he was killed.

Still basking in the glory of his victory in court, Baird was suddenly confronted with the unenviable job of prosecuting a group of respectable tax-paying citizens for conspiracy to commit murder in the first degree. The task was made even more difficult when Trena named Clement as one of the killers. Consider Baird's dilemma: If he prosecuted Clement—an action that would be so unpopular in Nodaway County that he would certainly forfeit any hopes for a successful career there— it was unlikely that a local jury would convict him, no matter how much evidence was presented. But if he didn't indict Clement, Baird might expose himself to federal conspiracy charges and, at least, censure by the Missouri attorney general. Baird instinctively passed the buck to NMMIS.

During a ten-day investigation, NMMIS officers interviewed more than 100 people, many of whom were eyewitnesses. At the end of the investigation, the officers in charge urged Baird to indict Clement, arguing that failure to do so would encourage more vigilante killings. Baird, however, already knew how to escape the dilemma with both his professional integrity and his career intact. *The will of the people is the law of the land.* He would let the people decide what to do about McElroy's death.

Thus, in late July, a coroner's jury was convened. After hearing testimony from six witnesses—including Trena McElroy, who told them she had watched Del Clement shoot her husband—the jury determined that McElroy's death was the work of "a person or persons unknown."

The ball was back in Baird's court, and he was ready for it. He had already requested a formal grand-jury investigation—the first such request in Maryville in more than 13 years. It was granted, and for six weeks, the grand jury listened to testimony from more than 40 witnesses without issuing an indictment. Finally, on September 25, in a courtroom crowded with reporters, the grand jury was dismissed. There were television cameras outside the court, and Baird, aware that he would be asked to meet the press, was dressed in an elegant three-piece suit. A wide smile—composed in equal parts of relief and satisfaction—creased his chubby face. Not only had he weathered the storm that threatened to sink his career, but he had advanced himself in the eyes of his public as well.

"Did some weakness of the legal system force the people of Skidmore to kill McElroy by failing to protect them?" Baird was asked.

"I can't see any failure of the legal system that was responsible," Baird, the legal system's representative in Nodaway county, answered proudly. "We did everything that was possible to send McElroy to prison and we've done everything that's required to investigate his death. As far as I'm concerned, the legal system is working perfectly."

• • •

In late July, two weeks after McElroy was murdered, a full-page ad appeared in the *Maryville Daily Forum* that read, in part:

> The people of Skidmore are some of the best, friendliest and most hospitable people in the country. The courts should protect the innocent, not unleash the guilty on them to vent their anger. Let us give credit where credit is due . . . to the good people of Skidmore. Let us also give the blame for the problem to where it is due: the court system and their liberal attitude.

The ad was signed "Norman Robbins Associates." Because Robbins is generally considered to be the wealthiest, most powerful politician in the county, I went to see him at his office in Maryville.

Robbins is a man of about 60, whose wizened face is peppered with stubble. A veritable rogues' gallery graces one wall of his office: Nixon, Wallace, Reagan, Goldwater and General Curtis LeMay. All of the photos are autographed and addressed fondly to Robbins; the inscription from Curt LeMay is almost a love letter. On the same wall hangs a sign that says, YOU LOOT, WE SHOOT, and beneath it, a 50-channel police-radio scanner.

"You want to see what I call justice?" Robbins asked. He handed me a loaded Smith & Wesson .357 magnum that, when directed at the human midriff, would have an effect similar to that of a ten-pound sledge encountering an overripe watermelon. "This is what I call justice—judge and jury all wrapped into one.

"Listen, McElroy was scum," Robbins said. "He was a guy who needed killing. For years and years, he stole from everybody around here, and he was good at it. He was an expert thief and there just wasn't any way the law could catch him. People were losing hogs and tools and tractors, and they were fed up. They were scared of him, too.

"So they had that meeting. A trial is what it amounted to," Robbins continued, now, perhaps, mixing the mythology of vigilantism with what is actually known about the killing in Skidmore. "Everybody who was there had a chance to disagree with the verdict, but nobody did, and the sentence was agreed on. Then the $50 and $100 bills went down on the table; and, presto, an hour later, he was dead.

"Hell, you ain't seen the end of this by a long shot. There's eight more like McElroy been marked for death. Do you know that some judges in this state let criminals go free because they say the prisons are too full to hold them? Well, I got a solution for that: If you took the top ten percent of all the criminals in the state and eliminated them—you know, by *execution*—why, the prisons wouldn't be crowded at all. No sirree, this vigilante business ain't over. There's going to be a lot more killing until the courts start to give us some protection from criminals like McElroy."

I left Robbins' office and walked past the courthouse to the Shady Lady for a beer. It was a windy day in early October; the workmen repairing the courthouse steps wore gloves and mufflers; the weather had turned cold.

Inside the bar, I chose a stool beside a farmer I knew from Skidmore. He said that his wife had left him two days before and he had been drinking steadily since then. He appeared to be about as drunk as a man can be and still remain conscious. He asked if I'd found out anything about McElroy and the way he died. I told him I had learned quite a bit but nothing that offered much comfort. He nodded sympathetically.

"Ken was a pretty good old boy," he said, punctuating his speech with slugs of beer, "but he had no business tanglin' with all those people. Of course, nobody in Skidmore had any business rilin' him up like they did, either, and they certainly didn't have no business killin' him.

"Tryin' to understand what happened here is just like a cat tryin' to hold on to a big old steel ball. The harder that cat tries to get a grip, the quicker he slips off. This here thing just ain't got no heroes to it that I can see. This here is a case where everybody was wrong."

142

The Wiseguy
Next Door

by TOM ENGLISH
April 1991

I t was nearly 21 years ago that Michael Raymond, a beefy, Brooklyn-bred con man and stock swindler, got into a tight spot with the law. After a lengthy trial in Illinois state court, he received a four-year prison term for trying to use stolen Treasury notes to buy two small midwestern banks. A silver-tongued grifter with a robust appetite for the good life, Raymond had no intention of serving his sentence. Instead, he cut a deal with the feds.

What Raymond received, however, was far from your average, run-of-the-mill government deal. In exchange for testifying before a Senate subcommittee on stolen securities and the Mob, he was placed in what was then a new, top-secret federal program called WITSEC, short for Witness Security Program, now commonly referred to as the Witness Protection Program.

At the time, fewer than a hundred people had entered this experimental program, thought to be the government's most potent new tool against organized crime. Despite its controversial nature, the program had never actually been debated, or even proposed, on Capitol Hill. The U.S. Justice Department simply requested funds for "witness relocation," and the various appropriations committees gave it the rubber stamp. Over the next 21 years, the program would attract a vast following, not the least of which were the more than 13,000 criminals and their family members coerced into its ranks. Back in 1970, though, WITSEC was a theory to be tested. And like any new theory, it had bugs to be worked out—bugs like Michael Raymond.

As part of his agreement with the overseers of WITSEC, Raymond

143

was given a new identity and relocated to sunny southern Florida. The government also immediately began paying him $1500 a month, plus $50,000 for "job assistance." Over the next several years, "Michael Burnett," as Raymond officially became known, would learn to use WITSEC to underwrite one scam after another. During one deadly three-year period, three business associates of his disappeared under nefarious circumstances. One of them was a 67-year-old socialite and widow whom Raymond had been romancing. The woman was last seen getting into a car with him just hours after she cleared out her bank accounts. Raymond later became a prime suspect in her disappearance when an informant told local cops that he had bragged of killing her. "They're never going to find the stone she's under," he reportedly told the informant.

When Florida authorities began looking into the past of Michael Burnett, they were amazed to find that he had no personal history whatsoever. His life of crime as Michael Raymond had been effectively expunged, courtesy of WITSEC. Furthermore, the federal government helped Raymond disappear while the investigation was underway. He had intentionally violated his security, so the justice Department—unaware that its prize witness was also a primary suspect—relocated him to another region of the country and covered his tracks after he left.

In the years that followed, Raymond often caught the attention of federal crime fighters. Although the U.S. Marshals Service—the branch of the Justice Department that administers the Witness Security Program—believed that his life was in danger, he moved around like a man without worries. He drove Cadillacs and wore mink coats, and his fingers sparkled with diamond rings. A gourmet chef with a taste for fine wines, he allowed his waistline to grow in proportion to his criminal deeds, until he topped the scales at nearly 300 pounds.

Now 61 years old, Raymond/Burnett is no longer in WITSEC. His long, notorious life of crime finally caught up with him when, after he resurfaced in Chicago a few years ago as an informant in an FBI sting operation, the feds caught on to his act. In 1987, he went off to prison on weapons possession; there were no deals left to be struck. For more than 20 years, Raymond had feasted on the federal government's naivete and largess, turning the Witness Security Program into a criminal hideout.

The stupefying result of all this is that little has changed since the days when Raymond first made chumps out of the U.S. Justice Department. Although few inductees have abused WITSEC with the same panache as Michael Raymond, the 21-year history of the program reveals a virtual catalog of failures, from recidivism through bureaucratic ineptitude to government callousness and neglect.

Throughout it all, WITSEC continues to grow, amassing a rogues' gallery of inductees. "Almost everything that could go wrong (with WITSEC) has, at one time or another," says Donald Bierman, a former Justice Department official who is now a criminal defense attorney in Miami. Bierman has had several clients enter WITSEC, often against his recommendation. "If you absorb enough scandal, eventually you become immune," he says. "Ironically, because of the program's long history of failure, it has now become virtually scandalproof."

• • •

When 47-vear-old Max Mermelstein entered the Witness Security Program in 1986, it must have seemed like the last possible option. As the man who had run U.S. trafficking operations for the Colombian cocaine cartel for seven years, he had a criminal career that had escalated to a point beyond his wildest dreams. From 1978 to the time of his arrest, Mermelstein is believed to have smuggled some 56 tons of cocaine into Florida. In a five-year period, he ran $300 million in laundered currency through Colombia and Panama.

Mermelstein never planned on a career in crime. After marrying a Colombian woman he had met in Puerto Rico, he was introduced to Rafael "Rafa" Cardona Salazar, a major underboss for the Ochoa family, leaders of the Medellín cartel. On Christmas Day 1978, Rafa inexplicably murdered one of his fellow drug-runners after a long afternoon of freebasing cocaine. He and another smuggler then called on Mermelstein, whom he knew only casually at the time. They wanted Max to drive them around until they came down from their high. During their drive, Rafa, eyes ablaze, emptied five bullets into his roommate, who had been taunting him from the backseat of their rented van. "Just keep driving, Max. Don't say a fucking word," Mermelstein remembers Rafa saying.

Having witnessed, but not reported, a brutal murder, Mermelstein was an accessory to the crime, which effectively put him under the thumb of the cartel. His criminal associations with Rafa, Pablo Escobar and others flourished until June 1985, when he was jumped by a bevy of agents from the FBI, DEA, Customs and assorted other branches of American law enforcement. After searching Mermelstein's home, the feds had enough on his drug operations to put him away for many lifetimes.

Faced with a life behind bars, Mermelstein remembered the words he'd heard many times from the murderous Rafa: "There are only two ways you get out of trafficking coke, in a box or in a cell." Mermelstein proved him wrong; he agreed to cooperate with the government and go into the Witness Security Program.

"The day I got arrested was the best day of my life," says Mermelstein, now living under an assumed name somewhere in the United States. "If it hadn't happened, I'd be dead right now."

To initiate Mermelstein into WITSEC required extraordinary measures. Sixteen members of his family, mostly relatives of his Colombian wife, had to be relocated into the U.S. It presented the Marshals Service with a problem it has been forced to deal with more and more, as the so-called drug war escalates. According to the Justice Department's own statistics, nearly 80 percent of those now in the program are there because they or a family member testified in a drug-related case. More than one quarter of those are foreign nationals.

One might guess that with all the Colombians, Mexicans and Asians now entering the Witness Security Program, the Marshals Service would have devised a strategy for handling foreign refugees from our criminal-justice system.

Guess again.

Take the case of Arturo Jaramillo, Mermelstein's brother-in-law. Born and raised in Cali, Colombia, Jaramillo is described by his brother-in-law as "a quiet man who never wanted to be involved in drugs or violence." Still, he had been forced by Rafa to help dispose of his dead associate back in 1978, and he lived in fear of the Colombian drug merchants. When news of Mermelstein's "flip" reached him, he had no choice but to accept Uncle Sam's offer of a new identity in the United States. Although Jaramillo, his wife and young son spoke no English, they were inexplicably relocated to Memphis, Tennessee, a city not known for its racial tolerance.

The last time Mermelstein talked with his brother-in-law was November 13, 1986. "He was in a thoroughly morose mood," he says. "We tried to get an official assigned to his case to get him a Spanish-speaking psychiatrist—fast. What did the official do? He went on vacation."

One day later—on the day before his 49th birthday—Arturo Jaramillo was found hanged in a closet of the small apartment WITSEC had provided for him and his family. He had looped a rope over the hanger rod, tied it around his neck, then pulled on the rope with both hands until he strangled himself.

"I'll always blame myself, in a way, for what happened," says Mermelstein. "But I blame the program, too. Nobody involved (with WITSEC) understands the Latin mentality or the Latin people. They take my brother-in-law, his wife and kid, and stick them in a place like Memphis. Aside from the fact that it is one of the most bigoted places in the United States, nobody there speaks Spanish. They couldn't get a driver's license, because the tests weren't given in Spanish. They were just dumped in an apartment and left to fend for themselves." Echoing the sentiments of many currently in the program, Mermelstein adds, "Nobody cared. Those asshole inspectors out there just didn't give a flying fuck."

• • •

Back in the early Sixties, when Attorney General Robert Kennedy first made the pursuit of organized-crime figures a top government priority, a program for protecting high-profile informants and their families must have seemed like a dandy idea. As early as 1963, Kennedy hinted to the Senate subcommittee on organized crime that a program already existed on an informal level. Although official procedures had not been worked out, the means for protecting important witnesses were established that year when Mob hit man Joseph Valachi spoke before a Senate subcommittee on organized crime. His testimony was a revelation, and the fact that he dared give it at all was proof of the program's power.

Along with its potential as a crime-fighting tool, the concept of witness relocation contained a peculiarly American notion—a chance to correct past mistakes and literally become a new person. There was a kind of implied freedom in the program that suited the Great Society. The idea—that a lifelong criminal might somehow cleanse himself with the help of the federal government and emerge a chastened, productive member of society—was, of course, incredibly simplistic and naive. Yet so appealing was this concept that for years the public accepted the Justice Department's contention that the program was working, even as the horror stories mounted.

"In the beginning," says John Partington, a former U.S. Marshal assigned to WITSEC, "we never had any manuals or textbooks to go by. Basically, we were making it up as we went along. Soon the demands became so great we just couldn't keep up. It became like the uninformed talking to the misinformed." The program was devised to handle fewer than 30 or 40 elite witnesses a year, but during his 15 years as a regional inspector, Partington would personally guard, relocate and help falsify I.D.s for nearly 2,600 inductees.

"A big part of the problem," says Partington, now retired, "has always been that the program is run out of Washington. The bureaucrats don't seem to have any understanding of what's happening out there in the real world. They've never had to face up to their decisions."

For a long time, the Justice Department avoided making any written promises to witnesses. Only recently have inductees been required to sign a memorandum of understanding—known as an M.O.U. In the agreement, the Marshals Service makes it clear that while it will assist a witness in finding employment, it will not falsify credit or work histories. Thus, the witnesses are totally dependent on the government to find them work and are prone to look for outside income. Says Partington, "You've got people in the program who are being asked to take on a lifestyle they've never experienced before. We've got guys—lifelong gangsters—capable of making two and three hundred thousand dollars a year through crime, and here we are, asking them to work nine to five, five days a week, for maybe fifteen grand a year."

An even more insurmountable problem than the financial strains faced by those in the program is boredom. It doesn't take a criminal sociologist to figure that people accustomed to an exciting, high-wire lifestyle will have trouble adjusting to working-class sobriety. Such has been the case with thousands of inductees.

Henry Hill, the Mafia wannabe lionized in the book *Wiseguy* (the basis for last year's hit movie *GoodFellas*), is just one example. After a long career as a mid-level hustler affiliated with the Lucchese crime family in Brooklyn and Queens, Hill cut a sweetheart deal with the government in 1980 and testified against his former pals, Jimmy "the Gent" Burke and the late *capo* Paul Vario. Relocated to Redmond, a Seattle suburb, Hill found his new life to be interminably dull. As he put it at the end of the book and film, "Today everything is very different. No more action. I have to wait around like everyone else. I'm an average nobody. I get to live the rest of my life like a *schnook*."

The irony, of course, is that Hill did not wait around. In May 1987, he was arrested on federal drug charges after an undercover agent bought cocaine from two underlings who fingered him. Like their boss before them, Hill's henchmen turned canary and agreed to testify against him in court. A jury took two hours to deliver a conviction.

Hill had a strong incentive to stay clean, yet his addiction to the excitement and danger of crime—and the notoriety it provided—took precedence, a fact amply illustrated at the time of his arrest. When confronted by Washington state troopers, Hill is said to have asked pleadingly, "Don't you know who I am? I'm Henry Hill—the wiseguy."

• • •

It's not hard to fathom the appeal the Witness Security Program might hold for a career criminal facing a long prison sentence. Although inductees are often warned that life in the program will not be easy, the difficulties seem remote relative to getting whacked with a baseball bat or stuffed into a car trunk.

The assumption, of course, is that the government will be able to deliver on most of what it promises. "What the government says it can do and what it has the ability to do are two different things," says Mermelstein, who has been relocated four times in the past four years. "I've known lifelong criminals with more of a sense of honor than some of the people who run this program."

The prime appeal of WITSEC has always been the manufacture of a viable false identity, supported by all the documents. Although the government continues to insist that it can process records at short notice, the history of the program suggests otherwise.

"Every week I was on the phone," says John Partington, "with some witness shouting in my ear, 'My kid wants to play little-league ball and he needs medical records.' 'My daughter wants to get married and where's the goddamn driver's license?' And what about a birth certificate? You need a birth certificate before you can do anything.

"Most times, these are street-smart people—hustlers. They're not Billy Grahams. They'd say to me, 'Just gimme a week. I'll get my own documentation.' And I'd have to say, 'But that's not legal. You do that and you're back to your old ways.' It was frustrating. Why should it take the government months to do what these people could do in days?"

• • •

Despite the obvious failings of the program, there has never been a shortage of criminals trying to get in. During WITSEC's most ambitious period, the mid-Seventies, criminals were tripping over one another to cut a deal with the feds and get relocated. From 1971 to 1977, the annual number of inductees exploded from 92 to 450. The standards for admission broadened beyond organized crime to include people for whom the program was never intended—smalltime dope dealers, innocent victims of crime and white-collar stool pigeons. As those inductees worked their way through the system, new problems arose. Witnesses were told by the Marshals Service that they could no longer consider Atlanta, San Francisco or San Diego for relocation, because those areas were full.

If providing documentation and satisfying employment for lifelong gangsters with minimal job skills has presented the government with difficulties, finding adequate work for college-educated brokers and other white-collar types has proved an impossibility.

Consider the case of Marvin Naidborne, WITSEC's most notable white-collar failure. The bespectacled manager of a Brooklyn car-leasing agency, Naidborne had a character flaw: He was an inveterate gambler often in debt to loan sharks. Arrested in the late Sixties, he was given leniency and relocation and testified in a number of trials, where he fingered, among others, a bank president who had received kickbacks for extending loans to his buddies at the Italian-American Civil Rights League.

After relocation in the program, Naidborne, who had a degree in business administration, waited around for the government to come up with a job, as promised. One of the jobs was part-time work as a process server. "That's a great job," Naidborne later told a reporter. "I bump into someone who knows somebody in the Mob and I get killed."

In due time, Naidborne heard of an opening as general manager of a Volkswagen dealership that paid $42,000 per year. When he asked the Justice Department to vouch for him, his request was ignored.

Totally dependent on the government for subsistence, Naidborne spent the next few years working as a freelance rat fink. He would wander into a city, nose around and eventually present the government with a major crime case. He would collect informer's fees from the FBI or the DEA, witness fees from the Justice Department and sometimes insurance rewards for recovered goods. In one newspaper article, federal officials confirmed Naidborne's claim that he had accounted for arrests across the country involving drugs, stolen and counterfeit securities, stolen airline tickets and bookmaking rings. In a good year, he claimed he could make $30,000 as a Witness Security vampire. But it was a sorry, paranoiac life, said Naidborne, living on the run in bad motels. He blamed WITSEC: "They just don't care They leave you there, out in the cold like an animal. I don't want their money. . . . I just want a job, a chance to get my life straightened out."

• • •

150

Throughout WITSEC's troubled history, its flaws have frequently been fodder for investigative journalists. The Marvin Naidborne case led to a series of damning articles in Long Island's *Newsday*. In 1976, Fred Graham published a book called *The Alias Program*, a scathing view of WITSEC. The bad press resulted, in part, in hearings before the Permanent Subcommittee on Investigation, chaired by Georgia Senator Sam Nunn. Federal lawmakers finally took a look at a program they had been routinely funding over the previous decade.

The result was an abundance of saber rattling—one Senator called WITSEC "a body without a brain"—but little in the way of legislation. It wasn't until 1984 that Congress enacted the Witness Security Reform Act, a toothless capitulation to the powers that run the program. Since then, there have been no substantive congressional reviews, and WITSEC's budget has steadily increased, from $2 million in 1972 to nearly $44 million in 1988.

The program's most obvious deficiency has always been the degree to which it provides a framework for criminals to prey on unsuspecting communities, as in the case of Michael Raymond. Although the Justice Department claims that the current rate of recidivism among WITSEC's inductees is less than half the national average for felony offenders, this has never been very comforting for local cops. When trying to get information on someone they suspect might be a relocated witness, more often than not they find themselves butting heads with an intractable Justice Department.

One case that nearly singlehandedly sank WITSEC involved a bank robber and hardened lifer named Marion Albert Pruett. Pruett was released 11 months early from an eight-year prison term because he testified on behalf of the state of North Carolina in a murder case. After being relocated to New Mexico with his common-law wife, Pruett went on a violent rampage, murdering five people. One of those murdered was his wife, whom he bludgeoned with a hammer, strangled with a belt, then carried into the desert near Albuquerque, where he poured gasoline over her body and burned it beyond recognition.

When Pruett's case was brought before the U.S. General Accounting Office in 1982, it raised more than a few troubling questions. Local police in a number of jurisdictions had been trying to track him for years, but no one had been able to obtain information on his past. Even more pertinent was the degree to which informants like Pruett were supervised, and how closely they were monitored after their release from the program.

The Marshals Service may be correct in its claim that instances of people like Pruett's creating one-man crime waves are low, but there remain other troubling issues, such as the program policy toward innocent people who, for whatever reason, feel that they have been wronged as a result of WITSEC. In hundreds of cases, for instance, witnesses have used the program to dodge lawsuits and debt collectors. Some have even used it to keep divorced spouses from visiting their children. One such case, involving a Buffalo construction worker named Tom Leonhard, went as far as the U.S. Supreme Court.

A law-abiding patriot, Leonhard had been granted visitation rights to see his children each weekend by the courts of New York State. When they abruptly disappeared one afternoon with his ex-wife's new husband, Leonhard made the rounds of the local offices of the U.S. Marshals, the FBI and the U.S. Attorney. For two years, the Justice Department refused to admit it had had anything to do with his children's disappearance.

It was discovered that the children had, in fact, been relocated, so Leonhard sued the government. Ultimately, a U.S. appeals judge ruled that since the officials of the Justice Department had "acted in good faith," the federal court would not second-guess the officials' "rational exercise of discretion." Leonhard and the New York courts were bound by the decisions of WITSEC.

This example and others like it illustrate yet another flaw in the program—one that the Marshals Service has never been able to reconcile. In promising to protect the new identities of its inductees, the Justice Department is torn between its obligation to the witness and its obligations to the public. The result is that it is often unable to fully protect the interests of either.

• • •

In contrast to the complex and abundant reasons WITSEC has never really worked as intended, the justification for its continued existence—according to those who support the program—is short and sweet: The Witness Security Program brings about convictions.

"You cannot make an organized-crime case in this country without it," says Richard Gregorie, a former Assistant U.S. Attorney in Miami who initiated hundreds of people—including Max Mermelstein—into the program during his 17-year government career. "Our system of law requires firsthand evidence. Hearsay won't make a case. Unless you have someone who can put the criminal there firsthand, a conviction isn't going to happen."

There is no question that the U.S. Government has won a number of impressive victories in the past decade against what it likes to call "traditional organized crime." Together with the Racketeer-Influenced and Corrupt Organizations (RICO) statutes, the Witness Security Program has played an important role in these convictions. Virtually every major Mob case in recent years has relied heavily on turncoat witnesses. Invariably, the promises of the program have laid the groundwork for informant cooperation.

The fact that it works as a crime-fighting tool evidently carries weight with legislators and the public. Both seem resigned to accept the concept of a flawed WITSEC, believing, perhaps, that by fabricating new names and identities for people, our government is proving its daring and omnipotence. The problem, of course, is that by allowing government this power, we are only encouraging arrogance and cynicism, a fact amply illustrated by those who run WITSEC.

The program is now headquartered in Arlington, Virginia, and is run by Gerald Shur. Described by one witness currently in the program as "a small man with a small mind and a God complex," Shur is often cited by inductees as one of WITSEC's biggest administrative problems. He is known as something of a monomaniac in the J. Edgar Hoover mold and his decision-making process has been called "dictatorial and capricious" by one former WITSEC employee.

Shur almost never talks with the press, and he turned down repeated interview requests for this article. Doug Tillit, a spokesperson for the U.S. Marshals, responded by saying, "Our position is that there are some people who support the program and some who don't. There's nothing we can do or say about it." Shur has always preferred to let those who benefit most from the program—federal agents and government prosecutors—extol its virtues. As for its deficiencies, to say that WITSEC has engaged in a cover-up or two would be a quaint accusation. The program was designed to engage in deception.

It would be a mistake, however, to blame the failings of WITSEC entirely on Shur, or even on the inadequacies of the Marshals Service. The real question is not whether the program is badly administered but whether or not it can ever be administered.

No single group has a more acute understanding of this than the witnesses themselves. Dozens have turned to the press or the courts seeking an outlet, usually out of frustration with the Justice Department's lack of accountability.

Most witnesses enter the program in such a state of paranoia and fear that they willingly follow the government's lead. For every Michael

THE WISEGUY NEXT DOOR

Raymond or Marion Albert Pruett—lifelong criminals who see WITSEC as just one more exploitable branch of the system—there are hundreds whose motives are more confused. Once persuaded by the government to become informants, they have little choice but to see WITSEC in the most hopeful of terms, as a kind of redemption, a chance to cleanse their misbegotten souls.

Joe Labriola, a small-time gangster from Connecticut, was looking for just such a cleansing in 1987 when he was busted for trafficking in cocaine. At the age of 51, Labriola did not want to spend any more time in jail. Despite misgivings, he decided to become a government informant.

As with many criminals who do so, Labriola seemed to crave the approval of his masters. After each trial in which he testified against his former friends, he sought reassurance from the agents and prosecutors, who told him, "You did the right thing."

Had Labriola known that the suicide rate among inductees into WITSEC was many times higher than the national average, he might have asked himself an obvious question: Why? And he might have arrived at the obvious answer: that those in the program were, after all, criminals, just like himself. To believe that the government would ever truly concern itself with his welfare required the kind of wishful thinking of which only truly desperate men are capable.

Throughout his cooperation, Labriola sought to endear himself to the only friends he had left—the lawmen. Often he would cook meals for the police and prosecutors as they discussed his next day's testimony. Joe would regale them with stories from his Mob days, and they would all laugh and slap one another on the back. It was almost like old times, when Labriola had told wiseguy stories with his buddies until the dim hours of the morning.

But there was a difference. These men were cops and he was not. At the end of each day, they went home to their wives and kids, while he slinked around, feeling like a rat, hoping he wouldn't inadvertently blurt out some small fact that might betray his true identity. The contradictions in his life caused Labriola to suffer bouts of deep depression, which he sought to alleviate through the occasional use of cocaine and heroin.

In May 1990, Joe could take no more. Sitting on the bed in his tiny government-assigned apartment in Springfield, Massachusetts, he swallowed an entire bottle of medication he had been taking for high blood pressure, chasing that with illegal drugs. He left behind a suicide note in which he said he could no longer take the pressures of being a government witness. The last line, scrawled in what looked like a child's handwriting, read, "Don't be mad at me."

"You know," said a cop familiar with Labriola's case, "it's not all that shocking to me. Joe was in a lot of anguish. He never felt good about turning. It was an abrupt change in lifestyle. He was caught between two worlds and wasn't comfortable in either of them."

There were no federal agents at Labriola's funeral. He left the Witness Security Program the same way he entered it. Alone.

Lawrencia "Bambi" Bembenek

The Bambi Chronicles

by MARK JANNOT
July 1993

You believe her or you don't. There is no middle ground on Lawrencia "Bambi" Bembenek, the ex-blonde, ex-Bunny, ex-cop from Milwaukee who, in May 1981, either murdered or didn't murder her then-husband's ex-wife. You are her acolyte or her accuser. She is either a wronged innocent or a vicious murderer, ardent feminist or femme fatale, helpless repository of other people's desires or Svengali, media victim or media manipulator.

The anti-Bambi forces believe the crime went down like this:

It took her about 30 seconds to find the lock in the predawn dark, and another few beats to steady her hand enough to slip in the key. She opened the door and stepped into the house.

The carpet muffled her steps as she crept up the stairs and into Christine Schultz's bedroom. It wasn't hard to find—Schultz had left the TV on and its bluish light illuminated the room.

Bembenek didn't say a word as she roughly roused Schultz, gagged her with a bandanna and used a length of plastic clothesline to bind her arms behind her back. She waved her husband's .38 in Schultz's face before heading out into the hall.

The idea was to scare Christine so she'd reconsider her decision to stay in big, bad Milwaukee rather than move with the kids to her family's place up north, leaving this house to her ex-husband (and Bembenek's husband at that time), Fred, a police detective.

She stopped in the kids' room, across from Christine's, to put a little fear in them, too. She slipped another clothesline around the neck of Sean and pulled it tight, keeping a gloved hand on his face so he

157

couldn't get a good look at her. Still, he noticed her black police shoes, her military-style jacket (or was it a green jogging suit?), her reddish-brown hair tied in a ponytail.

But Sean screamed, and Bembenek suddenly realized that Christine wouldn't stay put for long. She let go of Sean and rushed across the hall, where Christine had managed to get off the bed and come toward her—close enough to see her face above Bembenek's mask.

Bembenek saw the flash of recognition. She grabbed Schultz, spun her around and threw her down on the bed, shoved the gun against her upper back, fired one shot, then fled down the stairs, out the door and back the way she'd come. She ran 16 blocks to the apartment she shared with Fred, the apartment they were leaving because it cost too much. Back in the house, 11-year-old Sean was frantically pressing his mother's wound with a roll of gauze, trying to stop the bleeding. She died within minutes.

If you believe that scenario, you are in the minority, along with the Milwaukee Police Department. If you care what other people think, you may prefer the pro-Bambi version:

The key worked like a charm. Hired thug Fred Horenberger—who got the key from former resident Fred Schultz, the sponsor of this hit—shoved the door open and motioned with a gun for his accomplice, Judy Zess, to get in the house. They'd never seen the place, but everything looked pretty much as Schultz had laid it out. When they got upstairs to the ex-wife's room, they found her with the TV on, giving them some light to work by. Horenberger trussed and gagged her, then passed the gun to Zess to stand guard while he went on a reconnaissance mission.

Horenberger stopped in the kids' room, across from where Zess was playing Ma Barker with the gun. The idea was to rouse the kids, let them get enough of a look at him to know he wasn't their father. They noticed his black shoes, his jogging suit (or was it a green military jacket?), his reddish-brown hair tied in a ponytail.

When one of the kids started screaming, it was time to get it done and get out. Horenberger rushed across the hall, grabbed the gun from Zess, plugged it into the woman's back and fired. Zess was already down the stairs when he raced past the kids staring in the doorway. They were out the door within seconds. Back inside, Sean was frantically pressing his mother's wound with a roll of gauze, trying to stop the bleeding. She died within minutes.

The third, Bambi-neutral scenario goes like this: Maybe none of them are guilty. Or all of them, including the entire Milwaukee Police Department. Anybody feel like confessing?

• • •

There's a problem with writing about murderers: They're murderers. They don't necessarily do things rationally. Small questions will come up, questions of technique or motivation, stuff that doesn't make sense. Why would Bambi jog 16 blocks in the black cop shoes that were noticed by the kids? Why would the kids describe a reddish-brown ponytail, when Bambi was blonde at the time? She was wearing a wig, right? But then why would she safely dispose of the clothesline and the green jogging suit but flush that wig down the toilet, where it would get clogged, as wigs in toilets will? Why would she use her husband's off-duty gun, then put it back in its place, as if nothing had happened? Hell, why would she marry Fred Schultz in the first place, only weeks after she met him, when she knew he had cheated on his previous wife?

Why did she kill Christine Schultz?

Who knows? Maybe she didn't do it. But if she did, how can we presume to understand what was going on in the murderer's mind?

None of this questioning has stopped the media from proclaiming Bembenek's innocence. *People, Vanity Fair,* the tabloids, *Geraldo* and *Prime Time Live* have fervently enlisted in the Bambi cause. Two television movies, both with the innocent-Bambi angle, have been produced: *Calendar Girl, Cop, Killer?*, which you probably didn't see a year ago on ABC, and the recent *Woman on the Run: The Lawrencia Bembenek Story,* a four-hour miniseries with Tatum O'Neal that you probably did see on NBC.

As a result of this exposure, Laurie (no longer Bambi to her friends) Bembenek's Q rating hovers around 100 in Milwaukee. More people have heard of her than have heard of Tommy Thompson, the state's governor. And of the 100 percent of Milwaukeeans who know who she is, the substantial majority simply knows she got a raw deal.

But if these people are right and she's not a murderer, how can we trust our judgment about Bembenek's friends and associates, half of whom have been accused of the murder by this or that Bembenek advocate in the ten years this case has been debated?

The trusting population of Milwaukee aside, there are at least a few Bembenek doubters. John Greenya, a writer who expanded a *Washington Post* piece into a still unpublished manuscript, *Did Bambi Kill?*, says, "I'm the only guy who's been following this for a long time who actually believes she's guilty."

Significantly, though, Greenya has never met Bembenek, and neither has the handful of other journalistic skeptics. The glue that holds the Bembenek-innocence theories together is a conviction that she is not the kind of person who could commit such an act. The one sure way to acquire such a conviction seems to be to meet Bembenek. She passes people's sniff tests. She's believable.

Or so I'm told. Bembenek says she's been burned too badly by her Bunny image (she once worked at a Playboy Club for four weeks and everyone thinks she was a Playmate) to get involved with the magazine now.

So, unable to get religion by means of direct contact with Bambi, I was left to pick through dueling theories of the crime. If you look at this story, it begins to seem as if Bembenek's entire life is a tapestry of circumstantial evidence and uncredible witnesses.

• • •

Bembenek entered the police academy—her lifelong ambition, she said—on March 10, 1980, at the age of 21. She graduated in early August and was almost immediately fired from the force for having filed a false police report that past May defending her friend and fellow recruit, Judy Zess, after her arrest for possession of marijuana at a Rufus and Chaka Khan concert. (The charge against Zess was later dropped.)

Bembenek claims the brass was looking for an excuse to drum her out of the department. In the following months, she would look into suing the Milwaukee Police Department for sexual discrimination and would accuse it of reaping federal money by hiring women and minority recruits and firing them at the slightest provocation.

To bolster her discrimination charge, Bembenek turned in a pile of photographs taken at a picnic in a public park near Lake Michigan. Among the revelers shown dancing around in various stages of undress, or ogling from the sidelines, were at least a couple of Milwaukee cops. If these guys can get away with such blatant lawlessness without sanction, Bembenek reasoned, how can they fire me for supposedly lying on a report? Pictured in several of the shots (and nude in a few that later surfaced) was the group's photographer and Bembenek's hubby-to-be, Detective Elfred Otto Schultz Jr.

Bembenek partisans often excuse her more glaring failures of judgment during this period by bowing to her age: Didn't we all make a few bad decisions when we were 21?

On reflection, though, the answer is no: I'm not sure we've all made decisions on a par with, say, marrying a newly divorced father of two, ten years our senior, whom we barely know but whose infidelities are infamous enough to have reached our ears, and who is an active, nude participant in parties we're trying to get the police department to investigate.

But that is, of course, just what Bembenek did. She and Elfred Schultz, who were barely acquainted when she turned in the picnic photos in December 1980, eloped to Illinois in January.

They spent the next few months moving in and out of apartments with Judy Zess (another odd decision, since it was Zess's subsequent report that Bembenek had been toking at the concert that gave cause for her firing). Zess got them evicted from their first place by throwing a wild party while the newlyweds honeymooned in Jamaica, and then broke the lease on their second place, forcing Schultz and Bembenek to shop for cheaper accommodations. This was the apartment they were packing up when Fred's ex-wife, Christine, was murdered at about two A.M. on May 28, 1981.

Bembenek didn't become a serious suspect until at least a couple of weeks after the murder. On June 24 she was arrested, based largely on three things: a wig found lodged in a pipe draining her toilet, ballistics tests that pegged Fred's gun as the murder weapon and damaging testimony by Judy Zess.

The motive was said to be money. Schultz was paying his ex-wife half his income in alimony and mortgage payments. That was putting a crimp in the fast life—designer clothes, fancy restaurants, exotic vacations—that Bembenek supposedly liked to lead.

But Sean Schultz and his brother, Shannon, the only witnesses to the crime, thought it was a man who'd killed their mother. Sean said that Bembenek couldn't possibly have done it, that even if she had been wearing football pads, she wouldn't have been as big as the guy.

Ultimately, though, the gun sealed Bembenek's fate. Fred Schultz and his partner inspected it the night of the murder and determined that it hadn't been fired. Remarkably, the department brass left it in Schultz's possession, without so much as recording its serial number. (This breach of procedure has since become a cornerstone of Bembenek-frame-up theories.) It wasn't until three weeks later that the department finally called the gun in for routine tests, just to cover all bases.

To the surprise of everyone, a top ballistics expert determined that it was, without a doubt, the murder weapon. Bembenek and Schultz were said to be the only two with access to it that night, and Schultz was on duty at the time of the murder. That evidence, and testimony from

THE BAMBI CHRONICLES

Zess that Bembenek had said "I would pay to have Christine blown away" and had asked Zess's drug-dealer boyfriend if he knew anyone who could do a hit, seemed to be enough for the jury members, who returned a guilty verdict. Bembenek was sentenced to life and sent to the Taycheedah women's prison in Fond du Lac, Wisconsin.

This is where the TV movies break for commercials and return with a block-lettered EIGHT YEARS LATER running across the bottom of the screen. But the real story was just beginning. Bembenek and her defense team encountered an unbalanced con man named Jacob Wissler, who proceeded to poison her motion for a new trial by paying, or promising to pay, witnesses thousands of dollars to testify on her behalf. One convicted murderer was supposed to confess to the killing but then clammed up on the stand.

It was also during this time that a private investigator named Ira Robins decided to make the Bembenek case his life's work. He began an eight-year (and counting) crusade that would see him dredging up all kinds of new evidence, both credible and incredible, that something fishy had led to Bembenek's conviction. He almost singlehandedly kept the story in the news.

He also honed a gift for loopy invective. He called Assistant District Attorney Robert Donohoo and District Attorney E. Michael McCann criminals and called a judge a "paid whore . . . prostituting herself for the government."

Even with Robins on Bembenek's side, two appeals failed. Nothing much else happened until, as Bembenek recounts in her autobiography, *Woman on Trial,* her "testosterone radar" went off one day in late August 1989 during visiting hours at Taycheedah.

"Ooooh, who's that!!!" she quotes herself saying—complete with three exclamation points—when she saw Dominic Gugliatto (he was visiting his sister) walking through the prison yard in white tennis shorts and a crisp white shirt. She and Nick met, began corresponding and saw each other at visiting hours. After a trademark whirlwind romance ("She doesn't have a real good track record with guys, period," her friend Wally Janke says), they were engaged.

On July 15, 1990, less than a month before the planned prison wedding, Bembenek squeezed out a laundry-room window, gashed her leg on barbed wire as she scaled a fence, then slipped into Gugliatto's waiting car. The next day they were in Thunder Bay, Ontario.

And there they stayed for three months while Bembenek's story took on renewed momentum. Fred Schultz appeared on *Geraldo* via satellite from his Florida home to say he feared for his life. "She would

162

do anything," he said. "I have no doubt in my mind. She'd kill again. If she wants something, she will kill." The camera then pulled back to reveal, sitting next to Schultz, Bembenek's original trial attorney, Donald Eisenberg, who dropped his own bombshell. "I also believe she is guilty. Everything I know points to the fact that she did it."

Meanwhile, Milwaukeeans donned Bambi masks, entered Bambi look-alike contests, slapped BAMBI ON BOARD stickers on their bumpers and hummed along to "Run, Bambi, Run," a novelty song that flooded the local airwaves.

In Thunder Bay, Gugliatto couldn't find a job, so Bembenek took two, one as a fitness instructor and the other, again using her renowned judgment, as a waitress at a busy bar and grill half a block away from a police station.

It was there that she waited on a tourist passing through from California who later, watching *America's Most Wanted*, saw a face that looked strikingly familiar. The Royal Canadian Mounted Police went to the bar to question her after the tip had been faxed in, and they later arrested the two fugitives as they were trying to make a break for it.

Gugliatto was immediately sent back to Wisconsin, where he was convicted of aiding the escape of a felon and was sentenced to a year in jail. He quickly faded from Bembenek's heart. (The two continue to juggle the hot potato of who dumped whom.)

Still in Canada, Bembenek made a plea for refugee status. "Her refugee claim was that she could not receive a fair trial anywhere in the United States," says Donald Macintosh, the Canadian Justice Department lawyer who conducted the government's case. "That is the single most preposterous allegation that any person has ever made in any court proceeding in either the U.S. or Canada." The architect of this defense was Frank Marrocco, a high-powered Toronto lawyer who wrote the book on Canadian immigration law. Marrocco spun out the proceedings for more than a year, virtually retrying Bembenek's murder conviction and squeezing out every drop of favorable PR he could while the Canadian government squealed that the whole thing was unfair.

Then, on the eve of the Canadian government's case—they'd dug up some stuff that might have tarnished Bembenek's Joan of Arc persona—the fugitive and her lawyers decided it would be more noble to return to Milwaukee, confront her persecutors in the district attorney's office and fight for justice toe-to-toe. Amazingly, that's how her retreat played out in the press: not as a brilliantly calculated public-relations ploy but as a courageous act of conscience.

At the time, a judicial inquiry called a John Doe had been launched in

Milwaukee to determine if Bembenek had been railroaded by the police department and the D.A.'s office in its investigation of the Christine Schultz murder. The decision came down in mid-August, about four months after Bembenek returned to the States.

It was largely a slap in the face to her defense. Not only had no crimes been committed, the special prosecutor said, but the pet theory of the Bembenek camp—that Fred Schultz had hired Fred Horenberger to murder his ex-wife, and that somehow Judy Zess was involved—didn't make sense.

But it did offer Bembenek a glimmer of good news in finding that "significant mistakes were made that cannot be condoned or excused" in the original investigation and in detailing seven particularly serious police blunders.

Enter Sheldon Zenner, Bembenek's latest high-powered defense attorney, whose influence waxed while Ira Robins' waned. Says Zenner, "We took the case out of Ira Robins' realm of 'I'm working out of the trunk of my car and I have a document I'd like to show you.'" Even those who have a healthy respect for Robins' bulldog approach think Zenner was smart to stiff-arm the guy. "I can see why they froze him out," says Duane Gay, a Milwaukee newscaster and veteran of the Bembenek case. "Robins became an embarrassment. One time, Ira had filed some motion and had been turned down, and he stood up in court, cursed at the judge, walked out and pissed next to the courthouse. Is that the kind of guy you want in your corner when you're arguing the case?"

Getting dumped on by Bembenek and her lawyers has made Robins extremely bitter. To discuss the case with him is to get an earful of bile. "I believe that Lawrencia Bembenek is not guilty in this murder," he says. "I also believe she's a board-certified cunt."

Robins is still pursuing Horenberger. It's easier to blame him now because he can't put up much of a defense: He's dead. That's not his only qualification for taking the rap. He used to hang out at one of the bars Fred Schultz frequented, was a convicted murderer and bur- glar whose *modus operandi*—military garb, wig, .38-caliber gun, gagging the victim—was apparently similar to the one used by whoever killed Christine Schultz.

While he was alive, Horenberger loudly proclaimed his innocence in Christine Schultz's murder, and Fred Schultz backed him up. Now that Horenberger is gone, eight confidants, mostly cellmates and other shady characters, have sworn that he confessed to them.

It's the way Fred Horenberger died that has Robins' conspiracy juices flowing. One morning in late November 1991, Horenberger and a friend decided to knock off a Milwaukee doughnut shop. The caper went awry, though, and after a chase, Horenberger, finding himself cornered with two elderly hostages in a south-side bungalow, went into the basement and blew his brains out.

"That he committed suicide, we have a problem with that," Robins says. "There were dog bites all over his legs from the police dog. These fucking people are not above murder. We're dealing with some people who are bad news."

• • •

In the legal profession, there's an old saw that goes: If the facts are against you, argue the law; if the law is against you, argue the facts; and if the facts and the law are both against you, attack the police department. After years of being pulled along by Robins' scorched-earth, attack-the-cops tactics, the Bembenek defense took a turn toward facts when Sheldon Zenner came on board.

The facts in this case are circumstantial and always have been. Both the judge at Bembenek's preliminary hearing and the one at her trial called it the most circumstantial case they'd ever seen. After years of scrutiny, the case hasn't gotten any less circumstantial. But Bembenek supporters have never been able to come up with anything but their own circumstantial evidence to battle the state's circumstantial evidence. The whole thing is a circus of circumstance, and may the best clown win.

Zenner filed a motion for a new trial. In the supporting brief he subjected the prosecution's original case to death by a thousand cuts. He took every piece of key evidence presented at the trial and cut it off at the knees, suggesting that witnesses were lying or that evidence had been tampered with.

A few examples:

• The wig. At trial the jury was shown a reddish-brown wig that had been removed from a drain common to the Bembenek–Schultz apartment and the one next door. The obvious implication was that Bembenek had flushed her disguise down the crapper. Recently, the neighbor, Sharon Niswonger, has come forward to say that she received an odd visit in early June 1981 from an acquaintance who said she was on her way to the gym and asked if she could change in Niswonger's bathroom. The next time the toilet was used, it overflowed. The visitor? Judy Zess.

- The strands of hair. The jury was told that color-treated blonde hairs—Bembenek was a hair tinter—had been recovered from the victim's body and from the gag in her mouth. At the trial, Dr. Elaine Samuels, who conducted Christine Schultz's autopsy, testified that the envelope the hairs were in was the envelope she'd put hairs in during the autopsy. But she was never told that the prosecution claimed that they were blonde hairs. Since the trial, Samuels has insisted that she never recovered any blonde hairs in her autopsy.

  Ira Robins discovered that during the police investigation the gag had been checked out of the crime lab and was unsealed so that it could be shown to a potential witness—Judy Zess. It was only after the gag was returned to the lab that the blonde hairs were found on it.

- The witnesses. Two key prosecution witnesses at the trial were Fred Schultz and Judy Zess. Because no one had written down the serial number of the gun Schultz and his partner had inspected the night of the murder, Schultz was needed to testify that the murder weapon was his off-duty gun, which had been in his apartment with Bembenek that night.

At the time of the preliminary hearing, Schultz was under internal police department investigation for dancing nude at the picnic and also for perjury—something Bembenek's defense team should have been told. When two officers went to District Attorney McCann to get a John Doe inquiry into Schultz's activities, McCann's response was, "Do you want Bembenek or do you want Schultz?"

Zess was used to connect Bembenek with virtually every other piece of prosecution evidence. She testified that Bembenek had owned a plastic travel clothesline, which was never found. She said she'd seen a green jogging suit at the apartment, though it was never discovered. She said Bembenek and Schultz often wore bandannas like the one the murderer had used as a gag. And she quoted Bembenek on having Christine Schultz blown away.

Zess has recanted her testimony (and then recanted her recantations) so many times since the trial that she would be crucified if brought before another jury.

None of this stuff is new, and Assistant D.A. Donohoo has developed an uncontrollable verbal tic when confronted with this kind of evidence. "So what?" he'll say. "So what?" Over and over.

Zess used the neighbor's bathroom before the toilet overflowed? "So what? All it proves is that Judy Zess is capable of going to the bathroom by herself."

As for Elaine Samuels' testimony about the strands of hair, Donohoo seems almost gleeful at the prospect of getting her up on the stand and tearing her apart. Samuels is an eccentric of the 50-cat-owning variety. She made headlines in the late Seventies for collecting jars of human testicles from her autopsy subjects, supposedly for a research project. More to the point, her job was abolished after she ruined key evidence in three murder cases and took too long to complete autopsy reports.

And while District Attorney McCann surely regrets asking if the police would rather go after Bembenek or Schultz, the underlying theory wasn't too outrageous: Schultz's perjury was for such things as lying on his marriage-license application. For that, you're going to let a murderer walk?

But Zenner's brief did highlight one piece of new evidence:

- The gun. According to members of the jury, it was Bembenek's access to the murder weapon that convicted her. But while Bembenek was fighting extradition in Toronto, her defense team struck on a novel argument.

When Christine Schultz was shot, the gun was pressed against her back. The pressure of expanding gases from a close gunshot forms a distinct reddish imprint of the muzzle around the wound. Mary Woehrer, a Milwaukee attorney and cohort of Ira Robins, had the inspiration to send photos of the wound, with measurements, and muzzle impressions made in modeling clay, to top forensic specialists in Canada and the United States. The finding, from five separate forensic pathologists, was that the muzzle imprint around the wound was two and a half times as wide as the muzzle of the supposed murder weapon. That gun, they said, couldn't have committed this murder. And if the gun was innocent, so was Laurie Bembenek.

But, of course, it isn't quite that easy. Donohoo produced his own expert, Dr. Vincent Di Maio, a man who has written a book on gunshot wounds and who says he often sees muzzle imprints two or two and a half times the size of the muzzle. Furthermore, Di Maio says his testimony is more credible than those of Bembenek's five experts. "They run medical examiner's offices," he says. "I run a medical examiner's office and a crime lab. I get the body and I get the gun. I just have to put the two together."

So it comes down to dueling experts, dueling theories, dueling contentions about the original evidence. No one knows how a new jury would have reacted, but it's hard to read Zenner's brief and imagine anyone finding Bembenek guilty beyond a reasonable doubt.

Donohoo was clearly struck by this once the brief was filed. He began negotiating with Zenner over a plea bargain for Bembenek. "Criminal prosecutions rarely improve with age," he said later at her plea-and-sentencing hearing. "This case is no exception, and the state has identified several areas that would make a second prosecution substantially more difficult than the first."

Bembenek was looking at spending three more years behind bars while justice was slowly grinding through a motion for a new trial, the trial itself (if granted) and the inevitable appeals. In the end she decided to sacrifice the hope of exoneration for the lure of freedom, and Zenner and Donohoo struck a deal. They would go to the original trial judge to vacate the conviction for first-degree murder and the life sentence that went with it. Bembenek would then plead no contest to a lesser charge of second-degree murder and would be sentenced to 20 years in prison, reduced to time already served plus parole.

On December 9, 1992, the actors appeared in court and played their roles to perfection. "They went in and basically said, 'Hocus-pocus, mumbo jumbo,' and then they walked out," says Jim Rowen, who covered the case for the *Milwaukee Journal*. "All the reporters swarmed around Zenner out in the hall, asking him what had just happened. He said, 'Oh, she's free.'"

Relatively free, anyway. Bembenek will be under court supervision through the Nineties and needs permission to travel. The government wouldn't let her fly to Toronto to watch the shooting of the NBC miniseries in March, but it did let her go to Los Angeles for a press conference, where she stood onstage in front of the entertainment press and listened while Tatum O'Neal summed up her saga: "She's been betrayed and yet she has so much strength and so much fight in her that it's like nothing could stop her. After spending an evening with her, I was just blown away."

• • •

It's early March in Toronto and the cast and crew of *Woman on the Run* are trying to shoot July in Milwaukee. Inside an office building, throngs of anxious media vultures mill about the lobby, then attack as "Laurie" and her lawyer emerge through the revolving door, over and over, from several camera angles.

Upstairs in the room where the crew hangs out, a large stack of accordion cardboard folds out to reveal a shooting schedule for the production, with tersely slugged scenes grouped by days. (Day 33: Nick Receives Laurie Letter. Sex Fantasy Now Reality. Laurie Succumbs to Love. Laurie Primps for Love. Bath Better than Sex.) By the time production wraps, the crew will have spent more than 40 days on set in Toronto and North Carolina, shooting most of the American scenes in Canada and most of the Canadian scenes in the United States.

"There's a pretty clear profile of what works in TV movies," says Todd Leavitt, executive vice president of NBC Productions. "Movies tend to attract a very strong women's demographic, so a story with a strong, appealing female lead is something you always look for. Another category that always works is true crime. The story of Lawrencia Bembenek fits both of those profiles. It has a strong central woman character and it's ripped from the headlines."

Still, NBC Productions optioned the story when Bembenek was in Canada fighting extradition; there was real concern about the risks of tackling a story that didn't yet have an ending. "If she's just extradited and reincarcerated, the story kind of stops there," Leavitt says. "It becomes difficult to make a statement about her innocence. Here, the system has validated our statement. At the ending, you bite your lip a little if you truly believe in her innocence."

Of course, there are those who would argue that a plea of no contest to second-degree murder isn't much of a validation of innocence. CBS, for one, didn't buy it, thereby killing Bembenek's opportunity for an Amy Fisheresque hat trick on network TV.

"CBS said, 'She just ruined the ending for your movie. She's pleaded to second-degree murder. Therefore, she's not in fact innocent,'" says Francine LeFrak, who was set to produce the network's entry in the Bambi sweepstakes, this one based on Kris Radish's authorized biography, *Run, Bambi, Run*. "I said to the network people, Are you kidding? Can you imagine what a dramatic moment it is when they take the shackles off Lawrencia and she hugs her parents in front of the judge? That isn't dramatic to you? And a crawl going up the screen saying she's pleaded no contest but she's still trying to prove her innocence? That's not powerful to you? You don't get goose bumps?' And they said, 'No.'"

Some people just can't tell a heroine when they see one.

Comrades in Crime

by ROBERT CULLEN
April 1994

The roots of America's Russian Mob run deep beneath Zagrebsky Boulevard in St. Petersburg, where Andrei Kuznetsov grew up. Built in the Soviet era, Zagrebsky is a place of brick factories and crumbling eight-story tenements, of weedy vacant lots and rattling trams. If there were truth-in-labeling laws in Russia, this part of the city would still be called Leningrad.

Andrei never bought the ideologically prescribed view of life on Zagrebsky Boulevard as a privilege, a reward to his father for 12 years of faithful service to the Soviet air force in Siberia. He saw it for what it was: a three-room apartment where somebody had to sleep on a fold-out couch and the piano had to go in the hallway. A daily trudge to the market to pick over the dirty potatoes and turnips. The old man, Innokenty Kuznetsov, a stalwart Communist, thought this was enough to make a man content in his middle age. His son knew better.

With ferocious determination, Andrei schemed to get out of Leningrad. His launching point, in the mid-Eighties, was the network of tourist hotels in the center of the city. These places—the Astoria, the Yevropeiskaya, the Pribaltiskaya—admitted only foreigners who had hard currency to spend. Typically, visitors stayed in the city for a few days, taking in the Rembrandts and Da Vincis at the Hermitage, traipsing through the imperial palaces and absorbing occasional lectures on the merits of socialism. Normally, the state tourist organization diligently shepherded them, but they sometimes broke away to explore the city for themselves. That was where Andrei found his opportunities.

If he could befriend tourists, for instance, he could persuade them to trade dollars for rubles with him instead of with the state. They got a better exchange rate, he got the means to buy jeans and Walkmans.

Andrei had a talent for befriending people. He was a good-looking boy, tall and slender, with wavy brown hair and blue eyes. He studied various languages, English first among them. He was particularly good at charming women. He wrote poems for them. He flattered them. He sensed when they wanted sex and when they wanted proof that he had something other than sex on his mind.

Sometimes, as part of a seduction, Andrei would take people home for a meal cooked by his mother, just to show them his sweet, boyish side. Women tourists loved him. In the mid-Eighties, while he was still technically a student at Leningrad State University, he began to prosper in St. Petersburg's black market.

That, unfortunately, brought him to the attention of the KGB, which had always monitored contacts between Soviet citizens and foreigners, however innocent. With the beginning of *perestroika*, the KGB also developed an interest in nonpolitical crime. KGB eavesdroppers listened in on all the phones in the tourist hotels. KGB operatives infiltrated the hotel and university staffs. In 1986, this net swept up Andrei Kuznetsov and sent him to jail for three years. The charge was currency speculation.

• • •

The KGB, like most things in Russia, has changed a great deal in the past seven years. It now calls itself the Ministry of Security of the Russian Federation. It has learned that in a democracy a police agency wanting to remain well-funded has to pay attention to public relations. It must crack down, or appear to be cracking down, on problems that concern voters. So nowadays, if a reporter wants to know about organized crime in Russia, he has only to call the Ministry of Security and ask for a briefing.

The reporter will be directed to walk past the glowering Lubyanka, symbolic headquarters of the KGB, to an old, pastel-blue merchant's mansion down the street. The waiting room has grimy brown linoleum flooring and matching chairs. A bust of Iron Feliks Dzerzhinsky, the KGB's founder, still occupies a place of honor. A few nervous Russians sit waiting for appointments. In a moment, Sergei Bogdanov appears.

Bogdanov is dressed in mufti, which means sneakers and a windbreaker with a label that reads DANNY. He sees reporters in the sort of barren, empty office where police in all countries talk to people who aren't suspects but who aren't exactly trusted, either. He is the number two man in the ministry's public relations office, where his duties include producing a weekly crime-busters show for Moscow television. He has read, he informs his interviewer, some of the standard American texts on the art of public relations. He has also read *The Godfather* in a translation that circulated within the KGB in the early Eighties.

Russian organized crime, he says, lacks the hierarchy of the American Mafia. There is no Russian Godfather. Instead, there are some 3000 gangs, ranging in size from five members to dozens. They first formed in the Sixties, as the fear of Stalinism gave way to a pervasive cynicism and a thriving black market.

"They started out in petty gangs, dealing in things like robbery and speculation," Bogdanov says. Speculation, in this context, means selling something for more than you paid. A gang might buy some meat, illegally, from the director of a state store. Then the gang members would sell it, at retail prices, while the store director reported a theft.

With the advent of *perestroika,* organized crime exploded. Gang members could form legal private businesses and avoid the messy Soviet necessity of working for the state. These businesses served as a place for gang members to invest their initial capital as well as a cover for their operations. Bogdanov recalls one case, in 1989, in which a gang stole titanium from a defense factory, made shovels with it and exported the shovels to confederates in Japan, declaring a tax valuation of three rubles per shovel. Titanium in Japan was going for about $19 per pound, perhaps 100 times more than the tax value of the shovel.

As the legitimacy of the Communist Party eroded in the late Eighties, the gangs found no shortage of bureaucrats for sale. Policemen, prosecutors and tax collectors were bribed. "Our estimates are that two thirds of the gangs bought an 'umbrella' in the law enforcement agencies," Bogdanov says. "Of the ones who have international ties, maybe 90 percent have bought protection."

And increasingly, Bogdanov says, Russian gangs look for opportunities abroad. As Willie Sutton once noted, that's where the money is. Ties with the U.S. began with the era of mass emigration from the Soviet Union, which began in the early Seventies and peaked in Gorbachev's last years in power. So far, more than 200,000 former Soviet citizens have come to the U.S. since 1975. "It's easy, when someone has a brother in New York or Los Angeles, to arrange some kind of joint venture," he says.

There is, in Bogdanov's voice, more than a hint of *schadenfreude.* The KGB, after all, spent the last years of the Cold War listening to American sermons about the need to liberalize emigration, the economy and the criminal justice system. If Americans now come to Moscow with concerns that these liberalizations have led to a new crime problem, one suspects that more than one KGB man is muttering "I told you so" into his vodka.

Bogdanov recounts the case of a Moscow gangster called Delyets, or "the Dealer." He began his career as a thief. Then he formed a gang that specialized in stealing icons and paintings. The Dealer branched out. He created two private businesses that smuggled automotive spare parts out of Russia, bribing customs officials to do so. He controlled prostitution around the Kiev subway station and the adjacent Slavyanskaya Hotel. He had a protection racket going with the truckers who needed a place to park outside the station. Delyets was arrested in February 1992, but after two months in jail, he paid an 800,000 ruble bribe to a prosecutor in return for the opportunity to make bail. Once he was back on the streets, the witnesses against him soon decided to forget whatever they had known about the Dealer's various enterprises.

During those two months, though, other gangs had muscled in on the Dealer's territory, typifying the anarchic nature of the Russian Mob. There is no "family," no structure to protect the business of a man who takes a fall. The Dealer, Bogdanov has heard, decided not to attempt the difficult and potentially bloody task of recapturing his turf. Nor was he interested in buying it back. Instead, rumor has it, he was pulling together the capital and the false documents he needed to go abroad. And Bogdanov has an idea where the Dealer wanted to go. "When he was arrested back in 1992," he says, "the Dealer had a ticket and a visa for the United States."

• • •

A ticket and a visa—those were the two things Andrei Kuznetsov most wanted when he got out of jail. He began the process of reinventing himself by putting his charm to work in the Leningrad art community. In the late Eighties, Western artists and art dealers began showing up in force in Russia. One of them was Serge Sorokko, a Soviet emigrant who was a co-owner of a chain of art galleries in New York, Beverly Hills and San Francisco. One of Sorokko's artists was another emigrant, Mikhail Shemyakin. In 1989 Sorokko staged an exhibition of Shemyakin's work in Russia. He needed a local factotum, and an ingratiating Andrei volunteered. Andrei then capitalized on the contacts he made through the Shemyakin exhibition. One dealer agreed to invite him to visit the U.S., a necessary requirement in the visa process. At the end of 1989 he left Russia for good.

Once Andrei was in the U.S., Sorokko set him up with a job selling art at his gallery on Rodeo Drive. It is a place where, in addition to Shemyakin's works, Hockneys and Warhols are sold to people who have blank walls and $10,000 or $20,000 to drop on a print. There is even a room of etchings done by Pablo Picasso, though these are from the artist's dirty-old-man period, mainly pictures of women diddling themselves.

A good salesman could earn $5,000, even $15,000, in commissions a month. Andrei was a good salesman, particularly with the Shemyakins. "He was a likable guy," his former boss recalls. "Great with people, could smell money and was very persistent."

In the space of a few weeks, Andrei had gone almost as far from Zagrebsky Boulevard as a man could go. The sights and smells of wealth assaulted his brain: leather from Bernini and Bally, perfume from Giorgio, diamonds from Cartier. He could cruise down streets lined with soaring royal palms and mansions so big the gardeners needed assistants. He bought a used BMW and then traded it in on a champagne-colored Mercedes. He rented a little house in West Hollywood, not far from Sunset Boulevard. It wasn't quite Beverly Hills, but it had a fireplace, a deck and a hot tub, and if he craned his neck he could see the tops of the palm trees in Beverly Hills. Andrei had reinvented himself.

Los Angeles was full of glamourous women—both Americans and Soviet émigrés—unlike any Andrei might have met on Zagrebsky Boulevard. Whether Russian or American, the women were equally responsive to a smile and a little poetry, and Andrei pursued them relentlessly. He generally had two or three little young women with him at exhibition openings. Frequently, they visited him during the day, hanging out at the gallery.

In the summer of 1991, he married a California girl whom we'll call Michelle. She was a 20-year-old blonde with long, tanned legs and cornflower-blue eyes. She was a saleswoman at Neiman Marcus when he walked in one day, introduced himself and asked her out. She declined. He got a Russian-American girl who worked at the store to act as a go-between, and Michelle finally consented. On their first date, he took her to his home in West Hollywood, where his mother, Galina Ivanovna Kuznetsov, visiting from St. Petersburg, cooked an enormous Russian supper. When he proposed, Michelle understood that Andrei wanted to marry her because he needed a green card. He was seeing, and would continue to see, other women. She loved him anyway, and she agreed. On their wedding night, he left her alone, going out with other people.

The money Andrei was making at the art gallery soon wasn't enough to attain the lifestyle to which he aspired, and he began to probe for ways to get more. One day the gallery's director got a call from a customer in Texas who had bought a picture with his credit card. The man said he had used the card only once in Los Angeles. But his latest bill had florists' charges on it, all for flowers delivered to women in the Beverly Hills area, including one bouquet to a woman who sold perfume at Giorgio. Andrei denied using the customer's card number, then said that a friend who had visited him in the gallery might have done it.

The gallery started to watch Andrei closely. One evening the phone rang, and a manager picked it up.

"Andrei?" a man asked.

"Yes," the gallery manager said, stringing the man along.

"You were supposed to send me two girls. Where are they?"

That phone call cast a new light on the pretty women who kept visiting Andrei at the gallery. He was fired, with the understanding that the gallery would not prosecute him if he never set foot in it again.

•   •   •

Andrei was hardly the first Soviet emigrant to the U.S. to dabble in fraud. The Soviet Union had a long tradition of producing grifters. In fact, the Russian language has several synonyms for the term, and the most beloved comic novel of the Soviet era, *The 12 Chairs,* is about a con artist named Ostap Bender. Finding a way to swindle the state was a survival mechanism during the declining years of Communism, and no one thought it wrong. It's no surprise that while most Soviet immigrants were looking for an honest path to a better life, some of them—arriving in a country where the police need a court order to tap a telephone and where there are vulnerable institutions such as checking accounts, credit cards, corporations and insurance companies— perceived their new home as a candy store without a proprietor. Fraud became the mainstay of the new class of Soviet-American racketeers.

Much of the fraud is directed against fellow immigrants. Some members of the Russian-speaking community devised new variations on the Ponzi scheme. At the time Andrei arrived in Los Angeles, an immigrant was getting rich by buying a small fleet of used passenger vans from hotels and car rental agencies, repainting them and putting them visibly to work in the streets. He then put out the word that anyone who invested $15,000 would own a van and receive a guaranteed $600 monthly profit. After selling each van a dozen or more times and using the new money to make a couple of $600 payments to his first customers, he sold the van fleet to Mexicans on the other side of Los Angeles and left town. When the victims located the new van owners and demanded their money back, they got only a shrug of shoulders.

Other Russian racketeers were involved in loan-sharking. An émigré might borrow money at 30 percent annual interest but be unable to make his payments. The loan sharks would arrange for the unfortunate businessman to borrow more money from other members of the Russian-speaking community, this time at 60 percent. The sharks would take a commission on the new loan, get their original money back and act as collection agents for the new loans. Typically, the borrower wound up hopelessly in debt to a wide range of people. When they had wrung all the money they could from the borrower, the loan sharks would settle the debt by taking over his business.

But the Ponzi schemes and loan-sharking are nothing compared with the fraud engineered in southern California by the Smushkevich brothers, David and Michael. Using pliant physicians and mobile clinics, the Smushkeviches offered free physical examinations. To keep the clinics full, they used telemarketing to find patients or, in some cases, went out on the streets to round up volunteers among the homeless. Once they got a patient into their clinic, they hooked him up to a few electrodes and diagnosed him with ailments ranging from heart disease to diabetes, even if the patient were healthy.

They billed insurance companies, Medicaid and the California medical system an average of $8,000 per patient for treatments the patients neither needed nor, in many cases, received. When the Smushkeviches pleaded guilty in spring 1993 to charges of mail fraud and money laundering, among other crimes, their prosecutors estimated that the brothers had bilked American government agencies and insurance companies of at least $80 million.

In the New York area, the other U.S. center of Soviet immigration, the federal government has allegedly become the dupe in schemes involving gasoline taxes. Under the law, distribution companies known as producers can buy and sell gasoline among themselves without paying the federal excise tax. When the gasoline finally goes to a retailer, the tax must be paid. According to an indictment handed down in New Jersey last May, racketeers from the former Soviet Union set up dummy corporations, including one known as the burn company. They shuffled the gasoline among dummy corporations, leaving the tax liability on the burn company. When the government came to collect the unpaid taxes, the burn company disappeared, along with the entire chain of dummy corporations that led to it.

According to the U.S. attorney for New Jersey, various permutations of this scheme have cost the federal government as much as $2 billion annually. The New Jersey indictment involved about $60 million in unpaid taxes. It named Victor Zilber, who emigrated from the Soviet Union in 1979, as the man operating many of the dummy companies. And it revealed a link between the Russian racketeers and the Mafia. According to the indictment, the Russians had been in partnership with the Gambino family in the tax-fraud business.

Comrades, they must have been asking themselves, is this a great country or what?

• • •

By the time Andrei Kuznetsov left the art gallery, he was ready to set up his own racket. A co-worker recalled that Andrei had long been fascinated by checking accounts. The idea that he could sign his name to a piece of paper and actually buy things with it intrigued him. How did the banks handle the paper? How long did it take them? What happened if there was no money to cover the check? He made it his business to learn and exploit the answers to those questions.

He soon found several weaknesses in the checking system. A merchant might call a bank to make sure that a customer presenting a check had the funds to cover it. But after the merchant accepted the check, it might take a day or so for it to arrive at the bank. If the bank delayed the processing for a day or two more, there would be time for a determined swindler to use the same money to write checks in dozens of stores. The banks and the police would eventually come after him. But what could they do if the swindler had gone back to Russia?

Of course, Andrei did not want to leave Los Angeles. But back in St. Petersburg there was an almost unlimited supply of people who would like nothing more than to come to California, shop for a week or so, take a small cut of the proceeds and return to Russia. They could be his foot soldiers.

Now he needed allies in the major banks, so he worked hard to meet women in the check-clearing departments. Soon, he was boasting to associates that his checks would linger in the bank for days before being presented for payment.

He needed customers. That was easy. He put out the word that he could get virtually anything for his friends at half price. "He was quite open and arrogant about it," recalls one Los Angeles woman to whom Andrei offered a $9,000 Cartier watch for $4,500. "He said that if I ever saw something in a store that I wanted, I shouldn't buy it. I should tell him and he'd get it for me."

Once Andrei's operation was up and running, it worked simply. He usually had a couple of shoppers working for him in Los Angeles and two more in training. He would rise early in the morning and go over his books and his orders. Then, promptly at 10 A.M., he, the shoppers and a driver would hit the streets in the Mercedes. Andrei would stay in the car and tell the shoppers precisely where to go and what to buy. They shopped steadily, all over Los Angeles, from the time the stores opened until they closed. As time went on, he found computer equipment to be a particularly lucrative specialty, but he also bought and sold rugs, antiques, cameras and jewelry.

His shoppers' checking accounts had fake addresses and names, but they had money in them while the checks were being written. And Andrei never let them spend more in a single store visit than the account held. So, if a store manager telephoned the bank to verify that the funds were on deposit, he would be told that they were. But by the time the checks were presented for payment, perhaps after being stopped or delayed for a couple of days by one of Andrei's helpful friends, he had withdrawn the money. And by the time the police started looking for the shoppers, they were back in Russia, their usefulness over after no more than two weeks.

In the meantime, Andrei had been training new shoppers in the proper ways to speak, dress and sign their names in an American store. He told associates he was netting as much as $50,000 per month from this racket. He was talking, according to police sources, of branching out by expanding his occasional pimping into a full-fledged escort service using Soviet émigrés.

He spent his money as fast as he made it, living what a Leningrad boy might imagine to be the exotic and glamourous life of a Hollywood man-about-town. He cruised at Bar One and Roxbury on Sunset Boulevard. He entertained lavishly. The champagne at Andrei's was chilled and abundant. He sent Michelle to New York, saying he didn't want her to be involved with the business he was doing in the house. He began dating another California girl, whom we will call Amanda. She became pregnant and told him she wanted to have his baby.

By then, Andrei was touching the fringes of Hollywood celebrity. He dated skier Suzy Chaffee. On the night of January 26, 1992, he was planning to attend a party at Bar One for Brigitte Nielsen, then midway between Sly Stallone and oblivion, but a movie star nonetheless. He was going to the party with Randy Webster, a Hollywood guy with a gold chain around his neck, a chiropractor who had left that profession in favor of more interesting enterprises: a modeling agency, a private investigation service and the inevitable film production company. Webster had found that going to bars with Andrei was a sure way to meet women.

But Andrei had miscalculated the temper of his new assistants, Sergei Ivanov and Aleksandr Nikolayev. Like Andrei, Ivanov and Nikolayev came from the Leningrad black market, where they had worked as a waiter and a bartender in tourist hotels and speculated in currency on the side. Each had emigrated to New York and knocked around in menial jobs for a year or so until they heard via the Russian grapevine that Andrei Kuznetsov was willing to pay good money for short stints of work in California.

They arrived in California late in 1991 and lived in Andrei's house for two months. Nikolayev made himself useful by cooking and cleaning house. Ivanov served as Andrei's chauffeur. They trained for their shopping spree, working on their English and their penmanship. But they chafed at being treated like servants while Andrei entertained his American friends and his women.

The precise motivation for what happened in Andrei's house on the afternoon of January 26, 1992, is a matter of dispute. Ivanov maintains that he and Nikolayev decided they did not want to shop for Andrei but were told they had no choice, because, among other things, he had their passports. Detective Dirk Edmundson of the Los Angeles County Sheriff's Department believes that they simply wanted to take over Andrei's business. Within Los Angeles's Russian émigré community, rumors swirled that Andrei had run into trouble for not passing on a percentage of his profits to the right people.

Whatever the motive, late that afternoon, Andrei returned from an expedition to an antiques show. Ivanov and Nikolayev were ready. They had left the house earlier that day and bought surgical gloves at a Rexall store on Santa Monica Boulevard in preparation for Andrei's elimination. Ivanov waited until Andrei was heading for his bedroom, then pulled out a new Beretta .380 pistol, purchased a couple of weeks before at a store called Gun Heaven. He shot Andrei once in the back. Andrei turned, stumbled and fell to the floor. Then, as Andrei lay dying,

Ivanov finished the job by putting a bullet into his chest and another through his handsome head.

Ivanov and Nikolayev cracked a bottle of champagne to celebrate. Then they donned the surgical gloves and, using a kitchen knife, cut off Andrei's fingertips and stuffed them into an empty beer bottle. They thought that the body, if found, would be harder to identify and trace without its fingerprints.

Ivanov and Nikolayev were caught, by pure chance, five hours later. While they waited for late night, when it would be easier to dispose of the body without being seen, they left a car in the driveway with the engine running. A neighbor called the sheriff's office, which sent two deputies to check on the car. When they knocked, Ivanov answered the door. The deputies noticed blood on his hands and asked him about it, and shortly thereafter, Ivanov pulled out his gun. After a short struggle, he and Nikolayev surrendered. The police found Andrei Kuznetsov's mutilated body, half covered with plastic garbage bags, awaiting interment.

The police carted away the remnants of Andrei's American career: five computers, four printers, four photocopiers, assorted rugs, watches, jewelry, telephones and cameras, a case of Moët & Chandon and 22 checkbooks. They found six messages from different women on the answering machine. Michelle, now a widow, came back to California for the funeral but decided to return to New York. Andrei's mother flew in from St. Petersburg and took her son's ashes home. She buried them next to his grandmother in a village called Ropshe, not far from Zagrebsky Boulevard. She reports that a young woman named Irina, whom Andrei knew, has collected some of the poems he wrote before he emigrated and hopes to publish them. Galina Ivanovna returned to Los Angeles in 1993 to visit Amanda, who went ahead and had the baby she was carrying when Andrei was killed. It was a boy, and she named him for his father.

Andrei Kuznetsov's murder, and the subsequent statements by Ivanov and Nikolayev, helped the police in Los Angeles fill in their picture of what is often misleadingly referred to as the Russian Mafia. Testimony about Russian rackets is hard to come by. Like all immigrant communities, Russian-Americans protect their own. Only because they were facing the death penalty did Ivanov and Nikolayev speak freely about their erstwhile boss's business. The picture that emerges suggests several major differences between the Russian gangs and their predecessors.

Unlike La Cosa Nostra, the Russians have yet to develop a disciplined hierarchy of families, captains and bosses. The Russian Mob is, for the moment, truly a mob—leaderless. No links have been found between

Andrei Kuznetsov and the Smushkevich brothers, or to any of the other Russian gangs known to police in southern California. After they were caught, Ivanov and Nikolayev were entirely on their own, represented by court-appointed attorneys. And Andrei's lifestyle suggests a criminal subculture in which every man is responsible for his own discipline, or lack of it.

Still, some law enforcement experts think it is only a matter of time before the ex-Soviets catch up to the Italian-American Mafia in discipline and organization. "They're now like the Mafia was back in the Twenties and Thirties. But I think that they'll far surpass it," says Detective Terry Minton of the organized crime intelligence division of the LAPD. "They're more ruthless and they'll learn from the mistakes that La Cosa Nostra made." Minton is particularly fearful that the Russian gangs will make a connection to the desperate Russian armaments industry, and that he will soon be seeing AK-47s and heavier weapons on the streets in Los Angeles.

But the ex-Soviets have to overcome some major disadvantages before they rival La Cosa Nostra. Prohibition and the profits from bootleg liquor turned Italian gangs from neighborhood thugs to entrenched and powerful American organizations. Drugs are the analogous source of money and power for organized crime in the Nineties. Russian gangs have entered the drug business in a small way by becoming middlemen in shipment schemes designed to fool customs agents not trained to think of Eastern Europe as a point of origin for dope. But Russia does not have the climate to be a major drug producer and lacks the hard currency to become a major market. And Russian gangs will have to displace entrenched black and Hispanic gangs if they want a big share of the business.

The Italian gangs established themselves on these shores on the crest of an enormous wave of virtually free, legal immigration around the turn of the century. That wave provided a pool of recruits and a substantial base of businesses in which to launder money. Immigrants from the former Soviet republics have to compete for places in the immigration queue and their numbers will remain comparatively small. Of those who do come, there will be many who are educated and want only a chance to compete for a legitimate role in the American economy.

But there will inevitably be more people like Andrei Kuznetsov. They will be graduates of the tough school of rackets in Russia. They will see America as a soft touch, a land of golden, illicit opportunity. And their careers will reflect all the chaos and cruelty, the romance and greed of the culture that produced them.

Nicodemo "Little Nicky" Scarfo

The Mob's Last Civil War

by GEORGE ANASTASIA
September 1994

The sun was burning the dew off the lawn in front of John Stanfa's Medford, New Jersey, home as the 53-year-old Mob boss left his house. He and his son, Joseph, 23, were on their way to work. It was early morning and their driver had just pulled his slightly beat-up 1976 Cadillac Seville up the driveway. Stanfa, balding, with thick, sloping shoulders and a broad chest, eased into the front passenger seat. Joe sat in the back. This was how they went to work every morning. They left the house at the same time, took the same route to work, rode in the same car. On August 31, 1993, the routine nearly killed them.

It takes about an hour, during the morning commuter rush, to drive from Medford to Continental Imported Food Distributors, a warehouse in the Grays Ferry section of South Philadelphia. Continental, which distributes imported Italian foods to restaurants and bars throughout the area, is owned by Joe Stanfa and his sister, Sara, 26. On most mornings the Stanfas, father and son, would be in the warehouse by eight A.M. Joe seemed to do most of the work around the place, supervising crews that loaded the trucks, even doing some of the bull work if deliveries were running behind schedule. John, on the other hand, would hole up in an office conducting business that investigators believed had little to do with the price of provolone.

The Cadillac Seville traveled west on Route 70 and then south on Interstate 295 toward the Walt Whitman Bridge, joining the flow of thousands of commuters heading over the Delaware River and into Philadelphia each morning.

At around 7:45 A.M., near the Vare Avenue/Mifflin Street exit on the

THE MOB'S LAST CIVIL WAR

Schuylkill Expressway, a white Chevy van caught up with the Caddy. In a flash, two 9mm machine pistols popped out of portholes cut into the side of the van and began strafing the Cadillac. John Stanfa ducked down as the spray of bullets shattered the window. Joe, in the backseat, wasn't as quick as his father. One of the bullets caught him above his right cheekbone. He slid to the floor in agony. Stanfa screamed for the driver, Fred Aldrich, to stop the car, that Joe had been hit. Instead, Aldrich rammed the side of the van, forcing it onto the Vare Avenue exit ramp. Then he gunned the engine and continued west on the Schuylkill for another half mile, exiting at University Avenue.

Police would later credit the burly Vietnam war veteran with saving the lives of the Mob boss and his son. But the fact remained that if Stanfa had not been so arrogant, if he had listened to some of his people and left the house at different times, taken different routes, the ambush could have been avoided altogether. But Stanfa had always underestimated the kids—the younger generation of mobsters in Philadelphia.

With smoke and the smell of burning rubber trailing in its wake—the rear tire, punctured by a stray bullet, was now in shreds—the Cadillac lurched around the corner at 34th and Wharton streets and pulled up in front of the Continental warehouse. Joe Stanfa was hustled out of the car and into another vehicle. Rushed to the emergency room at the Hospital of the University of Pennsylvania, he was conscious, alert and, police said, uncooperative.

The hit took everyone by surprise. The victims, of course, but also the public, terrified by the wanton display of violence, and even the cops, who had never seen anything like it during 14 bloody years of Mafia turmoil in Philadelphia. They were used to finding wiseguys with bullet holes behind their ears, wrapped in blankets and cast aside. This was different, crazy. An ambush in the midst of rush-hour traffic, with total disregard for hundreds of innocent people who might have been caught in the crossfire or crushed in a mass pileup. It was out of character—it was more Sicily than South Philadelphia. But that was just the point.

Everyone suspected that the kids were behind it. They were sure that Joseph "Skinny Joey" Merlino, the 32-year-old son of a Philadelphia *capo*, was sending a message to Stanfa, a man born in an Italian village not far from Palermo and raised in the Old World ways of the Mafia. The message was: Get the fuck off our corner. Get out of our city. Go back where you belong. It didn't matter that the hit failed. The kids had pulled it off; they were not about to back down. Philadelphia's civil war was entering a bloody new phase.

184

• • •

If you want to know about the decline of the American Mafia, look at Philadelphia. The Mob war that is raging there now—the gun battles that have left a dozen mobsters dead or wounded, the turncoat testimony that has brought a series of sweeping Mob indictments, the pending trials and prosecutions that could leave Stanfa and most of his top associates in jail for the rest of their lives, the bloody generation and culture gaps that have continued to widen—is part of a saga that may signal the end of the American arm of La Cosa Nostra. Three of the Mob bosses in the city have been indicted. Two have been murdered. A once low-key and highly efficient crime family has turned on itself. Fueled by greed, treachery and by what appears to be an insatiable bloodlust, the organization is self-destructing.

To track its demise, look to John Stanfa and his misguided attempt to bring the kids under his control. "Stanfa was not CEO material," says Richard Zappile, chief inspector with the Philadelphia Police Department and one of the point men in law enforcement's war on the Mob. "He didn't have the strategic planning ability it takes to lead. He didn't exercise enough control and he allowed things to build up."

Zappile, 46, is a South Philly guy. Take Brooklyn and shrink it to less than a tenth of its size and you have South Philadelphia. About 200,000 people live there, many in white ethnic neighborhoods that have changed little over the past 30 years. Loyalty, honor and family are celebrated in South Philly, as are its most famous sons: Frankie Avalon, Fabian and James Darren, all of whom grew up in the same area, around 10th and Jackson streets, where Joey Merlino was raised. Gangsters are just a small portion of the population, but for decades their impact on the city has far outweighed their numbers. Angelo Bruno, a longtime crime boss in the city, was never a candidate for South Philadelphia Man of the Year, but he was probably better known than contemporaries operating at his level in other lines of work.

The area has also produced its share of cops. Zappile grew up around the corner from Bruno. As a rookie cop, Zappile walked past wiseguy hangouts on his way to work. Later he was a sergeant in a district where several of Bruno's top associates lived and operated. Over the years, Zappile has seen changes in the mobsters' style: The shift from low-key to high profile, from sly and cunning to bold and arrogant, was accompanied by the loss of values, however repugnant, that had once made the organization seem invincible.

At a back table in a deli not far from police headquarters, Zappile

185

nurses a cup of coffee and talks about the vanishing older generation of mobsters in Philly: "Those guys didn't particularly like one another. But guess what? They pooled their resources for the good of the organization. They didn't flaunt it. Who knew what judge they controlled, what politician they owned, what cop they were paying off? It wasn't something that was talked about, you know? The guy who can sit in the back, in the dark, and wield that kind of power, that was a real mobster. Bruno was the boss and he kept them all in line. What did he have over them? It was that code, that honor. *Omerta*. It kept them together. They believed in that. That's what's missing now."

Bruno was killed in 1980. A year later he was succeeded by Nicodemo "Little Nicky" Scarfo, a paranoid despot who assumed control in 1981 and over the next ten years bankrupted Bruno's organization. Scarfo and more than a dozen other top Mob figures are now in jail, serving long-term federal prison sentences as a result of a series of prosecutions that began in 1987. But their legacy continues, carried on by sons, brothers and nephews who still hang out on the street corners and in the clubhouses that are the nerve centers of the organization.

"That's the biggest difference," Zappile says. "Today you've got these kids. They see the movies. They see Joe Pesci. They think that's what it's all about."

The kids. In South Philadelphia, it always comes back to the kids.

• • •

If there is a Mob prince in Philadelphia today it is Joey Merlino, the son of former Scarfo family underboss Salvatore Merlino. "Joey knows all the moves," says Nicholas "Nicky Crow" Caramandi, a former Scarfo family soldier and one of the first in a long list of Mob turncoats whose testimony brought down the Scarfo organization in the late Eighties. "His father and his uncle were both involved. He grew up with it. Plus, the kid always had a lot of balls."

Joey Merlino had one shot to go legit. As a teenager he worked for a horse trainer. Short, wiry, with great balance and arm strength, Merlino was soon a good apprentice jockey. His attorney now says Merlino outgrew the job and had to give up a promising career.

His uncle, in a recent interview from prison, tells a different story. "He was good," said Lawrence Merlino, who is now a cooperating government witness. "When he was 16 or 17 he was one of the leading apprentice jockeys. We used to go watch him race. Scarfo liked the kid. He knew he had a lot of guts and he wanted him with us. He used to go down to Maryland when Joey was racing there. Nicky would take him out for crabs. He told the kid that horse racing wasn't the life for him. It was dirty mucking stables, and he could get hurt." It was odd advice from a Mob boss who used violence as a management tool; his eight-year reign was marked by more than two dozen Mob murders.

Joey Merlino's father and uncle climbed the Mafia career ladder with Scarfo, both assuming positions of authority once Little Nicky became boss. Salvatore Merlino was the hands-on supervisor of the organization in South Philadelphia. Lawrence Merlino, who operated a construction company in Margate City, New Jersey, was a Mob *capo* who provided the organization with an entree into the casino-gambling boom of the early Eighties.

Early in 1987, Scarfo, the elder Merlinos and many others were jailed on a series of charges ranging from extortion and conspiracy to first-degree murder. They have been in prison ever since. When the older generation was sent away, Joey Merlino got his big chance.

• • •

Cops like Zappile refer to Joey Merlino as a "snot-nosed punk," but in certain underworld circles he is feared, if not admired, for his guts and swaggering street-corner style. Investigators are convinced that Merlino was behind the Schuylkill Expressway ambush, but have been unable, thus far, to prove it. In fact, Joey Merlino had built his reputation long before the bullets started flying.

Dark-haired and handsome, with brooding eyes, Merlino looked, dressed and acted the part of a wiseguy. He and his associates—the sons, brothers and nephews of convicted Scarfo crime-family members—hung out at the best spots in the city. They could be spotted in the funky joints along South Street and at the trendy bars, restaurants and nightclubs that sprang up along the Delaware River waterfront. Merlino was the accepted leader of the group. And because of his father, he also had the ear of some established, older Mob figures. With a foot in each camp, he was positioned to become a major player in the changing Philadelphia underworld.

He also had a certain flair that attracted both young and old. There is a story, confirmed indirectly by Merlino himself, about a Christmas party held two years ago at a beauty salon in South Philadelphia where he and some of his friends used to go for manicures. Merlino had arranged for an associate in the catering business to put out a spread—lunch meats, cheeses, fruit, bread, desserts—and all day long customers who came in were invited to join the feast. At one point, several young black kids from a nearby neighborhood drifted in and began eyeing the food. The owner of the beauty shop saw them and started making up platters for them. Then Merlino stepped in.

"What are you doin'?" he said to the owner. "That's not the way it's done."

Merlino pulled a wad of cash from his pocket and proceeded to hand a $20 bill to each of the seven or eight kids.

"This is how it's done," he said with a smile. "Merry Christmas."

"Joey was the kind of kid, if he had $5,000 in his pocket, he'd go out and spend $10,000," said Richie Barone, a government witness who fingered Merlino in a $352,000 armored-truck heist.

On the eve of their trial, Barone cut a deal with the prosecution and Joey was left to stand alone. Convicted and sentenced to four years in prison, he politely told U.S. District Court Judge Norma Shapiro, "Thanks for a fair trial." Assistant U.S. Attorney Robert Goldman sought a stiff sentence for Merlino, arguing that the mobster saw the prison term as the price of doing business. Merlino's attitude, he said, was "all you get is a couple of years in prison."

In fact, Merlino served a little more than two years behind bars. The money has never been recovered.

• • •

John Stanfa emerged as the new Mob boss while Joey Merlino was away. Like Merlino, he brought legitimate Mafia credentials to the table, although his pedigree was from a different time and place. Stanfa came to this country in 1964 from Sicily where, the Pennsylvania Crime Commission would later note, two brothers and a brother-in-law were members of the Mafia. He arrived in New York with a letter of introduction to Mob boss Carlo Gambino. Gambino then asked his good friend, Angelo Bruno, if he had anything for Stanfa to do in Philadelphia. Bruno welcomed the newcomer. Stanfa started a small construction company—his specialty was brick and masonry work—and was listed by law enforcement officials at the time as a low-level fringe player in the Bruno organization.

And that's what he remained until the night of March 21, 1980, when he was asked to drive Bruno home from dinner at Cous' Little Italy, a popular, Mob-run South Philadelphia restaurant. To this day, no one but the killer is certain how the plot unfolded and how Stanfa was in position to drive the don home that night. What is certain is that as

Stanfa pulled his car in front of Bruno's row house, a man wearing a raincoat walked out of the shadows on the corner, put a shotgun to the passenger-side window and blew a hole in the back of Angelo Bruno's head. That's when the Philadelphia branch of La Cosa Nostra began to careen out of control.

In rapid succession, the mobsters suspected of being behind the Bruno murder turned up dead, targeted by both Bruno loyalists in Philadelphia and the Mob hierarchy in New York which, in a display of understandable self-interest, decided it could not condone the murder of a sitting Mafia boss. Of those linked to the plot, only Stanfa managed to survive the bloodletting that followed. He disappeared after being indicted for perjury while testifying before a federal grand jury investigating the Bruno hit. Nine months later he was discovered living under an assumed name in a small town outside of Baltimore, working at a restaurant linked to the Gambino organization. Brought back to Philadelphia, he was convicted of perjury and sentenced to eight years in prison. He served more than six years and was released in 1987.

When Stanfa left prison, powerful underworld forces in both New York and Sicily interceded on his behalf. Several Philadelphia mobsters who are now cooperating with federal authorities tell the same tale. At first leaders of the Gambino family, as a favor to their Sicilian brethren, prevailed upon Scarfo and other Bruno loyalists to win a reprieve of the underworld death sentence placed on Stanfa's head. The deal was that Stanfa would return to Sicily after his release. Then John Gotti asked Scarfo to allow Stanfa to stay in this country. So it was that Stanfa went to New York after getting out of prison.

By that point, the Philadelphia Mob was in disarray. Scarfo's bloody reign brought death, destruction and disorganization. Not only were two dozen mobsters killed—including a generation of potential leaders—but nearly as many were convicted and sentenced to lengthy terms behind bars. Even more troubling, however, was the fact that six "made" members of the organization had become cooperating witnesses. Scarfo's slash-and-burn mentality had driven some of his closest associates to the witness stand, the only viable refuge for anyone who had a falling-out with the murderous crime boss. The repercussions would eventually be felt throughout the underworld.

Stanfa, born and raised in the old country, a product of the old ways, was sent down from New York to fix things up. He set about reorganizing around a small group of local mobsters whom he could trust. The idea was to get back to the way Bruno had run things, to avoid publicity and attention, to focus on making money rather than making news.

But too much time had passed and too many things had happened. After all, this was Philadelphia, not Palermo. There was a new generation out there. Stanfa just never figured on a problem from the kids. He never realized that for them, La Cosa Nostra begins and ends in the neighborhood.

"From the beginning, they perceived John as an outsider," said a local gambler familiar with the current underworld crisis and who, in the interest of his security, asked not to be identified. "They didn't look at it as a Mafia thing. They thought of it as a South Philly thing. Their fathers and uncles were all in jail and this guy comes rolling into town and they thought, Who the hell is he?

"Stanfa has a meeting in this restaurant with Joey Merlino and some of the other kids, and he thinks he's got everything settled. But he didn't know who he was dealing with. These kids, they turn on you in a minute. And the funny thing is, if the kids had listened, all this bullshit could have been avoided. Now, it's all falling apart. See, they're not global. They don't have the long view. To them, it's their corner and he's trying to take over."

The first signs of trouble came in January 1992, when a gambling dispute erupted over control of the weekly street tax bookmakers were supposed to pay. An old-time Mob bookmaker named Felix Bocchino was collecting for Stanfa, but some Merlino associates were apparently trying to horn in on the action. Bocchino was gunned down in an early-morning ambush near his home.

In retaliation, two shotgun-wielding assassins set a trap for Michael Ciancaglini, one of the so-called Young Turks running with Joey Merlino. Ciancaglini, 30, was walking home one night when the two hit men jumped out of a car parked near his house. The young mobster took cover, narrowly beating the gunmen to his front door. Shotgun blasts peppered the front of the brick row home and shattered a window, but Ciancaglini escaped unharmed.

Ciancaglini, like Merlino, was the son of an imprisoned mobster. His father was Joe "Chang" Ciancaglini, the enforcer for the Bruno organization who later became a capo under Scarfo. Joe Chang had three sons. The oldest, John, was doing a seven-year stint in federal prison on an extortion rap. Michael was the youngest. In between was Joe Jr., who was not as tough as Michael, but was said to be considerably smarter. Young Joe sided with Stanfa and, in a move designed to stanch the bloodletting and bridge the generation gap, Stanfa elevated him to the rank of underboss. "Joe was supposed to be the bridge between Stanfa and the kids," said the gambler. "It made a lot of sense."

The fragile peace held for several months and solidified in September 1992 when Stanfa held a formal "making ceremony" and inducted five new members into his organization—including Joey Merlino (who had just been paroled in the armored-truck case), Michael Ciancaglini and Biaggio Adornetto, a young Sicilian newly arrived in the city. Adornetto, one of three Stanfa confidants now cooperating with the government, told prosecutors he couldn't understand why Stanfa was making Merlino and Mike Ciancaglini because he knew the Mob boss didn't trust them. As Stanfa was taking him to the making ceremony, Adornetto said he asked about this and Stanfa said that he wanted to keep them close, but that he knew he would eventually have to kill them.

In the South Philadelphia underworld, the game of intrigue intensified. Behind the scenes, both sides were lining up their shots. Secretly recorded conversations, made public after Stanfa and 23 others were indicted on March 17, 1994, show the Mob boss ranting and raving about Merlino and his young associates. They didn't understand, he said. They had "no respect." He talked of importing hit men from Sicily. He threatened to take a knife and cut out the tongue of one Merlino loyalist. "And we'll send it to the wife," he said.

When the peace was broken, however, the shots came from the other direction. Joe Ciancaglini, Stanfa's underboss, his bridge to the Young Turks, was gunned down early on the morning of March 2, 1993. Two masked gunmen entered the garage of a luncheonette he owned just down the street from Stanfa's Continental Foods and opened fire. Ciancaglini was hit five times in the face and neck. He survived, but barely. Today, his face disfigured, his hearing and speech impaired, Joe Ciancaglini is no longer able to function as underboss. The shooting, which seemingly pitted brother against brother, ended any thought of reconciliation. Stanfa's attempt to merge the young and old factions into one cohesive crime family was over.

Angry, frustrated and bent on revenge, Stanfa began making plans to kill Merlino and his supporters, and FBI bugs picked up much of his plotting on tape. Some of the most fruitful listening devices were planted in the Camden, New Jersey, offices of Stanfa's criminal defense attorney, Salvatore Avena. Federal authorities later charged that Stanfa used the pretext of visiting with his attorney—and the cover of lawyer-client privilege—to meet with other mobsters.

Two months after the Joe Ciancaglini shooting, Stanfa and Sergio Battaglia, a young mob associate, met in Avena's office to plan the murder of Merlino, Michael Ciancaglini and Gaeton Lucibello, another Merlino loyalist. In a burst of confidence, Battaglia began discussing how to dispose of the bodies once the hits were carried out. He suggested that the remains be dumped outside the Philadelphia area. "Maybe we'll take one to New York, one down to Delaware," Battaglia offered. "We spread them out."

Then Stanfa had a better idea, perhaps drawing on his background as a mason and bricklayer. "No, no," he said in his fractured, heavily accented English. "What we do, we put a little concrete. They got already-mixed concrete. As soon as we do it, we put [the body] in the trunk, at night. This way the concrete hardens and we'll go dump them."

Talk then shifted to the proper technique for a shot to the head. Both Battaglia and Stanfa agreed that a bullet should enter at an angle. It was likely to destroy more brain matter that way.

"Over here," said Stanfa, evidently gesturing at the prime point of entry. "It's the best. Right behind the ear."

The next day Stanfa and two other associates were recorded planning a hit at the South Philadelphia clubhouse where Merlino, Mike Ciancaglini and Lucibello were hanging out.

"I don't want to mess it up," Stanfa told the others. "All three, they gotta go."

• • •

In underworld and law enforcement circles, the smart money was on Stanfa. "Joey's living on borrowed time," said one detective. "He's a walking dead man and he knows it," said another. Federal authorities warned Merlino, Ciancaglini and several other young Mob figures, but the kids just laughed it off.

On August 5, 1993, they stopped laughing. Ciancaglini and Merlino met late that morning in their clubhouse at Sixth and Catharine. The two-story brick building was formerly the storefront office of Greenpeace, the environmental group, whose sign still hung over the door. Now it was Merlino's headquarters in the war against Stanfa.

The place was under constant surveillance. The FBI trained a hidden camera on the front door. Arrivals and departures were clocked and recorded. Merlino and Ciancaglini walked out a little after one P.M. and headed, on foot, up Sixth Street and off camera. As they walked, a white Ford Taurus crept slowly up the street behind them. Less than a block from the clubhouse door, the car stopped and two men jumped out, opening fire. Ciancaglini slumped to the sidewalk, dead. Merlino turned to run and took a shot in the buttocks. He made it back to the clubhouse as the Taurus sped away.

Five days later, Michael Ciancaglini's funeral Mass was held at the Epiphany of Our Lord Roman Catholic Church at 11th and Jackson. He left the church in a box that day. Joey Merlino walked out leaning on a cane. That about summed up law enforcement's view of the young, renegade faction of the Mob. Stanfa was in control. Or so they thought. Three weeks later, the Mob boss and his son were ducking for cover on the Schuylkill Expressway and the blood was flowing again.

In the weeks that followed, three more mobsters were hit. One, a Merlino associate named Frank Baldino, was killed, shot behind the wheel of his Cadillac. Police, concerned about the wanton disregard for innocent bystanders in both the Schuylkill ambush and the Baldino shooting, started a street-level crackdown. Eight gangsters were pinched for weapons offenses, and the cops confiscated various handguns, mostly .38s and .380-caliber revolvers found under the seats and in the glove compartments of some of the cars that were stopped.

Merlino remained number one on Stanfa's hit list, targeted in a series of bizarre murder plots. A sniper staked out the apartment of a woman with whom Merlino sometimes lived, but he didn't show up. A bomb was planted under his car, but it failed to go off. It was planted again, and again the detonation device malfunctioned. In an even more ludicrous plan, Stanfa hoped to use a go-go dancer to poison Merlino. The woman, who did not agree to carry out the plot, was told to dress up and go to one of the nightclubs Merlino and his friends frequented. She was supposed to get close to the group, and then drop cyanide into Merlino's drink and the drinks of anyone who was with him, said a federal prosecutor.

The FBI probably saved Joey Merlino's life by taking him off the street before that plan could be carried out. Merlino was supposed to be working for an aluminum-siding company as a salesman and, according to parole terms in the 1990 armored-truck robbery case, was prohibited from associating with known felons. The FBI camera trained on the clubhouse door at Sixth and Catharine told a different story. At a parole violation hearing, federal prosecutor Robert Goldman documented Merlino's presence in the clubhouse on days when his work records indicated he was out giving estimates for installation work. It also showed him in the presence of wiseguys. Judge Norma Shapiro sentenced Merlino to three years in jail.

In March 1994 Stanfa and 23 others were indicted in a sweeping federal racketeering case and they, too, were taken out of circulation. The charges, a conspiracy built around the Racketeering-Influenced and Corrupt Organizations Act, include the murders of Michael Ciancaglini and Frank Baldino, plus nearly a dozen conspiracy and attempted-murder charges—including the various plots to get Joey Merlino—along with one kidnapping charge and numerous counts of extortion and gambling. Stanfa, if convicted, faces life in prison. Most of his top associates are looking at potential prison terms of 20 to 40 years.

Three top associates, including the hit men in the Mike Ciancaglini killing, are now cooperating and are expected to testify when the case comes to trial later this year or early in 1995. In addition, there are hours of taped conversations in which Stanfa and several of his co-defendants discuss murder plots, extortions and various other racketeering gambits. The case is an echo of the 1987 RICO indictment that sent Scarfo and 15 of his top associates to prison. It is also similar to the series of Mob indictments that put Gotti and the leaders of other New York crime families behind bars. And it is yet another nail in the coffin of the Philadelphia Mob, more evidence that La Cosa Nostra is dying.

Missing from the indictment, however, are Joey Merlino and most of the members of his Mob faction. They are said to be the targets of a separate federal investigation, one built around the Schuylkill Expressway ambush and several other acts of violence aimed at the Stanfa organization. Whether the feds have enough to bring an indictment, however, remains to be seen. Thus far, nobody from Joey's side of the street is talking. Nobody is cooperating. Nobody has been before the grand jury.

This has surprised no one. The kids all grew up together. They hung out around Tenth and Jackson. That was their corner. They fought the guys from Tenth and Porter or Third and Wolf, but never each other.

They know about loyalty.

It's a neighborhood thing.

MOB SCENE: WHO'S WHO IN PHILADELPHIA

THE BOSSES

ANGELO BRUNO: Philadelphia Mob boss whose March 21, 1980, shotgun murder set in motion the bloody internecine struggle that continues today.

PHILIP "CHICKEN MAN" TESTA: Bruno's underboss and successor, killed in a March 15, 1981, bomb blast.

NICODEMO "LITTLE NICKY" SCARFO: Testa's *consigliere* and successor. One of the most violent Mafia bosses in America. Many mobsters died during his 10-year reign of terror. Currently serving consecutive 14-year and

55-year prison terms following federal convictions on conspiracy and racketeering charges.

JOHN STANFA: Sicilian-born mobster who took over the Philadelphia crime family in 1991. Backed by the Gambino family in New York and by Mafia leaders in Palermo, but unable to control younger members of the local organization.

THE PLAYERS

JOSEPH "CHANG" CIANCAGLINI: Bruno enforcer who became *capo*, or captain, under Scarfo. Currently serving a 45-year sentence on federal racketeering charges.

SALVATORE MERLINO: Scarfo underboss. Currently serving a 45-year sentence on racketeering charges.

LAWRENCE MERLINO: Salvatore's brother. Became a cooperating witness after convictions on racketeering and murder charges. Now in the protective custody wing of a federal prison.

NICHOLAS "NICKY CROW" CARAMANDI: In 1986 he became one of the first "made" members of the Philadelphia Mob to turn witness for the state by testifying against Scarfo and dozens of others. A series of trials based in part on his testimony brought down the Scarfo organization.

JOSEPH "SKINNY JOEY" MERLINO: Son of Salvatore Merlino and leader of a young, renegade faction of the Mob that is bucking Stanfa's rule. Survived an August 5, 1993, street-corner ambush.

JOSEPH "JOEY CHANG" CIANCAGLINI JR.: Son of Scarfo crime family *capo* Joe "Chang" Ciancaglini. Named underboss by Stanfa. Wounded in a March 2, 1993, ambush at a South Philadelphia luncheonette he operated.

MICHAEL "MIKE CHANG" CIANCAGLINI: Younger brother of Joey Chang. Aligned with Joey Merlino against Stanfa. Killed in an August 5, 1993, street-corner ambush.

JOSEPH STANFA: Son of Mob boss. Wounded in an August 31, 1993, highway ambush.

GAETON LUCIBELLO: A member of the Merlino faction, targeted for death by Stanfa.

SERGIO BATTAGLI: Stanfa loyalist recorded on secret tapes discussing the right way to pop a bullet into an enemy's head.

FRANK BALDINO: Merlino associate killed in the parking lot of a South Philadelphia diner on September 17, 1993.

Teena Brandon

Death of a Deceiver

by ERIC KONIGSBERG
January 1995

Teena Renee Brandon's mystery was over the moment her body was discovered, facedown on a bed in a farmhouse in Humboldt, Nebraska. It was early in the morning on December 31, 1993, and lying dead with Teena were two others. Each of the three had been shot twice, execution style, with a .38 revolver. "Through and through" is how the coroner would classify their wounds, meaning the bullets had entered the victims' heads from one side and exited the other. In addition, Teena had been stabbed in the liver and her skull had been crushed. She was 21.

Word of the triple murder raced through Humboldt, a town of 1,003. At a bar called Big Mike's, townspeople gathered around a police scanner awaiting identification of the victims, and by dark the news came: The first was a local woman, and the second a young man, a friend of hers. The name of the third fatality, the one whose skull had been crushed, was Teena Brandon.

"Brandon?" The locals were perplexed. The barmaid remembered a boy named Brandon living in that house. He had shown up in Humboldt a month or two before and hung out with kids from nearby Falls City. He told people he was from Lincoln, about two hours away. He was small, 5'5" or 5'6", but good-looking: blue eyes, a wide mouth, heavy eyebrows, and sandy hair combed into a halfhearted ducktail. He wore Western shirts and looked so young they had carded him at the bar. "Brandon Ray Tenna," his ID had read. "Date of Birth: 12/10/72. Sex: M."

The folks at Big Mike's pieced together bits of news and speculation, and came to a bizarre conclusion: Brandon Tenna, the boy who had

197

waltzed into Richardson County and charmed a local girl off her feet, was dead; and Brandon Tenna had actually been a woman.

Teena Brandon was killed, prosecutors now maintain, by John Lotter and Tom Nissen, jealous friends of a girl she'd been dating. She was killed, essentially, because she was too successful in passing herself off as a man. She underestimated her own attractiveness and the envy it wrought.

• • •

Teena Renee Brandon was born to 16-year-old JoAnn Brandon on December 10, 1972, in Lincoln, Nebraska. Teena's father, Patrick Brandon, was a housepainter who had died in a car accident eight months before her birth. She was named for her father's German shepherd, Tina Marie.

JoAnn is a Lincoln native, doe-eyed and slender, who at one time modeled children's clothing for department store ads. She raised Teena and her sister, Tammy, who was three years older, in a trailer park in northeast Lincoln. She was remarried once, from the time Teena was two until she was seven, to a man Teena didn't like. After that, JoAnn said, "it was Tammy and Teena and me against the world. We were the three musketeers."

Where Tammy was prissy and popular, Teena was awkward and impish, tattling to her mom when she caught Tammy kissing a boy. Even though JoAnn didn't have much money, she aspired to do good by her daughters and tried to teach them middle-class values. She bought them nice clothes and sent them to Catholic schools—St. Mary's Elementary and Pius X High School.

But Teena wasn't much of a student, and Pius's strict environment, coinciding as it did with her adolescence, made her feel out of place. She argued with her religion teacher, Father Fucinaro, whenever he lectured on the virtues of abstinence, and she rebelled against the dress code by wearing pants and a tie. She kept her hair short and told people she was allergic to makeup. She was into weight lifting. Teena's friends say she had crushes on a few boys, but she never dated. Her only close friend at Pius was a girl named Sara Gapp, whom Teena cared for so much that when Sara became pregnant, Teena offered to get legal permission to raise the baby with her.

During the fall of 1990, her senior year, an Army recruiter visited Pius. Operation Desert Shield was under way and Teena thought she had found her calling. She planned to enlist and began parading around her mother's trailer in fatigues, but couldn't pass the written entrance exam.

"She was real upset," JoAnn said. "And other things in her life started happening. She started to change."

• • •

One day in late December 1990, not long after her 18th birthday, Teena was in her mother's living room, lying on the couch, watching TV. When the phone rang, she answered it. A girl had dialed the wrong number. Five minutes later, the phone rang again.

"Hello?" Teena said. It was another girl this time.

"My friend just told me a really hot-sounding guy lives here," the girl said.

"Oh," Teena deadpanned. She knew she had a husky voice.

"What's your name?" the girl said.

Teena drew a breath. "Billy Brinson," she answered, using her uncle's first name and a variation of her own surname. The two girls flirted on the phone for a few minutes. The caller was 13. They made plans to go roller-skating on New Year's Eve.

• • •

Teena arrived at Holiday Skate World accompanied by Sara Gapp and a few other friends. She had explained the date to them as a gag, a dare for herself. "We just wanted to see if she could get away with it," Sara said later.

Teena wore her usual clothes—Dockers, tennis shoes and a button-down shirt—and wrapped her breasts with an Ace bandage. She hooked up with the 13-year-old girl and made it through the evening undiscovered. She even took her hand for a couples' skate, grinning like a loon each time she passed Sara, who watched anxiously from rinkside.

Within a couple of weeks, Teena hit it off with one of the girl's friends, Heather Kuhfahl. Heather was a petite, blonde ninth-grader in the Lincoln public school. She was 14. The two of them began to date, Teena still posing as Billy. Heather was Teena's first kiss.

Thus began the double life of Teena Brandon: uneasy tomboy by day, cool lady-killer by night. As a girl, Teena had never received the kind of fawning she so comfortably unloaded on Heather. And it was reciprocated. Teena's former life seemed disconnected and thin. She became a glutton for attention and got into trouble trying to impress Heather.

DEATH OF A DECEIVER

She took money from her mother's bank account and bought Heather clothes and a stereo. Together they hustled beer with Heather's mother's credit card and cruised O Street until four in the morning.

School had never been much fun; now it was a big joke. Here was the new Teena Brandon: class clown and queen of the senior pranks—locking pigeons in a classmate's car and removing the toilet seats from the girls' washroom. But she got carried away and stole another girl's leather jacket, and she was failing classes. Just a couple weeks before graduation, Teena was expelled from Pius.

With school out of her life, the evolution of her male persona lurched forward. Teena started shaving her face, stuffing socks down the front of her pants and using the men's room in public. She went through her mother's photo albums and tore up all the pictures of herself wearing dresses. She was absolutely certain that this was what she was meant to be. A boy.

But how convinced was Heather? At one point early in their relationship, she had seen Teena's driver's license and read the name, Teena Brandon.

"It's an Irish name, *Tenna*," Teena offered. "Most people just call me Brandon. I was only kidding when I said my name was Billy." Somehow, that was enough for Heather. "He was always joking around about things, making up stories," Heather recalled. Like almost everyone who knew Teena as a boy, she still refers to her with masculine pronouns. "I just figured it was like him to make up a name on the phone when he told my friend his name was Billy."

Heather was the type of person Teena would stray little from as she traveled on her path of seduction. She was younger than Teena, sexually inexperienced, naive and poor. And like Teena, Heather had been raised by her mother, who worked several jobs and was rarely at home. She was needy and had never had a boyfriend. In Teena's estimation Heather was a girl she could outsmart and win over, largely because Heather's longings were not that different from her own. "I depended on having Brandon in my life so much," Heather said. "No matter what sex he turned out to be, I wanted him."

• • •

The two had been dating only a few months when Teena moved in with Heather and her mother on Holdrege Street. Teena had a number of jobs—pumping gas, working at convenience stores—but couldn't keep one for more than a few months. Once, she was fired when a manager

200

caught her making out with Heather behind the cash register.

JoAnn Brandon blamed Heather for what was happening to Teena—the dressing as a boy, the expulsion, the firings, the stealing. By now, JoAnn and her other daughter had started to follow Teena. They had seen her carrying on with Heather, but they insisted it was some kind of experimental phase that Teena could, with guidance, snap out of. "All I want is to have my daughter back," JoAnn cried to Teena's friend Sara. "Do something." So Sara paid Heather a visit. When she arrived, Heather was on the phone.

"Tenna is really Teena," Sara said to Heather. "She's a girl. Look." She produced Teena's birth certificate.

Heather feigned surprise. "Oh, really?" she said distantly and went back to the telephone.

But if Heather already had some idea, her mother somehow hadn't. The next day, after Sara stopped by the bowling alley where Heather's mother worked and told her Heather was dating a girl, Mrs. Kuhfahl made Teena move out and insisted she leave Heather alone.

• • •

In January 1992, Sara Gapp, at the behest of JoAnn Brandon, tricked Teena into a car, telling her they were on their way to Hardee's. Instead, Teena was taken to Lincoln General Hospital, where the Brandons were waiting. After a consultation, a psychiatrist informed Teena that she was having a sexual identity crisis—as if she hadn't known—and dispatched her to the Lancaster County crisis center. She was released three days later, after doctors decided she wasn't a suicide threat.

JoAnn and Tammy persuaded Teena to attend the counseling sessions the doctors required, and sometimes they accompanied her. At first Teena refused to participate, sitting in her chair expressionless and cracking jokes. She was too embarrassed to discuss her sexuality with her family in the room.

JoAnn refused to give up. "I asked her point-blank, 'Hey, we can work through this. Are you a lesbian?'"

"That's disgusting," Teena replied. She had some gay male friends in Lincoln but refused to accompany them to parties where there would be lots of homosexuals. "I can't be with a woman that way. I love them the way a man does. It's like I'm really a man trapped inside this body."

Teena insisted she hadn't been physically involved with Heather. She leaned forward, elbow on table, hand to chin. "I'm going to be a virgin until the day I die," she announced.

They talked some more before Teena got to the subject she'd been blocking out for 10 years. "Mom, I was raped," Teena said, choking on her tears. It had happened when she was a little girl, by a male relative who had also sexually abused Tammy. All three Brandons sobbed. Teena and her sister had never discussed it. Their mother was mortified by the revelation.

From that point on, it was virtually impossible to get Teena to talk to her psychiatrists. She preferred not to dredge up any more unhappy or complicated feelings, and no resolution was made about her identity or future. "They called her a compulsive liar," JoAnn recalled. "She stopped attending the sessions after two weeks. They said she didn't need any long-term care and let her go."

"After that," Tammy said, "we didn't know anything."

• • •

Transsexuality, a predisposition to identify physically with the opposite sex, is a largely uncharted phenomenon, though it is not uncommon. Roughly one in 50,000 people is diagnosed as transsexual, and recent reports indicate that it is almost as likely among women as it is among men. Although sex-change surgery has been performed in America and Europe since the Fifties, many people who consider themselves to be transsexual have chosen to live as homosexuals, and sometimes transvestites, and to hold on to the bodies they were born with.

Some people consider transsexuality to be nothing more than repressed homosexuality. Indeed, some gay men and lesbians say that when they first became aware of their sexuality, they felt trapped, held captive in a body of the wrong sex. Some were also revolted by homosexuality, much like Teena. It is difficult to know whether Teena was a transsexual or a young woman struggling to come to terms with being a lesbian in an unyielding environment—brought up Catholic in a conservative town, with a grandmother who once called her and a gay cousin "faggots."

• • •

Enjoying a popularity she had never known as a woman, the male Teena Brandon lived a peripatetic life. From the time that Teena met Heather to the end of 1993, Teena changed residences at least 19 times, moving in with newfound friends or, when she had to, bunking with family. "If

202

he could stay somewhere one night, then turn it into two or a week, he was happy," said one friend.

Constantly running from anything that grounded her to her old life, Teena's behavior grew increasingly troublesome. She continued to steal from people whenever she could. While living with Sara Gapp, she ran up an $895 phone bill and stole Gapp's automatic teller machine card. Teena forged checks from the account of her grandmother, who was angry enough to press charges. Her grandmother wasn't the only one to report her. From March 1991 to the end of 1993, Teena was charged with 18 crimes, mostly for forgery or failure to appear in court. She served several short jail terms. Most of the time, Teena stole only to buy her girlfriends gifts. If she made them happy enough, she figured, they wouldn't leave her.

During those three years, there were perhaps a dozen girls who claimed Billy Brinson, Brandon Tenna, Tenna Brandon, Brandon Teena or Brandon Yale as their beau. "Most of them were high school age and would go out with him for, like, a week, until they found out," said 18-year-old Daphne Gugat, who dated Teena in the fall of 1993. "But even after that, he would totally convince you that he was a guy." In fact, there were a few girls who were easily convinced and stayed with Teena for months.

With only 200,000 people, Lincoln didn't allow Teena to run far from her past. Often, when she had found a new circle of friends, an old acquaintance (or even a jealous former girlfriend) would arrive on the scene and blurt out that she was a woman. Other times, she would bump into a former schoolmate who would greet her as Teena.

Teena usually extricated herself from the confusion by telling people she was a hermaphrodite. "It means I was born with both sexes, but deep down inside I am a man," she would say. She had learned the term in biology class, but it didn't serve her that well. Most girls, even if they believed her, were scared away by its sheer freakishness. Time and again, a paramour would profess never to have suspected anything abnormal about Teena; one even said she saw Teena urinate standing up, and two girls, at the same time, claimed to be pregnant with Teena's baby.

In any case, Teena didn't seem to have trouble finding new people to con, new women to woo—women who desperately wanted to be charmed by a man who understood their needs. Her relationships were with girls whose ideal of a man had never been realized until they met Teena, girls with mostly troubled relationships with the men in their lives. Teena was their savior, attentive and affectionate. She was less awkward at 19 or 20 than most of the 16-year-old boys who were her competition. She had charisma. She wrote her girlfriends silly poetry, did their laundry and held their hands in public.

• • •

But how did Teena satisfy their sexual needs? That was the trickiest part of the routine, requiring ingenuity on her end and perhaps some denial from her partners, most of whom were virgins. And there was the realistic plastic penis that she attached to herself.

Teena liked to begin sexual encounters with extended foreplay—lots of kissing and ear-nibbling, undressing her partners, sucking on their breasts. But she never allowed anyone to undress her. With all but a few girls, she kept her undershirt and boxer shorts on.

"One time I tried to go down on him," said one of the girls, "and he stopped me. I thought, Great, a guy who doesn't like it even more than I." But when Teena returned the attempted favor, it was glorious. For one of the first times in her life, the girl had an orgasm.

"After that, I don't think there was a time with him when I didn't come," the girl said. "Orally, going all the way, even dry humping." Teena's sex life depended on a population of girls who considered sex nothing more than something they did for their boyfriends. With Teena they began to understand what all the fuss was about.

"Brandon was my great awakening: Sex could be fun and natural," said a girl who had slept with only one boy before meeting Teena. It had been dull with her ex-boyfriend. She would spend a night at his parents' house every weekend and wait for it to be over, staring at the ceiling and looking at the *Star Wars* wallpaper, the *Star Wars* curtains.

Teena didn't rush girls into intercourse but instead asked them to let her know when they were ready. She told them she was a virgin. Most of the girls, meanwhile, were too inexperienced to realize that Teena was using a dildo and too shy to look at or touch what they thought was their boyfriend's penis. "I noticed that he could go a long time, and that he usually pulled out as soon as I had mine," recalled another girl-friend, one of the few girls to actually see Teena naked or discover the dildo. "But it wasn't until after he said he'd had a sex-change operation that I noticed it stayed hard afterward. When I asked him about it, he said it was because the only options after the surgery were for it to be hard all the time or for him to use a pump.

"Still, it was funny," she said. "Sometimes I'd feel through his pants and it'd be small, and sometimes it felt like he had a lot more."

• • •

There were times when Teena hung around a cousin's dorm at the Lincoln School of Commerce looking for something to do. One day, in March 1993, Teena met Gina Bartu, a freckled 19-year-old secretarial student. It took Teena two days to ask her out, and in another three days, each had told the other "I love you." Soon, Teena had Gina's name tattooed on her arm. "You better not break up with me or I'm gonna have to date only Ginas," Teena would say.

What was it about Gina? Sometimes Teena sat up late at night with her buddies from work and talked about it: Heather had a killer body and knew how to have a good time. Some of the other girls were pretty cool if you told them what they wanted to hear. But Gina—well, she was shy and kind and had her act together. She was a farm girl from Crete, Nebraska, a college student, and she had a job. The kind of girl you could marry, Teena said.

And so one afternoon in late May, Teena sat on Gina's bed and waited for her to make her way back from class.

"I don't know how to say this," Teena said. "But will you marry me?"

"Yeah," Gina replied.

"He didn't have a ring yet," Gina recalled, "but he started planning our engagement party right away. He was a hopeless romantic."

The party was the biggest blowout Teena could manage. She rented three rooms at the Harvester Motel and wore a tuxedo. Only about 30 guests came, since Teena couldn't invite any friends from her past. But a few ex-girlfriends and a guy Gina had dated showed up. Teena ordered cigarettes and film from the front desk and snapped pictures all night. Pizzas were delivered, and a hot tub was filled with ice and beer.

Midway into the evening, Teena pulled Gina aside. "See, Gina, has anybody ever done anything like this for you before?" she said. She took Gina's hand and got down on bended knee: "Everybody, quiet." Teena delivered a formal proposal. "Brandon made a speech about how he was settling down," said Kendall Hawthorne, a friend Teena had met working at the state fair. "We all saw him as a ladies' man, but now he said it was time for him to stop looking. Gina was loving it."

They set May 28, 1994, one year from that night, as their wedding date.

• • •

DEATH OF A DECEIVER

The truth is, Gina had some reservations about Teena. Two of Teena's ex-girlfriends had told her Teena was a girl and had even shown her a yearbook photo. She confronted Teena immediately, and Teena, flustered, dug her hands into her armpits and explained: She had been raised as a girl until the eighth grade, she said. Then she had had an operation in Omaha.

Soon after, Gina noticed Teena's small breasts. Teena said they would "take a while to go away completely," and Gina remained credulous.

"Of course it bothered me, but I let it go," Gina said. "People believe what they want to when they're in love, you know? I mean, I just couldn't understand why a girl would trick you into that if she knew you liked the opposite sex."

Even more so than Heather, Gina clung to Teena, moving with her into a house shared by two gay men in their late 20s. Teena didn't have many belongings but always carried a faded photo of her father at the age of 18. "He loved to compare that picture to himself," Gina said. "They did look a lot alike."

• • •

Such pathos swelled in Teena's psyche, such fear of rejection, that she continued her life of petty crime. She forged checks to buy groceries rather than simply allow Gina to pay. When Teena was brought to court on one charge, Gina reluctantly posted the $345 bail. Driving Teena home, Gina was livid. She had seen the arrest summons. What was with this "Teena Renee" business?

Teena confessed that she hadn't yet had the operation that would make her a full-fledged male. But, she insisted, she planned to, and some steps were already under way.

"He told me how all his other girlfriends had treated him like crap when they found out," Gina said, "and it made me really angry. I started thinking, What does it matter what a person is like physically? He was a man to me, and I'd never been happier in my life. I told him to get the operation if that's what he wanted to do. I said I'd stay with him."

Next month the mastectomy, Teena promised. When a month went by, Gina inquired about it. Teena responded, "I don't have the money." When she eventually confessed that she couldn't go through with it, Gina protested.

"All you care about is what society thinks," Teena said. "You think I have to fit society's definition of a man."

"If you aren't going to do it," Gina said, "then this has to end. It would just be too hard to deal with."

In late August, Gina got her own place and asked for some time to think. Teena grew desperate, stealing Gina's Montgomery Ward credit card and using it to buy her a diamond ring. When Gina got the bill, she confronted Teena, who denied the theft. They fought all over the house, upstairs, downstairs, in the bedroom, in the kitchen. It was their only real fight.

"We're not getting married, Brandon!" Gina screamed. "What were you thinking?"

"I always told you I'd come through with the ring," Teena said and smiled weakly. The two girls erupted in laughter. But it was too late.

Teena felt she had come so close to succeeding with Gina. It was like high school, the Army, old girlfriends all over again: She had come this close to what she wanted. She was devastated and began calling Gina and showing up at her apartment at all hours. Sometimes she would drop letters through Gina's mail slot. "I often think of what it would have been like if I had told you the truth from the beginning," one letter said. "Would you have stayed with me or gone away? I wanted to let you know how good I could treat you before you found out."

Gina didn't know what to do. She had been so enamored, but did this relationship make her a lesbian? She never answered Teena's letters.

• • •

It was in November, two months after Gina ended their relationship, that Teena fled Lincoln. She owed money to too many people, some of whom had threatened her physically. She didn't tell her family or Gina when she took up residence two hours away in tiny Humboldt, crashing at a farmhouse shared by two girls, friends of someone she had dated in Lincoln. The house rented for $100 a month and stood on a modest hill, shedding gray paint and fronted by a wooden step porch.

Teena didn't stay single for long. In December she began dating Lana Tisdel, whom she had met at a party in Falls City. Lana was a 19-year-old strawberry blonde who was as easily won as Teena's previous conquests. "Other guys in this town don't give a girl flowers," Lana told her friends.

For more than a week the two were inseparable, sharing a couch at Lana's house every night, watching the country music television channel all day. Lana's mother was impressed by Teena's politeness, and

DEATH OF A DECEIVER

Lana's friends—including her former boyfriend John Lotter, 22, and Tom Nissen, 21, whom she'd also dated—got on well with Teena also.

Even within economically anemic Falls City, families such as the Tisdels, Lotters and Nissens were outcasts. Lana's mother, Linda Gutierres, supported a family of six with a $346 disability check she received monthly as the result of a stabbing by a former husband. John Lotter lived with his mother, an older brother, two sisters and three of his sister's children in a small three-bedroom house. To their peers in Falls City, they were marginalized, unpopular dropouts and derelicts.

The pokey, backwoods character of Falls City blinded Teena to the narrow-mindedness she was up against there. For all their lack of sophistication, those in Teena's coterie in Lincoln were permissive people, and quite a number had had gay friends, black friends and other associations considered vagaries in parts of rural America. But Teena's friends in Falls City were a different sort entirely.

The beginning of the end came December 15, when Teena arrived at the courthouse for a hearing on a charge of alcohol possession. She handed over her fake ID, but when it was discovered that she had forged a friend's check, Teena was jailed—in a women's cell.

During Teena's eight days in jail, much of the town learned she was in a women's cell. Lana visited her several times and, naturally, received the hermaphrodite story.

Seeing Teena locked up and crying, Lana was distraught. Like the girls before her, she was confused by the issue of Teena's gender. She still cared for Teena and wanted to post her bail.

"Don't you dare," her mother said. "And don't get any ideas about letting him in this house ever again."

On December 23, Lana took a signed, blank check her father had given her for a perm and cashed it in order to post Teena's $250 bail. Because Lana was under 21, she had to find somebody else to tender the money. She asked Tom Nissen, a gaunt fellow with a sparse mustache and light brown hair. "The agreement," Nissen told me from jail, "was that Brandon was going to show her what sex he was."

Indeed, Lana's friends and family were troubled by the way Lana was still drawn to Teena. Lana's mother suggested committing her daughter to a psychiatric unit for a month "so she could drill it into her own mind that Brandon is actually a she."

• • •

Although they were roughly the same age, John Lotter and Tom Nissen had met only recently, through Lana. Tom had lived with his father in Mississippi, but at 13 moved in with his mother, Sharon, near Falls City. He had run away from home several times, and his mother sent him to Blue Valley Mental Health Center. "I said, 'This child's not right. I don't know what it is.' If he'd done something wrong, or if you were mad at him, he'd just stand and let you scream at him.

"He was never violent, except to himself. He shot himself in the shoulder and blamed someone else. If you saw him with all his clothes off, you'd think he'd been in an accident—there are scars all over his body. Three years ago he cut his arm so bad with a butcher knife they had to take him to a plastic surgeon. It was like he'd tried to saw it off."

When he was 19, Tom married Kandi Gibson, a girl he had known in high school. In 1991 Kandi gave birth to a daughter they named Tiffany. The next year Tom went to jail for arson. He had burned down a neighboring house and garage.

Tom spent nine months in jail in Lincoln. He wrote often to his mother, "He did all right when he was there," she said. "He got his GED, he was working with computers, he got counseling. He said he was sorry." Tom went back to Falls City in May 1993. Although Kandi was pregnant with their second child, Tom soon started dating Missy Gutierres, Lana Tisdel's 18-year-old aunt. Then he got involved with Lana. It was confusing, but Tom seemed happy with the arrangement.

More of a follower, Tom yearned for the acceptance of a rake like John Lotter. John was boorish, with beady eyes and a wild mane of dark hair. His kindergarten teacher remembers him biting children and calling them motherfuckers.

John was away from his family for most of his youth—in foster homes, Boys Town, even jail (for stealing a car). But in 1990, at 18, he returned to Falls City and dated Lana on and off.

Mostly it was John's temper that got him into trouble. He once ran seven guys out of Kwik Shop all by himself when they made fun of Lana's lisp. It had been years since he and Lana had gone out, but loyalty was his subscribed virtue. He told friends he would still do anything for her.

• • •

On Christmas Eve Teena was supposed to meet Lana at a party at Nissen's house, a white stucco box in the middle of Falls City. Although Teena had been out of jail for a day, Lotter and Nissen still didn't think Lana knew that Teena was a woman. Lana said they were intent on proving it to her. Nissen, in a phone interview that took place from jail nine months later, maintained that Lana should have known what was to come. Lana denied having any knowledge of what Tom and John were going to do.

At the party, Lana's eyes flitted around the living room. There were only about a dozen people there, some whiskey, some beer, a Christmas tree listing in the corner. Where the hell was Brandon? She wandered toward the bathroom and found Teena, Tom and John standing next to the tub, poised for a showdown.

"Has he shown you?" John asked Lana.

"Shown me what?" She pretended not to know.

"What's in his pants," John said.

"I don't care what's in his pants!" Lana said. "It doesn't matter to me what's in his pants!"

In a single motion, Tom grabbed Teena and pulled her arms behind her back. John tugged her jeans and boxer shorts down around her ankles. Lana covered her eyes.

"Look at him," John said between gritted teeth. "Look, or Tom is gonna keep holding him like that." Lana turned her head and peeked between her fingers.

John and Tom then marched Teena out of the bathroom and held her in front of the guests.

"Yep, it's a girl," Lotter announced.

"Ain't got no thing hanging down there," Nissen said.

Soon everyone, including John and Tom, filed out of the house and went to a bar called the Oasis. Lana walked with Teena to the nearby Stephenson Hotel, where Teena telephoned her roommates in Humboldt to come get her. John and Tom showed up at the hotel and told Lana that they had run into her mother, who wanted her home. Lana told Teena she'd be back in a second. "Don't leave me" was the last thing Teena said to Lana that night. John and Tom took Teena back to Tom's house. It was now Christmas Day.

• • •

According to sources in the Richardson County Attorney's office, the following events then took place: With John Lotter looking on, Tom Nissen beat Teena. He struck her in the face, kicked her in the ribs and stomped on her back. The chief of the Falls City police, Norman Hemmerling, would later testify that Teena had a welt shaped like the sole of a boot on her back. According to Lana's friends, the two boys

210

had told Teena that they were angry that she ripped off their friends. Lana had used her father's money to bail Teena out of jail, they said, and now Lana was in big trouble with her parents.

John and Tom forced Teena into Lotter's Ford Crown Victoria. "All three of us were in the front seat," Nissen recalled. "Brandon was between me and John. We started riding around with her, and I think John said he was going to fuck her. Then Brandon said, 'Come on, guys, it doesn't have to be like this.' The car got stuck in a ditch off the road, and I just had on my windbreaker. And when Brandon got out to help me jack up the car, he kept offering me his jacket. I said, 'No. You better keep it on.' Then me and Brandon went across the road to this building that must have been an old schoolhouse or something, looking for bricks to put under the tires to get some traction. I came back and told John I could see a yard with a light on, and I went to get this farmer to tow us out."

John Lotter concealed Teena in the backseat while Nissen and the farmer towed the car back onto the road. Nissen drove further, finally turning off behind a Hormel pig-buying station. After he cut the engine, the boys attacked Teena in the backseat of the car. She put up a struggle. "You can either have the shit beat out of you or not," Nissen told her, "and then have it happen anyway."

Then Lotter and Nissen raped Teena.

"I went first," Nissen said. "Then John. I think it just sort of happened. I'd never done it before. I don't know that it wasn't more of an ego thing. I felt like I'd been fucked. Me and Brandon had a long conversation that evening, in the bathroom. I told him, 'I don't have anything against you. If you had just been straight with me, I would have understood.' Brandon started to feed me another line how he was going to have a sex operation. John was really upset with the whole situation. Maybe he still wished he was going out with Lana."

Perhaps, for John Letter and Tom Nissen, it was the only retribution they could exact for the embarrassment they felt in being duped by an ex-girlfriend's new boyfriend. After all, it was just before Lana met Teena that she had been sleeping with Tom. And John dated Lana for years.

At six A.M., Teena was at the Tisdels' door, barefoot and with no coat, out of breath and bleeding from her mouth. Her jeans were muddied up to the knees. Her hands were dirty. And her undershirt—she always wore an undershirt—was missing. An ambulance was called to take Teena to the hospital.

• • •

DEATH OF A DECEIVER

The phone rang in Tammy Brandon's apartment. She hoped it would be Teena. It was Christmas Day and she hadn't seen or heard from her sister in weeks. She didn't even know where to find her these days.

"Tammy?" Teena seemed to be hyperventilating.

"Calm down," Tammy said. "Where are you?"

Teena told Tammy about her exodus to Humboldt, about Lana, about being raped. In a way, it taxed her heart more to talk about it than to endure it.

"Do you hate me for what I am?" Teena asked. She was so ashamed, her reputation now shot to hell in the worst way she could imagine. She didn't know if she could tell her mother.

"Let me call Mom first," Tammy said.

"Tammy?"

"Yeah?"

"Well, I didn't cry the whole time. I wasn't going to give them the satisfaction."

• • •

Charles Laux, Richardson County's sheriff, came on the case dogged by problems of his own. Laux was being investigated by the Nebraska attorney general for selling used cars without a dealer's license. A city clerk says the town had temporarily withheld two of his paychecks for inadequate service.

According to the Brandons, Laux was not much help to Teena. When he questioned Teena on the afternoon of Christmas Day, Laux reportedly asked her, "Why do you prefer females?" and "Why did you take your pants down for those boys?"

Although a report from the Falls City hospital confirmed that Teena had been raped, Laux said he found inconsistencies in her statement: Initially, she claimed to have been raped once, then said twice. And she said both John and Tom had beaten her, but then said it was just Tom. Deputy Sheriff Tom Olberding, a friend of Lotter's, saw Teena that day, too. "There was no doubt in my mind it happened," he would say the following week, "but you have to get statements from the other side. You just can't go running around arresting people."

So Olberding and Laux didn't bring John and Tom in for questioning until three days later, on December 28. The two men denied raping Teena. Tom admitted to Olberding that he had heard Teena say "Don't hurt me" when John got in the backseat of the car with her, and he conceded that "clothing was removed," according to Olberding's sworn statement. Still, no arrests were made.

• • •

JoAnn Brandon felt helpless when she heard about Teena's rape, just as she had when she learned that Teena had been molested as a child. But she also felt some relief just to hear from Teena and know that her daughter would still come to her in a time of crisis. All that week Teena called home. She had a few things in Falls City to straighten out before she could come home—the alcohol and the forgery charges—and had a court hearing on the 31st. In the meantime, Teena said, she could be reached at the farmhouse in Humboldt.

Tammy phoned the State Patrol and, a few times, called Sheriff Laux, asking why no arrests had been made. Teena wasn't safe with those boys at large, Tammy pleaded. They had told Teena they were going to silence her permanently if she talked about the rape.

Back in Falls City, Lana Tisdel's sister had fought with her boyfriend, Phillip DeVine, who was visiting from out of town. Teena had seen Phillip in Falls City on Thursday, the 30th, and suggested that he stay in the farmhouse with her and one of her roommates, Lisa Lambert, whom Phillip also knew. It would be the three of them that night, plus Lisa's nine-month-old baby, Tanner.

By Thursday, Sheriff Laux's investigators decided that they had enough information on the rape case. They put reports calling for Nissen's and Lotter's arrests on the desk of County Attorney Douglas Merz. Merz said he was in court that afternoon and that the arrests would have to wait a day.

• • •

Sometime before one A.M. on Friday, John Letter had shown up at the house of his friend Eddie Bennett. Eddie was sitting in the living room. John went inside and stayed for less than 10 minutes. He knew Eddie kept a .38 revolver in his sock drawer. On New Year's Day, Eddie would report the gun missing.

Around one A.M., John and Tom Nissen arrived at Lana Tisdel's house, staggering and slurring their words. John was wearing gloves, which he didn't normally do. Tom asked Lana's mother where Teena was. "I think she's out in Humboldt," came the reply.

DEATH OF A DECEIVER

"I'm going to put a knife in my hand and kill somebody," he said to Lana's sister. Then he looked at Lana and added, "And you're next." Lana would later say that she didn't think Lotter was serious. It didn't occur to her to call the farmhouse in Humboldt and warn Teena, or to phone the cops.

Lotter and Nissen drove to Humboldt. "Basically, we said 'Let's go scare the shit out of them,'" Nissen said, describing the murders. "From the way events took place, I would say John probably had a plan. There wasn't much conversation." Nissen said the murders took him by surprise, that he and John had not discussed them beforehand. "This is the way it went, okay? John kicked in the door and we entered the residence. I found a light in the living room and turned it on. We entered Lisa Lambert's bedroom. Lisa had picked up the phone and was trying to call someone. John took the phone out of her hand and hung it up.

"There was a waterbed in Lisa's bedroom. Brandon was on the floor at the end of the bed, covered by a blanket, hiding. I pulled Brandon off the floor and sat on the edge of the bed. Lisa said to me, 'Tom, don't let him hurt me,' because John had the gun. I was kind of surprised when she said my name. I'd never met her but she knew me, because she had seen me around, I guess.

"I don't recall even a whimper from Brandon. Brandon was shot then. Both times. I don't know how to put it in words, to be honest with you," Nissen said. "If I had known that they were going to be killed, I think I would have run the car off the road into a telephone pole on the way there, killed us instead. But I couldn't have just turned back. It was kind of a matter of pride."

When asked about the knife that had punctured Teena's liver, and her skull being crushed, Nissen replied: "The report that her skull was crushed, that was caused by a bullet entering her head," he said. "The stabbing, well, that was me. It just kind of happened all so fast. I couldn't tell [if she was already dead]. I honestly don't know. Were you ever caught up in a moment before?"

Nissen said that after Lotter fired the gun, Lisa's baby began to cry. "So I picked him up, trying to get him to calm down. And she said, 'Tom, will you give me my baby?' And I said, 'Yeah,' and gave it to her. Then the gun was fired again. At Lisa. It hit her between the stomach and the chest, and she bled a lot. Then I remember I looked at John, and I didn't feel drunk anymore. I didn't say anything to him. Then Lisa said to me, 'Take my baby. Promise he won't be hurt.' So I put him back in the baby bed, gave him a bottle. Then Lisa was hit in the eye.

"So then I left the room and found Phillip in another bedroom, and

214

he started to holler, 'I didn't see nothing. I won't tell nobody. Can't we work this out?' At that point it was obvious no one was going to walk out of there. And we went into the living room and Phillip sat down on the couch. Then the gun was fired, twice.

"I thought about my kids and my wife. I do believe that if I had to do it over again, I would have stood in front of Lisa and taken her bullet. Brandon didn't deserve to die either. But I don't feel real guilty about killing her. I think she probably would have been killed by someone anyway. I've met people in prison who knew her in Lincoln. She had people out to get her. People said they knew people that wanted to do that to her too. But when I think about stabbing her, it pretty much does me in. With Phillip, I'd say I'm sorry he's gone. I feel pretty bad about just being involved in it. My biggest problem is with Lisa. She was a mother. I think about her little boy growing up. Someday he will find out that somebody murdered his mom. I'd imagine it could cause quite a bit of anger, growing up without a mom. Anger will make a person do terrible things. He could take some of the same paths I did. And I'd hate to see someone end up like me because of something I took part in."

The three bodies were discovered several hours later, on the morning of December 31, by Lisa's mother, who had worried when she heard that Lisa had not shown up for work. It was three years to the day since Teena's sweet, nervous date at Holiday Skate World, her very first appearance as a boy.

At five P.M. on December 31, local police pulled up to Tom Nissen's house and found Tom and John Lotter in the front room, playing cards. Eddie Bennett's gun and a folding knife were found the next day on the frozen Nemaha River just off Highway 73. Ballistics tests proved that the bullets used in the murders came from the gun.

Lotter was charged with murder, kidnapping and sexual assault and Nissen was charged with murder, kidnapping and aiding and abetting the assault. Both men are awaiting trials in the early months of 1995. If found guilty, both could face the death penalty. The two were being held at the same prison in Lincoln, though they were not allowed to see or speak with each other. Both have pleaded not guilty in pretrial hearings. (Nissen's words here mark the first public statement about the case from either man; Lotter did not respond to requests for an interview.) Nissen said his lawyer is encouraging him to testify against Lotter and cop a plea. After Lotter was moved to a higher-security prison for tearing the plumbing from his cell wall, locals began to speculate that he may try to get himself acquitted on some sort of insanity plea.

• • •

DEATH OF A DECEIVER

Although County Attorney Merz was initially slated to prosecute Lotter and Nissen, a judge has stepped in and appointed an independent prosecutor from Lincoln to help Merz. The Brandon family is in the process of filing a wrongful-death suit against Laux and Richardson County. They hope the state will determine whether Lana had any complicity in Teena's rape and murder. Even though Lana had helped her after the rape, Teena told her mother she was afraid of Lana. The Brandons were shocked to see Lana and her mother on *A Current Affair.* Michelle Lotter—John's sister and Lana's best friend—even accompanied the Tisdels on *The Maury Povich Show.* At the March arraignments for Lotter, the Tisdels talked and joked with him from the courtroom seats. For some time after his arrest, Tom Nissen continued his romantic involvement with Lana's aunt Missy.

• • •

Teena was buried in her favorite clothes—a black rugby shirt, matching cowboy hat and cowboy boots—beside her father, Patrick Brandon, at Lincoln Memorial Park Cemetery. At her funeral, mourners who knew her as Teena sat mostly on the left-hand side of the aisle. Those who knew her as a boy sat on the right. Today, dozens of girls who knew or dated Teena leave flowers and notes at her grave.

After the funeral, Teena's former fiancée, Gina Bartu, followed Lana Tisdel's car to a Long John Silver's. Something had been on her mind since she had learned of Teena's death.

"Did Brandon ever tell you about his friends in Lincoln?" Gina asked Lana.

"Not really," Lana said, "except for this one girl and how much that he still loved her."

Gina drove away feeling both better and worse than she ever had in her entire life. If only she had stayed with Teena, she thought, Teena wouldn't have gone to Humboldt and wouldn't have been raped and murdered.

Gina tried dating a man, but he balked when he learned about Teena. He said it made him "uncomfortable." Sometimes Gina fantasizes about moving away and starting over.

"I always hoped that if he'd work things out for himself," Gina said, "maybe someday we could still get married. The relationship was way too good to be true. But I don't regret one bit of it. He made me fall in love with him on the inside."

216

Toxic Terror

by **MIKE REYNOLDS**
November 1996

Americans grew nervous about terrorism this past summer. Someone set off a huge truck bomb that killed 19 U.S. servicemen. The
Bureau of Alcohol, Tobacco and Firearms busted members of a militia
unit, the Viper Team, that packed enough explosives and fire-power
to take down part of Phoenix. TWA flight 800 disintegrated off Long
Island, killing 230. Then a pipe bomb went off during the Olympics in
Atlanta, leaving one person dead.

If those events made you jittery, you had better stop reading. What
follows is a lot scarier.

The first rumblings could be detected back in the early Nineties.
Japanese authorities paid little attention to Shoko Asahara when he
began broadcasting charges that he and his Aum Supreme Truth cult
were the targets of a biochemical attack by a satanic New World Order
guided by Freemasons, Jews and the U.S. government. After two gas
attacks on unsuspecting Japanese citizens, the blind Asahara and his
apocalyptic cohorts were themselves facing charges of murder and biochemical terrorism.

The sarin attacks on the Tokyo subway and the village of Matsumoto
opened a new door for terrorists. "The attack in Japan has global implications," said Israeli terrorism specialist Yonah Alexander. "It's a quan-
tum leap to terrorism by mass destruction."

Several years ago the CIA warned that "clandestine production of
chemical and biological weapons for multiple-casualty attack raises
no greater technical obstacles than does the clandestine production
of chemical narcotics or heroin. One successful incident would significantly lower the threshold of restraint on their application by other
terrorists."

That nasty cat left the bag on the Tokyo subway in March 1995. The

217

attack showed that deployment of nerve gas, plague, anthrax or an infectious virus into a populated area is not beyond the capabilities of even a small band of enterprising terrorists.

Biochemical agents can be introduced easily into a building's ventilation system. Effective mass destruction can be accomplished with a payload aboard a single-engine Cessna such as the one that crashed into the White House a few years ago. If one crazed amateur can violate the airspace of what is supposed to be the most secure building in America and leave his plane piled up a few feet from the president's bedroom, a dedicated terrorist can manage a successful airborne biochemical attack on any major city in the country.

It is likely only curious coincidence that the Japanese cult was reportedly experimenting with and manufacturing biochemical-warfare agents at the same time several members of the Minnesota Patriots were concocting batches of a deadly material called ricin. Thomas Lavy, a former pipeline electrician who, on an April day in 1993, was driving a truck from Alaska to Canada, en route to Arkansas, was also implicated in carrying ricin. When Canadian customs agents searched the truck they found four guns, 20,000 rounds of ammunition, 13 pounds of black powder, neo-Nazi literature and three handy little books: *The Poisoner's Handbook, Silent Death by Uncle Fester* and *Get Even: The Complete Book of Dirty Tricks*. The first two books detail how to extract ricin from castor beans. Also present were a plastic bag filled with white powder, and about $80,000 in cash.

"Be careful," Lavy said to the inspectors. "Don't open that bag. That's ricin. It'll kill you."

A call was placed to U.S. Customs for a computer check on the man. It came back negative: no arrest warrants pending. The Canadians had Lavy fill out the proper forms for the cash and sent him on his way without the bag. They labeled it "unknown white powder" and put it on a storage shelf.

It remained there for weeks, 130 grams of a toxic natural poison. Had anyone been curious enough to open the bag, the inhalation of a single particle would have introduced its victim to exploding red blood cells—internal hemorrhaging.

Ricin is a toxin consisting of one or more proteins found in the common castor bean, *Ricinus communis*. Simple procedures can separate crude ricin from the bean into a variety of protein products that have extremely toxic effects. They all are deadly. Ricin is comparable in toxicity to the most potent synthetic nerve poisons. It is 6000 times more toxic than cyanide. There is no antidote.

Symptoms? If taken by mouth, after a delay of several days there are vomiting and high fever. Death can occur up to 14 days after the onset of symptoms. Injected or inhaled, the results are the same as if ingested orally, but the symptoms (fever, malaise, weakness) begin within several hours and death occurs in a few days. Death is from systemic failure, similar to shock.

Ricin is one of the deadliest plant toxins known. It is impossible to detect in an autopsy because it is a protein. It is odorless, tasteless, untreatable and fatal even in minute doses.

So what was Lavy doing with enough of the stuff to wipe out a large suburb?

Thomas Lavy took the answer with him when he hanged himself in an Arkansas jail cell two days before Christmas last year. He had been arrested on December 20 by FBI agents who had surrounded his little stone house in northern Arkansas. Inside Lavy's house agents found a tin Christmas fruit can filled with a pound and a half of castor beans and more recipe books for making ricin.

Lavy's attorney, Sam Heuer, said his client had planned to use his ricin for peaceful purposes, such as killing coyotes that threatened his chickens. "We have the right to have rat poison or coyote poison," said Heuer. "Just like we have the right to have a .357 Magnum."

Robert Govar, a federal prosecutor in Arkansas, countered that such claims "would be tantamount to saying you can use a thermonuclear device to protect your property from break-in or burglary."

When Lavy killed himself he was facing a charge of possession of a toxic substance with intent to use it as a weapon under the Biological Weapons Antiterrorism Act of 1989. Curiously, possession of ricin is not against the law. The law applies only if it can be proved that you plan to use it as a weapon. In Lavy's case it was clear that the amount of poison he had amassed was more than enough to kill every coyote in at least five states.

Were there others on Lavy's wavelength out there?

On the morning of May 20, 1992, Colette Baker walked into the Pope County, Minnesota sheriff's office with marital problems. She said her husband, Doug, had pointed a shotgun at her and threatened to kill her. While this was disconcerting enough, Colette said Doug had something else that might be of interest to the sheriff. She said Doug had some poison that could "kill a person on contact."

The next day Baker returned carrying a red coffee can and set it down on the sheriff's desk. She took out a baby-food jar, a fingernail-polish bottle, a pair of white rubber gloves and a scrap of paper with a handwritten note that read:

> Doug, Be extremely careful! After you mix the powder with the gel, the slightest contact will kill you! If you breath [sic] the powder or get it in your eyes, your [sic] a dead man. Dispose all instruments used. Always wear rubber gloves and then destroy them also. Good hunting!
>
> P.S. Destroy this note!

Colette added that her husband also had an arsenal of weapons and ammunition, plus a few explosives. Tellingly, Doug Baker's friend Richard Oelrich had run afoul of tax collectors and was being hit by the IRS for back taxes.

The banal assortment of household containers Colette brought into the sheriff's office was sent on to FBI chemist Thomas Lynch in Washington, D.C. Lynch identified the powder in the baby-food jar as *Ricinus communis*. Nearly a full gram of it. The green gel was dimethyl sulfoxide mixed with skin cream. The DMSO was a powerful enough solvent that any poison mixed with it would be absorbed through the skin and into the bloodstream in a matter of seconds.

Lynch was impressed by the Minnesotans' straightforward but clever delivery system. It wasn't so technically complex as what the Bulgarian secret police used on a defector 15 years earlier, but the results would have been the same: certain death. In 1978 a Soviet-sponsored assassin reached out with the tip of his umbrella outside a London Underground station and touched the thigh of Georgi Markov. The fitted tip injected a tiny perforated pellet filled with ricin beneath Markov's skin. At the autopsy all that was found were the remains of the pellet, which was slightly larger than a pinhead. The ricin, being protein-based, had been completely absorbed by Markov's system. The only trace detectable was in a microscopic fragment of the pellet.

If the biotoxin and DMSO cream were smeared on a door handle or steering wheel, the ricin would disappear by the time a medical examiner laid hands on the victim.

The FBI and U.S. Marshal's Office in Minnesota obtained court-ordered records from phones believed to be used by Doug Baker, Richard Oelrich and others. A federal cooperating witness said he heard who had the poison, who paid for the castor beans and who processed the beans into ricin. Eventually the feds discovered who was targeted. At the top of Oelrich's hit list was U.S. Deputy Marshal Bill Ott in Minneapolis. He also added "any other deputy marshal" who got involved in the seizure of Oelrich's property.

One year after Tom Lavy crossed the Canadian border with his quarter pound of ricin, some members of the Minnesota Patriots Council were arrested on charges of possessing ricin. Court papers claim that the men discussed blowing up a federal building, killing a law-enforcement officer and obtaining assault weapons.

In February 1995 Leroy Wheeler, 55, and Douglas Baker, 30, were convicted in federal court of possession of ricin. Dennis Henderson, 37, and Richard Oelrich, 55, were convicted of similar charges in October. These Minnesota rustics with their deadly ricin were the first terrorists convicted under the Biological Weapons Antiterrorism Act of 1989. Two months later Tom Lavy faced the same charge.

Christian patriot, militia and white supremacist publications routinely feature articles on biological and chemical warfare. Detailed instruction on the manufacture and deployment of poisons, nerve gas and other deadly chemical agents are available in such books as *Assorted Nasties* and *Silent Death*. These can be easily obtained on the Internet and through various mail-order houses that cater to the paramilitary movement.

Assorted Nasties, published by Desert Publication of El Dorado, Arkansas, is 138 pages of detailed instruction for the manufacture of 22 of the most highly toxic substances known. It also outlines several delivery systems for these agents such as poison bullets, toxic smoke grenades and contact poison applicators.

Silent Death, one of the books Lavy had in his truck, is the classic do-it-yourself guide to biochemical terrorism. From "Nerve Gas: The Poor Man's Atom Bomb" to "Time Delay Poisons" to the toxin of mass death, "Botulism," *Silent Death* covers all that any fanatic needs to know to kill a single enemy or wipe out several thousand people at a cost of around $1 per acre. "I'm sure you'll be surprised how easy to make and use these little gems are," concludes the introduction. "Read and enjoy."

The item that put biochemical weaponry into the hands of the Minnesota boys and Tom Lavy was a cheap little terrorist kit called *Silent Tool of Justice*. The book was advertised in hardcore Christian patriot publications as "including instructions for extracting the deadly poison ricin from castor beans. Agent of choice for CIA, KGB, etc. A single bean will kill an evildoer. Interesting suggestions for preparations and delivery, etc."

For $12, Maynard Campbell of Maynard's Avenging Angel Supply in Ashland, Oregon, would supply 10 castor beans and an instruction booklet detailing the manufacture of ricin.

Campbell, a white supremacist Christian, is now serving time in prison for threatening to kill federal officials. He was in an armed standoff with Oregon police for nearly 12 hours, and was sentenced to more than ten years in prison. Campbell had written *Kingdoms at War,* a guerrilla manual that has been distributed among patriot extremists. It advocates autonomous terrorist cells and assassinations as necessary tactics in a war against the federal government. "Corrupt judges," writes Campbell, "should simply be shot dead."

In May 1995 Aryan Nations member Larry Harris, 43, of Lancaster, Ohio, was arrested for illegally buying three vials of bubonic plague bacteria through the mail. Harris ordered the freeze-dried bacteria using an identification number from the food-testing laboratory where he worked. In a subsequent search of Harris' house, hand-grenade triggers, homemade explosive devices and detonating fuses were discovered.

On January 18, not far from where the feds turned up Harris' stash of explosives and plague, a shoot-out occurred between a suspect in a two-year stretch of bank robberies and FBI agents. Peter Langan exchanged gunfire with the authorities until he was slightly wounded and placed under arrest. Three days earlier Langan's suspected accomplice in 19 flamboyant bank heists, Richard Guthrie Jr., had surrendered to police after a brief car chase through Cincinnati.

The Midwestern Bank Bandits—as they were known—had taunted the FBI with letters to newspapers, bought getaway cars in the names of agents, dressed in a variety of disguises and spoke with each other in gibberish. Their trademark was to leave behind pipe bombs inside or in front of the banks they hit in Missouri, Kansas, Iowa, Wisconsin, Nebraska, Ohio and Kentucky. The robberies netted at least $200,000, none of which has been recovered.

By the time the FBI agents sorted through the evidence recovered from Langan and Guthrie's safe houses, vans and storage units, they found that the two were not routine bank robbers but a unit of an underground terrorist faction called the Aryan Republican Army.

Like Harris, Guthrie and Langan are members of Aryan Nations. The men had been in and out of Aryan Nations' headquarters in Hayden Lake, Idaho, since the Eighties. In July 1995 Langan and Guthrie took time from their fund-raising to attend Aryan Nations' annual world congress.

Hours after Guthrie was processed into the jail in Covington, Kentucky, he tapped an inmate who was being released and gave him a Pennsylvania phone number. Guthrie said to call the number and deliver this message: "The Ohio connection is dead." After police learned of the call, they found that the phone number belonged to a major Aryan Nations leader and Christian Identity minister.

The searches of storage units, safe houses and vehicles linked to Guthrie and Langan netted explosives, weapons, pipe bombs, phony U.S. Marshal IDs, and jackets and caps marked FBI—all of which are believed to have been used in the bank robberies. The feds also found a copy of *Mein Kampf* and stacks of white supremacist screeds from Aryan Nations.

But the most startling discovery was a recruitment video for the ARA hosted by a masked Peter Langan, who identifies himself as Commander Pedro. In the course of the two-hour production, stacks of money are piled up on a table before Commander Pedro, who enjoins white viewers to take action against the government. He holds up "essential reading" for potential ARA cadres, including neo-Nazi William Pierce's race-war fiction *The Turner Diaries* and Richard Kelly Hoskins' *Vigilantes of Christendom,* which includes a recap of the underground terrorist movement known as the Phineas Priesthood.

Included among those linked to the Phineas Priesthood are the assassin of Medgar Evers (Byron de la Beckwith) and Paul Hill, the killer of an abortion doctor and his escort. In Hoskins' book, he cites as Phineas heroes the two killers of Denver talk-show host Alan Berg.

Four years ago, two men were convicted of an Oklahoma bank robbery. One of the men told the *Tulsa Tribune* he had used the stolen money to support the Phineas Priesthood in Oklahoma before being captured after a gun battle with police.

This past year on April Fools' Day at 2:30 in the afternoon, ten weeks after law enforcement busted Guthrie and Langan, a custom van pulled up behind a suburban office of the Spokane, Washington, *Spokesman-Review.* The van's driver wore a ski mask and camouflage. A passenger, a younger man wearing a ski mask, hopped out of the van and dropped a foot-long pipe bomb at the newspaper's back door. The resulting detonation smashed into the building, showering the parking lot with shards of glass and steel.

As police and emergency units responded to the scene, two masked men were entering a Spokane Valley bank not far from the smoldering *Spokesman-Review* office. They pulled out their weapons and relieved the tellers of nearly $100,000. They then dropped another length of galvanized pipe to the lobby floor and ran before the bomb exploded. The resulting blast took out the front of the bank.

At the first bomb site, police found copies of the following computer printout scattered at the scene.

TOXIC TERROR

To: the leaders and rulers of nations and people; all kindreds, nations, peoples and tongues; the sheep of his flock, who hear his voice, his remnant, wherever you may be: Greetings.

Thus says Yahweh, Behold I will raise up against Babylon, and against them that dwell in the midst of them that rise up against me, a destroying wind. . . .

Three months later, in July, another bank robbery and a bombing of a Spokane Planned Parenthood clinic were linked by the FBI to groups with ties to Christian Identity—and to the Phineas Priesthood. FBI agents were struck by the similarity to the April Fools' Day bombing.

• • •

Get to know this.

It is the voice of America's jihad. Consider the foreword to Hoskins' *Vigilantes of Christendom*: "As the kamikaze is to the Japanese, as the Shiite is to Islam, as the Zionist is to the Jew, so the Phineas priest is to Christendom." On the Aryan Republican Army video its face is disguised. It appears wearing a begoggled, rubberized gas mask and a white biochemical-warfare protective suit. This eerie apparition is a homemade angel of the apocalypse bringing to mind words from the Phineas Priesthood's April declaration:

And after these things I saw another angel come down from heaven, having great power. And he cried mightily with a strong voice, saying Babylon the great is fallen, is fallen, and is become the habitation of devils, and the hold of every foul spirit, and a cage of every unclean and hateful bird. Shall her plagues come in one day, death and mourning, and famine, and she shall be utterly burned with fire.

A year ago, right after Thanksgiving, the following message appeared on an Internet newsgroup where paramilitary extremists, white supremacists, militiamen and would-be terrorists gather:

The smart boys who have hidden in the crowd will be walking around on the busy street looking harmless—while setting fires, planting bombs, creating sabotage, dispersing poisons.

There is a terrorist war going on in this country. It is not hypothetical and it is not symbolic. It is as obvious as more than two tons of explosives going off in Oklahoma City and as silent as a quarter pound of biotoxin riding on the seat of a rental truck. It is as real as the bombs exploding at abortion clinics and newspaper offices. Its grim clues can be found on recruitment videos and on Internet newsgroups. Do not be fooled by the ties to obscure religious sects or alien racist groups. The tools of terror have become ever more accessible and lethal.

There are vipers in the grass. And they are poised to strike.

Lawrence Schiller

Lawrence Schiller

the PLAYBOY INTERVIEW
February 1997

It was only days after O.J. Simpson's ill-fated Bronco run. Robert Kardashian, Simpson's close friend and confidant, was worried and confused—and positive that his house was being bugged. So he met at midnight with an old acquaintance in the noisiest place possible, a parking lot next to one of L.A.'s busiest freeways. Lawrence Schiller's discussing this most infamous murder case in the dark of night would surprise only those who don't know him. Like some real life Zelig or Forrest Gump, Schiller has a talent for popping up, inexplicably, in the middle of historic events. A photographer, filmmaker, author, interviewer and entrepreneur, Schiller has phenomenal instincts and even better luck. He was in Utah when killer Gary Gilmore was executed—but before Gilmore died, Schiller had been astute enough to tie up Gilmore's movie and book rights. He was in Texas when Jack Ruby shot Lee Harvey Oswald, and within hours he owned the rights to the photo of the murder. Schiller has worked his odd magic with Charles Manson, Marilyn Monroe, Richard Nixon and the family of Lenny Bruce.

What irks people about Schiller, besides his success, are his methods. He finagles and manipulates his way into major stories while those in the establishment media sit helplessly on the sidelines, immobilized by the weight of ethical considerations. Schiller's unerring nose for news leads him to a story and he lets nothing stand in his way. As a result he has been involved in some of the most compelling and unusual works of journalism, film and photography of the past three decades.

"The only real surprise about Schiller was that he took several months to surface in the Simpson affair," wrote *New Yorker* reporter Jeffrey Toobin in his Simpson book, *The Run of His Life*. Even Toobin didn't realize how quickly Schiller had managed to ingratiate himself into Simpson's camp. Immediately after the murders, Schiller, who knew both Simpson and

227

millionaire lawyer Kardashian casually, "had a hunch" that Simpson was hiding out with a mutual friend—Kardashian.

Soon Schiller had succeeded in meeting with Kardashian and Simpson's lawyers. It was no easy chore to win over the lawyers, but Schiller did. His first task was designed to help Simpson's image and get Simpson some cash. At a time when every reporter in the country was trying to gain access to Simpson in jail, Schiller visited him on 11 occasions. He arrived at the jail in different cars, always along different routes, so no one could discover what he was up to. Inside, he sat on one side of a glass wall, Simpson on the other, a tape recorder running, recording conversations that Schiller turned into *I Want to Tell You*, a book that sold well but was vilified by many critics. *I Want to Tell You* earned Simpson—who was in desperate need of cash to pay his legal expenses—$1.4 million (Schiller pocketed $170,000).

By then Schiller had become an unofficial member of the defense, helping to direct a PR campaign to aid Simpson both inside and outside of the courtroom. Schiller leaked stories to the press that were calculated to improve Simpson's image. He volunteered to edit the taped interviews of Detective Mark Fuhrman that were eventually played in the courtroom and so effectively undermined the prosecution's case. Schiller became so important to the defense that when one day he didn't get his usual seat in Judge Lance Ito's courtroom, he complained to Simpson lawyer Johnnie Cochran, who took it up with the judge. Schiller was immediately returned to his spot.

Schiller's tie to Simpson continued after the not-guilty verdict was delivered in October 1995. He was the only photographer to document (with his fiancée, Kathy Amerman) Simpson's acquittal party (after making a deal with Simpson and *The Star,* for which he earned about 20 percent of Simpson's $640,000 fee).

Schiller, meanwhile, was working on a project that was out of their control. Using his access to Simpson's lawyers and friends, he conducted hundreds of interviews about the case for his own book, *American Tragedy: The Uncensored Story.* When the book came out this past October, it shocked the Simpson camp and the country. Schiller had done the unbelievable for a Simpson insider—he had switched sides and written, with James Willwerth, a headline-making book that pointed the finger of guilt at his friend and onetime partner. The book contains revelations: that Simpson had tried to kill himself, that the defense lawyers were constantly at one another's throats, that Simpson failed a lie detector test soon after the killings and that the lawyers redecorated Simpson's home in preparation for a visit there by the jury, replacing a nude picture of Paula Barbieri with a photograph of Simpson and his mother as well as hanging up a Norman Rockwell print of a black girl walking to school accompanied by federal marshals.

Even more impressive, Schiller persuaded Kardashian to give his perspective: Kardashian served as the main source far Schiller's book (and was compensated for his effort). *American Tragedy,* for which Schiller received a $1.25 million advance, was an instant best-seller and was launched at a celebrity party hosted by Norman Mailer and Dominick Dunne. Attacked by Robert Shapiro, Cochran, Alan Dershowitz and others, it earned rave reviews in the *New York Times* and the *Los Angeles Times,* which called it the best-written and best-researched book on the Simpson case yet.

Schiller, 60, is a man with a confounding reputation. His demeanor and tactics make him seem like the perfect reporter for the *National Enquirer.* But his work has often been masterful. He earned accolades for the picture book *Minamata* that he produced with photographer W. Eugene Smith on the crippling effects of mercury pollution in Japan. He worked on a highly respected television miniseries, *Peter the Great,* and the Academy Award-winning *Man Who Skied Down Everest.* He collaborated on a series of books written by Norman Mailer. Yet he is loathed by some former sources, by colleagues and by many journalists. Toobin described Schiller as a "perfectly amoral profiteer." Producer David Susskind—against whom Schiller competed for the rights to one sensational story—once said, "Schiller swoops down on tragic events vulturelike and ghoulishly, salivating all the time."

Little in Schiller's life hasn't been controversial. Born in New York, he was the son of a discount merchant. When he was seven, the family moved to San Diego, where his father opened a camera, appliance and sporting goods store. As a child Schiller permanently damaged one eye in an accident. But by the age of 12, he was a passionate photographer. The hobby led to a college scholarship at Pepperdine and to an early career shooting historic photos for *Life, Look* and *Paris Match.* He photographed Richard and Pat Nixon, Vietnamese dragon lady Madame Nhu, Ann-Margret, Barbra Streisand and two popes. He also conducted interviews with some of his subjects for audio albums and books, such as the one that documented LSD culture in the Sixties. A photographer on the set of many movies, he took nude photographs of Marilyn Monroe after she achieved stardom. One famous shot from Schiller's session appeared in PLAYBOY in 1964. He shot numerous pictorials for PLAYBOY, including the first shots of pubic hair to appear in the magazine, in 1969. Moments after hearing the news about the assassination of President John F. Kennedy, Schiller headed for Dallas. He was present when Jack Ruby shot Lee Harvey Oswald and later conducted the last interview with Ruby before he died. Schiller also ingratiated himself with the Manson family and interviewed member Susan Atkins, collaborating with her on a book. He managed to get hundreds of hours of exclusive interview time with the widow of Lenny Bruce, which became the basis for the book *Ladies and Gentlemen, Lenny Bruce!*

For *Marilyn,* a book of photos of Monroe, he persuaded Norman Mailer to write the text and thereby began a tumultuous, though productive, relationship that led to a number of collaborations with the writer. The most significant of these was *The Executioner's Song.* By spreading around his money and charming Gary Gilmore's friends and family, Schiller sewed up the rights to Gilmore's story, just as Gilmore was about to be executed in a Utah prison. In typical Schiller fashion, he became a central figure in events that surrounded the execution and brought the story to Mailer, who wrote *The Executioner's Song* with the help of Schiller's research. Schiller went on to direct the television movie of the story, based on Mailer's script.

Mailer's most recent book on Lee Harvey Oswald was also brought to him by and researched with Schiller. *Oswald's Tale,* which relies on interviews with members and former members of the KGB, with Marina Oswald and with many other sources, came out of a relationship Schiller built in Russia when he made *Peter the Great.*

Schiller has been divorced three times and is now engaged to Amerman, a photographer. He has five children from his first two marriages. Although he had made millions of dollars on various projects, he filed for bankruptcy in 1991 after spending $600,000 in an ill-fated attempt to make a movie about Chernobyl. He's back on his feet again, in part because of the Simpson case. He also may have a new career because of his current book. Mailer once wrote that Schiller was sometimes "ready to cry in his sleep that he was a writer without hands." But Jason Epstein, his editor at Random House, says Schiller learned to write during the course of this book. "The final draft is all Schiller's," Epstein says. We sent Contributing Editor David Sheff to track down Schiller for this "Playboy Interview." Here is Sheff's report:

"I met with Schiller at his suite in the Plaza Hotel in Manhattan soon after he was subpoenaed to appear at the civil trial against Simpson. He seemed delighted 'They're going to ask me to reveal my sources,' he says. 'Of course, I won't. If I wind up in jail, it'll be great publicity for the book. . . .'

"The suite was equipped for business with a fax machine and a laptop. We sat facing each other with my two tape recorders on the coffee table between us. Before I asked my first question, Schiller carefully examined the recorders. 'I conducted my first interview with a wire recorder,' he said, 'the same kind used decades ago by the KGB. When I got in to see Ruby before he died, I had a tape recorder hidden inside a Neiman Marcus briefcase. For one session with O.J., the one that I knew would be used to introduce the audio version of *I Want to Tell You,* I used a DAT recorder. The guards were impressed.'

"During our long interview sessions Schiller often apologized for being 'inarticulate.' In fact he is a gripping storyteller with a remarkable memory for detail. I was struck by his desire for respectability, something that has eluded him despite his triumphs. Clearly, Schiller craves more than anything to be a man of substance. 'He has worked hard to purify himself,' Norman Mailer told me in a telephone conversation. 'He has changed more than any person I know. He is now very much a man of substance.'"

PLAYBOY: Let's start with the obvious question: Did O.J. Simpson get away with murder?
SCHILLER: If he committed these crimes—and the blood evidence certainly said he did, though the time line says he didn't—I think he must have repressed them completely.
PLAYBOY: You were close to Simpson. Which side of the issue do you come down on?
SCHILLER: Since I didn't talk to him today I come down on the side of guilty.
PLAYBOY: Meaning?
SCHILLER: If I had had a conversation with him today, I would probably say he is innocent. He is that persuasive.
PLAYBOY: Does he really believe he's innocent or could he be a convincing liar?
SCHILLER: I think he believes he's innocent. Bernard Yudowitz [*a psychiatrist who evaluated Simpson in jail*] said certain atypical killers are so repulsed by their actions that these actions become submerged. The actions cease to exist in their universe. They have to destroy any evidence that their crimes do exist. The episode I report in my book about the drainpipe [Simpson frantically cleans a drainpipe in his home because he fears it could have his blood in it] is very interesting. He is trying to wipe out evidence of the crime not because of a fear of prosecution, but because he wants to wipe out the crime itself.
PLAYBOY: You interviewed him in jail for 36 hours. In all that time, did

you discover any holes in his story or any evidence that he was lying?

SCHILLER: No. But since then I've seen another side of him.

PLAYBOY: What have you seen?

SCHILLER: Simpson called me about 10 days ago. He was very upset about one story in my book that was reported on TV. I wrote about the lawyers making over his house for the black jury, replacing the pictures of white women on the wall with pictures of Simpson's family and a Norman Rockwell print of a black girl. He was incensed. He was screaming. I kept saying to him, "Read the book, O.J. Stop it! Wait until you read it in the book. It's out of context." I said, "I didn't say you changed the pictures. I didn't say you knew about it or wanted it done." But he continued screaming. For the first time in my entire relationship with him, I felt the heat of his anger—not the anger, the *heat* of his anger. The words were on top of one another; they were out of control. I wanted to get off the phone, and I'm the type of person who never wants to get off the phone. It's not because I didn't want to discuss it—I'll fight for the book. But I wanted to get away from that terrifying heat. That may have said more to me than some of the evidence.

PLAYBOY: Why would this one revelation infuriate him? He's been accused of worse things than that.

SCHILLER: I think it is an affront to his view of himself—a powerful affront. He has some deep-seated concerns about the way he is perceived. So I wonder: Is that the sign of insanity? Could it have come out with Nicole? Could it be a doorway into his insanity to see that he cared so much about the perception that he was party to altering his home? I don't know. Throughout my career, I've interviewed a lot of criminally insane people. I interviewed Adam Berwid, who was in jail in Mineola, New York, for killing his wife. There was a guard in the room the whole time. The day after I completed the interview, his lawyer went to see him, and Berwid stabbed him in the neck with a pencil or ballpoint. For a long time I wondered if I had left my pen or pencil there—nobody knows how he got it. There was never a doubt: Here was a person who was genuinely and clearly insane. Another time, I interviewed two guys who had been sentenced to death and had figured out that the only way they could escape their sentences was to prove they were insane. They met in prison and decided to cut off each other's toes and fingers and other limbs with a hacksaw. They didn't use anything to numb the pain. There are extremes you will go to that are themselves acts of insanity. So now I have to ask, "Is there insanity in the reaction I got from Simpson?" I'm not certain.

PLAYBOY: Had you been a juror, would you have found Simpson guilty or not guilty?

SCHILLER: Not guilty. The blood evidence is hard to ignore, but the time line offers reasonable doubt. The key is the young couple, on their first date, who walked down Bundy at 10:25 and didn't see the paw prints of the Akita. I re-created it and it's pretty convincing. It says that he couldn't have committed the murders. On the other hand, the blood evidence is difficult to explain.

PLAYBOY: You reported that Johnnie Cochran was always troubled by Simpson's inability to explain in a reasonable and consistent way the cuts on his hand. Do you agree those wounds indicate Simpson's guilt?

SCHILLER: Of course. There's no logical explanation for those cuts.

PLAYBOY: Yet you would still vote not guilty.

SCHILLER: Yes. But my view isn't the point. I wrote the book to put forth the story. I want readers to draw their own conclusions.

PLAYBOY: How exactly did you get involved with this case?

SCHILLER: Years ago, my first wife and I lived across the street from Simpson, though I never really knew him. Suzanne, my oldest child, babysat for Arnelle and Jason and became very close to O.J.'s wife's sister. I got divorced and we moved away from the neighborhood and that was the end of O.J. Simpson, the celebrity who lived up the street. Later, with my second wife, I met and became friends with Robert Kardashian. Years later, the murders happen. I knew that Robert and O.J. were very close. I just figured out that he must be with Robert. I called and left a message on Robert's machine. He called me back five days later.

PLAYBOY: Next you and Kardashian had the clandestine meeting by the freeway. What happened?

SCHILLER: He was so scared. He was sure his house was bugged. That's why I suggested the freeway. If he was being bugged with parabolic microphones, the freeway noise would muffle our conversation. I told him that this case was going to become bigger than he imagined. We met again—by then he was no longer worried about being bugged—and I told him to keep a meticulous record of everything that happened.

PLAYBOY: Did you call because you already wanted to get involved in this story?

SCHILLER: At that point, I didn't know what I wanted to do. Right after the murders, I heard from my daughter Suzanne, who lives in Philadelphia. "Dad, I hope you're not going near this," she said. My son Marc said to me, "He's guilty. He did it. Don't get involved with another killer"—something like that.

PLAYBOY: Was there a chance you would take their advice and stay away?

SCHILLER: I guess not.

PLAYBOY: Why? What attracts you? Murder? The media frenzy?

SCHILLER: The challenge. Everyone wanted to get to O.J., and I thought I would be the one. I also thought I would attempt to do something respectable. I know it sounds self-serving, but I felt I could. I wanted Suzanne to end up saying, "You did it the right way this time."

PLAYBOY: Were you waiting for a way in?

SCHILLER: That's right. And I found it when I learned about the mountains of mail coming in to O.J. I came up with the idea for the book that became *I Want to Tell You.* The defense needed money. Robert had tried but wasn't able to get a loan on O.J.'s house; nobody would give O.J. a loan. So I proposed this project and it was approved.

PLAYBOY: Did you indeed get 20 percent of O.J.'s take of $1.4 million?

SCHILLER: I got 20 percent of whatever it was, although I had to pay the expenses out of my share. But the money was unimportant. It was the challenge. How do you think I felt the first day I walked in to see Simpson in jail? On subsequent visits I drove to the jail in various cars with different license plates. Do you realize the challenge? Talk about an adrenaline rush.

PLAYBOY: You were allowed in to see Simpson not as a journalist but as a material witness for the defense. Was this a ruse?

SCHILLER: At the time I denied it, but of course it was. Kardashian got Shawn Chapman [an attorney in Johnnie Cochran's office] to put me on the list to get in.

PLAYBOY: Describe the Simpson you met in jail.

SCHILLER: I was worried that I would have to sell him on the idea and on me, to persuade him to talk. But he just started talking. I saw him in every mood: depressed, angry, crying. He was a caged person who was nonetheless trying to live like a king. He didn't know what he was saying half the time. He was struggling just to keep his persona, very much like the Gatsby character. He was different in different interviews. I did 11 interviews with him. It was many moods. It was multilayered. But what came out was consistent. There was never an inconsistency in his story or in his view of himself as innocent.

PLAYBOY: In what ways was he trying to live like a king?

SCHILLER: They brought in people to make him happy, from his golfing buddies to neighbors. He was chained to the floor in the room where he met people, but it was open. There was glass between him and his

234

visitors, but they could breathe the same air. With Judge Lance Ito's consent, he was given a material-witness list that was designed to let anyone he wanted to see come visit with him. Once, Paula Barbieri showed up with seminude pictures of herself that had been taken for a fashion magazine or something. I'm in there, she's there showing him the pictures through the glass. These were sensual, sexy pictures. She asked if he wanted some prints for his cell. He said no. "I don't want them. Some guard may steal them and leak them to a tabloid: 'This is what O.J. has in jail.'" She was holding up all these pictures and they were the type of pictures that would make a guy horny. How can I put this: In a joking way, he pretended that he was enjoying himself.

PLAYBOY: That he was masturbating?

SCHILLER: In a joking way. She is showing him picture after picture after picture. Is that not taking care of the king? Another time she was there for four hours addressing Christmas cards with him. But Ito had to respond when *I Want to Tell You* came out. It was such an obvious breach of the material-witness list that Ito put his foot down because the sheriff was embarrassed. They basically took O.J.'s material-witness list away—it went down to 12 or 18 persons and there had to be an affidavit that stated why each person was a material witness. Before that, all his friends were on the list.

PLAYBOY: Before meeting with Simpson, did you think he was guilty?

SCHILLER: I didn't know.

PLAYBOY: If you had become convinced that he was guilty, would you have continued with the book?

SCHILLER: I would not have. Truly.

PLAYBOY: So you believed that he was innocent?

SCHILLER: I don't think anybody in the world in November or December 1994 could have sat opposite him for more than an hour and believed he was guilty. He was that persuasive. When I walked away from Gary Gilmore, I knew. He was a cold-blooded killer. I understood how you could be looking him straight in the eye, carrying on a conversation, and he would be sliding a shiv into your heart. In the process of conducting the interviews with Gilmore, we asked him if there was a crime worse than killing. His answer impressed me: "Yes," he said, "there is. It is worse to irrevocably alter someone's life—to take a hammer and hit someone in the head so he or she lives the rest of his or her life like a vegetable." It showed how clearly Gilmore knew what he was doing. He was a murderer. But with O.J., there was no way of knowing.

PLAYBOY: More than half the country thought they knew.

SCHILLER: But nobody had interviewed him since the murders. Maybe I didn't have the intellectual capacity to draw the correct conclusions, but I didn't see him as guilty. I don't think I'm exaggerating the power he had to convince people.

PLAYBOY: Did you have any qualms about helping Simpson at that time?

SCHILLER: Why would I have qualms? Dominick Dunne was asked on a talk show if he would have visited Simpson in jail if he had gotten a call. He said, "I would have been there before the sentence was completed." Anyone would have.

PLAYBOY: But *I Want to Tell You* was pure propaganda designed to elicit sympathy for Simpson.

SCHILLER: That was the point. We wanted to present an image before the jury was impaneled. At the time, Robert Shapiro [Simpson's original lead attorney] was asking television stations to play *Twelve Angry Men* for the same reason.

PLAYBOY: But you said you didn't know if Simpson was guilty or not.

SCHILLER: I guess I have to say that the ego of being the guy to pull it off is what ruled here. The best part was that we were able to keep it a secret for so long. Everybody who worked on the book lived in the house. The publisher's copy editors, everybody. We changed the phones. We put on digital scanners. We shredded the garbage. The dining room became a writing room. The bedroom became the layout room.

PLAYBOY: Do you understand why many people loathe that book?

SCHILLER: Sure, and a journalist may not have done it. It would taint his reputation. But to Schiller, this was an opportunity that might pay off. It was a way of ingratiating himself to Simpson and the defense team. I admit it! Not proudly, but I admit it factually. At the same time, I knew that the shadow of this book would stay with me for the rest of my life.

PLAYBOY: Are you proud of *I Want to Tell You?*

SCHILLER: Not of the book, but I am proud that I was able to pull it off. And you must remember that I spent 11 days interviewing Simpson before we had a deal. I could have made millions of dollars with those tapes. I could have become a millionaire overnight. But here is an example of Larry Schiller keeping his eye on the prize. This was just a step. I had ingratiated myself into his camp. Milking it for the last dollar was unimportant.

PLAYBOY: You also volunteered to edit the tapes of Mark Fuhrman that were eventually played for the jury. Why?

SCHILLER: It was another way to ingratiate myself with the defense.

PLAYBOY: Did you realize how important they would turn out to be?

SCHILLER: As soon as I listened to them, I knew what would happen. I listened to them all and edited 41 sections. Nobody knew how much the judge would allow. I know every word by heart.

PLAYBOY: At what point did you decide to write your own book on the case? Was that the reason you spent so much time with the defense?

SCHILLER: I didn't know exactly what I wanted to do, but I knew I had a unique perspective. Though I wasn't able to get law students and professors inside the defense, I was inside. My first idea was to ask Jeffrey Toobin [who covered the case for the *New Yorker* and eventually wrote his own book] to collaborate with me. He would write the prosecution's story and I would write the defense's story in alternate chapters. He wasn't interested.

PLAYBOY: In fact he was critical, even contemptuous, of you in his book.

SCHILLER: I knew it was coming. It doesn't bother me.

PLAYBOY: When you decided to write this book, were you afraid that your involvement in *I Want to Tell You* had destroyed any credibility that you might have?

SCHILLER: Yes. I was particularly disturbed when I realized how good a book I could write. But I also knew I had credibility because of my material. My interviews and research gave me all the credibility.

PLAYBOY: Your primary source was Kardashian. Why did he cooperate so fully with you?

SCHILLER: I think because he trusted that I would represent him accurately.

PLAYBOY: You also paid him.

SCHILLER: Robert was paid on an hourly basis for his time like the other lawyers.

PLAYBOY: Does he have a stake in the success of the book?

SCHILLER: No.

PLAYBOY: What if the book is a runaway best-seller and you make millions of dollars?

SCHILLER: If I make millions of dollars I will be very happy to share it with the people who contributed. Robert will not be singled out.

PLAYBOY: How much money was Kardashian paid?

SCHILLER: With all due respect, Connie Chung doesn't tell me how much she pays for interviews.

PLAYBOY: The point is that you paid your chief source.

SCHILLER: I'll tell you that the highest-paid lawyer, based on hourly rates, was not Kardashian. He just gave me more hours, so he wound up getting a little more money. But he was not the highest paid.

PLAYBOY: The fact is, no reputable journalist pays his sources, and you know it.

THE PLAYBOY INTERVIEW

SCHILLER: I wouldn't think of not compensating people for their time. Johnnie Cochran was paid more than $4 million for his time. Shapiro was paid $1.5 million.

PLAYBOY: They were paid for writing their books. It's not the same as paying sources.

SCHILLER: Do you really think Carl Douglas would have given me more than 20 hours of time for nothing? Come on! There's nothing wrong with paying him his normal hourly rate.

PLAYBOY: One thing that's wrong is that paid sources are unreliable. They have a financial incentive to embellish their stories.

SCHILLER: I don't rely solely on any one source. My book is multisourced. I checked everything and cross-checked it.

PLAYBOY: Kardashian is being attacked by members of the defense team and other lawyers for revealing secrets that are protected by his professional relationship with Simpson. Do you agree that he has crossed the line?

SCHILLER: No. Maybe he made a breach when he told Barbara Walters [during a *20/20* interview] that Simpson miserably failed the lie detector test he took right after the murders. But I didn't rely on Robert for that story. He was not the first, nor the only, source for it.

PLAYBOY: But did Kardashian know about the polygraph because he was Simpson's lawyer?

SCHILLER: Robert didn't have a bar license. He had studied law. He had passed the bar, but he never pursued it as a profession. I don't think he's worried about being sanctioned by the bar.

PLAYBOY: Does Kardashian have a responsibility to Simpson as a friend? Did he betray Simpson?

SCHILLER: Kardashian said to me on many occasions, "Simpson never asked me to withhold anything. He never told me to lie. He never said I shouldn't talk, and only he will know whether I have betrayed our friendship." Kardashian doesn't believe he has. He believes that if Simpson reads the book, he will end up admiring Robert for what he's done.

PLAYBOY: That's self-serving. It's unlikely that Simpson would agree with that.

SCHILLER: Robert did this because he needed to rid himself of it so he could have some peace in his life. This guy is going through hell. Every place he goes people spit on him and cuss at him. They write "murderer" on his car. Whether he is seen as supporting O.J. or being against him, he is attacked. So he wanted to purge himself.

PLAYBOY: How about you? Do you acknowledge that you betrayed Simpson and his lawyers in order to cash in?

SCHILLER: There was no betrayal. There is no question that I exploited the situation, but it was not to make money.

PLAYBOY: After your bankruptcy because of *Chernobyl,* didn't you need money?

SCHILLER: I have five children. Three are grown, one is in college and another is a junior in high school. I want to earn money, but this is motivated by something else. If I were to stand in the bathroom with no clothes on and look at myself in the mirror and ask, "What was your real motive, Larry?" it's that I wanted to be the person to do it. Maybe the means were not perfect at times, and I am not saying that the end justifies the means, but I don't think anything would have stopped me from trying to reach my goal.

PLAYBOY: What is it? Notoriety?

SCHILLER: I've already had notoriety. It's the sense of accomplishment, the sense of leaving something to my family that they might be proud of, something that juxtaposes the criticism and the controversies of my life. I am as proud of my book about the case as I am of anything I've done.

PLAYBOY: But we'll ask it again: By writing it, did you betray Simpson?

SCHILLER: No. I followed through with every agreement that I made with O.J. I made him lots of money. I helped influence public opinion. I edited the Fuhrman tapes, which were key to his trial. In my agreement with him, I always had the option of doing my own book. Because of my agreement with O.J., I didn't rely on any material that I had. Listen, there are, in my goddamn closet at home, a stack of O.J.'s diaries, the notes he kept throughout the trial. I never even read them because I didn't want to be tempted to use the material. Because of our contract, I couldn't use any of the material from my interviews with Simpson. But I was free to do my own work.

PLAYBOY: You said the means may not have been perfect. What was wrong with the means?

SCHILLER: There were things I did. At one point, at the end, after the acquittal, there was a time when I hugged him. I did feel very guilty. When he got out of the van and he was walking into the house, holding the Bible up, he passed me. I gave him a hug and said, "You did it, you did it!" I felt guilty for that.

PLAYBOY: Why?

SCHILLER: I don't know. In the emotion of the moment, I just gave him

239

a hug. Everyone else was giving him hugs and I didn't want to be. . . . I don't think a certain type of journalist would have given him a hug.

PLAYBOY: So you felt guilty because you felt it was unprofessional?

SCHILLER: That's right. It was stepping over the line.

PLAYBOY: Perhaps you were acknowledging that your role in this case was confused. Had you become his friend and colleague or were you a journalist who would write a book that would be viewed as a betrayal?

SCHILLER: I never felt as if we were friends. I would call us acquaintances, not friends. When I hugged him, I was caught up in the moment. That's all. It was an emotional day. I saw what was yet to come. At the acquittal party, Kathy [Amerman, the photographer, Schiller's fiancée] and I were taking pictures. We'd divided up the house. People would come up to O.J. and I would ask them to stand closer together so I could take a picture. But no one would. They moved away from him. They said, "Oh, that's okay, we don't need a picture." They said, "No thanks. That's all right." Outside, in the cars, on our way there, first we heard cheering and that faded into the cries of "Murderer, murderer." Then we were inside among his friends and no one would stand close to him to be photographed. It was very illuminating of what was to come.

PLAYBOY: Does it surprise you that his lawyers feel you betrayed them?

SCHILLER: It depends who you're talking about. Some are embarrassed by things I've reported about them, sure.

PLAYBOY: Have you heard from Robert Shapiro?

SCHILLER: He's been out of the country since the book came out.

PLAYBOY: Johnnie Cochran has denied some of your charges. Specifically, he denies having made a comment after seeing Simpson the night before his closing argument to the jury. You reported that Simpson attempted to sculpt Cochran's closing remarks and that there was an argument. Afterward, Cochran said, "It's a good thing I don't have blond hair."

SCHILLER: Only four people were in the car when that was said. I can tell you that Cochran said it. I understand that his persona is important to him. Of course he won't admit to saying it.

PLAYBOY: Has F. Lee Bailey responded to the book? He comes off as exceedingly incompetent.

SCHILLER: He hasn't said that anything in the book is untruthful. He has said he believes that Kardashian has breached his responsibility as a lawyer, but not that I breached my agreement with him. His incompetence is obvious when you read the transcripts. But what's more humiliating to Bailey is what Carl Douglas told me: that they wouldn't allow him to have a copy of the Fuhrman tapes. Bailey was pleading with him: "Why can't I have them?" "Well, you can't be trusted." That's what is humiliating to him. But it's history. I'm not going to sacrifice the truth of history to remain a friend of F. Lee Bailey. At the same time, I hope he will respect me more because I haven't done something just to make a friend of him.

PLAYBOY: It's unlikely.

SCHILLER: I don't know. It depends on how big a man he is. I would say it's unlikely with Johnnie Cochran.

PLAYBOY: After watching these lawyers in action, who would you call if you needed a defense attorney?

SCHILLER: Barry Scheck. Definitely. If he believes in something, he believes in it honestly. He doesn't have hidden agendas. He will be realistic. If he took your case, he'd be working.

PLAYBOY: As opposed to?

SCHILLER: Bailey would be out partying. Shapiro would be at concerts or boxing matches. Cochran would be out speaking about it and making enormous amounts of money—I think he made close to three quarters of a million dollars giving speeches.

PLAYBOY: In the course of your research, did you interview Marcia Clark?

SCHILLER: I never interviewed her or had any direct conversation with her. I wound up in an elevator with her once, on the day the Fuhrman tapes were being played. I said "Hi," but she didn't lift her eyes. She was going up and the elevator arrived for her. Although I was going down, I got on—what reporter wouldn't? But she never lifted her eyes nor her head. She never said a word.

PLAYBOY: Is she responsible for the not-guilty verdict? Could another prosecutor have stood up to that defense team?

SCHILLER: She blew the case. I think she blew it because she became emotionally involved with the relatives of the victims. That worked against her. When we would arrive in the mornings, she'd be sitting in seats with relatives of the victims. Because of that, she thought this should be a case like others she had tried that involved stalkers and spousal abuse. She thought O.J. was just another one of those. If Bill Hodgman had handled the case, it would have been different. He was dispassionate and very clever. When he got sick, it gave her too much control of the case. Marcia's arguments were very persuasive. She's a good orator. But all her emotion did not win the jury. She made a critical mistake thinking that the case was a slam dunk based on blood evidence. She didn't realize the blood evidence could be unraveled, and Scheck unraveled it. He convinced the jury there was reasonable doubt. She thought the blood evidence was a sure thing. She said the blood matched Simpson's.

But Scheck said you can't use the word "match"—it's not like finger-prints. All you can say is that the blood is similar. It was the first thing he did. Well before that, she turned off the jury.

PLAYBOY: How?

SCHILLER: There was an arrogance that came through. And all her prick-teasing with Johnnie Cochran.

PLAYBOY: Prick-teasing?

SCHILLER: All the eyes and giggling and whispering in his ear. I thought, When is she going to put her tongue into his ear? That's what seemed like the next step. At one point she whispered to someone that she was wearing crotchless panties. She was joking, but she still said it. There seemed to be a miniskirt competition going on between her and Jo-Ellan Dimitrius [a defense jury consultant]—who could wear shorter skirts. But all the sex stuff just didn't work. It stopped when Johnnie's wife, Dale, put her foot down. Johnnie stopped engaging her. Before that, they would almost hold hands walking up to a sidebar. I felt it was repulsive. She tried to use her sexuality in every way she could—to engage Cochran on that level and have it work for her. But it didn't work.

PLAYBOY: How could it have worked?

SCHILLER: Maybe to distract him. Her big mistake was that she didn't understand this trial at all. She didn't listen to her jury consultants. The jury consultants for both sides said the same thing: That middle-aged black women looked at Nicole in a negative way and O.J. in a positive way. Marcia Clark never understood that.

PLAYBOY: Do you have a higher opinion of Christopher Darden?

SCHILLER: No. Everyone talks about Darden's brooding. But what was he brooding about? He just went out half-cocked. Look at his attack on screenwriter Laura Hart McKinny—practically accusing her of hav-ing a love affair with Fuhrman. I felt he was desperate. That may be to Johnnie's credit. I think Johnnie was successful in disarming Darden. Darden never felt comfortable in the courtroom as far as I could see. He never had strength, security or confidence. Johnnie not only rattled Ito, he also rattled Darden. Johnnie won every battle with Darden. Even Bailey got Darden. He taunted him once: "You've got the balls of a stud field mouse." Darden's book was great because it had his real anger in it. Real, believable anger. He took the high road in his book about Marcia Clark—said they didn't have an affair, that they bonded because she was supporting him while his brother was dying of AIDS. I don't think she'll take the high road in her book.

PLAYBOY: Was the defense team contemptuous of the prosecution?

SCHILLER: The defense always felt the prosecution was lying and cheating. They also felt that the prosecution never developed a scenario of what actually happened the night of the killings. They never had a clear story. And they never really knew what triggered the murders. What triggered the murders? That helped lose the case. If they could have convinced the jury that something triggered O.J., they might have won. The closest they came was that he was mad because he hadn't been invited for dinner. That was no trigger. Why didn't they tell the story of O.J. showing up at the house and watching through the window while Nicole was giving head to this guy when the kids were upstairs, with the bedroom door open? Because if that hadn't triggered a flip-out and caused him to murder Nicole, nothing would.

PLAYBOY: At what point did the prosecution team feel it had won?

SCHILLER: After LAPD criminalists Collin Yamauchi and Dennis Fung got off the stand, the defense felt that they had a hung jury at the minimum [as a result of sloppy police work]. At that point, as Shapiro put it many times, all they had to do was "be sure we don't step on our dick." In other words, "Don't mess up."

PLAYBOY: Did the defense lawyers feel that the prosecuting lawyers were in their league?

SCHILLER: No. They felt they were up against amateurs. The prosecution became so defensive that their prosecution case was a rebuttal to the defense from the beginning. Every single witness was a rebuttal to the defense. They were starting to anticipate the defense so much that they lost sight of an affirmative prosecution.

PLAYBOY: How did Cochran rattle Ito?

SCHILLER: He did it all the time. He drove Ito from the bench twice—got him so mad he had to take a break. Throughout, Cochran was able to push Ito's buttons. Ito left the bench so disgusted and Cochran would never back down.

PLAYBOY: What was the defense team's view of Ito?

SCHILLER: Alan Dershowitz and Scheck had disdain for him, looked down on him. Shapiro was afraid to offend him. Cochran couldn't give a fuck. Cochran was in control. He couldn't give a fuck.

PLAYBOY: Have you spoken with Cochran since your book came out?

SCHILLER: No. But I heard he said I should retitle it *The Enemy Within*.

PLAYBOY: Did you interview him after the trial?

SCHILLER: Never on the record. But often during my interviews with Carl Douglas, Johnnie came into the office. He never interrupted. When he talked, it was always off the record. He said he couldn't talk as part of his book deal.

THE PLAYBOY INTERVIEW

PLAYBOY: Did the defense team feel that the Fuhrman tapes assured the not-guilty verdict?

SCHILLER: Yes. They assured an acquittal. They knew they would at least have a hung jury without tapes. Reasonable doubt had already been proved. Stalking had not been proved. Neither had spousal abuse. The tapes sealed it.

PLAYBOY: Why were you entrusted with such important evidence?

SCHILLER: Because I was there. I offered to do it. I was, once again, the right man in the right place at the right time. It was not that they trusted me. There were goddamn bodyguards on me. The tapes were probably worth $2 million to $3 million at that time. Here is another example of me thinking about the future of the project, not just the moment. I wasn't going to do anything to blow my access. I kept thinking about Norman Mailer and *The Executioner's Song*. The fact that I stayed friendly with my sources was crucial.

PLAYBOY: But many members of Gary Gilmore's family think that you ripped them off.

SCHILLER: I told every one of them to get their own representatives and attorneys. I didn't deal with them directly. I wanted them protected so they'd never feel they were taken advantage of.

PLAYBOY: Your plan didn't work—some clearly feel you cheated them.

SCHILLER: Some expected more money than they got.

PLAYBOY: One, Vern Damico, Gilmore's uncle, still says you owe him money.

SCHILLER: Yes, but we agreed that he and the others would be paid with what was left after defending any lawsuits that were brought. One was brought by the insurance companies that paid the victims' families. I paid to defend that suit. Still, Vern says I owe him $157,000. I don't. There's something else that happened with Vern. I stayed close to Nicole Baker [Gilmore's girlfriend] and several other people for a number of years because I felt I couldn't just walk in and out of their lives. I felt responsible for them. But Vern was a shoemaker, a family man whose children had grown. He seemed self-assured. I pulled away from him because it didn't seem as if he needed anything more from me. Maybe I pulled away from him too fast. I think he was resentful.

PLAYBOY: Lenny Bruce's widow, Honey, charged that you not only owed her money but that you also got her strung out on drugs in order to get her story.

SCHILLER: It was her lawyer, trying to get money in a lawsuit. Honey was dead broke and needed money. I didn't hold that against her. I never once blinked.

244

PLAYBOY: Do you deny supplying her with drugs?

SCHILLER: Do I look like someone who's involved with drugs? I never dropped acid in my life. Timothy Leary held that against me until the day he died. I don't smoke and I don't drink. I've never been involved in drugs. But Honey was dead broke—she asked me for money. I turned her down because of the way she asked and because the amount she asked for was utterly obscene. There was a settlement for $8000. And it wasn't me who paid. Those people complained, but the work that came from those experiences is brilliant. The Gilmore story led to *Executioner's Song*. It won Mailer a Pulitzer. Lenny was just brilliant work on my part. Who else would have moved Honey Bruce into his house for six months to get her story? Once she was sitting with my daughter Suzanne, teaching her about sea horses. She said she had to go to the bathroom. Two hours later she came out of the bathroom. She shot up in there, came out and continued talking about sea horses without missing a beat.

PLAYBOY: Let's go back to the Gary Gilmore story. How did you become involved that time?

SCHILLER: I was in the middle of producing *The Trial of Lee Harvey Oswald* and picked up the paper and read an article about this girl—Nicole— who had been persuaded to attempt to kill herself by a convict who had been sentenced to death. She had two children. What attracted me was the question, "How could one human being have the power to persuade another to take her life when she had two small children?"

PLAYBOY: You headed to Utah. But so did swarms of media. Why were you able to get to Gilmore and his family when no one else could?

SCHILLER: Because I was the Fuller Brush man. I was the Avon salesman. I was able to knock on the door, get my foot in. Once again, I walked in and ingratiated myself.

PLAYBOY: In order to ingratiate yourself in this or other instances, does anything go? Do you lie?

SCHILLER: No. I just figure out what is required. I don't know why people trust me and open up to me, but they do. I sometimes am surprised at how much people tell me. Women seem to respond in particular. Nicole told about when Gilmore was able to respond to her sexually, when they played together in the bathtub, when he shaved her pubic hair. She cried after she told me how her husband felt she was unable to satisfy him sexually. She felt she was such a bad lay he must have thought it was like fucking the wind. It was devastating to her. Why would she tell me that? Why would Marina Oswald write to me and my wife asking if she should have a hysterectomy? I guess it's almost like talking to a girl-

245

friend, not talking to a guy. I feel like a rabbi sometimes. Someone you can cry to. I never go for the jugular in my interviews. I take my time. I tell stories about my own life. Sometimes I adapt my life so it works better to make a point. I react with a certain innocence.

PLAYBOY: Is it genuine or rehearsed?

SCHILLER: I don't know the difference.

PLAYBOY: You have said the fact that you could get into the jail to see Gilmore helped persuade him to trust you. You said, "The fact that I got in showed that I could buck the system, and that impressed him."

SCHILLER: There's no question about it. But I could never have gotten in without Gilmore's help from the inside. He told me when to come—what shift. He told me which guards would look the other way. Guys on death row make friends with their captors very quickly. Some of O.J. Simpson's closest friends now are his former jailers. They go to his house all the time. I'm not going to give you the names of the officers, but I know them.

PLAYBOY: You witnessed Gilmore's execution. How did it affect you?

SCHILLER: The execution was just like a military operation. It was detached, cold. He was a cold-blooded killer. He wanted to die. He didn't want to be butt-fucked in jail for the rest of his life. So he was a partner with the State of Utah in his execution. I had no problem with it.

PLAYBOY: How did you persuade Norman Mailer to write the Gilmore story?

SCHILLER: I knew that what was going on around Gilmore had tremendous social impact. There were conflicts between religion and capital punishment. I saw the power of Gilmore's personality, that he could control Nicole to the extent she would try to kill herself for him. I saw this world of Mormons and Jack Mormons in Utah. But I've always had this problem: I am unable to express myself. I knew that a writer such as Mailer had the ability not only to absorb the material but also to filter it in a way that would mean something to society. I didn't think twice about making the approach. He was convinced because of the material.

PLAYBOY: Describe your relationship with Mailer.

SCHILLER: Over the years, Norman and I developed a language. He no longer was a writer to me. He was a rabbi. He gave me guidance, encouragement. He never put me down. Sometimes we fought, sometimes we didn't speak for months, but there was respect. He respected the work I did for him. No one else could have gotten him *Executioner's Song*.

PLAYBOY: You first worked together on *Marilyn*. How did that come about?

SCHILLER: I was in L.A. on the set of *The Misfits,* photographing for *Paris Match*. Another photographer and I were the only ones on the set, shooting side by side. The night before, Marilyn's publicist told us she was going to do a semi-nude swimming scene. The next day, there she was. Marilyn almost nude, wearing nothing except a pair of panties. So we shot the pictures. I immediately went to the telephone and made two calls, to *Paris Match* and *Life*. I said, "You won't believe it. We have Marilyn Monroe in the nude." The only previous nudes of her were the ones that appeared in the first issue of PLAYBOY. The other photographer walked by the phone and I stopped him. I convinced him that two sets of pictures of Marilyn would drive the price down and we should become 50-50 partners. Marilyn had approval of the pictures. I went over to her house in the evening. She said, "Let's go to Schwab's." She drove—I think it was a T-Bird convertible—and ran into the store. She came out and asked for the pictures. Out of a paper bag, she took a pair of shears she had bought at Schwab's. She held my 35mm strips of film and, with only the light of a streetlight, began cutting through the shots she didn't like. Thank God I didn't bring them all, because not many survived.

PLAYBOY: You didn't bring them all? But you had an agreement with her.

SCHILLER: I guess I was more worried about the pictures than the agreement. I went down to the printing plant and waited for the first issue of the magazine to come off the press. I took it to Marilyn to show her. Back to her house, late at night, she sat there with Dom Perignon, looking at the magazine. She loved it and started talking and talking. Finally, I said, "Marilyn, I've gotta go home. My wife is going to fucking kill me." She asked where I lived and I told her the address. Then she left the room and didn't come back for 25 minutes. I didn't know what was going on, but I didn't feel as if I could get up and walk out of the house. I sat there for all that time. Finally, she came back. We're schmoozing. I don't know if she wants to be fucked or what. I wasn't so fat then as I am now, but I was still a little heavy. But it was just Marilyn and me. I'm a chickenshit. I don't make a move. Finally, I leave. She gives me a kiss. I say, "Thanks for making me famous." I drive home and I'm ready to start making apologies to my wife, but she wasn't mad at all. She wasn't mad because Marilyn had sent her two dozen red roses. The note said something like, "Sorry for keeping Larry." That's what she had done in the 25 minutes.

PLAYBOY: Your photographs of Monroe appeared in PLAYBOY soon afterward. Were they from the same session?

SCHILLER: Yes. One was one of those we never showed Marilyn—a black-and-white—which I knew would be valuable to Hefner. It wasn't the best picture of her, but it was the only shot that showed her nipple. I had the photo colored and offered it to Hef. I told him that the pictures were worth $25,000 or worth nothing. I wouldn't negotiate. He agreed to buy them. I was told that that was the highest price he had ever paid for photography at that time. After that, Marilyn agreed to pose for the cover of the magazine, but she died before we were able to shoot it.

PLAYBOY: Were the Monroe pictures your first in PLAYBOY?

SCHILLER: I had shot Playmates. My pictures of Paula Kelly, the dancer, were the first ones that showed pubic hair in the magazine. I persuaded her to do the spread by telling her I wanted to do dignified, artistic nudes. She liked the idea, but was worried you would see her genitals. She wanted to wear a patch over them until I explained that it could pick up a light that you might see in the pictures. Since her pubic hair was black against her dark skin and we were using rim lighting, I said that you'd never see anything. She was very cooperative; she threw away the patch. The staff loved the pictures. I got a call from Vince Tajiri, the photo editor, who said, "It's the first time we've gotten away with pubic hair in the magazine!" I said, "What pubic hair?" I was worried because I had promised Paula there would be none. I went and looked closely and for the first time saw it. You could definitely see the black pubic hair in three of seven exposures. It was a breakthrough, but I thought Paula would go ballistic. Yet she never said a word to me about it.

I also did sports and celebrities for the magazine. One time, Paula Prentiss and Elliott Gould were doing *Move* and I got them to agree to a nude shot in a bathtub to promote the movie. We were all set up. Elliott was in the bathtub and Paula was supposed to come out, but she wouldn't. Elliott went in and tried to convince her to come out and then I tried. No way. I noticed that she was completely flat-chested, but I had no idea this had anything to do with it. Dick Benjamin, her husband, finally went in and talked with her and came out and said, "She just can't do it today." I said, fine. Three or four weeks later, they told me she would do it. This time Paula walked out of the dressing room without any coaxing. I'll tell you: She had the biggest fucking set of knockers in the world. Now, I can't swear to you that she didn't have the knockers the first time around, but she looked pretty flat-chested to me. I don't know what changed, but she was a fucking knockout when she walked out the second time.

PLAYBOY: At what point did you cross over from photographer to interviewer and journalist?

SCHILLER: I began doing interviews for spoken-word record albums. I did an essay for *Life* magazine on LSD culture and that started me doing a record. I also did ones on homosexuality and the American male, one on JFK and the one on Lenny Bruce that was the basis for the book. Those interviews were all for record albums. Three became books.

PLAYBOY: What was the story behind your book with Charles Manson follower Susan Atkins?

SCHILLER: I was called by Paul Caruso, a famous divorce attorney, with a tip. "A buddy of mine who's a public defender has a client by the name of Susan Atkins who is in jail for a series of murders. She told her lawyer that she was involved in the Tate-LaBianca murders. Would you like to talk with her?" I interviewed her. I wrote a book under her name, set up a trust for her child and took half the money. The publishers chose the title, which was terrible, the worst exploitation: *The Killing of Sharon Tate*. But it was sold all over the world. Before the article about the book was published, I was with President Nixon in the White House shooting a campaign commercial. Afterward, we sat around and talked. The president asked me what I was up to and I told him about the Atkins interview, that she confessed to the Manson murders. I never imagined he would take this information and make this incredible statement that was a front-page headline the next day: The president said Manson was guilty of those murders. It was because I had lunch with Nixon and I was bragging! It threw the trial into a tizzy.

PLAYBOY: Was it a coincidence that you were in Dallas when President Kennedy was shot?

SCHILLER: I wasn't in Dallas at the time. I was there within $3\frac{1}{2}$ hours of the assassination. They kicked off all the passengers on the next plane there from Los Angeles and it became the first press flight. I was working for the *Saturday Evening Post*. I was in the basement when Lee Harvey Oswald was being moved. He came out and somebody stepped in front of me and there was a flash, a flash, and then a pop and then another flash. Somewhere in there, I saw somebody shooting somebody, but I never got the fucking picture. Oswald immediately was picked up and taken away, and they're all on top of this guy who did it. I realized one or two photographers had the picture and I didn't. There were two labs being used in Dallas and I raced to one. Someone walked out of the darkroom with the picture: the famous Bob Jackson photograph of Jack Ruby shooting Oswald. I asked what rights were available. I offered $10,000 for world magazine rights and got the original print. I sent it to the *Post* and we made sales to *Paris Match, Stern* and other magazines around the world and made five times the $10,000. Jackson won the Pulitzer Prize for that picture. I have the original print framed at home.

PLAYBOY: You met up with Ruby again, conducting the final interview of his life before he died in the hospital in 1967. How did you get it?

SCHILLER: I had been in contact with his brother and sister over the years. I was doing the record of JFK when I got a call and was asked if I wanted to see him. It was a pure coincidence.

PLAYBOY: What revelations came from that last interview?

SCHILLER: Most of all, that he stuck to his story on his deathbed. He had acted alone. There was no conspiracy.

PLAYBOY: Yet you visited the conspiracy theory again, both with *The Trial of Lee Harvey Oswald* and your research for Norman Mailer's book *Oswald's Tale*. Why the preoccupation with that story?

SCHILLER: It is probably the greatest unsolved mystery of our time. Particularly with *Oswald's Tale*, I had access to incredible information— all the KGB files.

PLAYBOY: How did you get them?

SCHILLER: I had a name in Russia. I was invited to Mikhail Gorbachev's peace conference and then to be a negotiator on the bilateral talks in Russia between the U.S. government and the U.S. Information Agency. I couldn't believe it. So I went back to Russia a second time as a delegate of the U.S. government under President Reagan. This time I looked up Ludmilla Peresvetova, a translator whom I had met but had not worked with. She was one of the most skilled translators in Russia. Although she denied it, I knew from others that she also had worked in some context for the KGB.

PLAYBOY: She became your third wife.

SCHILLER: Yes, but it was not a sexual relationship yet. I was invited back the second year by the government to negotiate. This time it was held in Washington and we brought Ludmilla to be my translator. Finally, I decided to do a film based on the Chernobyl disaster. I convinced the Russians. I hired J.P. Miller, who wrote *Days of Wine and Roses*, an Emmy Award–winning screenwriter. I always surround myself with the best people. Ludmilla is helping me again. I put a lot of my own money into it, almost $600,000. My wife—still my second wife—and I were just ready to kill each other. I told her that we were going to have to go into bankruptcy in 1991. That was the greatest humiliation for her. The lawyers told me how to do it to protect my family, but my wife wouldn't accept it. It was the end of our marriage. Six months later, Ludmilla showed up in the U.S. to visit her daughter. Gorbachev by then had gone far in hacking his own window to the West. I was having many problems with *Chernobyl*—my backers fell out. There was one problem after another. But I knew there were other great stories in Russia. I was interested in three: Alger Hiss, the Rosenbergs and Lee Harvey Oswald. One night, I asked Ludmilla to talk with her friends in the KGB about them. She returned to Moscow and then called me: "Come to Moscow." She introduced me to a former KGB agent who told me there was nothing in their files on Alger Hiss except news clippings. He said there was a lot about the Rosenbergs, but nothing more than the West already knew. "What about Lee Harvey Oswald?" "There's a lot." I asked, "How do I get it?"

PLAYBOY: How did you?

SCHILLER: More negotiating. I told them I wanted to bring in a writer. I called him the American Tolstoy. I had to sell them on Mailer even though I hadn't yet sold Mailer on the project. I knew this was a story for Norman, but I had to convince him.

PLAYBOY: How did you?

SCHILLER: I went back to New York and told him I felt I could get the KGB files. I said, "It's the one part of the mystery that nobody knows anything of. They bugged him." I said, "Nobody has ever seen Oswald interacting with people. Here are his fights, depressions, it's all in there." I said, "Here is a chance to be flies on the wall inside Lee Harvey Oswald's life. Nobody else is ever going to have that."

PLAYBOY: Why were you given those extremely valuable files? Did you bribe the officials?

SCHILLER: From the beginning I was told that I would have to pay with shoes and sardines, not money. That meant that I would pay with whatever goods they couldn't get. But I had to convince many people who were not bribed. The Supreme Soviet learned what we were doing and attempted to stop it. They wanted to know why a Western writer should get them. The FBI heard about it through the American Embassy and made a push for the files. Ludmilla in the meantime was getting so fucking scared that the government might swing back [to the Communist regime] and she would be put in jail for working for Americans. One time the KGB showed us a report on us conducted by the local KGB which said that Mailer was working for the CIA and Ludmilla was an operative. She became even more scared then. Now it was in the KGB files that she was working for the CIA, it became obvious that I had to marry her. I'm not saying I didn't love her, but we got married for that reason. We went to the U.S. and got married and returned to Russia to work. The marriage was a tough one. It was not a marriage based on real love or devotion or understanding. When the project was over, the marriage was annulled—after she got her green card. She now lives in Washington, D.C., and is a translator for the Securities and Exchange Commission. Living a happy life.

PLAYBOY: Years earlier, you had interviewed Marina Oswald, most extensively, for *The Trial of Lee Harvey Oswald*. Did she have to be persuaded to talk again?

SCHILLER: Yes. And it was very difficult. Of all the people I have interviewed who feel betrayed by me, she feels the most betrayed.

PLAYBOY: Was she?

SCHILLER: I didn't betray her. But in Russia we had learned a lot about her early life. She had relations with many men. I wanted to get her to talk about it. I convinced her. "What does it matter?" she wanted to know. But, I said, if something as small or as large as this affected Oswald, it gives us a better understanding. In the hands of Mailer, perhaps society will learn something. So she talked to me, but she despised the book. She says Mailer depicted her as a whore. But she is not depicted as a whore. She is depicted as someone who had a horrible experience with a stepfather. She was thrown into the street and locked out. She feels betrayed by everybody.

PLAYBOY: Does that make you feel bad?

SCHILLER: I don't lose any sleep over it, but I feel bad because she does not accept the fact that the best has been done with truth we know, and that society does learn. Again, Schiller is in the middle of history. We filled in a piece of history with that book, just as we had with *Executioner's Song*.

PLAYBOY: You clearly are obsessed with making a mark on history. Have you analyzed why?

SCHILLER: It is doing something important, something my children can look to proudly. When I was a child, my father was very proud of my brother, who was an incredible athlete. When he beat me in the 11-and-under category in tennis, that was the end of my tennis career—and my brother is two years younger. My father was a marathon runner. I couldn't compete in that arena, but I found other ways to compete. I participated in athletics when I was a child by being a photographer. It was my way of participating. Maybe everything comes from this.

PLAYBOY: Did the accident that hurt your vision in one eye affect your decision to become a photographer?

SCHILLER: I don't think so. My father was a portrait photographer. He owned a camera store on 42nd Street. We went to California and he opened another store, this time selling sporting goods, cameras and appliances. So he had more to do with it than anything else, I think. And photography is what opened doors for me. It got me to college. I never had the grades, but I got a journalism scholarship for my photographs.

PLAYBOY: Do you think that most of what you've tried to prove in your life goes back to your father?

SCHILLER: It's not only my father. My children and ex-wife and I once went to see *The Mosquito Coast*. There's a scene in the film where Harrison Ford tries to explain to his wife and one of his sons what he's all about—why he's brought the family to this hellhole in the middle of the jungle. He explains his dream, for the first time communicating who he is to his family. His wife and son look at him in the worst way. You can see by their faces that they are horrified. When I saw that, I broke down and cried in the theater. It was so much about me at that moment in my life. My wife was so embarrassed that she took my children and moved to another part of the theater. She wouldn't sit next to me. That was the end of my marriage as far as I was concerned. She didn't know it, but it was. We had a big fight that night.

PLAYBOY: What exactly did you relate to in the movie?

SCHILLER: How misunderstood he was. And when my wife moved away, it proved how much I was misunderstood, too. I see things a certain way. I've made a lot of mistakes in my life. I've done things that are wrong for which I deserve to be criticized and torn apart. But the story of Schiller is not only those things.

PLAYBOY: Yet like it or not, along with all of your accomplishments come the labels: you as a carrion bird, as "O.J.'s sleazy friend" and as an exploiter. Do these bother you?

SCHILLER: They no longer bother me. I used to be concerned for my children, but they and those who know me are used to it. This new book is something they can be proud of. The reviews that have come in—from the *New York Times*, the *Los Angeles Times*, *Time* magazine—are all a vindication. I mean, I cried when I read the *New York Times* review. I was in a restaurant with Kardashian on my left and Kathy on my right and I just started to cry.

PLAYBOY: Why exactly did you cry?

SCHILLER: It was an acknowledgment by a stranger who is considered to be important. It acknowledged all the work I put in.

PLAYBOY: Did you feel legitimized on your own at last, independent from Mailer?

SCHILLER: Maybe. Yes.

PLAYBOY: For that you have O.J. Simpson to thank.

SCHILLER: But I pulled it off myself. I pulled it off.

PLAYBOY: Yours is the 40th or so book about O.J. Will the interest in this case ever subside?

SCHILLER: The obsession with the case will die down, although it will reappear whenever big events in O.J.'s life come along. It will reappear when he gets married again, especially when it is to a white blonde; when he has another child. The biggest news will be when his wife ends up dead again. A knife. Blood. A glove. [*Smiles*] Actually, the biggest news will be when they find the knife and the real killers. Imagine: Somebody confesses and everything finally fits together. A killer with blood so close to O.J.'s or something. Think about what that would do to America. I know it's unlikely, but that would be something, wouldn't it?

Versace's Paradise

by **PAT JORDAN**
December 1997

The Normandy Plaza Hotel has the sad pretension of a faded beauty whose best days are only a memory. It lies at the wrong end of Miami Beach, at Collins Avenue and 69th Street. The chic art deco hotels are a few miles south, on South Beach. The Normandy is garishly made up with a hot-pink exterior, purple trim and green awnings.

The lobby of the Normandy, with its peeling linoleum floor, is barren except for two soda machines, a deserted metal bar that hasn't served a martini or manhattan in decades and a few black-and-white photographs of Marilyn Monroe on the walls. Monroe once stayed at the Normandy. So did Clark Gable and Carole Lombard. The Normandy's most recent guest of note was Andrew Cunanan. He checked into the hotel on May 12 and left on July 14, the day before he murdered Gianni Versace.

"He was so well-mannered," says Miriam Hernandez, the hotel manager. "He had a beautiful smile, and beautiful teeth."

Teeth are something Miriam would notice at the Normandy Plaza, whose guests tend to be missing teeth. Miriam herself is a soft-spoken Cuban woman with a sweet smile. She is about 60, with short gray hair worn like a stocking cap, and a faint mustache. She wears a chain with a cross around her neck.

"Sometimes the guests make me feel afraid," says Miriam. "But he was not a rough person. He was very gentle and nice." A man who is drinking from a can of beer stops at her desk for his room key. Miriam opens the cabinet behind her to get it. A semiautomatic pistol hangs from a nail on the back of the cabinet door.

Cunanan paid for his room in cash because the Normandy does not accept personal checks or credit cards. He did not give Miriam a $10 deposit to turn on his phone. He received no phone calls, no visitors,

VERSACE'S PARADISE

no mail. He talked to no one.

He never opened his curtains. He sat in his tiny room that smelled of Lysol and listened to the hum of his window air conditioner. He sat on a pink velvet chair at a kitchen table covered with linoleum, or he lay on a pink-and-blue polyester bedspread. He never cooked on the tiny, dented, rusted Fifties stove. He went out during the day to buy fast food, perhaps a pizza, a sub, a McDonald's hamburger, and some fashion magazines or a gay porno magazine. He returned immediately to eat and read. After he ate, he slept. When he woke at night to take a shower, he turned on the faucet and let the rust-colored water run out before he stepped in. After he dressed, he tidied up his room so neatly that the maid did not have to clean it. He went out late at night to Hombre and Twist and Liquid and Warsaw, gay bars and dance clubs on South Beach. He'd heard they were frequented by Versace.

But Cunanan got his information wrong. His timing was bad. That was the old Versace.

Versace lived four miles from the Normandy Plaza, on Ocean Drive, in Casa Casuarina, a restored 1930 Moorish castle patterned after the home of Christopher Columbus's son Diego in the Dominican Republic. It cost Versace $2.9 million, and more than $30 million to renovate in a style best described as gay baroque.

Casa Casuarina is the home of a Roman emperor—a Nero, not a Caesar. It is all decadent excess. It is a confluence of influences (Greek and Roman, for starters), with busts of Cupid and Pocahontas and Columbus and Confucius and Benito Mussolini. It is the mansion of a man whose philosophy of fashion was once summed up by his sister, Donatella, as, "Less is not more. Less is less." He once spent $3 million in two hours on furnishings for his Miami home. He was so excited by how much he had spent that when he returned home, he said, "I started to dance. I wanted to kiss myself."

In many ways, Versace's mansion typifies South Beach, a bouillabaisse of people of every nationality, race, religion and sexual persuasion. The district has a beach's laissez-faire lifestyle and a chic city's frenetic pace. At the same time there is palpable condescension toward anyone considered to be without style or beauty, which are the only moral virtues here.

Versace liked to throw lavish parties at Casa Casuarina for celebrity friends. There was no reason to leave his home at night, he once said, because it was the best place to be. He did occasionally venture out at night to a dance club, but mostly he found his pleasure in South Beach during the daylight and early evening, on the beach and the

256

sidewalks, in cafés and restaurants and shops. He liked South Beach, he said, because it was the only place where he could relax. He moved effortlessly and usually unnoticed through the heavy human traffic, day and night.

"Everybody loves me," Versace said, and in South Beach almost everyone did love him. Except on the day of the murder. Before Versace left his house, the surveillance camera at the News Café picked up the shadowy image of Andrew Cunanan hanging around on the sidewalk, as if he were waiting for someone.

• • •

"South Beach was becoming what it is in 1988, three years before Versace came here," says Jerry Powers, publisher of *Ocean Drive,* the model and celebrity magazine that chronicles the lives of South Beach's beautiful people.

Powers is a balding man with thick eyebrows. He is someone else whose success is tied up with the life of the place. His first office, where he put together the premiere issue of his magazine, was over the News Café. One morning he looked out his window and saw Versace sitting below at a table. He hurried downstairs to introduce himself to "the maestro" and ask him for an interview. Versace told him to contact his PR people, but when Powers did, they said the maestro was too busy.

"I told Versace what they said," says Powers, "and he said, 'Come to my hotel; I'll give you all the time you need.' He even got us Claudia Schiffer for our first cover."

Conventional wisdom has it that Versace came to South Beach to relax. But he did do business there. "He got inspiration from the styles of the street kids," says Powers. "He saw the tans and the color of the water and the pastel colors of the buildings and it affected him. Before, he used mostly primary colors. And he could take it all in while letting his guard down. You know, in Italy they kidnap you for ransom. But America is a violent society. We had 18 homicides in Miami during the week of Versace's murder."

In the early Eighties, South Beach was a decrepit stretch of crumbling deco hotels inhabited by retirees waiting to die, crack dealers, Mariel boat people, a few surfer dudes and some brave people who wanted to live a pleasant life on the beach.

Then German photographers discovered it as a beautiful, cheap locale to shoot their summer catalogs. They began to bring in their models, some of whom stayed to live here. The models attracted men and art directors. Today there are 20 modeling agencies on the beach, and at any given time 4,000 young men and women work or wait to work as models.

The Michele Pommier Building at 81 Washington Avenue in South Beach is a silver art deco structure with a circular entranceway of glass blocks. Inside there are floor-to-ceiling mirrors. Michele Pommier herself sits at a glass table and the walls around her are covered with photographs of the beautiful people she represents. Pommier, a conventionally pretty woman of 50, opened her modeling agency in 1988. She says it was South Beach's first agency and it is certainly one of the most successful today.

Pommier says the models were the founding settlers of this American Riviera. "Claudia Schiffer used to Roller-blade down Ocean Drive five years ago," she says. Then came the clubs like Liquid and Bar None, the restaurants like China Grill and the local magazines like *Ocean Drive.*

"The magazines and the clubs find us," says Pommier. "The girls don't get work because they're in *Ocean Drive*. *Ocean Drive* needs the models to exist, not the opposite. The same with the clubs." And then, according to Pommier, came the celebrities. She included Versace in this list. "He introduced South Beach to the fashion world by making his home here," says Pommier.

Pommier's assistant enters the room with two mugs of coffee. She puts them down on the glass table. Pommier glares at the mugs, then at her assistant. "Don't we have napkins?" she says. The assistant leaves and returns moments later with napkins. No one trifles with Pommier, especially not the models and the media.

A few days later, at midnight, dozens of models crowd the VIP room of Bar None, waiting for Pommier to arrive. Most of the models are men. They lie back, insouciantly, on couches against the wall, deep in conversation. The women stand around looking over their shoulders for celebrities.

The male models are all handsome. The female models are exotic looking, but not conventionally pretty. They are dressed in retro outfits—short Qiana shirts that expose their navels, bell-bottom pants and platform shoes. They stand in that model's pose, stomach thrust forward, shoulders rounded like predatory birds on a branch.

Actor Peter Weller, who is in Florida directing an Elmore Leonard movie, *Gold Coast,* is on hand, sitting unnoticed in the VIP room. He stands, looks down at the bar, turns and waits for someone to recognize him. A model goes over to him and introduces herself. They talk intimately, with their faces close.

Well after midnight, a light appears at the entrance to Bar None. Pommier enters, followed by a television camera crew. The camera's light is so close to her face that she's the only person in the room who's clearly visible. "*Extra* [the TV show] has been filming me all night," she says. "First at the Forge, then at the China Grill, now here." She smiles. "See what happens when you put 'Michele Pommier' on an invitation?"

• • •

"We're still trying to answer the question of how Cunanan went undetected during his time in Miami Beach," says Alfred Boza, a Miami Beach Police Department detective and spokesman. "He was not moving about with impunity. Someone at Miami Subs recognized him and called us, but he was gone when we arrived. The problem is Miami Beach's congestion. Sixty percent of the people on the beach are not permanent residents. They're from Miami or New Zealand or wherever. The influx of strangers is so great and Cunanan's look was so average it was hard to pick him out. He fit the description of any number of Latins on the beach. In fact, we grabbed a guy at Versace's memorial service who turned out to be a *Miami Herald* reporter."

• • •

In the late afternoon sun, the beach is still crowded with sunbathers. Beautiful blonde and brunette women walk into the pale green water to cool off, then return to their blankets to sunbathe topless in thong bikinis. An older man with a perfect tan and a dyed blond ponytail tosses a Frisbee to his skinny boyfriend at the water's edge. The old guy, too, is wearing a thong, exposing his small, drooping ass.

Ocean Drive is crowded with exotic cars moving slowly north and south. The drivers and passengers lean out the windows and shout at pretty girls walking up the crowded sidewalk. The walkers stare at the people sitting at the outdoor café tables. The patrons stare back. Staring at people is the major activity on South Beach. It is less a place of conversation than it is a place to worship beauty.

At Wet Willie's, boys in bathing suits that show off their chiseled abs (chiseled abs for boys are big in South Beach) and their girlfriends in low-cut bikinis that show off their tiny waists and navels (navels for girls are big in South Beach), are getting rowdy as they drink. The girls sit on their boyfriends' laps, kicking up their legs and laughing loudly.

VERSACE'S PARADISE

Their boyfriends nuzzle their necks, shout from table to table and yell into their cell phones.

A little farther south, the outdoor tables of Café Milano are filled with a more chic clientele in their late 20s and early 30s. The crowd is dressed stylishly in Seventies retro for a late lunch. Café Milano is the kind of place Andrew Cunanan would have frequented before he fell on hard times and had to eat subs in his room at the Normandy Plaza.

Inside, the restaurant's darkly wooded dining room is deserted, except for a few waiters in yellow shirts, sitting at a table, speaking Italian. The walls around them are decorated with faux Picasso prints and drawings.

"We opened in 1990," says Milano's owner, Massimo Barracca. "Versace was our first customer. He ate macaroni with mozzarella, tomatoes, basil and extra virgin olive oil. He would sit at a table with friends. Only at lunch. He was a lunch person, not a night person. He could go to late-night clubs in any city. He loved South Beach because it has such a large gay community. He could be himself here. He was accepted as a normal person. He felt free here. There's no real gay community in Italy. South Beach is just a village, though, like Italy in a lot of ways. A little city on the beach. It reminded Versace of Italy."

At the News Café, the sidewalk tables are filled with beautiful people and tourists who stare at the beautiful people. Inside, however, the small bar is deserted except for a gray-bearded man in a Hawaiian shirt watching *Oprah* on the television over the bar. Oprah's guest is Madonna, dressed in a pale-blue suit that makes her look fragile, like a suburban mother. It's a look Madonna has cultivated ever since her daughter, Lourdes, was born.

"So tell me," says Oprah. "What are you going to teach Lourdes about men?"

Madonna giggles like a girl, and blushes. The audience hoots, laughs and applauds.

A waitress walks by the TV and stops. "Oh, look! Madonna! I served her last week."

Oprah says, "What do you have to say about Dennis Rodman?"

The audience whoops and applauds and shrieks again. Madonna, looking quite stern now, waits until the noise dies down before she says, "I have no respect for a man who kisses and tells." The audience applauds her answer. People must have forgotten her documentary, *Truth or Dare,* in which Madonna exposes the foibles of her friends and her then lover, Warren Beatty.

Madonna was a friend of Versace's. They used to alternate New Year's

Eve parties every year. One year, Versace sent only ten invitations to Madonna and she was insulted. So she boycotted the party.

The Versace Boutique is around the corner from the News Café. It is often deserted, except for a few muscleboys dressed in black, who stand with their arms folded across their chests at each of the four corners inside the store. They look like bodyguards, but what are they guarding? Versace's baroque prints?

Versace's reputation as an outrageous, risk-taking designer isn't really accurate. He was not a daring designer, but a timid one. His designs were derivative, influenced by classical Greek and Roman designs right down to his trademark Medusa's head. They were mathematically and geometrically plotted out, as if by an engineer. They were balanced, a rose on the left breast, an identical rose on the right breast. Then Versace colored them in with primary colors in the manner of a child compulsively unable to color outside the lines. Versace was a structured man, at least in his work, and, his friends say, in his life, too. That may be why he loved South Beach. It is unstructured. It is all soft edges blurring into one another. Its colors are muted pastels that bleed, one into another. Life on South Beach is blurred with people of every class and race mingling in the same clubs and restaurants like paella, until they all become one.

• • •

"I'll bet everyone loves your hair," says Kevin, as he snips and cuts.

"Why?" asks the silver-haired man in his 50s.

"It's so thick and soft," says Kevin. Snip. Snip.

"Yeah, but it's gray."

"Oh, I have boys come in here all the time and ask me to put silver in their hair. It's to die for."

Kevin gets some gel from his station and begins rubbing it into the man's hair. Kevin is tall and thin, with long blond hair cut like Prince Valiant's. He was Versace's hairdresser at Oribe, on the corner of Collins and Ninth. The walls of Oribe are decorated with giant paintings of naked mermaids.

"I was called to their Bal Harbor store one evening to do Donatella's hair," says Kevin. "She liked what I did so I was summoned to their house one day to do Versace's hair. He was down-to-earth. So shy. Which made me not nervous. After that, he got me this job with Oribe."

Kevin blow-dries the man's silvery hair, fixing it just so with his fingertips. "The murder was an awful thing," he says. "I'm afraid celebrities will be fearful about coming here now. They thought it was so free before."

The silver-haired man thanks Kevin for his haircut and goes to the front desk to pay his bill. The haircut costs $75. He leaves Kevin a $10 tip. The last haircut Andrew Cunanan got in South Beach, at Supercuts, cost him $11. He didn't bother to get a shave because after he murdered Versace he let his beard grow as a disguise.

"I heard they were going to sell the house," says Antonio Martucci in his accented English. "The family can't bear to live there now and be reminded everyday of the murder." Martucci is standing behind the bar of his restaurant, Farfalla.

"I heard Mike Tyson was gonna buy it," says a man eating linguine with clam sauce at the bar. "The furnishings and everything for $45 million."

"I heard that, too," says Martucci. "But I don't think the family will sell it to him."

Farfalla is an old-world Italian restaurant in the middle of South Beach where Versace used to order pizza and, on occasion, stop for an early dinner.

"He'd come in at 7:30 P.M.," says Martucci. "He'd sit by the window with his boyfriend. He was a quiet person, not like a typical Italian. You know how we are—we scream. His sister, now, she wore lots of gold and talked a lot."

Martucci says Versace tended to frequent mostly Italian places in South Beach ("Not gay places," he says) because they reminded him of his birthplace, Reggio Calabria. Martucci points across the street, at an ice cream store, Cocco Fresco.

"After dinner he always stopped there for a gelato because the owner was Italian. But now it's owned by Middle Easterners." He shrugs. "Versace loved it here because he wanted to re-create Italy in South Beach."

After dinner at Farfalla and a gelato at Cocco Fresco, Versace liked to walk north on Washington Avenue so he could window-shop. On rare occasions, he'd stop in the gay bar Twist for a glass of wine. Cunanan stopped in Twist, too, the day before he murdered Versace.

It's an innocuous-looking bar, no different from any other bar except that its customers are all men. A blonde woman stops in not long after the murder. One of the patrons questions her.

"Are you lost?"

The woman says, "No."

"Then you must be a tourist."

"No." She looks annoyed.

"Don't you know what kind of a bar this is?"

"Yes, I know." She finally tells him she is there because she's doing research on Versace for a magazine article.

"Oh, yes, he stopped in here once or twice. Very quiet. Then he left. I heard the family is going to sell the house. I hope someone beautiful buys it." He shrugs. "But who cares?"

• • •

Andrew Cunanan also frequented the late-night dance clubs Warsaw and Liquid, which he'd heard Versace frequented. But according to Versace's friends and employees, the stories that made the rounds were not true. At one time, perhaps, but not after the mysterious change in his lifestyle that happened several years ago.

"He never went to such clubs," says a servant. "He would go only as a courtesy to guests. Oh, I'm sure he had a wild side when he was younger and it served him well."

"He used to go to clubs like Warsaw in his early years in South Beach," says Tara Solomon, the *Miami Herald* columnist known as "the queen of the night." But, she adds, "not after he got sick."

A few years ago, the press reported that Versace was suffering from a form of inner-ear cancer. It was also rumored he had AIDS. When he appeared healthier, he was quoted as saying he was thrilled to have more life to live. But he was different, more sedate, quiet. Perhaps Versace had come to feel uncomfortable in the world with which he had become identified.

South Beach club behavior is "freaky, unabashedly hedonistic and decadent," says Solomon. "The scene encourages uninhibited behavior that many people believe is spiritually bankrupt." Solomon has covered the scene for several years and has strong opinions. "You know, Versace came here to get inspiration. He drew as much from the beach as we did from him. South Beach existed before he got here and he just knew a good thing when he saw it."

Tara Solomon is a short, curvaceous, 40-year-old woman with unlined, ghostly white skin. She doesn't wear clothes, she wears costumes. And she doesn't much like Versace's colorful shirts. "I mean, you can't wear Versace every day," she maintains.

Solomon, dressed like Irma la Douce, arrives at Liquid at two A.M. "They're all so dark, loud, smoky and dirty," she says. "To strangers it's just another dark club. But dark places are appealing to celebrities because they can be anonymous in them." The music is deafening. Couples, mostly women (it's "girls'" night at Liquid), are dancing in the smoky darkness. Solomon moves around the dance floor to a banquette and sits down. Around her, girls in black leather and bustiers are kissing. Tough-looking Hispanic boys walk past, staring at the girls. The crowd looks as if it was plucked en masse from a Calvin Klein ad. One guy, shirtless, is wearing his pants so low around his hips that his assiduously ruffled pubic hair is showing. There's a pornographic cartoon playing on the wall behind Solomon. "These people come to distract themselves," she says, shouting to be heard. "That's what it's all about. Distraction and denial. They think that they're invincible. They reinvent themselves every night."

Tara sees Ingrid Casares, the club owner, who is famous as the gal pal of such celebrities as Madonna and K.D. Lang and Versace. Ingrid looks like a Latin Audrey Hepburn, with closely cropped black hair and big black eyes.

Recently she hosted a party for Lang, who had to share billing with RuPaul. Lang sat in the same banquette Tara is sitting in. She complained about the music.

"I hate fucking disco," Lang said. Then, "Jesus, it's fucking cold."

When it was time for Lang to take the stage with RuPaul, Casares led her through the crowd. RuPaul was talking into the microphone. Finally RuPaul handed Lang the mike and she thanked the audience for coming and returned to her seat. A man asked her, "How does it feel to be upstaged by a no-talent drag queen?"

Lang said, "The fucking shit I got to do. Tomorrow I go to an AIDS benefit." She raised her eyebrows. "On Ivana Trump's yacht."

When Cunanan went to Liquid during his stay in Miami, he reinvented himself, too. He struck up a conversation with some drag queens, telling them he was working on a research paper for graduate school.

It's 3:30 A.M. when Solomon leaves Liquid for the short walk around the corner to the gay men's club Warsaw. The atmosphere inside Warsaw is not much different from Liquid's, except that all the clubbers are boys. The huge ballroom dance floor is packed with what Tara calls "genetically blessed and testosterone-filled boys," shirtless and muscular, dancing manically as if there will be no tomorrow. Solomon shouts above the din, "More people have a need to lose themselves than they do to find themselves." She walks past the stage where a lone, muscular guy, wearing only a gold lamé G-string, is gyrating and thrusting his hips at the dancers below him.

Tara goes to the upstairs bar and orders a drink. "They usually have amateur strip nights on Wednesdays," she says. "Just good clean fun." Tara prefers gay clubs to straight clubs, she says, "because I feel protected. Gay men are peacemakers. Gay clubs are also more uninhibited when it conies to sex."

One local straight bachelor says he loves to go to Warsaw with female dates because "when they see two men having sex it turns them on. They get so aroused, they're all over me."

Versace liked to go to Warsaw, too, before he "got sick." He would come with some "pretty young boys," according to Max Blandford, Warsaw's manager. Versace shunned the VIP sections and preferred to spend his time in the trenches with the wildly dancing boys.

• • •

It's 4:45 in the morning and there's still a line of clubbers trying to get into Liquid. The streets are crowded with young women and men, their eyes glassy, staggering down the sidewalks. In the street in front of Liquid, a policeman has handcuffed a man who is bent over the hood of his car. Across the way the 13th Street parking garage entrance is crowded with homeless men.

The 13th Street garage is where Cunanan parked the red Chevy truck he stole from William Reese, the man he killed in New Jersey. It's also where he ran to change his clothes after he murdered Versace.

At five A.M., the late-night clubbers wander down to the News Café for breakfast. The café is still playing loud dance music over its speakers. When the last of the late-nighters leaves after six o'clock, a woman with gray hair comes out with a hose and begins hosing down the tables, chairs and sidewalk. The stereo speakers switch to soft and soothing chamber music. The breakfast waiters begin to arrive.

The older, early-morning crowd begins to arrive a little later. Men in jogging shorts and flip-flops and women in spandex bra tops, shorts and sneakers sit down with their newspapers and order coffee. This is the crowd Versace was a part of when he left his mansion on the morning of July 15. He talked briefly with a waitress and began walking back toward his mansion at 8:40 A.M. He was unaware he was being followed by a disheveled, backpack-toting man wearing a white baseball cap, a white shirt and black shorts.

When Versace got to the stone steps of his mansion at 8:42 A.M., the man following him spoke to him, according to witnesses. Then the two men began to tussle. Versace tried to pull away from the man. The man pulled out a gun and shot Versace in the head. As Versace fell to the steps, the man aimed his gun at him and shot Versace a second time in the head. Then he turned and calmly walked away.

Inside, Versace's chef was preparing his breakfast (waffles and fruit). Antonio D'Amico heard the shots. He came running out the front door to find his lover dying on the steps. He screamed, "Gianni! Gianni!" Then he saw the killer walking away. He ran after him, shouting. The killer turned and leveled his gun at D'Amico. D'Amico stopped, backed off and ran back to his dying lover.

Inside the mansion, a servant was screaming into the telephone at the 911 operator, "A man's been shot!"

• • •

What did Cunanan say to Versace when Versace reached the steps to his house and began to open the wrought-iron gate?

Perhaps it was, "Gianni, it's me! Don't you remember?"

Versace turns to see a man who has fallen on hard times. Even if he had once met Cunanan when he had been a pampered young lover of older men, Versace probably would not have recognized him now. To Versace, this man was probably just another of those annoying people who accosted him because he was famous. "I refuse to be molested," Versace once said. "I put a DO NOT DISTURB notice on my life." So Versace turns to the man and says, "No, I'm afraid I don't know you." He turns to go through the gate.

"But we met once. You must remember. You must!"

The stranger reaches out a hand to grab Versace's arm. To make him remember. To force him to stay there until he does remember. And when he does, when Versace's face breaks into a broad smile, and he says, "Oh, of course, now I remember. How are you? Come in. Come into my life," then the stranger's life will be righted again. He will return again to that privileged, indulgent life of his recent past.

But Versace does not remember. He tries to pull his arm from the younger man's grasp. In that instant, rebuffed again by a wealthy, older gay man, Cunanan becomes infuriated. Without thinking, without having planned it, he reaches for his gun. He points it at the older man's head and pulls the trigger, as so many spurned suitors have done in the heat of rejected passion.

Don't Worry, We Only Kill Each Other

by **JAMIE MALANOWSKI**
May 2000

From Don Corleone to Tony Soprano, the mob has had an uncanny grip on our imagination. Colorful characters? Fuhgeddaboutit. These guys are killers.

Let's face it: Deep inside every man there is a mobster yearning to breathe free. He may be a small mobster, a weenie among mobsters, a mobster who doesn't do anything but put on a pinkie ring occasionally. Why? It's simple. We all want to seem cool, we all want to seem tough, we all want to look like we know our way around a broad and a pool cue and the business end of a calamari. Like the Old West, mob life is one of America's great myths, and we can't get enough of it. The mob has provided an alter ego for each American era. It doesn't matter that real mobsters, men like Sam Giancana and Albert Anastasia and Carmine "the Snake" Persico, were and are brutes and thugs and sociopaths who would without effort turn us into sausage meat. Inside all of us is a little mobster yearning to breathe free.

Vito Corleone of *The Godfather* was the mob's first hero. Thanks to Vito, men who had previously rooted for Eliot Ness, who for years listened to Sinatra without detecting a hint of subtext, suddenly began picturing their enemies asleep with the fishes. *The Godfather* is set in the Fifties, but it is truly a Seventies picture. Vito rejected authority while living an ethical life—at least within the norms of the society he inhabits. The little mobster inside was delighted.

Hollywood fed us more mobsters after *The Godfathers*, all less magisterial than Vito: the over-the-top *Scarface*, the scheming outerborough thugs of *Goodfellas*, the pathetic small-timers of *Donnie Brasco*, the downsized Michael of *Godfather Part III*. Filling the gap fell to John Gotti, who offered the public glamour, bravura and some Teflon-coated escapes. He ruled while establishment types were acting like mobsters: Savings and loan officials looted the safes, Oliver North stonewalled Congress, George Steinbrenner paid for dirt about Dave Winfield, Mike Ovitz allegedly said he would send his "foot soldiers up and down Wilshire" to destroy a screenwriter. A celebrity mafioso was just part of the parade. Then the show drew to a close. Gotti turned out to be a bad don whose lapses proved so disastrous that, unlike Trump, Ovitz, Milken and Steinbrenner, he has yet to enjoy a comeback.

The mafioso of the moment is Tony Soprano, a middle-aged, suburban mobster dad with a family and headaches and an SUV that gets lousy mileage. Mobsters used to be guys from the old neighborhood, but Tony is from our neighborhood. We like him for his modern virtues. He's a good boss, a considerate family man, a guy who's getting in touch with his inner feelings. If he's short-tempered, well, haven't we all succumbed to a bout of road rage now and then? And just because he's a killer, who among us doesn't have an issue or two to work on?

The beauty of the mob myth lies in how it has adapted to change. It's a prism through which we view ourselves. We've seen the magisterial mob and the downsized mob, a "Take the cannoli" mob and a "Take the Prozac" mob. And we will keep watching, of course. Who in 2020 won't tune in to see what Meadow Soprano does with her dad's organization?

THE QUOTABLE MOBSTER

In mob history, turning a phrase is second only to turning informant.

ON OPTIMISM

"I'm only going out for a few minutes. Besides, I'm wearing thermal underwear."—Genovese crime lieutenant Tony Bender, in the last words spoken to his wife before his 1962 disappearance

ON POPULARITY

"Senator, I'm the best goddamned lay in the world."—Actress Virginia Hill, at Senate hearings, explaining why so many mobsters liked her

THE PRINCIPLES OF BUSINESS

"Don't worry, we only kill each other."—Bugsy Siegel, trying to calm Flamingo builder Del Webb

ON BEING CAREFUL

"I take the Fifth on the horse and the broad."—Chicago hood Fifi Buccieri, on the rumor that his brother had given a horse to his girlfriend

ON ANSWERING TO A HIGHER AUTHORITY

"God is a fucking fag."—John Gotti

ON UPHOLDING APPEARANCES

"I'm sorry, counselor. I'd rather blow the goddamn case."—Frank Costello, known as the Prime Minister of the Underworld, refusing his attorney's advise that he dress less sharply while on trial

ON REGRETS, I'VE HAD A FEW

"Jesus, I'm sorry to hear that."—Vincent "The Chin" Gigante to John Gotti, after Gotti announced his son had become a made member

"I've learned too late that you need just as good a brain to make a crooked million as an honest million. These days you apply for a license to steal from the public. If I had my time again, I'd make sure I got that license first."—Lucky Luciano

ON MATH

"It was 49, Your Honor."—Convicted murderer Richard Pagliarulo at his sentencing, interrupting the judge who'd pegged his body count at 48

ON PAYING THE CONSEQUENCES

"The guy really pissed me off. When I shot him in the head, his blood spurted all over my car. And I had just washed that goddamn car."—Anthony "Gas Pipe" Casso

BY WAY OF EXPLANATION

"I'm going to shoot some pheasants."—Capone torpedo and avid golfer Sam "Golf Bag" Hunt, explaining to inquisitive lawmen the presence of a shotgun in his golf bag

DON'T WORRY, WE ONLY KILL EACH OTHER

Are you ready to join our social club?

1. Bonanno family capo Nicky Marangello was known by three nicknames. Which of these was not among them?
(a) Nicky Glasses. (b) Nicky Cigars. (c) Little Nicky. (d) Nicky the Pooh.

2. In federal prison, boss Vito Genovese gave hit man Joe Valachi a kiss. What happened next?
(a) Nothing. They remained good friends. (b) Joe filed a sex harassment suit. (c) Joe slipped him some tongue. (d) Recognizing the kiss of death, Joe turned informer.

3. Which sentence uses the word fugazy the way a mobster would?
(a) "This diamond is fake. It's a fugazy!" (b) "When the moon hits your eye like a big pizza pie, that's fugazy." (c) "The secret to my scungilli is that I marinate it in fugazy." (d) "Fugazy inna girl's eyes, maybe later she put out."

4. What mobster is featured in a Bruce Springsteen song?
(a) Phil "Chicken Man" Testa ("Atlantic City"). (b) Pico "Rosalita" della Mirandella ("Rosalita"). (c) Benedetto "Tom Joad" Croce ("Ghost of Tom Joad"). (d) Lorenzo "Dancing in the Dark" Borgia ("Dancing in the Dark").

5. What did mobster Longy Zwillman keep in his wallet?
(a) Ten dollars in mad money for emergencies. (b) His Dick Tracy Junior Crimebusters ID card. (c) A photo of Sinatra. (d) A lock of Jean Harlow's pubic hair.

6. What does a mobster mean when he says he's "bringing both sets"?
(a) His wife and his girlfriend. (b) The books the boss sees and the books the IRS sees. (c) His Callaways and his Pings. (d) Two pinkie rings.

7. When mobsters send a floral arrangement to the funeral of a fellow mobster, what does the ribbon customarily say?
(a) SEE YOU IN HELL. (b) R.I.P., YOU RAT BASTARD. (c) HOW COULD THIS HAVE HAPPENED? (d) OUR PAL.

8. What was the biggest regret of Louis "Two Gun" Alterie?
(a) Not finishing school. (b) Not spending more time with his kids. (c) All those cannoli! (d) When he began packing a third gun, the press did not redub him "Three Gun."

9. Why is Baldwin-Wallace College in Berea, Ohio referred to as Mafia U?
(a) It has a fine criminology program. (b) Danny Greene went there. (c) It offers courses in loan-sharking. (d) The school has cooperated with the Witness Protection Program in creating false identities.

10. What does "buckwheats" mean to a mobster?
(a) A good source of fiber. (b) Alfalfa's friend. (e) A commodities scam. (d) Torturing a victim prior to execution.

11. What did Joe Colombo do to Carlo Gambino that Gambino had him hit?
(a) He forgot to send Carlo a Christmas card. (b) He made disparaging remarks about the way Carlo's social club was decorated. (c) He referred to Carlo as "Gam-WEEN-o". (d) He spit in Carlo's face.

12. What did Godfather Joseph Profaci keep in his basement?
(a) A foosball game. (b) A washer and drier. (c) Meat hooks and a band saw. (d) An altar for family mass.

13. What is the name of this tightly knit West Coast group known for its muscle?
(a) Mickey Mouse Mafia. (b) The Gazpacho Gang. (c) The Starstruck Syndicate. (d) Miramax Films.

14. What does "omertà" mean?
(a) Manliness. (b) Let us pray. (c) Shut up, asshole. (d) Scrambled eggs with roasted peppers and parmesan.

15. What, besides his name and address, did Al Capone have on his business card?
(a) KING OF THE UNDERWORLD. (b) PRODUCT OF A BROKEN HOME. (C) SECONDHAND FURNITURE DEALER. (d) HIT TEN, GET THE NEXT ONE FREE!

Answers:
1. d, 2. d, 3. a, 4. a, 5. d, 6. a, 7. d, 8. d, 9. d, 10. d, 11. d, 12. d, 13. a, 14. a, 15. c

MOB RECORDINGS

Thanks to the efforts of law enforcement officers, there are now more recordings of mobsters than there are of Frank Sinatra, Dean Martin, Tony Bennett, Vic Damone, Buddy Greco, Jerry Vale, Louis Prima and Jimmy Roselli put together. Here are some hits:

DON'T WORRY, WE ONLY KILL EACH OTHER

Consigliere Joseph Russo and capo Vincent Ferrara, of the Patriarca crime family of New England, prepare for a secret initiation rite in 1989:

RUSSO: "Okay, we could put some seats over there, and some over there. Christ, these seats take up a lot of fucking space."

FERRARA: "You could put some there."

RUSSO: "A lot of fucking space. And the food's going to take up a lot of space. What are you putting over there?"

FERRARA: "Ashtrays."

RUSSO: "Fuck, Vinny, I told you this is a nonsmoking house. I don't want to see any ashtrays. If she smells smoke when she comes back, she's going to have a fit. These guys don't hate me enough, now I'm in charge of this."

FERRARA: "We got to do the best we can, Joe."

RUSSO: "I know."

FERRARA: "And they're all stupid. What do you care what they think?"

RUSSO: "Look, I don't want any criticism from anybody in any way, shape or form."

John Gotti, recorded in federal prison in January 1998, speaks to his brother Peter and to his grandson. Gotti encourages the boy to study hard and become a lawyer. The boy says he'd rather be a professional athlete:

GOTTI: "To be a good basketball player or baseball player, first of all, you got to be a good liar. A good lowlife and an imbecile. And you got to take steroids! You must take steroids, and anybody who takes steroids is a garbage pail."

BOY: [Softly] "Fine. Then I'll be a crook."

GOTTI: "I don't care if you'll be nothin'! You think you're being spiteful with me? You'll get an ass-kicking from me! I know how to raise children!" [The boy drops his head against his chest.]

GOTTI: "You ain't doing me no favor coming to see me and talking sass to me! I will put my foot right up your ass. Don't you look at me like that! I'm more serious than cancer! You can look as sad as you want. Now, give that phone to your uncle and get out of here!" [The grandson flees the cubicle, head down.]

GOTTI: [To his brother] "These visits, I got to keep them to a minimum. When I go back upstairs to my cell, it breaks my heart. Let's try and salvage some of this visit. You know anything good? Anything good anyone wants to talk about?"

PETER: "Not really, everything's normal."

GOTTI: "That's perfect. That's terrifying. Normal. Normal in this family is terrifying, that's for sure. Normal in this family is terrifying."

Members of the DeCavalcante family of New Jersey—capo Anthony Rotondo and several soldiers, one of whom is an informant wearing a wire—talking before a sit-down on March 3, 1999:

JOSEPH "TIN EAR" SCLAFANI: "Hey, what's this fucking thing 'Sopranos'? What the fuck are they?"

RALPHIE [cooperating with the feds]: "You ever watch it?"

SCLAFANI: "Is that supposed to be us?"

ROTONDO: "You're in there. They mentioned your name in there."

SCLAFANI: "Yeah, what did they say?"

BILLY [last name unknown]: "'Watch out for that guy,' they said. 'Watch out for that guy.'"

ROTONDO: "Every show you watch. More and more you pick up somebody. Every show."

SCLAFANI: "Yeah, but it's not me. I'm not even existing over there."

ROTONDO: "One week it was Corky. One week it was, well, from the beginning it was Albert G., the guy that died and had stomach cancer."

BILLY: "They had the guy die with stomach cancer?"

SCLAFANI: "Yeah, but where do they get this information from?"

BILLY: "I'm telling you. You got to watch."

SCLAFANI: "So what they say?"

ROTONDO: "Aren't they funny? What characters. Great acting."

THE NUMBERS RACKET

Annual interest rate percentage, according to one investigation, charged by a typical Manhattan loan shark: 3000

Net worth, in millions, of Meyer Lansky at the time of his death in 1983: $400

Number of slugs found in the body of Joseph Aiello, Chicago mobster, in 1930: 59. The slugs added more than a pound to Aiello's body weight.

Number of putts taken on the sixth green by an upset Sam Giancana when he discovered himself under close personal surveillance by half a dozen FBI agents: 18

Age at which Bugsy Siegel was already heading his own gang: 14

DON'T WORRY, WE ONLY KILL EACH OTHER

Weight in pounds of Peter "Fat Pete" Chiodo, Lucchese family enforcer: 547. His avoirdupois enabled him to absorb seven bullets from a hit man and live.

Cost, in cents, of a bunch of parsley to restaurant owners in Manhattan in the early Eighties: 5

Cost, in cents, after the Mafia got control of the parsley market: 40. Remarkably, in defiance of the law of supply and demand, restaurant owners increased their orders.

Number of dollars received by bandleader Tommy Dorsey for releasing Frank Sinatra from his contract, after the intercession of mobster Willie Moretti: 1

Amount per year the World Trade Center paid to a mafia-connected trash hauler: $1.2 million

Amount paid when a legitimate businessman replaced him: $150,000

MAFIA MAN

New York Attorney Lou Diamond estimates that he has handled more than 10,000 criminal cases during his career. Among his clients have been bosses, acting bosses, underbosses and consiglieri.

What's the best part of representing monsters?
There is no best part now. Ten or 15 years ago I would have given you a completely different answer. Then they constituted the most exciting cases a criminal trial lawyer could handle, action at a very high level.

What's been the big change?
Drugs. And the penalties for dealing drugs. Back then, you had higher-quality clients, old-timers who had honor. They didn't give up people. You didn't have everybody looking to become a cooperating witness.

What's the worst part?
Not getting paid. Some of these guys would rather eat their children than pay me. There was a lawyer who had his arm broke a couple years ago. He told everybody it was a mugger trying to get his Rolex. Later it came out Gotti had somebody break his arm because he kept asking for money for court transcripts.

Gee, that makes them seem like cheapskates.
They don't have the money anymore. They're on the run. Look at

274

the crimes they're committing. Acts of desperation. One guy I know, when he got straightened out, he got depressed. He told me, "Before, I was good earner, made a good living. Now I got this one-way ticket to jail or to the graveyard."

What's the future of organized crime?

The Europeans, particularly the Russians. They're like the Sicilians who came over at the turn of the century in that they're hard and ruthless. But they're also very sophisticated and well financed.

Is "The Sopranos" realistic?

Absolutely. If anything, they haven't shown how hilarious the really stupid stuff is that they do. Shooting a bakery clerk in the foot over some cannoli? I got that case yesterday. That happens all the time.

THE REAL DEAL

As lovable as mobsters may be, it's important not to forget that deep down, many of these colorful rogues are actually sadists of the most vicious sort. Tony Spilotro, Chicago's man in Vegas, once crushed a man's head in a vise until his eyes popped out. Riccardo "Richie the Boot" Boiardo, a legend in the Lucchese family, maintained a crematorium on his New Jersey property where he sometimes roasted his victims alive. The kill-happy members of the DeMeo crew would pop victims then hang their corpses in the shower until the blood drained out; they became so bloodthirsty Big Paulie Castellano had to have them killed. William "Action" Jackson, a 300-pound bag man from Chicago who was suspected of being a stoolie, was hanged for two days by his chained feet from a meat hook by Mad Sam DeStefano. He'd been beaten, shot, carved with a razor and burned with a blowtorch; a fed bug caught one of his killers gleefully reminiscing about the ordeal, regretting only that he died too soon. Finally, consider the case of the architect who worked on Gas Pipe Casso's million-dollar home and submitted a $40,000 bill. Gas Pipe dismembered the architect, but not until he worked him over with an acetylene torch and gouged out his eyes with red-hot spoons.

275

Biker Wars

by JAMES R. PETERSEN
November 2000

DATE: November 22, 1994

FROM: Bureau of Alcohol, Tobacco and Firearms, Washington, D.C.

TO: All Federal, State and Local Law Enforcement Agencies

SUBJECT: Officer Safety Advisory

Since October 1993, a series of escalating violent acts and conflicts have taken place between Chicago-area Outlaws and Hell's Angels motorcycle clubs. This growing feud is the result of a territorial conflict involving the conversion of Hell's Henchmen Motorcycle Club to Hell's Angels. The Outlaws are vehemently opposed to the Hell's Angels' establishing a Midwest chapter and are aggressively protecting their territory. To date, as a result of this feud, there have been three documented homicides and six bombings in the three-state area. All law enforcement personnel should take extreme caution when stopping or encountering members of Outlaws or Hell's Angels motorcycle clubs.

• • •

This fax may be the first document to recognize the range war between two of America's largest biker gangs, which seemed to take Washington by surprise. In 1987 the feds arrested archangel Ralph "Sonny" Barger and dozens of his associates on charges related to a plot to blow up the Chicago clubhouse of the Outlaws. (The plan had been concocted by an undercover provocateur.) News accounts had predicted that biker gangs would just fade away without leadership. The stories were wrong.

The incident credited with escalating the conflict occurred on June 25, 1994. Peter Rogers, a.k.a. Grease or Greased Lightning, was riding his Harley-Davidson on the Dan Ryan Expressway in Chicago. A van pulled up behind him, the occupants opened fire and the regional president of the Outlaws took a bullet in the leg and another in the gut before escaping up an exit ramp.

Word of the shooting spread throughout the Midwest. The next day, the Outlaws made their annual run to the Illiana Motor Speedway for the motorcycle drag races and a swap meet. Spokesmen for the gang warned a BATF agent on the scene that if the Invaders (a club associated with the Hell's Angels) showed up, there would be "dead bodies all around." No Invaders attended, but after the event, police pulled over the Outlaws' fortified war wagon—an armor-plated van with a gun port. Inside it were handguns, rifles, a submachine gun, bulletproof vests, smoke grenades, ammunition and walkie-talkies.

The day after that, June 27, David Wolf, a former member of the Insanity Motorcycle Club and a would-be Outlaw, saw an opportunity to prove himself. Kevin "Spike" O'Neill, president of the Wisconsin/Stateline chapter of the Outlaws, gave Wolf a map of Rockford, Illinois, with a circle around a motorcycle shop owned by a Hell's Henchman. O'Neill wanted Wolf to check out LaMonte Mathias, a nationally known drag racer and leader of the Henchmen's weekly runs. According to Wolf, O'Neill was vague at first. "I'm not going to ask you to kill the guy. I'm not going to come right out and ask you. If the opportunity comes up, do what you can." Then the Outlaw indicated by a gesture that he wanted Wolf to cut the enemy's throat. If Mathias were there with his old lady, the instruction continued, kill them both.

Wolf traveled to Rockford with Harvey "RV" Powers, a former member of the Death Marauders, who was also a probationary Outlaw. Accompanying them was Alan "Big Al" McVay, a hang-around friend of the club. The trio partied in the car, did a few lines of coke, checked into a motel and then cruised the nudie bars.

The next morning the hit squad overslept. Because Wolf had no tattoos that might warn his intended victim, he volunteered to check out Mathias' motorcycle shop. He tucked his unruly hair under a baseball cap, entered the shop and bought some spark plugs from a man who matched the description of Mathias.

Wolf left the shop but returned a few moments later and asked to exchange the plugs. Sensing something, Mathias dove through a door to the back of the shop. Wolf opened fire with a .45. Three slugs tore into the target's shoulder, head and neck. Mathias was still alive, but Wolf then bludgeoned the biker with enough force to break off a section of the gun's butt. Wolf tried to flee out the back of the shop but found the door locked. He came out through the showroom and found Mathias alive and cursing. Wolf picked up a screwdriver and repeatedly stabbed Mathias in the throat. (A coroner would later characterize the lacerations as "frenzy wounds.")

After the attack, the hit squad drove to the farm of a biker friend and used an acetylene torch to melt down the murder weapon. They tossed the remaining blob of metal into a pond. Wolf then burned his blood-soaked clothes.

According to Wolf, Powers telephoned O'Neill. "The head gasket you wanted us to look at is blown," was the cryptic message. "It was leaking like a sieve when we left it."

Mathias was buried in full Angel colors. More than 300 Angels and members of affiliated clubs rode through Rockford, honoring him with the sound of rolling thunder.

For his enterprise and initiative, Wolf was made a full member of the Outlaws, given a belt buckle with the twin lightning bolts of the SS and treated to a weekend at the FantaSuite Hotel.

CRY HAVOC

Three months later, Wolf would defend the colors a second time. On September 25, 1994, the Outlaws confronted Angels at the Lancaster Speedway, near Buffalo, New York.

Someone had tossed two grenades into the house of Walter "Big Wally" Posnjak, head of the Buffalo Outlaws. His wife and daughter, home at the time, escaped injury. Posnjak had called for support and carloads of Outlaws arrived from around the country.

Armed with bats, brass knuckles, ax handles, knives and handguns tucked into waistbands, between 20 and 50 Outlaws invaded the speedway. In the middle of the pit, they tangled with a small group of Hell's Angels. Wolf and a red-haired guy from Ohio pulled down an Angel, trying to cut the colors from his jacket. Don Fogg and Randy "Mad" Yager, two Outlaws from the Gary chapter, did the same to another Angel.

A third Angel fired one shot from a Charter Arms .44-caliber automatic. The bullet lifted Big Wally off the ground and threw him backward several feet.

The melee evaporated with Outlaws and Angels running like characters in a Monty Python movie, climbing fences, throwing knives in garbage cans and guns under cars.

Michael Quale, a Hell's Angel, was rapidly bleeding to death from multiple knife wounds.

Police stopped a carload of Outlaws about 45 miles from the Speedway and retrieved a set of blood-stained colors. After taking names they let

278

the bikers go. In all, police recovered 23 guns, none of which was traceable. Blood on a bowie knife and a folding knife matched the DNA of Quale but the weapons had no useful fingerprints.

Local papers covered the funerals and spoke of the Angels' winning the war over bragging rights. Almost 400 motorcycles and twice that many mourners turned out to honor Michael Quale. In contrast, only about 100 bikers turned out for Posnjak's funeral.

The rumble was too big to overlook. Police arrested Robert Herold, a member of the Rochester Angels. A pistol recovered from his house matched shell casings found at the speedway, but a senior firearms examiner cleaned the rusted gun with a brass brush before test firing, changing the ballistic markings. Herold was acquitted.

Don Fogg, the Outlaw found with the blood-soaked colors and a primary suspect in Quale's death, was less fortunate. In late January police found Fogg's body next to his truck, three bullet holes in his head. Was it retaliation, or was Fogg killed by his own club? During Herold's trial, a story circulated that Fogg was a police informant. Others suggest that Fogg was out of control, inviting heat by wearing an upside down death's head as a trophy of the Lancaster killing. In 1997, the government indicted Harry "Taco" Bowman, the Detroit-based president of the Outlaws, for the murder of one of his own.

THE TAPES

The case against the Outlaws was the gift of Patricia Wolf. Outraged at her husband's flagrant womanizing, she'd come home from a bar one night in February 1994 and called the Crimestoppers' hotline. She described the car Wolf would be driving and told them he was carrying cocaine.

The next day, a Lake County Sheriff's Department investigator called. Patricia agreed to inform on her husband.

The night before LaMonte Mathias was killed, Patricia warned her police contact that David was going to Rockford "to surveil a Hell's Henchman for three to five days and then do him." The agents did not warn Mathias, and there are conflicting accounts as to whether the motorcycle shop was put under surveillance. According to one BATF agent, they were meeting for coffee and doughnuts when the biker was murdered.

Again, nine days before the Lancaster shootout, Patricia Wolf told her contact that her husband was going to the speedway to confront Hell's Angels. No preventive measures were taken.

Was the BATF willing to risk lives to gather information, to let the war rage on while it built a case? There is evidence that agents leaked the names and addresses of Outlaw members to Henchmen and Hell's Angels. O'Neill would later claim that a Chicago police detective passed along the names and addresses of local Hell's Angels to the Outlaws.

Members of the investigating team leaked details to a reporter for Indiana's *Hammond Times*. One "bike watcher" suggested that the only way for the Outlaws to avoid all-out war was to sacrifice (i.e., murder) the entire Stateline chapter. The tactic—incite, observe, arrest—is known as stirring the pot or tickling the wire.

Agents gave Patricia a lamp with a concealed transmitter to place in the Wolf residence, along with a bugged telephone. When Kevin O'Neill admired the lamp, Patricia gave him a similarly equipped lamp.

The listening devices were installed without a court order (the BATF would argue that the Outlaws bugged themselves). Eventually agents secured a Title III wiretap authorization and commenced the surveillance. During the next four months, the Trojan lamps and bugged phone captured hundreds of hours of conversation.

The lamps picked up not only hours of talk but sound bites of what was happening in the background. The tapes reveal the foot soldier's view of the war.

Tape C-23: As they're listening to what sounds like an *Our Gang* episode or the Cartoon Network, David Wolf, Harvey Powers and Robert Kruppstadt discuss a blood run, how best to carry weapons, how to poison guard dogs, how to kneecap a victim so he'll never ride a motorcycle again.

POWERS: "If it's in the right spot, we're talking about clunking their kneecaps and shit. Spike says fuck that, if we're going to do that, why not just stick the guns in their fucking knees and fucking blow their kneecaps out with a gun, with a pistol? What would be the difference?"

WOLF: "Get before the judge, when it comes to that——"

POWERS: "Yeah, when it comes before the judge, you tried to cripple the man. It doesn't matter what you cripple him with."

WOLF: "You savagely beat him with a wrench, which makes things worse than popping them with one bullet."

In another tape, Wolf and Kruppstadt watch a TV news report on the Oklahoma City bombing.

KRUPPSTADT: "That's one devastating bomb. We need to learn more about these techniques."

WOLF: "You know, when they showed that building, you know, destroyed, but then they show the rescue workers how, like—shit, they look like ants on there—that's when you realize how much fucking rubble there was."

On tape, Outlaws joke about the high cost of the "prime fucking filets" used to knock out guard dogs, that the club is running out of nonfelons to use as gun-bearers, that they need better bombs, that they can't even burn down the Angels' clubhouse. They talk about killing Angels with Uzis, then cutting their heads off. Maybe even keeping the heads as trophies.

KRUPPSTADT: "If I get caught with it, what am I going to do?"

POWERS: "You would have gotten away with it, friend, if you wouldn't have taken the head with you."

WOLF: [*Laughing*] "Son of a bitch, I'll remember next time not to do that."

The rec-room tapes capture Kevin O'Neill debriefing a fellow biker on April 9, 1995, about an Outlaw meeting in Tennessee, how presidents from other regions had expressed dismay at the escalating war in the Midwest: "I stood up, and I says, Hey, you know, I don't know if you think we started this war or what the deal is up there in Wisconsin. Them Angels were circling around us. LaMonte Mathias lied to us saying that them Angels weren't around, and I said, if things wouldn't have started when they did, there'd be double the amount of Hell's Angels in Chicago right now. So whoever did what, did it for a good fucking reason. I didn't admit to nothing you know. I said when we got in this club we were told that any chance we got at them fuckers coming through our fucking state to go for it. That's the way I was brought up."

On another tape, he dismisses the presidents of other clubs.

O'NEILL: "Fucking ungrateful motherfuckers."

Within a few days of the Mathias murder, the Outlaws heard that the police suspected two Outlaw probates. And, it was said, the wife of one of the probates was a snitch. It was against club rules to talk club business with "cunts." Wolf, who after each escapade would have sex with his wife and tell her everything, began to suspect that Patricia was the informant.

The Outlaws acquired a government training tape about how agents could get biker old ladies to turn on their guys.

Tape C-264: On March 12, 1995 Wolf put the training tape into his

VCR and turned up the volume. The bugged lamp picked up the dispassionate voice of the narrator: "Stopping biker groups requires skill, planning." David Wolf and Harvey Powers scream at Patricia:

WOLF: "You are a stinking piece of shit cunt. Maybe if you didn't spend so much fucking time worrying about other fucking shit that doesn't even concern you, you'd have time to remember this shit, wouldn't you? Wouldn't you? Maybe if you didn't spend all your time thinking I was with some fucking cunt, you'd take care of business at home and I wouldn't even think about it."

POWERS: "Property of Outlaws, shit. You keep fucking around you're going to find out real soon what fucking 'God forgives, Outlaws don't' really means, baby."

The two dragged Patricia out to the car. The agents in the command center, fearing for her life, intercepted the car and staged a mock arrest of Patricia on drug charges.

Seventeen days later, Patricia called Wolf, saying she had just spoken to the grand jury. The tape begins with her announcement that "they know a lot about that fucking murder in Rockford."

PATRICIA: "Listen to what I got to say. okay?"
WOLF: "On this phone?"
PATRICIA: "On this phone. I don't give a fuck."
WOLF: "I don't know nothing about that thing."
PATRICIA: "Well, fine. I don't give a shit what you're going to say right now, I told Spike."
WOLF: "You what?"
PATRICIA: "I told Spike. I told him I knew about that murder."
WOLF: "Why would you do that? I don't know nothing about it."

She tells Wolf that a prosecutor "offered me witness protection if I would testify. He gave me his pager number and I think you should consider calling this number."

WOLF: "I should?"
PATRICIA: "Yes."
WOLF: "Why?"
PATRICIA: "Just so you have an option. Okay?"
WOLF: "Who, me?"
PATRICIA: "Yes, take the number."

WOLF: "Tricia, can't we talk in person, please?"

PATRICIA: "Take the number."

WOLF: "Please, Tricia."

PATRICIA: "Take the number."

WOLF: "Tricia, you're scaring me. What are you talking about?"

PATRICIA: "I'm not going to see you. Take the number. Get a pen."

WOLF: "Hold on. Tricia, no, don't do this, don't do this, Tricia. Oh God, Tricia, don't do this."

PATRICIA: "Take the number."

The tape catches the sounds of Wolf crying, screaming, sobbing, hyperventilating, then vomiting in fear.

The wire had captured multiple beatings and an unspecified number of blow jobs. Now the wiretap captured Patricia Wolf's revenge.

Within a month, Kevin O'Neill discovered the lamp bugs. Fearing reprisals from his own club, David Wolf turned himself in and began cooperating with the government, telling his stories to all who would listen.

JANET RENO'S WAR

In 1994 Janet Reno declared war on violent crime, authorizing government agents to use all the tools at their disposal—the "federal weapons" of grand jury investigations, wiretaps, pretrial detention, mandatory minimums and racketeering statutes. In 1996, she announced her goal: to "dismantle" gangs. At the top of her list were the Hell's Angels and the Outlaws. They were, she would say, among the top 15 crime cartels in the U.S., evoking images of empires built on blood, bodies and illegal drugs.

The government launched investigations against the Sons of Silence in Denver, the Breed in Asbury Park, New Jersey, the Vagos in San Diego and southern Oregon, as well as the Outlaws in the Midwest, North Carolina and Florida.

The Outlaws would later claim that they were the victims of a BATF image crisis, that in the aftermath of Waco and Ruby Ridge, the government went looking for more-conspicuous bad guys. Indeed, during this period, the feds shifted from "one man, one gun" cases to crusades against criminal enterprises. Washington, like Hollywood, knows that before you can have a hero, you must create a villain.

Bikers are one of the most identifiable subcultures in America, the subject of movies, documentaries, magazines and gallery exhibits. American originals, they were pop culture figures in the Sixties, the brawny version of the Beats, the darlings of academics and journalists. Somewhere in the memory of every baby boomer are images of Angels tongue kissing, of Angels sporting chrome Kaiser Wilhelm helmets and Nazi regalia, riding in funeral processions to honor the fallen. Bikers were the guys who volunteered to go to Vietnam and kick butt. Out of prison, Sonny Barger, now 62, recently toured the country to promote his autobiography. Imagine, a biker doing book signings at Borders. As Barger's book rolled on to the *New York Times* best-seller list, his website hawked sculptures of *Sonny Barger: An American Legend,* as well as Sonny Barger's Kick-starting Hellfire Sauce.

Bikers made tattoos and black leather a national obsession. Harley-Davidson sells 200,000 motorcycles a year; in the same period, it sells millions of T-shirts, leather jackets, bandannas, boxer shorts, coffee mugs, chip and dip trays, desk clocks, playing cards and key fobs. Every March, some 500,000 middle-aged men take Harleys to Daytona to pretend to be bad. They bring home the official Harley-Davidson Barbie doll, a.k.a. "Biker" Barbie, for their daughters. The BATF wanted to strip bare the myth that bikers were harmless antiheroes. Among the lovable misfits, there were monsters.

Agents moved slowly, issuing indictments against 17 Outlaws on May 30, 1997. The investigation involved more than 25 law enforcement groups, with costs running into the millions of dollars. Almost three years later, on March 8, 2000—after compiling some 30,000 pages of documents, 750 tapes, 900 pieces of evidence and 141 witnesses—the government put the range war on display.

SHOW TRIAL

The federal courthouse in Milwaukee wasn't designed for a show trial. The 100-year-old gray stone building still has wall plaques directing citizens to the offices of steamship inspector, lighthouse inspector, inspector of locomotives and the oleomargarine department. Heavy oak doors open onto a vast terrazzo-floored atrium. The modern touches seem out of place: Passing through metal detectors and X-ray machines, one looks up to see five tiers of courtrooms and government offices, an iron-framed skylight, rose-colored columns, gold leaf everywhere. Beige plastic tarps shroud the third floor, where the trial of the Outlaws Motorcycle Club rumbles on. The defense team has objected to a cordon of black curtains in the hall outside the courtroom, saying it gives jurors "the impression that something sinister, evil or dangerous lies behind these curtains."

The judge tells the jury the tarps cut noise and distraction, that if they want a tour of the historical court building they should save it for after the trial. But the curtains serve an obvious purpose: They block lines of sight for those who might want to intimidate witnesses or jurors.

During opening statements, Assistant U.S. Attorney Eric Klumb takes two and a half hours to sketch the government's case: The Outlaws had waged war against the Hell's Henchmen and Hell's Angels. They had attacked Angels in bars, cutting the death's head patch or colors from their backs. They had set off car bombs outside of clubhouses, conducted "Angel hunts" or "blood runs" in war wagons filled with automatic weapons, looking for enemies to kill or count coup. They had taken lives with guns, knives and screwdrivers to the throat. They had assaulted the enemy with baseball bats, pool balls, gun butts, table lamps. They had committed robberies, dealt drugs and counterfeit money, stolen cars and motorcycles to fund their evil enterprise.

"They did it all for this," explains Klumb, throwing down a black motorcycle jacket with a red-and-white image of a Charlie, the teeth-bared-skull over crossed pistons, "the right to wear the colors of the Outlaws Motorcycle Club."

The court was not designed for multiple defendants or multiple law-yers. At the head table sit three members of the U.S. Attorney's Office joined by two agents from the BATF. The Outlaws sit with their own lawyers. At the front of the room sits Kevin O'Neill, the alleged mas-termind of the Stateline chapter of the Outlaws, the man who stands accused of sanctioning or committing more than 20 criminal acts. A table set off to one side accommodates Randall "Madman" Miller, a club enforcer, charged with 14 acts of racketeering, including the murders of Donald "Domino" Wagner during a drug deal gone bad, and an elderly farm couple during a burglary. There are chapter presidents and vice presidents from Chicago and Gary, Indiana, whose only crimes seem to have consisted of showing up in the wrong address book or sporting the wrong tattoos. Some defendants have been Outlaws for more than a decade, a few had been members for a matter of months before being caught in the sweep. Of the original 17 indicted, six had pled guilty to lesser charges to avoid this moment. The Constitution prohibits guilt by association. As one defense attorney notes, "This courtroom almost assures it."

The court is awash in testosterone. Both the lawmen and the bik-ers sport goatees—they look like they're wearing merkins on their chins. These guys bulge. Maybe it's tension or their chewing gum, but their temples pulse, causing their sideburns and hair to move like gills. There is something inevitable about this dance. At the opening of the

BIKER WARS

1954 film *The Wild One,* two highway patrolmen watching bikers ride through town characterize the renegades this way: "Ten guys like that give people the idea everybody that drives a motorcycle is crazy. What are they trying to prove?" "Beats me. Looking for somebody to push them around so they can get sore and show how tough they are." It still applies. Outside the courtroom, one of the lawyers had warmed up by doing head-high karate kicks.

SHRAPNEL

The first witness is Hell's Angel Roger Fiebrantz, a boulder of a man with a shaggy beard and tattooed forearms. He hobbles into the courtroom, climbs into the witness box and, after coaching, leans toward the pencil-thin microphone. He bristles with hostility and reticence. He will not help the government against his alleged enemies—either from a standing attitude or because the clubs negotiated a truce after the indictments were handed down. Shown a picture of the charter members of the Hell's Henchmen, Fiebrantz can only recall the first names of men he had ridden with for years.

On November 13, 1990, he had found a wired-up fire extinguisher leaning against the door of the Hell's Henchmen clubhouse in Rockford. He'd called the police. The device exploded in the bomb squad's containment vehicle, sending a column of flame skyward and blowing out windows in the neighborhood. No, he had no idea who might have planted the bomb.

For Fiebrantz, the war would escalate dramatically in 1994. Klumb moves a pencil down a legal pad, checking off his questions, creating the story that the government wants told.

"Describe the events of October 12, 1994. Did anything particular happen on that day?"

"I started my truck. It ran for a couple minutes. Then it blew up. I put it in gear and it blew up."

Fiebrantz recalls seeing his leg on the dashboard, his wife, a towel wrapped around her head, screaming on the porch of their house. Nothing much after that.

Fiebrantz spent about four months in the hospital. By the time he got out, the Henchmen had patched over and become a Hell's Angels chapter. It was more than a year before he could walk. No, he had no idea who had planted the bomb. No, he'd never had a problem with any of the Outlaws.

Fiebrantz, currently serving a four-year sentence on a drug charge, isn't exactly a sympathetic victim. His wife, not bound by codes of

286

silence, is more forthcoming. She tells the court that the blast had stripped the meat from the back of her husband's legs. The severed veins and arteries protruded like hose pipes and he had no blood pressure. As paramedics pumped plasma in one end, it came out the other. Fiebrantz died a couple of times in the ER but the doctors had brought him back.

Once Fiebrantz had been released, his wife had to change the dressings four times a day, reaching into a "hole up to here"—indicating midway up her forearm—to fill the space with gauze.

The prosecution calls a policeman who had been sent to the hospital to collect two Tupperware containers holding the bomb and truck fragments taken from the victim's body.

The jury passed the hard candy hand to hand, trying to imagine this shrapnel in their own lives.

Bombs were the weapon of choice in this range war, though few were successful. In law, as in love, it's the thought that counts. Each of the following was considered as a conspiracy to commit murder:

On or about October 30, 1993, Illinois Hell's Henchman Eddie Murphy found a bomb attached to his truck. Thinking it was a joke, he removed it and tossed it onto the side of the road.

On December 15, 1993, a bomb destroyed a truck owned by Patrick Matter, president of the Hell's Angels chapter in Minneapolis. Matter didn't cooperate with the police.

On July 12, 1994, two Outlaws took another try at intimidating or killing Eddie Murphy. After a night of drinking, they put together a Molotov cocktail out of a plastic milk jug and diesel fuel. The device burned a patch in the porch. A neighbor saw the bungled attempt and phoned the police, and the two Outlaws were arrested a few miles down the road. Murphy slept through the incident.

On November 7, 1994, Hell's Henchman Michael Coyne discovered a bomb attached to the underside of his truck. While attempting to disarm the device with a water cannon, the bomb squad set it off.

On the same day, surveillance cameras recorded the destruction of the Grand Avenue Hell's Henchmen clubhouse in Chicago. Still photos, taken at 15-second intervals, show a Taurus parked in front of a two-story brick building. A city bus is caught in one photo. A flash of light in another.

One BATF agent called it the most powerful bomb he'd ever seen; another source called it the third-largest blast in American history, behind the World Trade Center and Oklahoma City bombings. The door of the clubhouse was blown clear through the building. The TV news that night began with this: "In scenes that look like Beirut. . . ." Intimidation comes in all sizes. One Outlaw tells of finding a rival's car and, not having a bomb handy, leaving a firecracker under the windshield wiper.

The indictment lists only those acts committed by Outlaws. Following the murder of LaMonte Mathias and the Lancaster rumble, Angels from around the country converged on Rockford for a war council. Among those spotted were Chuck Zito, a Hollywood stuntman, bodyguard and one of the stars of the TV series *Oz*. Police reports identified the Terror Squad—Angels designated to handle problems. An informant told police that two Angels were in town to bomb the Outlaws' clubhouse in Janesville, Wisconsin, with C-4 or dynamite. The local paper ran an article warning neighbors of possible violence. A tattoo studio owned by a Milwaukee Outlaw was the target of a bombing. Shortly after the Lancaster incident, the Toronto, Ohio, clubhouse of the Barbarians, a group affiliated with the Outlaws, was torched. Police caught two Angels on the southwest side of Chicago. A gym bag contained a pipe bomb made from PVC tubing and flash powder.

The war seems local, but it is part of a larger conflict that has raged for decades. On the first day of the trial, the defendants had passed around copies of *Hell's Angels at War*, a book by Canadian journalist Yves Lavigne that tracks the biker wars back to 1969. In Canada, the body count surpasses 140. In Scandinavia, bikers fire missiles stolen from a Swedish army base into rival clubhouses, or use grenade launchers to deliver presents to jailed enemies. In the Milwaukee courtroom, the Outlaws devour a photocopy of the chapter detailing their exploits.

BAR FIGHTS AND BRAGGING RIGHTS

Bombs have been called a coward's weapon, but the Outlaws were not afraid of confrontation. The jury hears accounts of fights at J.R.'s Watering Hole in Calumet City, Illinois; Club 51 in Rockford, Illinois; Slick's Tavern in Janesville, Wisconsin. Witnesses tell of Outlaws wrapping green bandannas around their arms so they can distinguish brothers from bar trash, Outlaws pulling up on motorcycles with baseball bats tied to the handlebars to beat the hell out of rival bikers, of fights brought to order when someone pulls a gun and fires into the ceiling.

Some of the accounts are humorous. A story circulates about a 450-pound biker named Roadkill being too large to get through the door of a bar. How Big Don, poking at tires in the parking lot with a knife, cut off the tip of his thumb. The bar owner kept the thumb in a jar, and the feds tried (and failed) to subpoena the piece to lift its print.

The government argues that the bar fights are a pattern of racketeering, a means of establishing dominance over other biker clubs, of protecting turf. Bar fights are their bowling league. According to biker etiquette, a fight isn't serious until you lose an eye or break a bone. As a lawyer for the defense points out, bar fights are consensual combat: When a biker puts on colors he adopts a code of honor. It is a mark of great shame to have your colors taken by a rival.

Outlaws and Angels live by a code—at least until they find themselves facing serious time.

SNITCHES ARE A DYING BREED

The witness list describes Houston Murphy as a former Outlaw. Murphy, a regional president from Florida, is in jail because he had been the wheel man on the murder of a member of a rival gang. He is testifying as part of a deal: The government will overlook hundreds of assaults, extortions, machine gun charges, drug dealings, the time he threw a guy off a motel fire escape—and shorten by years his time behind bars.

Murphy, the "turncoat Outlaw," is a professional snitch who goes from trial to trial describing biker hierarchy: "If you were a problem child, bodily harm could be visited upon you. You became subject to sanctions." On the other hand, if life was good, you got free drinks, parts and service for your bike, free time with the girls at the rub houses.

He tells of Outlaws' management techniques. He'd once invited a rival gang leader to the Outlaws' clubhouse. "As soon as he walked in I broke his nose. Then I explained why I had broken his nose." Apparently, the gang wore vests too similar to Outlaws' colors.

Murphy is an odd witness, but he sets a pattern for those who follow. The witness box is just another barstool. He flexes, preens, exudes bravado and bullshit, then obediently slides into betrayal. The government uses Murphy to describe an interstate hierarchy, a black leather menace, the specter of organized crime. He talks of war wagons, of tool or toy boxes—the containers of artillery and machine guns Outlaws keep handy for security. He explains the meaning of certain tattoos, patches and belt buckles. The twin lightning bolts of the SS mean that the wearer has killed for the club or taken care of business. AHMD means All Hell's Angels Must Die. GFOD means God Forgives, Outlaws Don't.

q: "And the slogan, Snitches Are a Dying Breed?"
a: "It means my life is in danger for being here."

BIKER WARS

He is there to prove that the Outlaws are the baddest of the bad, an interstate cartel that meets the RICO definition of criminal enterprise, a group that exists to dominate the biker world. But when asked how many members of the Outlaws there were when he became southern chapter president, he says "two." The number he'd presided over was anywhere from six to 19. Nationally, there were maybe 300 to 400 Outlaws.

He tells the court that in 1993, national president Harry "Taco" Bowman had called for an uprising of the Outlaws nation. Still, he acts surprised that the range war had broken out in the Midwest. Chicago Outlaws had gone from being the mother chapter to a relic. Chicago was a lot of talk, no action, the Windy City braggarts, bikers who "spent more time at poetry readings than taking care of business." They were known as the "sissy crew."

THE DRIVE-BY

In stark contrast to the bikers are the citizen witnesses caught up in the conflict. Randall Downs, a slight man with the sad face of a basset hound, tells the court of Jack Castle's last day on earth. Castle was a friend, a co-worker, a newly patched-over Hell's Angel. They'd met as they had every day for five years, for coffee at a diner on the northwest side of Chicago. They then drove in separate cars to Ignoffo Trucking. Downs had gone ahead to open the garage door.

"I put the key in the door, then heard something like the Fourth of July. I turned around. It was all over."

He saw the windows of Jack's Lincoln shattered, his friend slumped over.

"I reached in and shook him a little. He was a mess. He was tore up, his face, his neck. There was a few bullet holes in the door. The glass was shattered. There was blood on the windshield."

The detective on the scene adds detail: "Basically, the side of his face was shot away. There was brain matter on the windshield, the dashboard. On the sidewalk there were parts of bone—the jaw of the victim."

The jury views images of the crime scene. Castle is still clutching a Styrofoam cup of coffee, his Hell's Angels T-shirt soaking through with blood.

Dr. Nancy Jones, a forensic pathologist, describes the state of the body. Tattoos on the left forearm include multiple tombstones with different names. There were 11 entry wounds, no exit wounds. The bullets had begun to tumble after passing through glass. The marked destruction of the body and the broken bones were the result of high-velocity bullets fragmenting and scattering throughout the body. It's called the snowstorm effect. On an X-ray, the shattered bullet fragments show up like snowflakes in a snowstorm, so small they cannot be recovered.

"The victim," Dr. Jones says, reducing the horror to a line on a report, "died of multiple gunshot wounds." No one in the courtroom is accused of pulling the trigger. Some had arranged surveillance, or had helped dispose of the murder car; the killers had parked it a few blocks away in a handicapped parking zone.

According to the government, the range war ended with Jack Castle's death. On April 26, 1995, the Outlaws discovered the lamp bugs and realized they were under investigation.

The defense counters that the war ended because rogue Outlaw David Wolf was in custody.

The investigation was only beginning. The government had another informant among the Outlaws.

TICKLING THE WIRE

Mark "Crash" Quinn takes the stand. Of all the cooperating witnesses, he is the most enthusiastic, betraying his brothers with a booming voice.

He admits he is a liar, that he has committed perjury, and has in the past played games with law enforcement. During cross examination he tells of getting drunk one night and shooting himself in the hand as he tried to pull a loaded gun from his leather jacket. He told police he had been jumped by two guys. He admits he has told people he was responsible for the bombs, and claimed that he did Castle. But that, Quinn says, was bullshit. Now, in return for immunity, he is working for the government.

Quinn is a drug addict who in prison burned his retina with welding equipment in order to get a prescription for painkillers. In 1995, alone in a cell and 48 hours into withdrawal, he called the feds and offered to cooperate—anything to get into a methadone program.

For almost two years, he wore a wire and participated in controlled buys for drugs from fellow Outlaws. The jury hears a new set of tapes, the soundtrack of bikers counting money in the rest room of the Lone Star Café, while a jukebox plays "Lifestyles of the Not So Rich and Famous."

The jury hears a BATF agent order Quinn to try to lead another Outlaw into incriminating statements, "even if you have to put your hands around his throat"—and listens as Quinn recites his version of a pregame prayer. They hear the bikers discuss the finer points of motorcycle theft. On tape, Randall "Madman" Miller boasts there's no physical evidence to tie him to a murder, that the gun used was melted down to something the size of a quarter. On another tape Quinn brings up the elimination of Don Fogg. His brother Outlaw dismisses the incident: "Yeah, Big Don did have some problems though, I know that. He was pussy-whipped big time, you know."

The tapes capture Outlaws talking about betrayal, about who knows what and who is talking to the government. There are echoes of evil in the courtroom. No single version of a crime exists, and in the whisper stream, you can hear stories change.

After his arrest in 1997 Outlaw James "Preacher" Schneider began to talk to police. Like Wolf, he confessed to a murder and offered to testify in hope of a reduced sentence.

Schneider tells the court that in 1993, he was told that O'Neill wanted him to stake out Eddie Murphy's house, to slash the Hell's Henchman's throat and shove the biker's patch into the wound as a message.

Schneider never carried out that crime, but knives were wielded on or about April 8, 1993. The crime was not part of a turf war, just simple robbery. Morris Gauger, 74, ran a vintage motorcycle shop on his farm just east of Richmond, Illinois. His wife, Ruth, 70, sold ethnic and tribal rugs from a trailer on the property. They dealt in cash and were known to keep large sums of money in paper bags.

Schneider at first told police that Madman Miller killed both Gaugers during an early morning robbery. Then Schneider admitted he had killed Ruth, saying Miller had killed Morris. They had bludgeoned the elderly couple with pistols, then slashed their throats repeatedly. Mrs. Gauger was almost decapitated. They'd taken $15, tossed the knives into Lake Como and gone for breakfast. Schneider had been able to drink a glass of chocolate milk, barely. Miller had ordered a big breakfast and for months joked about being able to kill someone and then devour a huge plate of spaghetti "with lots of red sauce," without it bothering him.

On tape, Miller describes the crime to Mark Quinn, how the blood had poured out as if from a five-gallon bucket.

MILLER: "Preacher goes over there and goes, 'Oh come on, hurry up and die, you old fucker.' He's crying about that. At the restaurant, I says, 'You hungry?' 'No.' Well, I said, 'I'll have some, ah, French toast, bacon, a couple of eggs. Large milk, too. Cup of coffee.' He goes 'I'll just have a chocolate milk.' I said, 'You're not hungry?'"

QUINN: "How long did it take him to become normal again?"
MILLER: "Huh?"
QUINN: "How long did it take him to become normal?"
MILLER: "Never."

When Quinn testifies, he says Miller told him he could see what Morris Gauger had for dinner, that he could see the spaghetti in his victim's throat.

The Gauger killings are not part of the range war. Jurors wept at the crime-scene photos. The emotional impact taints every other act. This was not bikers killing one another; the Gaugers were innocent citizens.

Members of the Gauger family sit in the courtroom. For them this is just one episode in a long-running nightmare. There is no closure: When police arrived at the crime scene they interrogated Gary Gauger, the victims' son, for almost 20 hours. They told him he had killed his parents in an alcoholic blackout, that there was physical evidence linking him to the crime. Gauger "confessed," was found guilty and sentenced to death. He was in prison when Quinn reported to his case officer that two Outlaws had committed the murders. A year passed before Gauger was released.

THE DEFENSE

For three days the defense attorneys try to undo three months of testimony. They argue that no physical evidence connects individual Outlaws to any of the crimes. There were no fingerprints, no DNA, no ballistics, nothing. Heinous crimes were committed, but the perpetrators were in the witness box working for the government. The witnesses were "admitted perjurers, pathological liars, cold-blooded killers and paid informants who spoke their lines well." The BATF's case, said the lawyers, was itself a conspiracy. Agents were accused of "misconduct," their testimony a shameful travesty. They put names in the mouths of witnesses and made deals with the devil. Assistant U.S. Attorney Klumb admits the witnesses are not perfect. If Klumb had his way he would call his high school English teacher, a priest, his colleague's mother. "But English teachers, priests and mothers don't know the inner workings of organized crime."

The biker war, in the end, comes down to the power of storytelling. The Outlaws who had bragged "we got another Angel" found themselves trapped by that "we." Share the bravado and the bullshit and you become part of a criminal enterprise, branded by consequence.

BIKER WARS

On June 14, 2000, after 40 hours of deliberation, the jury found the defendants guilty of RICO conspiracy. (The sentencing was scheduled for October.)

The prosecution announced that the trial—the longest federal criminal trial in Milwaukee history—had sent a message to Outlaws: Stop doing this.

"The most important thing to note," said a press release from the prosecutor's office, "is that in the aftermath of the investigation and prosecution of this case, the killings, bombings and the war between members of the Outlaws and the Hell's Angels motorcycle gangs appear to have stopped."

Perhaps. But in the summer of 1999, an Outlaw in a Chicago suburb was found dead on his porch, the victim of multiple gunshot wounds. A visit to the Outlaws' website reveals a controversy over the death of another Outlaw, Robert "Honest Bob" McGillis. He was killed during an altercation with two men (identified as John Doe and James Roe) in the parking lot of the Brat Stop near Kenosha. The DA report says the death was justifiable homicide. "McGillis grabbed Doe's finger, placed it in McGillis's mouth and then tried (in Doe's estimation) to bite Doe's finger completely off. Doe tried in many different ways to extricate his finger from McGillis's mouth to no avail. Finally, Doe commenced strangling McGillis until Doe was able to remove his finger from McGillis' mouth. It appears, in retrospect, that the reason McGillis stopped biting Doe's finger was that he was dead." The range war may be over, but the violence evidently is not.

L.A. Hookers, Russian Gangsters, Sex and Death

by **WILLIAM STADIEM**
August 2002

According to the cops, Leyla Ismayilova was a high-class callgirl, though she refused to admit it even if her life depended on it. Leyla was a 28-year-old, nearly six-foot-tall Ukrainian goddess. She had huge dark blue eyes, high cheekbones, higher heels and couture by Versace. How else, they figured, would she know that the victim, Lyudmyla Petushenko, another beautiful young Ukrainian, who had been beaten and then executed in her Studio City apartment? Having been in the U.S., illegally, for only three months, the leonine, blonde Lyudmyla had been making more than $10,000 a month as a callgirl. She was also recruiting new girls from the Ukraine to join her stable. Ambitious and driven, Lyudmyla was moving fast. Too fast, the cops surmised. Speed kills, especially in what was becoming known as the whore wars, the battle among ruthless Russians to take over the big-buck sex turf left vacant by the incarceration of Heidi Fleiss.

Heidi Fleiss—the chic Jewish American princess who lived in Michael Douglas's former estate and partied with Jack Nicholson and Mick Jagger—was the second supermadam to hook up Los Angeles prostitutes with a big-name clientele. The first, Madam Alex Adams, had built a multimillion-dollar business selling sex to her black book of stars, moguls, politicians and oil sheiks who would take Alex's charges on trips that started at $10,000 a weekend. After Alex ran afoul of the Los Angeles Police Department, Heidi took over the business and made

295

it even bigger, but her flagrant enjoyment of the elite sex trade also spelled trouble. Eventually, it got her three years in prison. Madam Alex died while Heidi was doing her time, and by the late Nineties the field was relegated to a large number of minimadams and thousands of Internet sex ads. Starlet-level callgirls, even in Hollywood, became increasingly difficult to find. Enter the Russians, who had the looks, brains and greed.

The investigators suspected that Leyla was one of Lyudmyla's callgirl colleagues. Leyla conceded she had befriended Lyudmyla prior to her final bloody morning of Thursday, August 17, 2000. But she steadfastly denied that business of any sort was involved. The two Ukrainians had met at a Russian market in West Hollywood and had bonded. As for tricks, "Never," said Leyla. She said she was the daughter of a small-town police chief, and that she had a rich boyfriend in Los Angeles. She had no need to turn a trick. Her version of events on the fateful morning of August 17, however, did not entirely satisfy the cops.

According to Leyla, Lyudmyla was planning an outing to Magic Mountain amusement park with a Russian friend. A late sleeper, she had asked Leyla to give her a wake-up call at nine A.M. After 11 phone calls with no reply, Leyla told police, she began to worry. Just before noon, she drove her SUV from her West Hollywood apartment into the 90-degree heat and smog of the San Fernando Valley to 4150 Arch Drive. Because another car was entering the security garage the moment she arrived, she was able to enter without being buzzed in.

Walking up to the second floor, Leyla found the front door to apartment 211 unlocked. She entered and called Lyudmyla's name. No answer. Then she went into the bedroom. Lyudmyla was on the rug in a silk robe, bikini panties and heels. "I thought she was drunk," Leyla told the cops. When she started to shake her awake, a stream of blood poured out of Lyudmyla's mouth. Her body was cold. Leyla fled back to her car and called the Russian woman who had rented the apartment for Lyudmyla. Leyla asked her to call the police. Why hadn't she called herself? the investigators asked. "My English was no good," Leyla answered. Why didn't she wait for the police to arrive? She had no answer.

A team of policemen and criminalists from the LAPD's North Hollywood Division arrived early in the afternoon and didn't leave until after midnight. The corpse itself had awful bruises all over the head and neck, and a single, neat bullet hole directly above the left nipple, right into Lyudmyla's heart. There was no evidence of any sexual assault. The beige-carpeted modern apartment, where the air-conditioning had been turned down to a Siberian chill, had little furniture other than a large bed, nightstand, television and sound system. The closets overflowed with sexy lingerie and expensive shoes. There was an industrial supply of condoms in the bathroom.

The first search yielded no identity papers, no address books—only a lot of telephone numbers jotted on random scraps of paper. As the cops tried to track the calls on the phone Lyudmyla had been using, they made their most surprising discovery—her phone had been tapped by the FBI. As the LAPD was about to find out, Lyudmyla's death was no routine murder; it was a can of worms.

As soon as they learned the FBI was involved, the local police kicked the case upstairs, or actually downtown, to the Robbery-Homicide Division. The RHD, as it is known, is the elite corps of the LAPD. Robbery-Homicide handles the city's highest-profile cases: the big bank heists and big murders, such as the Manson carnage and the Nicole Brown Simpson–Ronald Goldman slayings. The Lyudmyla Petushenko case was assigned to two of the department's stalwarts, Charles Knolls and Brian McCartin.

Knolls, 45, had roots in the San Fernando Valley, where the victim had been found. He had worked his way up at Von's grocery chain from bag boy to the head office, when at 30, frustrated by corporate life and inspired by a brother-in-law in the FBI, he joined the LAPD.

McCartin, a wiry 42-year-old who "didn't like to sit still," served as an Army paratrooper as well as a New York City fireman before moving west to join the LAPD in 1983. The styles of the two detectives couldn't have been more different. Knolls, true to the laid-back California stereotype, likes to "sit back and let people talk and talk and talk," he admits. McCartin, who has a master's degree in behavioral science, likes to "get into people's faces. My training was based on boot camp," he says. "Take names and kick ass." As Knolls, in his understated way, says, "Brian has a tendency to do things a little quicker than I do."

What the two detectives had in common was a total inability to penetrate or comprehend Los Angeles's 250,000-member Russian community, a Byzantine agglomeration of Slavs, Jews, Armenians, Georgians, ex-KGB officers and ex-Communists—a citizenry as diverse as that of the old Soviet Union, united only by a common desire to make it in California. To lead the way through this maze, the RHD assigned Knolls and McCartin a new partner, 30-year-old Kiev-born, Valley-raised David Krumer, who'd recently joined the force after graduating from UCLA and Southwestern University School of Law. One of the rare Jews and rarer native Russians in local law enforcement, Krumer

L.A. HOOKERS, RUSSIAN GANGSTERS, SEX AND DEATH

made an unlikely cop. With his Tom Cruise looks and James Stewart purity, he could have used his law degree as a passport to any number of high-paying law firms. Yet this son of a baker, who had recently gone back to the Ukraine to marry a pre-med daughter of a family friend, had his own unique take on the American dream.

Not wanting to be "one of those smart Jews who get beat up," Krumer had become a black belt and Kempo karate instructor. He was a pretty boy, but he was tough. He was also more interested in justice than he was in wealth. His parents were disappointed by his new career choice. "There are no bragging rights for a Jewish cop," says Krumer. Nevertheless, the new officer was thrilled to be on the force and working with such pros as Knolls and McCartin. What he wasn't thrilled about was experiencing the dark side of the Russian community that his parents had hidden from Krumer and his two sisters.

The initial meeting between the FBI and the LAPD smacked of a Mexican standoff. The always-secretive FBI did not want to show its hand; the LAPD had no hand to show. The ice was broken when a certain chemistry developed between the handsome Krumer and a woman on the FBI team. Aside from his looks, she was interested in his ability to access a world the FBI had been exposed to only via its wiretaps. Why not let the RHD do the FBI's dirty work? Knolls, McCartin and Krumer had no problem serving as the feds' truffle hounds.

The FBI offered its files, and the LAPD dived in, only to discover the complexity of the case. The feds' interest in Los Angeles's Russians involved not merely the FBI, but also the Immigration and Naturalization Service and the Border Patrol. The focus of all three agencies was the large-scale trafficking of Russians, particularly young Russian women, over the Mexican border. The route under investigation was from Kiev via Amsterdam to Mexico City, then to a Mexican villa in Rosarito and over the border at Tijuana to San Diego and the promised land. There had been hundreds, if not thousands, of people smuggled across in the past few years. The wiretaps showed that a ring was organizing the smuggling as well as conscripting the women to prostitution. One of the most frequently dialed numbers on Lyudmyla's phone was that of the suspected ringleader, a charismatic character by the name of Serge Mezheritsky, who is currently under indictment.

"That was the slickest piece of work I ever saw," says McCartin, who went with Knolls and Krumer to interview the 6'2", muscular, blond 35-year-old Russian in his multilevel home in the Hollywood Hills. There were five expensive vehicles out front, including the latest Mercedes. The cops later learned that Serge was planning to use a "Sex UV," a

298

converted pleasure van equipped with a bed and its own Jacuzzi, as a rolling brothel, ferrying johns and hookers up and down Sunset Strip. "He was sly, very ingratiating, like a nightclub shill," says Krumer. "He was so cocky and arrogant that he agreed to take a polygraph. When the results were inconclusive, he couldn't believe it. He was convinced the machine was defective."

To Serge, everything in America worked; it had always worked for him. The son of Jewish émigré parents and a graduate of Fairfax High School, Serge had made a lot of money in assorted schemes, claiming to be in the auto parts business. Whatever he called it, he did well enough to live large in the hills. Well enough, in fact, to run for City Council in West Hollywood. He lost, but he was intent on running again.

Cars were Serge's passion. Police theorized he was involved in an auto theft ring that sent stolen cars to Mexico. They have presented their evidence to the DA and as of May were still awaiting a possible indictment. Serge was no stranger to the LAPD's Burglary and Auto Theft Division. They had investigated Mezheritsky so often, and so unsuccessfully, that he felt he had not only an immunity from prosecution but also a relationship with the police. "He thought he had the same deal with us," Krumer says. "He told us tons of stuff," McCartin adds, "assuming that in return for helping us, we would protect him. But everything he told us was self-serving and mostly lies. He thought he was a genius, and we were flat-out stupid."

Without actually confessing to any personal wrongdoing, Serge told the police he was having a torrid affair with Lyudmyla. For free, of course. He also told them he was having affairs with a number of the other newly arrived Russian prostitutes. And always for free. He was that irresistible. He had no interest in how his lovers earned their living. Serge surmised that Lyudmyla had met her end at the hands of a jealous madam. Insisting that he wanted to see her avenged, Serge gave the investigators the names and numbers of several Russian callgirls.

Almost all the women Serge identified were extremely attractive— tall and tawny with great figures, the athletic beach-goddess types the world associates with southern California. The cops could see why these women were taking over the sex trade. American girls with these looks charged upwards of $500 an hour. The Russians had undercut them with a bargain rate of $150 an hour. Small wonder that Heidi Fleiss, upon her release from jail, hadn't gone back into the business. The Russians had priced her out of the market.

"One thing they are not is lazy," McCartin explains. "In the USSR they grew up with no religion, no morality. Prostitution is not considered a bad thing. In fact, it's considered a great way to make money. That's why it's exploding here. What we saw was just the tip of the iceberg." McCartin minimizes the notion of white slavery. "These girls didn't come over here expecting to be nannies. They knew exactly what they wanted and what they were getting into."

There were three ways that the women could enter the U.S. The most enterprising would pretend to be Jewish and request political asylum. With the liberalization of the new Russia, religious persecution has become largely a nonissue, making this ruse much more difficult to employ. Others would enter the country on a three-month tourist visa and simply never leave. And then there was the third option, the one the feds were trying to stop. It was called being trafficked, but, as McCartin notes, there were few unwilling participants. A fee, ranging from $2,500 to $10,000, paid to a "travel agent" in Kiev would get a girl to Mexico and a villa in Rosarito for about a month. There, to get the California look, she would work on her tan, start dressing in L.A. clothes—UCLA T-shirts or anything Gap—and be taught American inflection and slang like "totally" and "awesome."

Once in California, the girl would be auctioned to a Russian pimp or madam for anywhere from $2,500 to $20,000. The sum of the travel fee, the auction fee and a cost-of-living fee constituted what a girl had to earn out before she was free. In hooker accounting, the girl could credit only half of her sexual gross toward her goal of breaking even, then breaking out, which took the average girl about a year. With no English and few lucrative options, most of the girls elected to remain in the game. The most motivated of the lot would become madams and take their place in this pyramid scheme of commercial sex.

The prostitutes would be housed in apartments in Beverly Hills, West Hollywood and Studio City, places with big concentrations of entertainment industry types, the core clientele. The madams would advertise their charges on the Internet and in local alternative newspapers such as *L.A. Weekly* and *New Times*. In addition to the estimated thousands of Russian prostitutes in L.A., there was an elaborate support group of drivers, telephone touts, hairdressers, manicurists and bikini waxers to sell, transport and glamorize the girls, and another support group of lawyers, accountants and money launderers—almost always Russian—to keep track of the spoils. The system was decentralized. There were many small agencies, as the madam operations were known, and few ran more than 15 girls at a time.

For the past several years Mezheritsky himself was believed to have been in an alliance with an elegant 50-year-old Russian in the Valley named Tetyana Komisaruk. An indictment alleges that together they imported illegal aliens from Ukraine and sold some of them into prostitution. Tetyana's involvement was a family affair: Her 40-year-old husband, her pretty daughters, 31 and 25, and her stylish son-in-law, 29, were allegedly all part of a ring that included a number of Kiev-based Ukrainians on the supply side and a real estate agent in Los Angeles who laundered profits by buying and selling expensive property.

Serge had two pleasure crafts he used to transport Ukrainians from Tetyana's fancy beach villa in Rosarito to San Diego. He also had a Lincoln rigged with special shocks so that the car wouldn't look weighted down by the Ukrainians being hidden in the trunk. But Serge was getting greedy. Having learned the smuggling business from the Komisaruk family, police theorized that Serge wanted to jettison them and take on a single partner, namely the clever, hard-working Lyudmyla. Lyudmyla was well connected in Kiev; she could be Serge's new Tetyana.

Moreover, as the feds learned through wiretaps, Serge was concocting a far more ambitious prostitution operation, typified by such jazzy accoutrements as his Sex UV. He was talking about setting up video cameras in the apartments of his whores to blackmail rich and famous johns. Serge had seen how Hugh Grant and Eddie Murphy, apparently at sea without a madam like Heidi Fleiss, had suffered in the press for their street dalliances. The hush money he discussed would be as much as a quarter of a million dollars per celebrity. Serge also wanted to upgrade to "Heidi prices," so that the cream of his Russian beauties would each gross $10,000 a day.

As titillating as these details were, they were of no real help to Knolls, McCartin and Krumer. They had a murder to solve, and a month later there were still no tangible leads. Then they learned of a taped conversation between Serge and his Fairfax High classmate Alex Van Kovn, another Americanized Russian who had become a lawyer. Van Kovn was indicted for allegedly providing fraudulent documents for some of the illegal Ukrainians. He later pleaded guilty to harboring illegal aliens, witness tampering and making false statements in court. The cops listened to a tape on which Serge and Van Kovn discussed someone called Boxer. Van Kovn stated, "He killed your girlfriend, he killed my girlfriend, he killed your business completely."

"Absolutely, pal," Serge agreed. "He just totally killed my business." Then Van Kovn, who sounded as if he, too, had been sleeping with Lyudmyla, shared his regrets that Serge's "grandiose plans" had all been destroyed by Lyudmyla's murder.

Who was Boxer? The cops had the tape from the surveillance camera at the Arch Drive apartment on the morning Lyudmyla was murdered, and it recorded lots of people going in and out. The three cops pored over the grainy tape until they could identify each tenant, each delivery person, each handyman and maid. Finally, there were only two entries who could not be identified: a bald man and a woman who arrived together at 9:03 and departed at 9:23. It was a short stay, but time enough to have dispatched Lyudmyla.

After they showed the video to the FBI, the feds recognized a potential suspect. The man, Alexander Gabay, 36, was a classmate of Serge and Van Kovn at Fairfax High. Unlike Serge, however, Alex had gone straight. A former Navy Seabee, he had graduated from the prestigious Southern California Institute of Architecture. Alex's specialty was architectural welding, and he had a fancy clientele in Beverly Hills, Brentwood and Malibu. A killer? Not likely. But as Krumer worked the West Hollywood grapevine, he found out that before his family had immigrated to Los Angeles when he was 15, Alex was a kickboxing expert in Moscow. Hence the nickname Boxer, used only by Serge, Van Kovn and a few others in the high school circle.

The girl on the tape was identified as Oxana Meshkova, 23. She was one of six Kievans Serge had helped transport from Mexico to San Diego on July 4, 2000. She and three other fellow travelers were sold to Lyudmyla Petushenko at auction with the expectation that they would enter the business.

Lyudmyla became dissatisfied with Oxana, who clearly had no interest in play for pay. Lyudmyla tried to unload Oxana to other madams. None wanted her. Only Gabay, who had met Oxana at a party Serge had thrown for his new arrivals, showed any interest in the girl, who had lifted weights back in Ukraine. He invited her to move into his downtown loft on East Sixth Street. Alex and Oxana became the LAPD's prime suspects in the murder of Lyudmyla Petushenko.

Speaking perfect English, Gabay acknowledged having gone with Oxana to visit Lyudmyla on the day of her death so Oxana could pick up a bag of clothing she had left there. He found Lyudmyla alive and left her alive. In a separate interrogation room, Oxana, extremely anxious because of her illegal status, told the same story to Krumer, who translated it for his superiors. By the end of a long day, however, Oxana had changed her story several times, from Lyudmyla's being alive when she and Alex left to Lyudmyla's being dead when they arrived. That evening Alex and Oxana were arrested and charged with Lyudmyla's murder.

Alex Gabay's loft didn't fit with his image of being a successful architect. "It was a pit," says Krumer. "His mother would have been appalled." The bathroom plumbing didn't work, and there was nothing but a hot plate to prepare food. The walls were plastered with pornographic photos of Alex's assorted girlfriends, some of them with a naked Alex participating in kinky poses. Weapons abounded. There were crossbows and arrows, rifles, pistols and bullet casings. There were welding torches and clumps of metal the police assumed were Alex's art. "It was a junkyard," said Krumer. Although Alex did not seem like a killer, his lifestyle did nothing to establish confidence in his character.

Still, the LAPD case was by no means open-and-shut. For nearly a year after their arrest and incarceration in downtown jails, Alex and Oxana continued to insist on their innocence. Despite repeated police interrogations, they confessed to nothing. No witnesses to the murder came forward. None of Serge's prostitute friends knew Alex; he wasn't in that loop. A few of the Kievans had met Oxana when she arrived, but none had ever worked with her. As far as anyone knew, she had never turned a trick in America.

Serge Mezheritsky proclaimed his friend Alex's innocence, even after Serge himself was arrested in May 2001 by the federal task force. Serge, Tetyana Komisaruk and her family—in total, 18 co-conspirators—faced years in prison on alien-smuggling charges. Serge continued to bargain. "His lawyer came to me and said Serge would give us the information we needed if we got him released. I said no dice," McCartin says. "I had told him at the beginning that if I didn't get the truth, it would come back to bite him, and it did. He's convinced I screwed him." Feeling betrayed by his cop friends, Serge now claimed that the FBI's wiretaps of his conversations with lawyer Van Kovn, also indicted as part of the ring, about Boxer's culpability had been grossly misinterpreted. The alien-smuggling trial began this past April.

Unwilling to risk using any of Serge's doubletalk in a trial of Alex and Oxana, the prosecution got a break when DNA evidence linked a tiny spot on a pair of Alex's jogging shoes with Lyudmyla's blood. But no other blood was found on any of the alleged assailants' garments, and the spot didn't necessarily come from the commission of the crime. It could have been generated by casual contact with the splattered blood in the apartment after someone else had killed Lyudmyla. The DNA was helpful, but not enough to build a case.

As the cops waited for a bigger break, the smuggling case and the arrest of Serge and Tetyana had halted the supply of Russian prostitutes in Los Angeles. The only way madams could offer new faces and bodies to their insatiable clients was to raid the stables of their rivals.

L.A. HOOKERS, RUSSIAN GANGSTERS, SEX AND DEATH

What ensued were the "whore wars." In late August 2001, two Russian girls were lolling about in Gucci cocktail dresses in a fancy Sherman Oaks apartment, waiting for a client who had seen their Internet ad. When the man arrived, he had a gun in his hand and several large accomplices behind him. "You're working for us now," the intruder announced, as his heavies ransacked the apartment for cash and passports. The girls were blindfolded, packed into a van and taken to an equally luxurious three-bedroom condo off of Beverly Boulevard.

"The madam who organized this raid was making $4 million a year, laundered through Russian-owned banks in New York City," says a source in the LAPD. Adds Bret Richards, 44, the LAPD detective in charge of a series of felony kidnapping cases in the whore wars: "These are brutal people." A few days after the August abductions, another Russian madam's army invaded a rival's mid-Wilshire playhouse, kidnapping four more prostitutes. One of the abductees called 911 from the bathroom of the Beverly Hills penthouse where she had been taken, and the LAPD made its first raid. "But the girl got the Stockholm syndrome," Richards says. "She fell in love with the chief abductor and refused to testify against him." Richards has been frustrated that several of the other rescued girls, whose testimony is key to convicting the madams, have returned to Russia or New York. "Even if the girls stayed under our protection, they're terrified that they could be targeted for reprisal. It has been a tough case," say Richards.

As Richards worked to end the whore wars, Knolls, McCartin and Krumer finally got their break. Oxana Meshkova decided to testify against her lover Alex Gabay to get herself out of jail and out of trouble. "We made a deal with her," McCartin says. "But only because we believed she was finally telling the truth." Oxana now said that she and Alex had gone to Lyudmyla's to ascertain the whereabouts of Oxana's close friend, also a prostitute. Oxana had heard that her friend had been turned into a heroin addict, and she wanted to rescue this 19-year-old she referred to as her "baby sister."

According to Oxana, when Lyudmyla refused to reveal her friend's whereabouts, a fight followed. Alex nearly kicked Lyudmyla to death, then finished her off with a bullet from his .45. What gave Oxana added credibility was her revelation that a third person, Alex's buddy Marvin Graham, a Santa Monica bartender, had driven Alex and Oxana to Arch Drive that August 17.

Knolls had now been transferred from the RHD back to the beat work that he loved, so it was McCartin who found and questioned Graham. The interrogation proved extremely successful. Graham not only told him Alex had admitted to him that he had shot Lyudmyla, but also surrendered part of the murder weapon: the frame of a gun he had been hiding for Alex, who had melted down the .45 barrel but hated to let a good gun go to waste. With Oxana, with Graham and with the DNA, the DA was at last ready to go to trial.

Alex Gabay's mother and stepfather, a prosperous Russian businessman, hired ace criminal lawyer Ronald Hedding to defend Alex. Hedding passed up a plea bargain. In spite of the evidence, he believed that the cops' deal with illegal alien and would-be prostitute Oxana would not survive scrutiny in court. Why should she go free just to get Alex, whose own record was spotless? Hedding felt there was enough reasonable doubt to win an acquittal for his client.

The trial in the case of *California* vs. *Gabay* opened on January 2, 2002. Opposing Hedding was Deputy District Attorney Jane Winston, who looked like a surfer girl gone Armani. In the two-week trial, Winston would call a battery of witnesses, but her star was Oxana Meshkova, just as Hedding's was Alex Gabay. In the end, the battle of reasonable doubt would come down to he said–she said.

Oxana, dressed in jailhouse blues, with her even drabber prison pallor and greasy hair, was an unlikely callgirl. According to her, as explicated by a string of translators, she never was a callgirl, never intended to be one, nor had any idea that sin would be the price of her immigration to California. She recounted how, after Lyudmyla was reluctant to reveal her friend's location, a nasty argument erupted in which, after Lyudmyla ridiculed her as a "cow," Alex erupted in a lover's fatal rage.

In his cross-examination, Hedding challenged Oxana's entire story. Oxana knew precisely why she was here, Hedding said. He dragged out her weight-lifting past, which she minimized as an attempt to shed pounds. He also got her to admit she occasionally shot guns for target practice in Alex's loft.

Deputy District Attorney Winston ran a chaste prosecution. She stayed away from sex. She didn't bring up prostitution when she questioned wake-up caller Leyla Ismayilova. Serge Mezheritsky was barely mentioned. And so it went, until Alex took the stand in his own defense.

His head no longer shaved and his blond hair slicked back, Alex, in his navy Italian suit, could have easily passed as a European banker. In a mellifluous voice, Alex conveyed his incredulity that he could be accused of this murder. The inelegance of it seemed to offend him. He spoke of his teenage kickboxing laurels. His athletic physique spoke for itself. Why, Hedding asked him, would he beat a woman to death if he could have neatly killed her with one thumb pressed to her temple?

"She wouldn't have had a mark," Alex said. Yes, the gun that killed Lyudmyla belonged to him, for recreational use. But Oxana kept it in her purse "for self-defense," and it was Oxana who had shot Lyudmyla. According to Alex, weightlifter Oxana had beaten the madam to a pulp for her role in turning her beloved girlfriend into a heroin addict. After Lyudmyla called her a "fat cow," Oxana snapped, crushing Lyudmyla to the floor, stomping on her head and neck, and, as the coup de grâce, shooting her.

What did you do? Hedding asked. "I thought I should let them duke it out together," said Boxer, unaware of the depth of Oxana's rage. One witness said Alex loved Oxana as a "cultural girlfriend" who would please his mother. Alex explained that he had told Marvin Graham, who had simply stopped for them at Lyudmyla's en route to what was to have been a pleasant day at the beach in Venice, that he had shot Lyudmyla because "I didn't want Oxana to be implicated at the time. I think if he would have known that she did it, he would have just flipped" and turned Oxana in. As it was, Alex trusted his friend to protect him, if not his girlfriend.

Cross-examined by DA Winston, Alex Gabay had an answer for everything. Except for one detail. If Oxana had the gun in her purse, why was that purse not visible on the surveillance tape? Winston repeatedly played the entrance and exit of Alex and Oxana. Alex kept his composure, complaining that the tape was blurry and vague and stating that Oxana always carried her purse. So where is it? Winston pressed, and, for once, Alex could only shrug.

In summation, Hedding denounced the government's deal with Oxana, who had the motive of revenge against Lyudmyla, a motive Alex lacked. He was a gentleman who might stand up for this lost soul of a lover, but would he kill for her? Hedding said no.

After deliberating for less than an hour, the jury found Alex Gabay guilty of second-degree murder. Since he used a gun, he faced a mandatory prison sentence of 40 years to life. As always, Alex remained cool. His mother wept.

Oxana was released, but still faces deportation charges. "She has nothing to celebrate. Even if they were to let Oxana stay, God knows what could happen to her family back in Kiev. Russians do not forgive or forget," says Krumer, who went on to help Richards on the whore war cases. By April 2002, four male abductors had been sentenced to prison terms ranging from two to 12 years. None of the madams, however, was convicted, and the investigation continues.

"I feel good," says McCartin of the verdict. "There was a time when

Gabay was testifying that I questioned the jury's ability to come to the right decision. He was good." McCartin is off on another capital case now. He's relieved to be moving on from the prostitution scene. He'll leave the whore wars to other cops. "Gabay's conviction will have no deterrent effect" on Russian crime, McCartin says. "They're all back-stabbers. And there will be a lot more Lyudmylas. They're entrepreneurs. They're looking at $10,000 a month for turning tricks. For them, that's the American dream."

Run-DMC

The Last Days of
Jam Master Jay

by **FRANK OWEN**

December 2003

OCTOBER 30, 2002: MISCHIEF NIGHT

It's the day before Halloween in Jamaica, Queens. A cold, slanting rain falls in the streets, and it's unseasonably chilly—above freezing, but not by much. Jam Master Jay, the DJ who ran the turntables for the legendary rap group Run-DMC, pulls his black SUV into a parking space outside a two-story building on Merrick Boulevard. In the fading afternoon light he hustles inside and upstairs to the second floor, to Studio 24/7.

The small recording studio looks like a crowded bodega. Jay's longtime business partner and friend Randy Allen moves around in the control room—where tens of thousands of dollars' worth of equipment is on display—next to a tiny soundproof vocal booth. A glass window separates the two rooms. Jay greets Randy as the others slide over to make room for him in the lounge, a modest sitting area with two couches. Randy's sister, Lydia High, the studio bookkeeper and secretary, is there, as are two other people: a homeless friend who sleeps in the studio and a hanger-on named Uriel Rincon.

From the studio window Jay can see the red brick building that houses the 103rd Precinct. The police station overlooks PO Edward Byrne Avenue, a street that was renamed to commemorate a police officer assassinated in 1988 on a local drug dealer's orders. Behind the studio building sits a large open-air bus depot, a onetime hangout of the South Side Crew, which long ago waged turf battles with Jay and his boys, the Hollis Crew.

Jay lets Randy do most of the fussing. Randy has a lot riding on their

309

THE LAST DAYS OF JAM MASTER JAY

current project, a duo called Rusty Waters, consisting of Randy and Jay's nephew Boe Skagz (born Rodney Jones). Their debut album is due at Virgin Records in a matter of days. Consumed by details, Randy sends Boe to the barbershop to get a haircut for an upcoming promotional tour.

Amid this usual activity the little group in the studio is taken by surprise: A stranger appears at the door. She explains that she's a friend of a friend and has a demo tape she would like to give Jay. On the otherwise bare white walls she sees gold and platinum records, a reminder of Jay's glory days as the musical mastermind behind Run-DMC. The stories of Jay's generosity are matched only by his accessibility. The young woman with the tape has heard of others making this pilgrimage. Now it's her turn.

In fact, Jay doesn't generally listen to tapes from strangers, but Randy agrees to. Despite the looming deadline, the vibe in the studio seems relaxed and peaceful, no doubt helped by the joints being passed around. But in the fragrant clouds of smoke, Jay is on edge, possibly fearing for his life; he is armed with a .45 automatic. With all the traffic moving in and out of the studio, it is not entirely clear whom he fears most.

A Rusty Waters song called "Cornbread" booms out of the speakers: "Cornbread, all head / Macaroni and cheese / Where the collard greens at? / Y'know, you know that." Jay settles into a tan couch in the lounge to play one of his favorite Xbox football games with Rincon on the widescreen TV. They're focused on their game rather than on a four-way split-screen monitor hooked up to closed-circuit video cameras in the hall. It's about 7:30 P.M. According to this version of events, pieced together from multiple sources, including people present in the studio that night, everything is about to change forever.

Downstairs, two men dressed in dark clothing enter the building lobby and move past a camera. Undetected, they climb the narrow staircase single file from the street to the second floor. At the top of the stairs the smaller man stops. The other man, about six-foot-two and 180 pounds, bursts through the door—and all hell breaks loose.

"Look at the ground!" he shouts as he swiftly pushes Lydia aside. He has a .40-caliber pistol.

"Oh, shit," Jay cries. "Grab the gun!"

It's too late. The man's weapon is inches from Jay's head, behind his left ear. "What about this? What about this?" says the assailant. He pulls the trigger.

The bullet passes through Jay's head, and he collapses. The gun is so close to him that powder burns scorch his shirt. In the confined space, the gunman falls over Rincon, who has bent down to get his cell phone. A second shot goes off and hits Rincon in the leg. Before he has time to register the pain, the assailants are running down the stairs.

Randy is in the control room with the curtains drawn, listening to playbacks, when he hears the shots. He and Mike B., the homeless friend, rush into the lounge. Randy picks up "the studio gun" they keep handy and pursues the killers into the street. He loses them in a nearby parking lot, where he drops the weapon.

None of this effort helps his friend Jam Master Jay, who dies where he fell, next to a brown leather hat and wearing his trademark snow-white Adidas.

OCTOBER 30, 2002: THE MOURNING

The news spreads rapidly through the streets of Queens, by cell phone, pager, radio and TV. The neighborhood kids, Jay's business partners, even guys who had beefs with Jay—his death shocks them all. They gather outside the studio, in numbers that increase throughout the night. Everyone knows this is a landmark event. The first scratches on a record average Americans had ever heard came from Jay's recordings with Run-DMC. More than that, the band always had a social conscience, speaking out about prejudice and violence.

Standing by yellow police tape and caught in the rain and the periodic sweep of TV spotlights, the crowd is possessed by a mournful nostalgia. In the age of gangsta rap the party jams of Run-DMC suddenly seem more naive than ever. Chuck D of Public Enemy stands out in the glare of a camera. "Run-DMC was the Beatles of hip-hop," he says.

Jay was a kid from the rough neighborhood of Hollis who raised himself up and tried to bring others with him. "Jay was always trying to get his friends who strayed back on the right path," says his friend Hurricane, who credits Jay with saving him from a life of crime by getting him a job as the Beastie Boys' DJ. Jay paid rents. He bestowed gifts. He taught chess to young kids in the park. He was a local hero. Soft-spoken and amiably aloof, he'd wear a small smile on his face, as though he were paying only half a mind to the matter at hand and couldn't wait to get back to his music. Even after two decades of success he never took on the airs of celebrity or the pose of the thug, and he embraced all kinds of hip-hop.

NYPD personnel carry the body bag down the back stairs.

Jay could have left Queens countless times, but he always returned. "He stayed here because of me," his sister, Bonita Jones, Boe's mother,

311

would later say. "A long time ago his wife wanted to move out of New York, but he said, 'I'm not leaving my sister.' That's the man he was."

But who exactly was Jam Master Jay? Long before the night was out, questions were raised about almost every aspect of his murder. As the list of suspects—and possible motives—grew, it became clear that there was more to Jay than the good-guy image he had maintained for years. It also became clear that this would not be an easy crime to solve. After a flood of early reports, information dried up, the mystery hardened, and people stopped talking—until now.

The man originally known as Jason Mizell led a secret life that involved guns, drugs and murky business deals. The answers to why he was killed lie in the story of his final few months alive. It all comes back to a place called Hollis, Queens.

JULY 2003: SCOON AND PEP

At Masta Kutterz, a scruffy Hollis Avenue barbershop, foam padding peeps through the peeling plastic-covered chairs. Magazine pictures featuring braiding and weaving styles adorn the purple-and-blue walls. A sign instructs patrons: NO SMOKING. NO LOITERING. NO PROFANITY. Masta Kutterz is a place one goes to chew the fat and exchange gossip about what's going on in Hollis. "Barbers always get the news first, know what I mean?" says the genial owner, Preston Harts.

On a sweltering afternoon, a rogue's gallery of ex-criminals in spotless sneakers starts to congregate outside, but not to get a $10 trim. News has filtered through the grapevine that Curtis Scoon is back in town. As recently as 10 years ago Scoon was a prominent fixture of Hollis street life. Since shortly after Jay's death he's been living in Atlanta (to pursue a career as a screenwriter, he says). He gained a brief moment of noto- riety following Jay's death when his name was plastered all over the newspapers as the prime suspect. Like Jay, DMC (Darryl McDaniels) and Run (Joseph Simmons), Scoon grew up in Hollis.

Soon a steady parade of former comrades in crime comes by the bar- bershop to say hello. Scoon has persuaded some of his press- and cop- shy friends—now older, somewhat calmer and decidedly thicker around the waist than in their hell-raising heyday—to divulge what they know about the circumstances of Jam Master Jay's tragic demise.

Pep, a friend of Scoon's, rolls up and squeezes his wide girth out of a Nissan Maxima. Scoon and Pep (whom some call Pep the Pimp, though not to his face) go back a long way: The two were co-defendants in a 1985 robbery-and-kidnapping case in which they were both acquitted.

He's dressed in a baggy Washington Wizards shirt with a thick platinum chain around his neck.

"Am I getting paid for this interview?" Pep wants to know.

Most of the people at Masta Kutterz initially claim they won't talk to a journalist. Why risk it, especially when they aren't getting paid for their trouble? "We're skating on very thin ice here," says one. But after a little prodding they begin to gossip like a bunch of Park Avenue matrons.

Few people in the neighborhood believe Scoon killed Jam Master Jay, but at one time the rumor made a certain amount of sense. A notorious argument between the two men is part of Hollis street lore. "Everybody knew Scoon had a beef with Jay," says Pep. "It was easy to believe that Scoon did it."

The dispute originated in the early 1990s when Scoon and Jay had a business arrangement. Many in the neighborhood say it was a drug deal gone bad. They say Scoon and Jay put up cash ($15,000 apiece is the figure bandied about), and a third party ran off with the money. Scoon, however, says it was simply a small loan that Jay failed to repay promptly. Whatever the truth, Scoon, who readily admits he has "a checkered past," felt that Jay owed him and wanted the debt paid. At six-foot-four and 250 pounds, Scoon is a big man with a booming voice and an easygoing wit, though one gets the impression his mien can darken in an instant. "If Jay was dealing drugs, it wasn't with me," insists Scoon. "He paid the debt. I had to get a little heavy with him, but he paid. Jay did not owe me a dollar at the time of his death. I hadn't been in contact with Jay for at least four years."

"Jay always hung on the block," adds Pep. "He always came back to the neighborhood. There was no real hate out here for him." Still, nearly everyone interviewed for this article agrees that Jam Master Jay's murderer must have come from nearby—someone familiar to Jay and intimate with his movements either killed him or set him up. Scoon claims it was common knowledge that Jay was mixed up in narcotics trafficking. The perception is that as he traveled around the country, he served as a middleman—putting buyers and sellers together and taking a cut of the profits without ever handling the drugs. "Everybody in Jay's inner circle knows that Jay was involved in arranging deals," Scoon maintains, "but nobody wants to talk about it because they don't want to tarnish his image. Jay kept a gun on him because he was in a lot of business disputes. He owed a lot of people money. He was so broke he was pawning his jewelry to drug dealers. Everybody loved Jay except the people he did business with."

In the middle of our chat, undercover detectives, seeing this OG reunion on the corner, drive by in an unwashed sedan to check us out. "Five-O, Five-O," the warning goes up, and we all trek back inside the barbershop.

Ten months later the questions surrounding Jay's death have only deepened. Detectives have admitted to the New York tabloids that their investigation has been stymied by the uncooperative attitude of Jay's friends in the studio. Nearly all the murder details have come into question. Various parts of the accepted scenario—Boe's haircut, Jay's gun, how the killers entered the studio—have been filtered through police leaks, conflicting tabloid accounts and sometimes contradictory sources. Either the security cameras were inoperable or the tape is missing. There is even confusion about the number of witnesses, who was actually in the studio and whether the gun Jay was said to be carrying was in fact a .380 (the description of the so-called studio gun). THE STREETS IS WATCHING BUT NOBODY'S TALKING blared MTV.com in an article about the stalled probe.

"It's bullshit to say that the street don't talk," scoffs Scoon. "The street always talks." Just not necessarily to law enforcement officials.

When Scoon ambles outside, whom should he see gliding down Hollis Avenue on luxury German wheels but Randy Allen, making one of his few brief appearances in the neighborhood since Jay's death. At first Scoon can hardly trust his eyes: Here is his nemesis, the man he believes put out the story that he shot the beloved rap icon. As Randy drives past in his Mercedes, Scoon fixes him with an icy stare. Randy looks at Scoon, incredulous.

OCTOBER 30, 2002: JAHLIEK VERSUS BOE

It's one hell of a convoluted tale, a story told by myriad street sources, some of whom are dangerous individuals with serious criminal records, many of whom have never before spoken to the press or the police. The drama unites some of the biggest names in hip-hop with a cast that ranges from street-level hustlers to big-time drug suppliers. The narrative reaches as far afield as the underworlds of the Midwest and Baltimore. But in the end, it all comes back to Hollis.

In 1987 Jay moved to nearby Parkside Hills, to a three-story house with wrought iron gates, ornamental trees and a carriage lamp in the front garden, but he always kept one foot in the streets of Hollis. It was where his inspiration came from.

The Bronx may be the Mecca of hip-hop, but a strong case can be made that Hollis and the surrounding neighborhoods are rap music's

Medina. A 30-minute train ride from Manhattan, this tight-knit neighborhood of modest single-family homes has raised an extraordinary number of rap's movers and shakers; it's where hip-hop pioneer Russell Simmons, older brother of Joseph "Run" Simmons, got his start dealing weed at the local high school. In addition to Simmons and Run-DMC, rap heavies from Hollis and the nearby environs of Jamaica and St. Albans include LL Cool J, A Tribe Called Quest, 50 Cent, Ja Rule and local radio personality Ed Lover. Hollis is also the birthplace of Irv Gotti (a.k.a. Irving Lorenzo), founder of the rap label Murder Inc. (which bills itself as "the world's most dangerous record company"). Gotti grew up several blocks from Jay, who taught the young Irving how to deejay. Gotti too is suffering from his association with street toughs, and his label is currently the subject of an FBI probe.

Tension between lower-middle-class respectability and the siren call of the streets characterizes life in the neighborhood—a decent address before white flight in the 1970s and crack cocaine in the early 1980s turned the prosperous and racially integrated community into a suburban ghetto. During the day Hollis has a village vibe, like a place where everybody either is related to or knows everybody else, and strangers draw perplexed stares. But at night respectable residents retreat indoors. Outside it's guns, drugs and crime.

Within hours of Jay's death, mourners gather on 203rd Street, outside the house where Jay grew up. His sister, Bonita, lives there now. A friend of Bonita's named Jahliek, who regularly crashes on her couch, hears a commotion outside and investigates. According to Jahliek—a tall, thin man with cornrows—he finds Bonita's son Boe Skagz shouting at the crowd clustered in the light of the street lamps and the shadows of nearby trees. Boe sees him, he says, and then attacks him, cracking him over the head with a gun and leaving a serious gash. "He was angry," says Jahliek. "Later he apologized. He said he was upset because certain people had told him a bunch of bullshit that I was affiliated with his uncle's murder." Instead of going to the hospital and attracting the police, Jahliek uses Krazy Glue to close the wound. "I wasn't going to make a fuss, so I doctored myself," he says. Aversion to fuss is common in Hollis—just ask the cops.

NOVEMBER 5, 2002: REQUIEM FOR A DJ

Police cruisers block off several Jamaica streets. Throngs of onlookers pack the sidewalks and press against barricades as an NYPD helicopter hovers overhead. Plainclothes officers shoot video from rooftops and take photos as stretch limos disgorge hip-hop dignitaries: Queen

THE LAST DAYS OF JAM MASTER JAY

Latifah, Kurtis Blow, Foxy Brown, Chuck D, Russell Simmons, the Beastie Boys, P. Diddy and Grandmaster Flash. A glass-covered carriage pulled by four white horses comes down Merrick Boulevard.

Jam Master Jay's funeral is a grand and sober affair, not unlike a statesman's. Fans, family and friends pack the Greater Allen Cathedral in Queens, where some 2,000 mourners hold their hands aloft and bow their heads in prayer. Church ladies dressed in white robes dispense tissues and water to the crying masses.

Funeral wreaths, including a floral arrangement in the shape of twin turntables, adorn the altar. Pallbearers wear black fedoras, leather jackets and unlaced shell-toe Adidas—the look Jay invented for Run-DMC. According to witnesses, Lydia High, who was in the studio the night Jay was murdered, barges to the front row—traditionally reserved for family members—and tries to sit with Jay's mother, Connie Mizell. Mizell tells her to sit at the back with her brother, Randy Allen, who, the story goes, has arrived at the funeral accompanied by a bodyguard. Randy greets a guest and gasps, "I can hardly breathe. I've got to get out of here." (As Lydia leaves the service, witnesses say, she is picked up by NYPD detectives from the 103rd Precinct and whisked away to be questioned again.)

From the pulpit Darryl McDaniels, a.k.a. DMC, fights back tears and eulogizes his friend: "Jam Master Jay was not a thug. Jam Master Jay was not a gangster. He was the personification, the embodiment, of hip-hop."

OCTOBER 2002: A HOLIDAY WITH SHAKE

In the week before his murder Jam Master Jay spent four days with his friend Eric "Shake" James at Shake's bachelor pad, an unremarkable aluminum-sided house in a Milwaukee suburb. It was a personal visit. "We were just popping shit and hanging out," says Shake. Jay seemed relieved to be out of Hollis. He was reluctant to go home but had to be in Queens to put the finishing touches on Rusty Waters' debut album. Afterward Jay was to travel to D.C. to spin during halftime at a Wizards–Celtics basketball game.

"Jay told me he was going through some problems," Shake says. "It was regular everyday bullshit. People owed him money."

Jay also told Shake about a recent incident in Jay's studio involving an acquaintance named Goldie. Goldie allegedly owed Jay money from some sort of fishy business arrangement. When Goldie walked into the studio sporting a new set of clothes, a perturbed Jay demanded his money. "I need to get my cheese," he insisted. Goldie thought Jay wasn't serious and laughed off the request. Jay whipped out a .45 automatic and waved it in Goldie's face. "I was shocked when Jay told me that," says Shake.

Except for a brief trip to Chicago to see 50 Cent at the House of Blues, Jay and Shake spent most of their time together in the living room, playing an NFL video game. Jay loved games and would sometimes play for 24 hours at a stretch. After playing awhile, he turned to Shake and said, "I ain't going home. I'm happy out here." The memory pains Shake. "He kept saying that he'd rather stay in Milwaukee and chill," he says. "But I kept telling him that he had to go home and take care of business."

While Jay was there the mother of rapper Mos Def called and asked Jay to write the music for an upcoming play she and her son were producing. To Shake it seemed that Jay's career must be booming again, but his street-regal exterior masked his worrisome involvement in numerous beefs. "Randy is taking my money, man," Jay told Shake. "I'm glad that Rusty Waters is signed to Virgin. I'm happy that Randy is finally out of my pocket."

"Jay didn't suspect Randy was stealing from him," says Shake. "He *knew* Randy was stealing from him. It had been going on for a while." The last conversation Shake had with his old friend was the day after Jay left Milwaukee. "He'd forgotten his two-way, and he called me from a sandwich shop near the studio and asked me for 50 Cent's number," Shake says. "He was with Randy, and they were just about to go upstairs and work on the album. That was the last time I ever heard from him. You can't imagine how bad that makes me feel, knowing I was the one who persuaded him to go back to New York."

JULY 30, 2003: LOVEY AND THE BURGLARY CREW

Lovey sits in a barber's chair at Masta Kutterz, reminiscing about how he and 15-year-old Jason Mizell ran wild in the Hollis streets. Now a rotund, balding 38-year-old with fading tattoos on his arms and a day job, Lovey recalls those years with pride and fondness: "Me and Jay grew up together on 203rd Street. I was the first person he met when his family moved to 203 in the late 1970s."

Growing up, Jay was a good, if rambunctious, kid, a member of a close-knit family. He was expected to speak proper English at home and developed an early interest in music—first learning the drums, then the bass. He also learned to navigate the neighborhood, and to feel safe he needed everyone to be his friend. As Jay explained to Bill Adler, author of the Run-DMC biography *Tougher Than Leather*, "If I was going to the store for my mother, all the wild guys would be there, so I had to be their friend in order not to be scared of them."

"When he was a kid, Jay was cool with a lot of drug dealers," says Lovey, "but he never sold anything for them." Jay may not have dealt drugs, but he was involved with a junior burglary crew that broke into houses in Jamaica Estates. "Me and Jay and Randy Allen and Randy's brother Frankie all used to rob houses together," says Lovey. "That's what we did." Others in the shop say they were joined by Ronald "Tinard" Washington and a guy everyone called Yaqin.

Lovey's revelation is significant. Every surviving member of the crew later figured prominently in stories about Jay's death. While Jay went on to legitimacy and success, his friends—whom he never abandoned, despite the trouble they might have caused him—went on to lead hard lives.

The fledgling posse targeted wealthy white neighborhoods—you don't get rich robbing the poor. Frankie Allen would stake out a place, often hiding in a tree or bushes until the residents left. Then the crew would head inside.

"We'd take everything," says Lovey. "Jewelry, guns, money, drugs, stereo equipment, televisions—even food for a meal afterward. Jay had a strict father, so we tried to keep him out of a lot of stuff, because we knew his mom and pop would be angry. But Jay held stuff in his basement, where his parents didn't go."

Whenever the others allowed it, Jay tagged along. In Hollis, crime is practically a rite of passage—the occasional heist or drug deal does wonders for your reputation.

"One time Jay decided he wanted to come with us," remembers Lovey. "He wanted his own money. So we took him on a score." As they were leaving a house in Jamaica Estates, a private security guard spotted them and fired several shots, one of which nearly hit Jay, says another of the crew. "That was his wake-up call," says Lovey. "He didn't want to do that no more."

When Jay's parents found out about their son's extracurricular activities, they were furious. Jay's mother burst into tears. Scared straight, Jay began concentrating on his true passion—deejaying, which he practiced religiously in his bedroom.

The others continued down their crooked paths—Frankie Allen died from an overdose and Randy landed in jail on a felony charge—but Jay used his ill-gotten proceeds to set himself up as a professional DJ. He played outdoor parties at Two-Fifth Park, a concrete playground with a hoops court, situated just around the corner from his house. The new sound of hip-hop was rocking New York City's outer boroughs. MC after MC took the microphone to brag about pretty girls they didn't have or fancy cars they didn't drive. In the early 1980s the parties attracted crack dealers flush with cash and carrying weapons. It wasn't uncommon for the boisterous events to end with a mammoth brawl or gunshots. But at Two-Fifth Park, Jay's skills caught the attention of two up-and-coming local rappers, Run and DMC.

1986: RAISING HELL

Run-DMC attained heights unimagined by any previous hip-hop act. They were the first rappers to be featured regularly on MTV. They were the only hip-hop performers to play Live Aid. The group's debut was the first hip-hop album to go gold. The second, *King of Rock*, eventually sold 4 million copies. Their third and best album, *Raising Hell*, sold millions more worldwide, fueled by "Walk This Way," the hit collaboration with Aerosmith. They played London, Tokyo, Sydney and Paris; they made as much as $150,000 a show. They also scored a major endorsement deal in 1986 when they signed a $1.5 million contract with Adidas. Jay was rich beyond his wildest dreams. So why was he virtually broke at the time of his death?

"Jay hadn't had a hit record in 10 years. Why would he have a whole bunch of money?" asks Russell Simmons, who managed Run-DMC in the 1980s.

Part of the problem was Jay's extravagance. He wore mink when the rest of Run-DMC wore leather. He had the most jewelry. He had the flashiest cars. Jay didn't drive one automobile but several—a Lincoln Continental, a Mercedes, a Toyota Land Cruiser, a Jeep Wrangler and his favorite, a seven-passenger Lincoln Navigator. He also purchased showy rides for his sister, brother, mother, wife and at least two close friends. As his fame grew, so did his entourage. He thought nothing of dropping $3,000 a night on champagne at a nightclub.

"As far as I know, he had no effective management in the last 10 years of his life, which is not unusual in the rap world," says one industry figure who worked closely with Jay. "But he must have been profligate to die broke."

Jay's financial woes started early, according to Tracey Miller, Run-DMC's longtime publicist. A six-figure tax bill incurred during his *Raising Hell* heyday mushroomed over time to nearly $500,000. "Jay couldn't keep up with all the penalties and interest," says Miller. "It kept compounding and compounding. Eventually the IRS put a lien on his earnings. He was allowed to keep a portion to live on, but most of his performance fees went to the tax man. Russell Simmons was their manager and made millions. Why didn't he instruct Jay to manage his finances and pay his taxes?"

An angry Simmons retorts, "To say I made millions from Run-DMC is an absolute lie. Everybody got jerked. That's how it was for rappers in those days. Tracey is not in a position to know what I did for Jay. I did the best I could to advise him and to find opportunities for Jay. I'm not a business manager. I introduced him to financial managers, but I couldn't force him to pay his taxes. He was a grown man."

In 1988 Simmons sued the band's label, Profile Records, to break their contract. The dispute effectively put Run-DMC's recording career on hold for nearly two years, an eternity in the fast-paced world of rap. When they finally released a new album, their momentum had dissipated, and new rappers had taken their place.

According to their rhymes, Run-DMC were clean. But rap's first stars also had a dark side. Before he was ordained a minister, Run had a substance abuse problem, and DMC consumed eight bottles of malt liquor a day. As the group's record sales declined, Jay turned to side projects. He did solo gigs, helped start a turntablist school called the Scratch DJ Academy, bought a recording studio and formed his own label. In 1992 JMJ Records scored a huge hit with fellow Queens rappers Onyx ("Throw Ya Gunz"), but subsequent releases tanked.

Despite his dwindling fortunes Jay still had an ear for talent. In 1999 he helped get the then-obscure rapper 50 Cent signed to Columbia Records. But 50 Cent's deal showed that Jay was developing a reputation for ripping off his protégés. "My deal with Columbia wasn't a good deal," 50 Cent complained to the website AllHipHop.com. "It was for $250,000. I got $65,000 in advance; of that, $50,000 went to Jay and $10,000 went to the lawyers who negotiated the deal. I was left with $5,000. I was still selling crack." (After Columbia dumped him, 50 Cent hooked up with Eminem and his producer, Dr. Dre, and went on to release the platinum-selling *Get Rich or Die Tryin'.*)

It's an old story: A musician gets screwed, signs a bunch of his boys and treats them the way he got treated. "Jay was known for taking the lion's share of the money," says one music journalist, speaking off the record.

SUMMER 2003: RUMORS ABOUT RANDY ALLEN

The police at first thought Jay was a victim of a simmering rap war. All roads led to the doorstep of Irv Gotti and Murder Inc. and a contemporary of Jay's, Kenneth "Supreme" McGriff. A convicted crack kingpin,

McGriff gained notoriety in the 1980s as a leader of the Supreme Team, a murderous gang that controlled the drug trade in next-door Jamaica. The feds are investigating whether McGriff secretly bankrolled Murder Inc. with drug profits. There's also talk that he ordered the 2000 hit on 50 Cent that nearly took the rapper's life. After Jay's killing, the NYPD offered protection to 50 Cent.

Then Scoon's name hit the papers. When that lead turned cold, however, investigators focused on a felon believed to be the killer's lookout. In May 2003 Jay's mom vented her frustration with Randy in the press, publicly excoriating him for not visiting, not telling her what he saw the night of the killing and not helping the police. Then a new motive surfaced: Jay had been killed because of an alleged affair between McGriff and Jay's wife, Terri. This seems unlikely, since one would assume the FBI had McGriff under 24-hour surveillance and had his phones tapped.

The Greek chorus in Hollis connects all these developments with Randy Allen. The day after Jay's death, they say, Randy relocated his sister to Las Vegas, and he and Boe disappeared for three days, claiming they needed to rehearse for a Rusty Waters promotional tour. One family acquaintance says, "I was at Jay's mom's place, and I heard her say on the phone to Randy, 'If you don't bring my grandson back, I'm going to call the police and have you arrested for kidnapping.'" The suspicion is that they were trying to get their stories straight. "A detective I know told me he wanted to question them, but they kept dodging him," the Mizell family confidant says. "They were being uncooperative. Each story Lydia told was different. Her stories and her brother's didn't match."

Hurricane (born Wendell Fite), the former DJ for the Beastie Boys and one of Jay's oldest friends, blames Randy—who was best man at Jay's wedding—for starting the McGriff affair rumor. "Terri is a straight-up lady," he says, "a good mother and an excellent wife. I never saw Randy grieve once at the funeral. A friend of his gets killed, and the day after burying Jay he goes on some bullshit promotional tour for Rusty Waters."

AUGUST 2003: RANDY DENIES ALL

Five days after Jay's murder, a distraught Shake, who had traveled to New York City after Jay's death, met Randy Allen in a Burger King parking lot on 179th Street. Below the asphalt, trains rumbled into the last subway stop in Queens—the end of the line. Shake jumped into the back of a car with Randy. "He was upset and real agitated," says Shake.

THE LAST DAYS OF JAM MASTER JAY

"I asked him, 'Who killed Jay?' and Randy told me, 'The nigger who killed your best friend and mine is Curtis Scoon.' I asked him how he knew. He said, 'Because my sister Lydia looked him right in the face.' I asked to speak to Lydia alone, but Randy wouldn't allow it. Months later I heard Randy on Hot 97, and he told an entirely different story. He said Scoon didn't kill Jay. I was upset. Why would he lie to me like that?"

Shake says Randy also told him that after Jay's death the studio had been burglarized and equipment was taken. "But niggers on the street told me afterward that Randy did it," claims Shake.

While accusations are flying, Randy Allen agrees to speak on the phone. He vehemently denies meeting with Shake and fingering Scoon as Jay's killer: "No such meeting took place," he says. He also refutes the accusation that he was stealing money and equipment. "That's a bunch of bullshit," he says angrily. "Shake is lying. He's saying this for publicity. I didn't steal from Jay. I made money for Jay. Do you think Jay would have kept me as his business manager for more than a decade if I was stealing? Shake is just jealous of what I did for Jay." Other friends of Jay's, however, back up Shake's story. "It was well-known that Jay and Randy were not on good terms in Jay's final days," says Hurricane. "Jay knew he was stealing and confronted Randy. Jay and I asked Randy about missing money, and he denied it. They were definitely on the outs by the end."

Shake and others also say that prior to Jay's fight with Goldie, there was another disturbing encounter in the studio, which allegedly involved Randy's brother Teddy pulling a gun on Jay's cousin and saying, "This is my brother's studio, not Jay's. Get the fuck out of here."

Randy, his voice rising with emotion, professes his innocence: "A lot of people don't like me because Jay and me were together for a long time. I'm trying to find out who killed my best friend. I don't care what Hurricane or Shake says. If my boy Jay was here, he'd smack the shit right out of them for saying this bullshit. Jay would be turning over in his grave if he heard all this nonsense."

Bonita, Jay's sister, tells PLAYBOY that she too believes Randy was behind the burglary. After a chance meeting, Bonita, who doesn't want to submit to a formal interview, says she knew that Randy and Jay had taken out an insurance policy on each other and that in the wake of the killing Randy drained all the money from a joint bank account. (In May the New York *Daily News*, citing a police source, reported the policy's existence. Jay and Randy were listed as beneficiaries if either came to harm in the studio. Other police sources dispute the story.)

322

"The insurance policy doesn't exist, and there was no bank account," insists Randy. "All these people are talking about money, money, money. They should stop worrying about that shit. All this backstabbing is doing nothing to find the real killer."

"No bank account?" scoffs Shake. "The bank account was under the name Erotic Money. I even have the account number. If there was no bank account, what were all those checks Randy was writing when Jay wasn't around?"

JULY 31, 2002: TINARD DROPS A BOMB

Ronald "Tinard" Washington is a slim, tall and deceptively quiet career criminal who has been in and out of various correctional facilities for half his life. He was also a longtime buddy of Jay's—and a member of Jay and Randy's burglary crew. Speaking from behind bars following an arrest for allegedly trying to rob a Long Island motel, Tinard says that on July 31, 2002, he and Jay journeyed to Washington, D.C., in Jay's black SUV to meet with Uncle, a major-league drug supplier from the Midwest.

Tinard, who was sought by police after the murder, says Jay had a sit-down with the supplier at a local hotel. "Jay didn't put up any money," he alleges. "The guy from the Midwest, Uncle, fronted the coke to Jay. It was 10 keys, worth about $180,000, which could be sold on the street for about $280,000." Tinard says that Uncle expected Jay to pay him back in seven days. Another street source confirms the existence of Uncle but says he's from Los Angeles, not the Midwest.

The same night in D.C., Tinard alleges, he saw Big D, Run-DMC's former tour manager. (Big D says he has heard of Uncle but vehemently denies being in Washington.) "A lot of people came in and out of the hotel room that night to see Uncle," says Tinard.

The next day, according to Tinard, he and Jay left: "We took the coke to Baltimore because Jay had someone lined up who was going to sell it for him. But he was having trouble hooking up with the guy. Jay told me to take his truck and go home—he was going to fly back in the morning. Later Jay told me he met the guy—someone we grew up with in Hollis—and gave him the coke, but the guy never paid him. Jay went back to Baltimore and tried to collect the debt, but he couldn't get in touch."

Tinard refuses to name the Baltimore connection, saying only, "Me and the Baltimore guy used to be real close until we had a falling out. He's known for moving a lot of coke. He's also known for using his rep to burn people." Curtis Scoon thinks Tinard could be referring to a former associate whose street name is Yaqin. Scoon says he, Yaqin and Pep were co-defendants in the armed-robbery trial. Yaqin, who has reportedly done time for the attempted murder of an NYPD officer, was also part of the Hollis burglary crew. (Tinard was also reportedly imprisoned for shooting a cop during a jewelry heist.)

"I can't believe Jay would give Yaqin 10 of anything," says Scoon. "Yaqin's a piece of shit. He wouldn't think twice about ripping off someone like Jay. Jay wasn't that tough. You fuck Jay over and what's he going to do—make a song about it?"

Flash-forward to the afternoon of the murder. Tinard says that Jay called and asked him to come to the studio: "One of the first things he said when I got there was, 'Do you have a gun?' I didn't. So Jay showed me his gun—it was a .45—and he gave me $200 to get some bullets on the street. He was going to meet Uncle in Connecticut the next day. He said the guy wanted to get paid, but he didn't have the money. He asked me to come along for protection."

After purchasing the bullets, Tinard—the man cops at times have theorized was either the lookout or the shooter (he fits the physical description)—claims he was on his way back to the studio when he saw two figures ascending the stairs. They were about 20 steps in front of him. Tinard says he recognized the duo as Big D and his son, Little D. At more than 300 pounds, Big D is not hard to spot. Tinard ducked and went out back to the bus station, where he heard three loud gunshots—not the two shots reported in the media—then saw Little D rushing down the fire escape, looking agitated. "I'm positive it was Little D. I looked him right in his face before he ran off," Tinard asserts. After the encounter, Tinard says, he took the bus back to Hollis. Later that evening, he claims, he bumped into Little D on the street and asked him what had happened. "Little D told me, 'My pops wasn't supposed to shoot Jay. That wasn't supposed to happen,'" alleges Tinard. Tinard says he was shot at twice the following Saturday, and he then decided to get the hell out of Dodge.

A common assumption in Hollis is that Tinard fingered Big D to get a reduced sentence (his lawyer says there is no deal), to exact revenge on the man he suspects tried to have him clipped, and to collect the reward money.

AUGUST 31, 2003: BIG D'S REBUTTAL

Smoking blunts in his girlfriend's backyard and rehashing various forensic scenarios, Darren "Big D" Jordan doesn't seem like much of a killer. Murderers don't usually come with their vocation stamped across their forehead, but if Big D did whack his childhood friend, he's one hell of a cool customer. Big D was a pallbearer at Jay's funeral and grieved alongside the family. In the old days, Jay helped him get a job as Run-DMC's road manager after Big D ran into trouble with the law. In the mid-1990s he and Jay owned a fish store in Jamaica, Queens.

Big D, a Jesus medallion hanging from his neck, seems remarkably unperturbed for someone whom police want to question and whose son, Little D, is incarcerated on Rikers Island on an attempted murder charge for shooting Boe Skagz in the leg. The dispute wasn't directly related to Jay's killing: Big D says Little D was angry with Boe for writing a lyric about how someone linked to Murder Inc. fractured his jaw. But given Tinard's allegations and Boe's relationship with Randy, the bust was probably not coincidental.

"Tinard don't mean shit to me," Big D says. "He's losing his mind. He's lying. Tinard just wants to come off as a big man in prison."

If Big D seems composed, his girlfriend is anything but. We make a brief stop on 203rd Street to pick up some clothes at Big D's old place, opposite Bonita's, and she says, "If someone tries to pop your ass, I'm out of here."

Big D says he was home on the night of the killing. "One of Jay's cousins ran across the street from Bonita's, screaming that someone had shot Jay," says Big D. "We jumped in my car and made a beeline for the studio."

Big D is not easily mistaken for someone else; he's nearly twice the size of the killer in the standard description. So if he didn't murder Jay, who did? "I don't know for sure," he says. "Yaqin could be involved if the stakes are high enough. I'm hearing he's strong enough. If the 10 keys is true, that's enough to get someone killed."

As to why Tinard would implicate him. Big D says, "The only thing I can think of is that back when we were teenagers, my first wife had a beef with his sister. Tinard's sister got cut pretty bad, so bad she couldn't use one of her arms."

EPILOGUE

More than 10 months after the slaying of Jam Master Jay, an arrest had yet to be made. As this story went to press, sources told PLAYBOY that the police had placed Lydia High in protective custody to encourage her to open up. The case has been plagued by predictions that never come to pass—such as the gossip that Randy Allen was about to be charged with obstruction of justice and that Big D would be arrested on Labor Day. "As this is an ongoing investigation," says a detective at the 103rd

Precinct, "we can't say anything at this moment. Once it's out there you can't take it back, so you're not going to find anyone who will say anything."

Meanwhile, in Hollis, theories continue to swirl. "Whoever killed Jay ain't no stranger," says Shake. "It's someone from around the way. It had to be someone he trusted for the gunmen to get up that close on him. There were powder marks on his shirt."

"Everybody wants to whitewash Jay's life," says Scoon. "But Jay, like all men, had his flaws. He was no saint. What man is? But he can still be people's hero without being perfect. This isn't about tarnishing Jay's legacy. The attempt to cover up his business dealings and protect his image is why it's taking so long to catch his killer."

In the end Jay's loyalties probably brought him down. His attempt to straddle two worlds became untenable. He played a game he could not win with men he should not have trusted. The most startling realization, according to his friends, may not be that he got killed but that he managed to stay alive so long.

Stolen Screams

by SIMON COOPER

March 2005

On Sunday, August 22, 2004, Christina Vassiliou stepped inside the doors of a small art museum in Oslo. For Vassiliou, who was traveling with her mother, the vacation to Norway was a reward and a pilgrimage: a reward for her recent graduation from Rutgers University law school in New Jersey, a pilgrimage to see a work of art that fascinated her almost as much as its creator, Norwegian expressionist painter Edvard Munch.

The Munch Museum is situated in a northeastern neighborhood of Oslo, Norway's elegant, quiet capital city. There are narrow cobblestoned streets, trams, immaculate squares and well-tended parks. Every hour or so, delicate chimes ring from towers on the street corners, giving visitors the impression of a city set inside a music box.

The tourist season was waning. The streets were deserted that morning except for a few people walking to cafés. A little after 11 A.M., Vassiliou, 26, stood in front of the painting she had waited 10 years and traveled 3,700 miles to see: *The Scream*, the iconic depiction of human angst, which has become one of the most recognized images in the world.

The painting, created in 1893, is nearly as enigmatic and mysterious as Leonardo da Vinci's *Mona Lisa*. Is the man screaming, or is he shielding his ears from some infernal noise? Whatever the viewer sees, Munch's bold, thick brushstrokes conjure a creation whose power far exceeds the two-and-a-half-foot-by-three-foot frame that contains it. "It is the primal image of urban alienation," says Robert Rosenblum, a curator at New York City's Guggenheim museum. "It looks like an anxiety attack."

Vassiliou, jet-lagged and overwhelmed by the power of the painting she had read about for so many years, found herself deep in thought, lulled by the soft shuffling of the other gallerygoers, when she heard a man's voice cry out.

"Gun!"

This single word, shouted in English, echoed through the hushed interior of the museum. There were more shouts, this time in Norwegian, and a commotion erupted just out of sight, back in the main foyer.

Two men ran past the café and the little gift shop and up to the ticket booth. One pulled out a revolver with an enormous, Magnum-size barrel and held it to the head of a female guard. He shouted to the crowd to get down.

Vassiliou turned in the direction of the shouting. She saw the second man, dressed in a gray hooded top and wearing a black face mask and black leather gloves, heading straight toward her. Suddenly he veered away and moved toward an 1893 Munch painting titled *Madonna*. He banged it against the wall until it broke free, severing the gray wires that connected it to an alarm that sounded at the local police station. He took the paintings to a viewing area and continued to smash it against a wooden bench, obviously trying to break off its dark, ornate frame.

Then the man stopped and spun in a complete 360. He appeared to be confused, as if he didn't know what to do next. His eyes, the only part of his face visible behind the black mask, searched the walls. Then he saw what he was looking for.

With *Madonna* still in one hand, the man strode past Vassiliou and tore *The Scream* from the wall. The young American woman was frozen to the spot in fear. She stood close enough to touch the robber, who at six feet tall towered over her. She says she will never forget his blue eyes.

In an instant he was gone: back to the lobby, where he handed one of the paintings to his armed accomplice. They fled the building, dashing about a hundred yards over a lawn—one of them twice dropped a painting—to a waiting black 1992 Audi A6 wagon manned by a third member of the crew. The works were placed in the car, and the Audi peeled away, disappearing into the Norwegian capital's winding side streets.

In no more than two minutes the thieves had helped themselves to two modern masterpieces estimated to have a combined value of more than $100 million.

• • •

No alarm rang in the museum, and no guards gave chase. Despite a collection containing 1,000 paintings and more than 23,000 drawings and prints worth about $3 billion, the Munch Museum does not arm its guards.

The three men sped away from the museum, briefly hooking to the west on a street called Tøyengata before turning north, following a road that encircles the zoological gardens opposite the Munch Museum.

Inside the getaway car, the thieves were tearing away *Madonna*'s frame and hurling it to pieces out of the car windows: Fragments were later found lying on the sidewalk, in gutters and under parked cars, like a bread crumb trail marking the robbers' flight.

By the time they passed through a major intersection bisected by tram lines, they were out of the immediate vicinity of the museum. Up hills and through Sunday-quiet roads, they drove deeper into the sub-urban outskirts of the city, the roads getting smaller, until they pulled behind a block of modern apartments. There, in a muddy spot used to store construction materials, they broke off the final pieces of the frame and tossed them from the car. Turning around, the robbers con-tinued north. Only two or three minutes had passed since they exited the museum.

They took a road called Hasleveien into a residential area of Oslo, past a Bible school and over a graffiti-emblazoned railway bridge, then made a sharp left into the dirt parking lot of the dreary Sinsen tennis club. Sinsen is one of these drab neighborhoods so familiar to the out-skirts of all big cities: utilitarian, frayed at the edges, squeezed between highways and rails, a place you pass through to get somewhere else.

The thieves ditched the Audi in a parking lot and set off a fire extin-guisher inside it in an attempt to destroy any forensic evidence they'd left behind. It was smart thinking not to torch the vehicle, which would have drawn police to Sinsen; the car was not discovered for hours.

At this point police lost the trail. Perhaps another car or cars were parked there and the crooks simply swapped vehicles. Or maybe they exited the parking lot on foot. Only 10 feet of grass and weeds sepa-rated them from the railway tracks that run to Bergen and Trondheim. It would have been an easy stroll to the highway opposite and from there into the ether. There were too many possibilities.

• • •

Back at the museum there was chaos. Three guards were present that day, two women and a man. None seemed to have any idea what to do. Vassiliou remembers being told, "It's okay. They didn't get any paintings," the guard seemingly unaware of the blank spaces on the walls right in front of her.

Meanwhile the crime scene was being overrun. The guards hadn't closed the front doors, and tourists continued to enter, mingling with the witnesses to the heist. Vassiliou estimates it was at least 20 minutes before the first police officer showed up. Many witnesses had already left the museum.

A helicopter scrambled to scan the city for signs of the Audi, but by then the getaway car had been abandoned. The police did not find it until three P.M. Airports, ports and border crossings were put on alert, but this was a futile gesture.

The police stumbled across one bit of luck: some remarkable video-taped footage of the robbers leaving the building. The images came not from the museum's few security cameras but from the cameras of tourists disembarking from a bus in the parking lot.

"No glass in front of the paintings, no alarm systems as in French museums—where a bell rings if visitors have gotten too close—not even a cordon to keep people back a certain distance. There was no search of people's bags at the entrance, and the guards were nowhere to be seen." This assessment, given to a reporter by an indignant French witness named Francois Castang, was repeated in newspapers throughout Europe and the U.S.

Norway seemed to turn against the museum directors rather than the thieves. ALMOST AS EASY AS ROBBING A KIOSK, read the headline in the daily newspaper *Aftenposten*. Most of the world's media carried the news on the front page or in prime time, adding to Norway's embarrassment.

In Oslo, Munch Museum spokesperson Jorunn Christofierson responded defensively: "We have guards, but when thieves threaten the guards with a gun there is not much to be done."

A palpable sense of shame radiated not just from the museum but from Norway itself. Munch and his most famous painting are deeply embedded in the national psyche. They are examples of world-class achievement in a country of 4.5 million souls striving for a sense of identity among Scandinavian nations. From the upper reaches of the intelligentsia to the criminal underworld, every Norwegian knows Munch and his value to the national pride. The country was ashamed not just because of the ease with which one of Norway's national treasures had been taken but because, as it turns out, this wasn't the first time *The Scream* had been stolen in Oslo.

It is late September 2004, and in London's Gray's Inn—a large quadrangle inhabited by members of the British legal profession since the 1500s—fall leaves are being blown in tight eddies around a courtyard. *The Scream* and *Madonna* have been missing for a month. In a discreet third-floor office in a discreet redbrick building, Dick Ellis is poring over the details of the robbery. Like most stolen-art experts (he is a former member of a British police art-crimes squad), he fears it will be years before the paintings resurface.

Ellis, a former competitive rower, has settled into a comfortable middle age. In a dark blue suit, cream shirt and red tie, he gives off the confident, authoritative air of a career policeman, which he is. The son of a surgeon and a physiotherapist, brother to a doctor and a psychiatric nurse, Ellis figured out early on that he would not follow the family tradition. "I knew I didn't deal terribly well with people who are ill," he says. At the age of 19 he joined London's Metropolitan Police.

Early in his career a burglar broke into his parents' house and made off with the family silver. It was a clean, professional job; the crook drilled a small hole in a window at the back of the house before inserting a wire tool that lifted the catch. Ellis took it upon himself to investigate and two days later tracked the family's silver sugar bowl to a stall at a local market. His detective work resulted in the return not only of his parents' collection but also of silver belonging to their neighbors, all targeted by the same thief. Ellis went on to co-found Scotland Yard's Art and Antiques Squad in 1990 as a detective sergeant. Now retired from the Metropolitan Police, he runs his own consultancy, International Art Recovery, tracking stolen art and antiques for private clients and institutions.

"The stolen-art market works like any other market," he says. "Criminals are just businessmen who have made a career choice to earn their money illegally, and art is like any other commodity in which they deal, such as drugs or firearms. But when it comes to something as distinctive as *The Scream*, you're talking about an extremely difficult market. Yes, these paintings are incredibly valuable, but they are also so well-known they are unsellable."

Then what possibly could have motivated these three men to commit an audacious daylight theft of paintings that have little or no street value?

"It wasn't for the insurance," says Ellis matter-of-factly. "As any art thief worth his salt knows, such paintings are rarely insured, due to the prohibitive cost of the premiums." For ransom, then? Again unlikely, says Ellis: "The museum has no real money of its own, and the Norwegian government has clearly stated that it will not, under any circumstances, pay ransoms."

Criminals usually assign a stolen painting a value of about 10 percent of its highest publicly reported worth. The painting can then be used in negotiations for drugs, arms or other black-market items such as jewelry or silver. In 1990 a painting by Dutch master Gabriel Metsu was recovered in Istanbul, where it had been part of a heroin deal. And Vermeer's 1670 work *Lady Writing a Letter with Her Maid* was recovered from an Antwerp gem dealer, who had taken it as collateral against a loan he'd made to the thieves. "Paintings circulate like bonds," Ellis says, "like any other international commodity."

But Ellis ventures that something else may have been at work here. In the case of *The Scream*, he thinks the thieves may have decided to steal something "so significant nationally that it would be a big snub to the authorities. It would really catch the headlines and make a state-ment—a way of showing the police and their colleagues that these men are the number one criminals in Norway."

Bragging rights for the thieves—could that have been the motiva-tion? That deduction, the educated guess of a savvy art cop, turned out to be the key to solving the case of the missing 1994 *Scream*. Dick Ellis should know—he headed up the international investigation that recovered it.

Edvard Munch painted the harrowing figure in *The Scream* multiple times: in oil, in tempera and in a mixture of the two on cardboard. He created lithographs as well, and the originals of these are worth mil-lions, though not nearly as much as the paintings. In the early hours of February 12, 1994, two young criminals raided the National Gallery in Oslo and stole its copy of *The Scream*, which is called the first version of the painting and considered the most valuable of the four known ver-sions. The 2004 thieves stole the painting known as the second *Scream*, for the order in which it was painted. (It is also called, unkindly, the seasick *Scream*, for its livid green palette.) Version three is still held safely in the Munch Museum, and the fourth is in the hands of a pri-vate collector. Though less well-known, the thieves' other 2004 trophy, *Madonna*—a dark, erotic portrait of a woman—is considered another example of the artist's genius.

After examining the circumstances of the two robberies, Ellis has begun to believe that faint undercurrents may connect the heists. It's not a simple story. A full decade divides the two crimes, which involve three stolen masterpieces, half a dozen crooks, squadrons of police, art experts from three countries, $472,000 in cash and a murder. But tangled in the strands of the tale that follows may be tantalizing clues to solve the 2004 theft, as well as the reasons professional thieves have gone to such trouble to steal Norway's most famous painting—twice.

BAD BOYS: ELLINGSEN AND ENGER

"Thanks for the bad security."

These five words were handwritten on a postcard and pinned to the space on the wall where, a few minutes earlier, *The Scream* had hung. It was the early hours of February 12, 1994; a curtain twisted in the winter wind blowing through the window where the thieves had entered. A ladder led down to the street right outside the front door of the National Gallery in Oslo.

Grainy security camera footage would later document the crime for police and embarrassed gallery officials. At 6:30 A.M. two masked men came around the side of the museum. They propped their ladder against the museum's front wall; while one held it steady, the other began to ascend the rungs. He didn't make it to the top. Maybe it was the cold, maybe the rungs were slippery with ice, or maybe he was just so nervous that his shaking legs couldn't hold him, but 18-year-old William Ellingsen slipped and nearly fell on top of Pal Enger, his partner in crime.

Ellingsen quickly recovered and went back up, reaching the window. The teenager broke the window, went inside and simply pulled *The Scream* off the wall.

It was all over in 50 seconds. Fifty seconds to pull off the greatest and easiest art theft since 1911, when former Louvre employee Vincenzo Peruggia made off with the *Mona Lisa* tucked under his smock. That theft wasn't noticed for an entire day, but the masterpiece was finally recovered two years later from a trunk in a Florence, Italy hotel room. The ensuing publicity ensured that the *Mona Lisa* would become the most famous painting in the world.

Now *The Scream* was suddenly gone, and this 1994 theft also produced national embarrassment for Norway. Not only had the most famous and valuable painting by its most famous citizen been stolen, but it was taken on the morning of the first day of the Winter Olympics in Lillehammer, a town about 80 miles north of Oslo.

Police suspected the theft was a publicity stunt by a radical antiabortion group that had threatened to disrupt the Olympic Games. The group immediately claimed responsibility and announced it would return the painting if a graphic antiabortion commercial was aired on national television. For the Norwegian authorities, it certainly appeared to be a political crime. Little did they know that the assault had actually been planned and perpetrated by two friends from the poor Oslo neighborhood of Tveita.

Enger, 26 at the time, had played professional soccer for the Norwegian club Valerenga, but his first love was theft. In 1988 he made his first major score, walking off with Munch's *Vampire* from the ill-fated Munch Museum. Enger was quickly caught and jailed, and the painting—also worth millions—was safely recovered.

A few years later, out of jail and back in Tveita, Enger hooked up with the teenage Ellingsen, a young man with spiky blond hair, a slight build and an almost cherubic face. "We were like brothers," Enger later told a reporter.

In those heady days of winter 1994, Enger and Ellingsen must have been jubilant. Their 50-second snatch was famous, on front pages and in leading newscasts around the world. They were the toast of the Norwegian underworld.

But the duo could not be accused of thinking ahead. They assumed that the deep pockets of the museum's insurance company would pay the ransom they demanded. But *The Scream*, they learned, was uninsured. And as Dick Ellis could have told them, the Norwegian government would never pay a ransom.

Ellingsen and Enger found themselves in possession of a $60 million painting everyone wanted back but no one wanted to pay for.

They desperately needed a plan B.

CHARLEY HILL

Charley Hill is probably the politest man you'll ever meet. He asks if our interview can take place in London's Kew Gardens, a lush botanical paradise and former haunt of kings and queens of England. Once inside, he proceeds to guide a detailed tour, pointing out horticultural and architectural features and displaying an encyclopedic knowledge of the people and events that shaped the gardens. During a stop for a cup of tea and a slice of cake at Kew's café, he carefully thanks everyone—the attendant at the gate, the girl at the cash register, the busboy cleaning the tables outside.

This is not your typical cop. He looks and sounds like a university professor. He plays choral music in his car, a little silver Renault.

The son of a U.S. Air Force officer and an English mother, Hill was raised on both sides of the Atlantic. He attended George Washington

University in Washington, D.C., where, he says, he was "bored out of my mind." So he volunteered for the Vietnam draft and in 1968 found himself in the 173rd Airborne Brigade, fighting deep in enemy territory. "I was the intellectual grunt of our platoon," he says.

After Vietnam, Hill returned to his studies, winning a Fulbright scholarship that took him to Trinity College in Dublin. From there he experimented for two years as a schoolteacher before deciding he wanted to be an Anglican priest. Using money from a Veterans Benefits Administration grant, Hill completed a bachelor of divinity at King's College London. By the time he earned his degree, he says, the most valuable thing he had learned was that his strong faith had little to do with the Church. "So I joined the police," he says, and for the next 20 years he distinguished himself as a gifted, if maverick, detective. "I was not the Yard's idea of a good police administrator," he says. "I take that as a compliment."

In 1993 Hill was assigned as Scotland Yard's liaison to Europol, a European organization that tackles transborder crime. Stationed in The Hague, the Dutch capital, Hill commuted each week from his London home, catching a plane early on Monday mornings and flying back late on Fridays.

The Monday after *The Scream* was reported stolen, Hill got the call from London. Scotland Yard's Art and Antiques Squad had come into possession of a lead and wanted him to go undercover. Hill, who had spent much of his career in the Yard's Criminal Intelligence Unit infiltrating drug crews and organized crime gangs, was a natural choice. He had undercover skills and the intellectual pedigree. Now he was asked for a strategy.

"Give me a few minutes to think about it," Hill said to his contact before hanging up. He stared out his office window, gazing down at the canal below. A plan formed in his mind, and he called back immediately. "Here's what we'll do," he said. He would pretend to be a representative of the J. Paul Getty Museum in Los Angeles, which was at the time spending tens of millions of dollars in a major acquisitions spree. The thieves would be told the museum had decided to pay to retrieve the painting for the sake of world art. Hill theorized that, with the Getty's money as bait, the crooks would lead him to the stolen picture.

Dick Ellis, the Yard's point man for the *Scream* investigation, liked the plan. Now all they needed was for the thieves to make their move—and for the Getty to play along.

Ellis flew to California and arranged a meeting with the Getty's head of security. To Ellis's delight, the museum gave the plan its wholehearted support. It created a special post for Charley Hill, who would adopt the identity of Chris Roberts, a roving ambassador for the Getty. To ensure the charade was convincing, the Getty made up business cards and letterhead stationery, created a telephone number that would always be answered by a secretary and even put Roberts on the payroll, backdating its computer records to give him seniority.

Ellis returned to London triumphant. The trap was set.

DEALING WITH THE DEVIL

Charley Hill is explaining why crooks steal "smudges," art-trade slang for paintings. "You have to understand," he says. "There's nothing glamorous about this. It's not like in the movies. There's no Mr. Big in a castle on a hill ordering the theft of great works of art so he can hang them in his private museum. That's just crap."

The true face of art theft, says Hill, is rather more mundane, practical and brutal. Most stolen paintings are minor works, valuable but not too well-known and easy to slip into the hands of the many dealers who bridge the world between the black market and the legitimate one.

Art is bought and sold in a free-market economy, and within it the black market in stolen art is unregulated, unpoliced and uninvestigated. Stolen paintings are recycled through auction houses or private trades, often ending up in the hands of innocent purchasers.

According to Julian Radcliffe, chairman of the Art Loss Register, it takes seven to eight years on average for a painting to resurface from the black market. Forty percent of the 160,000 stolen items in the ALR's database are paintings, he adds.

Hill has scored a number of high-profile recoveries in the past decade, including that of *Rest on the Flight to Egypt,* a masterpiece by Titian, considered the greatest painter of the Venetian Renaissance school. The painting was stolen in 1995, and Hill recovered it in 2002. He adds that one option for art thieves is to use paintings as collateral to fund other illicit deals.

"What you quickly learn in this game," says Hill, "is that no crook steals art exclusively." Art theft is usually part of a lively portfolio of criminal activities, including burglaries, petty theft, drug deals and even bank robberies.

On the trail of a stolen painting, you must enter this world, and once there a deal with the devil is normally required. It is a deal that places most art recoveries on a fine ethical line.

In 2003 the Tate paid $6.7 million to secure the return of two J.M.W. Turners, stolen in 1994 and valued at $46 million. The money was paid to a middleman who brokered the deal between the crooks and the museum. Hill had similarly arranged for a $139,000 finder's fee to be paid to the middleman who engineered the return of the Titian.

The art world doesn't consider these deals to be ransoms, as they usually involve people steps removed from the thieves themselves. Still, it is dangerous territory. "Given the choice between never seeing these pictures again and getting them back, most people would prefer to get them back. If someone helps in getting them back, that person should get what is proportionately a small sum of money compared to what the art is really worth," says Hill.

These negotiations usually require time and patience, two qualities Ellingsen and Enger were not familiar with. They demanded outright ransom. In order to get *The Scream* back, police decided they would have to allow the crooks to get uncomfortably close to a huge sum of money.

PLAN B: OLSEN AND ULVING

With the hottest painting in the world on their hands and an ever decreasing number of options for getting rid of it, Ellingsen and Enger turned to an acquaintance in Norway's criminal underworld. Jan Olsen, who had completed an 11-year jail sentence for arson a few years earlier, was recruited to act as a go-between in negotiations for the painting's return. Olsen's major qualification for this role was his claim that he could get direct access to the chairman of the National Gallery. Olsen's tactic was to approach the gallery and tell the chairman that unless someone paid up, *The Scream* would be returned in pieces.

Olsen's inside track was a circuitous one. By chance, he'd been sporadically buying pictures from an art dealer and auctioneer named Einar-Tore Ulving. Over the course of their business relationship the two men had had several conversations, and during one exchange Olsen learned that Ulving's wife's cousin was the National Gallery's chairman.

Ulving remembers Olsen's first approach shortly after *The Scream* was stolen: "He called and said he wanted to meet me. He seemed very uncomfortable talking on the telephone. We met outside a hotel, and he told me he could get *The Scream* back and asked if I could arrange a meeting using my family connections." A meeting between the crook and the chairman was duly arranged.

Olsen was told that if things were to progress, he must provide absolute proof that he could deliver *The Scream*. "Read Dagbladet on Tuesday," Olsen told Ulving. "You'll get your proof."

Sure enough, the Tuesday cover story of this Norwegian daily news-

STOLEN SCREAMS

paper featured a nearly full-page picture of a fragment of *The Scream*'s broken frame, discovered near a bus stop in the small town of Nittedal, about 10 miles northeast of Oslo. The piece of frame had been found following an "anonymous" tip to the paper. "That was good proof," says Ulving.

On May 5, 1994, Charley Hill (as Chris Roberts) spoke with Ulving. It had been decided that the Roberts character should be based in Brussels to further muddy any possible connection between him and the London police. Hill flew to Brussels that morning to make the call. He told Ulving he would be in Oslo that evening and staying at the Plaza Hotel. Could a meeting be arranged between him and Olsen?

A little before 10 P.M. Hill walked into the lobby of the Plaza. Sporting a jaunty bow tie and looking every inch the art scholar, he strode up to the reception desk and loudly announced his name. Ulving and Olsen approached the man from the Getty.

Olsen made an immediate impression on Hill. Although in his 40s, he was clearly in superb shape, a good-looking, confident man who while in prison had become an expert kickboxer. Next to him stood Ulving the art dealer, shorter and balding, nervously smoking Marlboro Lights.

After some quick introductions, Ulving made his excuses and tried to leave. "I thought I was there just to introduce Olsen to this man Roberts," he says. He was rudely disabused of the notion. Olsen told him, "No, no, you're not leaving here. My English is not good. I need you to translate." Thus beginning what he described as a "long, long two days," Ulving reluctantly checked into the Plaza.

Hill went to his suite on the 27th floor to freshen up. Three floors below, an advance team, including a British undercover officer called Sid Walker (not his real name; his identity is still secret), had established a surveillance operation to monitor the sting along with Norwegian police.

That evening Hill, Olsen and Ulving sat in the lounge of the Plaza and began their negotiations for the return of *The Scream*. Olsen said the robbers wanted 3.15 million Norwegian kroner (about $472,000) to return the painting, a price Hill agreed to. Given the lateness of the hour, the men called it a night and arranged to meet again at breakfast.

At eight A.M. Hill and Ulving were taking the elevator down to breakfast when, Hill says, he began to get a bad feeling. When the elevator doors opened, he was confronted with a sight that filled him with horror.

338

"What was absolutely, staggeringly unbelievable was that the Scandinavian police were having their annual drug conference that weekend in the hotel," says Ellis. "Neither the Norwegian police nor the bad guys had thought to check the hotel out before our team turned up." Added to the mix of hundreds of cops were dozens of plainclothes Norwegian officers who had been drafted to monitor the sting operation. "It was a disaster," says Ellis.

Hill, Olsen and Ulving reconvened that afternoon in the Plaza's reception area, but this time Hill was accompanied by Sid Walker, whom he introduced as a guard for the money. While Ulving stayed in the lobby, Hill and Walker took Olsen upstairs to Walker's room, where Walker produced a sports bag filled with nearly half a million dollars in what police call flash money.

Police have an awkward relationship with flash money, says Ellis: "You need it because once you have flashed the bad guys the sight of a suitcase full of cash, they tend to go for it. Trouble is, you have to make sure you get it back." Hill and Walker were nervous about the sheer volume of cash now inches from the face of Olsen, a violent career criminal. Being that close to half a million dollars seemed to calm Olsen, though, who had become increasingly agitated by the police presence in the hotel. He left the two undercover policemen, saying he had a "short but important meeting" to attend, and returned an hour later having apparently received the authorization to proceed.

Because of the police conference at the Plaza, nobody argued with the suggestion that they move to the quieter Grand Hotel a few blocks away. While they switched hotels, Olsen ordered Ulving to drive him to the underground parking lot of an apartment building. Once they were inside, a man appeared from the shadows equipped with what looked to Ulving like some sort of metal detector. Olsen and the man spoke briefly, and then the car was swept for bugs and tracking devices. Satisfied the car was not under electronic surveillance, the men drove to a quiet side road near the city center, where Olsen ordered Ulving to stop the car and turn off the engine and lights.

They sat in the dark in Ulving's black Mercedes 300TE wagon for several minutes. Then a rear passenger door opened and a man slid onto the backseat. He was dressed in all black, with a cap pulled down over his forehead and a scarf pulled up over his nose and mouth. He positioned himself directly behind Ulving, preventing the driver from observing him. For the next 12 hours the man Ulving knew only as Mr. X would be his constant shadow, sent by the crooks to supervise the handover of the money and the painting.

STOLEN SCREAMS

"I had a very bad feeling. I was very unhappy," says Ulving of Mr. X's entrance. The hulking, silent man scared him.

Hill was in his room when the phone rang. He glanced at the clock; it was 11:30 P.M. Ulving was in reception. The deal was on. Hill went down to meet the three men. Sitting in the back of the Mercedes, he told them bluntly, "I am not going for a midnight walk in the woods with you."

"Then the painting will be destroyed," said Mr. X. "It's now or never."

It was Ulving who solved the impasse. "Look, why don't I go with Mr. X to see the painting, and Olsen can stay here with you and the money?" Everyone agreed, but as Hill got out of the car, Mr. X said, "If anyone follows us, my people will find out immediately, and the painting will be destroyed." He closed the door and turned to Ulving.

"Drive."

Ulving did as he was told. "We started to drive going out of Oslo," he says, "turning left, right, left, right, going straight ahead and through some tunnels until we ended up in Etterstad, in east Oslo. Mr. X told me to stop. He got out and walked about 50 yards to a phone box where, I assume, he made a call. He came back a few minutes later and told me to drive south on the E18 highway and not use my cell phone. He said someone would call and give me instructions. Then he walked off."

• • •

The E18 led straight to Ulving's home in the picturesque town of Tønsberg, 30 miles south of Oslo. An hour later there had still been no call, so Ulving decided to go home. It was two A.M. on Saturday, two days since he'd last seen his wife and children. Ulving pulled up in front of his house and went inside. As he opened the door to his house, his home phone began to ring. A man's voice told him to get back in his car and drive to a diner called By the Way, just outside Tønsberg.

Spooked at the realization that his house was being watched, Ulving did as he was told and five minutes later pulled into the diner's deserted parking lot. Five minutes after that he was still there, sitting alone in the dark. "Suddenly Mr. X appeared from behind the building, and he was holding something wrapped in a blue sheet," he says. "He put it in the trunk of my car and then told me to drive home. At that point I refused."

It was one thing to be at the beck and call of Mr. X (whom Hill describes as a psychopath). But Ulving says he drew the line at letting

340

the man into his home, where his wife and two daughters were sleeping. "My brain was racing," Ulving says. "There was no way I wanted this man in the same place as my family." A solution suggested itself. Ulving owned a summer residence a few minutes farther up the road in the old fishing village of Asgardstrand, which by coincidence also happened to be where Munch had a summer house and studio in a converted fisherman's cottage. Ulving knew the Asgardstrand house would be closed up for the winter and deserted.

It was freezing inside the summer house. The wrapped painting was placed on the dining room table. Ulving gingerly unwrapped the package.

He says it felt as though the air were vibrating around him. "When you are that close to genius, you can feel it coming out at you from inside the paint," he says. He rewrapped the painting and took it to the basement through a small hatch in the kitchen floor.

Mr. X ordered Ulving into the front room. It was now three A.M. For the next two hours they sat in cold, dark silence, the anonymous thug brooding silently, hunched inside his coat, facing the door. Ulving, exhausted but unable to sleep, was chain-smoking, reasonably concerned for his life. No one in all of Norway knew where he was at that moment.

An hour or so later, sick of waiting in the cold, dark cottage, Ulving hatched a plan to lure Mr. X out of the house. He promised the criminal the chance to drive his Mercedes 500SL, a tiny two-seat convertible that was not only expensive but rarely seen in Scandinavia. So the art dealer and his hulking bodyguard drove back to Ulving's family home, swapped cars and then spent a few hours killing time, driving the back roads between Tønsberg and the small town of Drammen, waiting for dawn to break and Ulving's cell phone to ring.

MAY 7, 1994: "I'VE GOT IT!"

For the first time since he'd gotten to Oslo, Charley Hill was enjoying himself. He was sitting in the backseat of a rental car watching his partner, Walker, put on a show for Olsen. Walker was giving the crook a master class in anti-surveillance driving. "Olsen was obviously impressed," says Hill. "He had no idea the man in the driver's seat was the most accomplished professional undercover officer in the London Metropolitan Police." Dick Ellis says of Walker, "He was just amazing."

The three men were on their way to Drammen, about 20 minutes southwest of Oslo, their destination a diner near a tollbooth where they had been told the exchange could take place. As they arrived Hill noticed a brand-new Mercedes 500SL parked outside.

Inside the diner at a table with his minder sat Ulving, looking miserable. Walker volunteered to get everyone coffee, and when he returned Ulving was confirming that, yes, he had seen the painting. So the robbers had seen the money, Ulving the intermediary had seen the painting, and now here they all were, sitting somewhere in the middle of nowhere without a plan. Nobody seemed to know what to do next. A tour bus began to unload its passengers, and the café started to fill up.

Walker suggested a solution: He would take Olsen and Mr. X back to the hotel, where the money was stashed, while Hill and Ulving went back to Asgardstrand for the painting. As Oslo was closer, it seemed to give the crooks the advantage of getting to the money at least half an hour before Hill and Ulving could get to the painting. It was agreed that Hill would call the hotel as soon as he had seen the painting, and the money would then be handed over by his partner, Walker.

Hill and Ulving set out for the summer cottage in Ulving's Mercedes 500SL. Hill says the journey took years off his life: "Not only was Ulving a terrible driver, but he was also groggy from exhaustion and lack of sleep and kept weaving all over the road. I was sure we were going to end up in a ditch or under the wheels of a truck." Eventually the pair arrived at Ulving's house and went inside. Ulving went to the kitchen and opened the hatch to the basement.

Hill never lost his sense of caution, even with the mild-mannered Ulving. "I'm not going down there," Hill said. Ulving shrugged and disappeared into the darkness, emerging a second or so later holding the wrapped painting. Hill took it from him and walked to the dining room table. He carefully laid it down and pulled back the edges of the sheet.

"Shit."

Hill found himself looking at a rather plain piece of board covered with a few scribbles and smears of paint. We've been had, he thought, before realizing he was looking at the back of the picture, which bears the remains of Munch's first, failed attempt to capture *The Scream*. Hill turned the painting over, and there in front of him at last was the famous howling figure. "The thing about a masterpiece is that it tells you it is a masterpiece," he says. "You can look at a thousand paintings, but when you look at something like *The Scream*—*boom!*—it comes straight out at you." The painting also bears telltale wax splatters caused by Munch blowing out a candle too close to it. The distinctive splatters are like a fingerprint Hill had memorized. "You can't blow a candle out twice the same way," says Hill. The wax marks he saw were the indisputable proof he needed.

• • •

"Oh fucking hell, what have I done?"

The painting was too big to fit through the door of Ulving's compact sports car. The two men opened the roof, and Hill managed to squeeze the painting behind the seats. Hill jiggled it and was able to push it down another inch or two—enough to close the roof. Hill then realized that, as he'd wrestled with the painting, he had accidentally pushed one of the Mercedes's headrests so far into the back of the picture that a small but noticeable lump had appeared in the screaming figure's shoulder.

"Oh shit."

He looked over at Ulving, who seemed not to have noticed. With his secret intact, the top secured and a slightly dented Norwegian masterpiece pressing into the back of his head, Hill let Ulving drive him to the nearby Asgardstrand Hotel. After renting a room Hill took the painting in through a rear fire escape and barricaded himself inside Room 525, pushing all the furniture against the door.

It was 10:30 A.M. Pouring himself a generous whiskey from the minibar, Hill picked up the phone and dialed.

"I've got it," he told the voice on the other end.

Back in Oslo, the Norwegian police surveillance operation had descended into fiasco. The team managed to miss Walker, Olsen and Mr. X walking in through the front of the hotel and going up to Walker's room. And Walker didn't know that the two-man police team that was supposed to be in the room next to his had wandered off to get breakfast, taking the bag containing the $472,000 ransom with them.

Walker sat in the room with the two crooks, unaware that he was totally alone and without backup. As the minutes ticked away, Olsen and Mr. X got more and more anxious. The tension in the room was rising to an uncomfortable pitch when the door suddenly swung open. Standing in the doorway were the two Norwegian policemen, in full uniform, holding Big Macs, cups of coffee and the bag of cash.

They had walked into the wrong room.

• • •

STOLEN SCREAMS

NOT A SCRATCH, began the story in *Dagbladet* heralding the safe return of *The Scream* on May 7, 1994. "They must have ironed the bump out," says Hill, "or not noticed."

Over the next few days Ellingsen, Enger, Olsen and Mr. X—revealed to be an old criminal accomplice of Enger's named Bjorn Grytdal—were rounded up and charged. Enger, it seemed, couldn't resist telling the world about his role. He was arrested after placing a notice about the birth of his son in a local newspaper, announcing that his son had arrived in this world *"met et skrik!"*—"with a scream."

The four conspirators were convicted, but the court decided that because Hill and Walker had entered the country using false passports, they had been there illegally; therefore their entire operation had been unlawful. Convictions against three of the four men were overturned on appeal. Only Enger's conviction of receiving stolen property stuck.

THE TEFLON KID

Norway has changed in many ways since the 1994 heist; separated by a decade, the two crimes provide a picture of just how much. Ten years ago, stealing *The Scream* was an almost civilized affair: Two unarmed young men used a ladder to pull off an almost comical robbery in the still hours of early morning. In 2004 thugs with guns barged into a museum in broad daylight, threatening staff and visitors in a highly calculated and professionally executed raid.

Lulled by a liberal, open and—thanks in part to oil—affluent standard of life, Norway has been slow to react to the rapidly changing face of modern crime. Only 4.5 million people live in this land about the size of Montana, and they enjoy a lifestyle most Americans would envy. The average family income is about 60 percent greater than that of American families, and health and education are heavily subsidized. The UN Human Development Index rates Norway the world's most livable country year after year. Despite this affluence, though, crime rates have risen across the board in Norway, with violent crime increasing nearly 15 percent in the past eight years. Yet there are few jails in this most liberal of countries, and the courts are loath to impose heavy prison sentences. Prisoners are often not remanded to holding cells before trial, and even when convicted they can spend months in the community waiting for jail space to open. Once inside, prisoners are released on leave after they serve a third of their sentence.

The system appears to be incapable of dealing with the highly mobile, professional criminal gangs that now operate across the open borders of Scandinavia and the rest of Europe. These criminals *sans frontieres* slip through the porous borders with impunity, carrying out raids in one country and escaping to another. In the past 10 years a highly violent hard core of professional armed robbers has evolved within Scandinavia. Not so much a gang as an informal network, this eclectic group includes Norwegians, Swedes, Albanians, Finns, Bulgarians, Pakistanis, Iranians—along with bikers and even neo-Nazis. Racial, cultural and spiritual differences are put aside when it comes to their work. They are real-life reservoir dogs, specializing in armed bank robberies planned and conducted with military precision. Among their number, according to Norwegian police, was the cherubic blond bandit William Ellingsen.

After walking away from his *Scream* charges Ellingsen entered this world. His crimes began to escalate. In 1998 he was implicated in a $170,000 bank robbery. He escaped to Costa Rica but was captured and deported to Norway, where he somehow managed to escape conviction. In September 2001 he was part of a team that pulled off what the Norwegian daily newspaper *Verdens Gang* called "the impossible."

Ellingsen and his crew drilled their way through the concrete floor of a bank and dropped into the safe-deposit vault, where they opened and emptied more than 500 boxes, getting away with millions in cash, jewelry and other valuables. Ellingsen was caught and charged, but as usual the police couldn't make the case stick.

He was the Scandinavian Teflon Kid, good-looking, intelligent and daring. But on February 6, 2004, his luck ran out.

That night a number of underworld enforcers and debt collectors— the Norwegians call them torpedoes—held a party in the posh Gabels Gate area of Oslo. The gathering was well attended by members of the city's criminal fraternity, including Ellingsen. When a fight broke out between a bouncer and two torpedoes, Ellingsen tried to intervene. One of the men responded by pulling a pistol and opening fire. Ellingsen was hit and killed.

He was buried on February 13 to the sound of "Amazing Grace" and Metallica's "Nothing Else Matters." Three hundred mourners attended his funeral, among them the crème de la crème of Norway's criminal elite.

On that cold Oslo day it was doubtful that those at the funeral were conscious of the poignancy of the date on which they were burying their friend and comrade. Exactly 10 years and one day earlier, at the age of 18, Ellingsen had first burst onto the criminal scene when he made off with the second-most famous painting in the world.

STOLEN SCREAMS

Of the four men involved in the 1994 heist only Pal Enger and Bjorn Grytdal (Mr. X) were still in circulation when the August 2004 robbery took place. Ellingsen was dead, as was Jan Olsen, who had died the previous year as a result of intravenous heroin use.

Enger, who'd become something of a celebrity criminal over the previous decade, engineering little stunts to keep his name and photo in the newspapers, became uncharacteristically media shy in the aftermath of the Munch Museum raid. "Weapons are not my style," he said in a terse interview following the heist. "I have always used the methods of a gentleman." After being pulled in for questioning by Oslo police, the normally ebullient Enger disappeared. His cell phone is now dead, and at the time of this writing he had not been seen for several weeks.

For Charley Hill, *The Scream* has stirred both memories and curiosity. Hill, an analyst of the Norwegian criminal landscape, believes that the solution to last year's robbery may lie in the past. And in a surprising twist, he says, there may be connections to the fallen Ellingsen.

Two months after Ellingsen's death, the most violent robbery in Norwegian history was carried out in the west coast town of Stavanger. On April 5, 10 armed robbers raided Nokas, a hub for Norwegian banks. The robbers first drove a truck into the parking garage entrance of the local police station and set it on fire. As police ran from the building, the robbers hurled tear-gas canisters, creating a blinding fog. Mobile patrols responding to the alarms were sprayed with gunfire by the robbers, who were armed with automatic weapons. It was, by all accounts, like a scene from the movie *Heat*.

The gang then attacked the bank, smashing its way into the counting room with sledgehammers. In 30 minutes the crooks managed to haul away $8.5 million, keeping the police at bay with bursts of suppressing fire. During this firefight, which occurred around 8:30 A.M., a police commander was killed.

The level of violence and the murder of the policeman caused outrage in Norway. The authorities responded by declaring war on the criminal fraternity they suspected of being behind the raid: Ellingsen's former comrades. Soon many of those who had attended Ellingsen's funeral were either behind bars or the subjects of intensive police searches, their names appearing on wanted lists around Scandinavia. They included one of Ellingsen's pallbearers, who police believed was the mastermind behind the Stavanger robbery. As police continued to turn up the heat on Ellingsen's former associates, rumors began to circulate in Oslo that another big score was imminent—one that would have significant symbolic value.

It is hard to deny that the theft of *The Scream* and *Madonna* perfectly fit the bill, says Hill. "Don't make the mistake of trying to rationalize a crime like this," he explains, "because both the 1994 and 2004 thefts were carried out by irrational people who see the world very differently from you and me. These people are short-term thinkers and planners. They live for the now, and they tend not to live very long."

Hill continues, "Crimes like this make sense to them because they feel they are showing the world what they are capable of. These are trophy crimes. They have nothing to do with money—they can make much, much more from drugs, prostitution or armed robbery. No, this is their telling the world, 'We can do what we like when we like, take what we like and fuck you.' For those involved in the Stavanger robbery, it would have made perfect sense to order this theft. The crooks would have seen it as a good way to get the police chasing after something else and a good way of telling the world they are still capable of pulling any job they want."

Sources close to the Norwegian police inquiry have admitted that one of the leading theories of the 2004 Munch theft is that it had been perpetrated to draw police and media attention away from Stavanger. Several newspapers and a Norwegian television station have run stories quoting anonymous sources confirming that the Stavanger crew ordered the robbery. The Norwegian television station TV2 reported that the robbers were paid about $30,000 to commit the crime.

In late December Norwegian police arrested an unnamed 37-year-old man and confirmed that they have identified two other suspects. The paintings remain missing. Iver Stensrud, head of the organized crime unit of the Oslo police department, said, "We don't know where they are, whether they are still in Norway or whether they have gone abroad." The Norwegian daily *Verdens Gang*, claiming to have information from criminal sources, reported that both *The Scream* and *Madonna* are still in Norway but that both works sustained damage during the robbery. *Madonna* was thought to be significantly damaged, while *The Scream* was described as "diminished."

Who Killed
Joey Gallo?

by CHARLES BRANDT
August 2005

Mary Gallo grabbed her son's coffin at Green-Wood Cemetery in Brooklyn and cried, "My baby, my baby son." She wailed, "Joey, why didn't you take him with you, Joey? Take Big Boy . . ."

It wasn't clear whom Mary Gallo was referring to. The prevailing belief about Joe Gallo's murder was that three Italian gangsters had come through the Mulberry Street door of Umberto's Clam House in Little Italy and opened fire. It was a Mob version of the shoot-out at the OK Corral. But Mary Gallo's meaning should have been clear. Joey's mother was berating her dead son for not killing his own assassin, the gunman who shot him three times in the back while Gallo was eating calamari. As his party celebrated his 43rd birthday in the small hours of April 7, 1972, Gallo became an entry on a police blotter, "Homicide GUN at 0520."

For nearly 30 years the identity of Big Boy was a mystery. Then Frank "the Irishman" Sheeran, a six-foot-four hit man, confessed to me that his godfather, Russell Bufalino, had ordered him to kill Gallo, whom Sheeran called "a fresh kid." In my 2004 book, *"I Heard You Paint Houses,"* I wrote about what Sheeran told me.

I had spent five years interviewing Sheeran, trying to understand what drove him to murder his friend and Teamsters mentor Jimmy Hoffa in 1975. Sheeran confessed in passing to shooting Crazy Joey Gallo after telling me how valuable Gallo was to Bufalino. The accepted version of his death had been that Carmine "Sonny Pinto" DiBiase led two unidentified Italian gangsters through a side door of Umberto's, and they blasted away. The source for this was Mob informant Joe

348

Luparelli. The authorities seemed to believe Luparelli, but no one was ever indicted for killing Gallo based on Luparelli's information. I've had plenty of experience as an interrogator, and I was satisfied Sheeran had told me the truth about Gallo.

Shortly after my book was published, Sheeran's account received additional support when writer Jerry Capeci corroborated that a lone gunman had shot Gallo. As a young reporter for the *New York Post*, Capeci said he had "spent a few hours at Umberto's Clam House on Mulberry Street in lower Manhattan during the early-morning hours of April 7, 1972." Capeci wrote that Al Seedman, chief of detectives for the New York Police Department, walked out of Umberto's and told reporters that all the carnage was the work of a lone gunman. The case was building for a necessary revision of an important slice of Mob history.

Then fortune brought me something extraordinary. Eric Shawn, senior correspondent with Fox News, called me to say he had discovered an eyewitness to the Gallo shooting. She was a journalist at *The New York Times* who wished to remain anonymous. He phoned her, and she admitted she had been at the scene and witnessed the shooting. Shawn said, "I understand three Italian types came in and started shooting." She said, "No, it was a lone gunman." He directed her attention to an Internet photo of Sheeran taken in the early 1970s, around the time of the Gallo hit. "Oh my God," she said. "I've seen this man before." Shawn immediately walked from Fox News on 47th Street to the New York Times building on West 43rd Street and gave her a copy of my book.

I told Ted Feury, a friend of mine and a retired CBS executive. With a big smile Feury said, "I know her. She was the best grad student I ever had at Columbia. She's a terrific gal, very bright, a great journalist and as honest as they come. I'll call her."

The three of us had dinner at Elaine's in Manhattan. Although other journalists knew of her presence at Umberto's, the eyewitness told us she still wanted anonymity. She drew a diagram of the scene for us, indicating her table in relation to the Gallo party's. "There were a lot of shots that night," she said. "I heard those shots for a long time afterward." She confirmed that they came from a single gunman, "and he wasn't Italian, that's for sure." She flipped through a display of photos, including ones of other gangsters, and when she saw a black-and-white photo of Sheeran from the early 1970s she said, "Like I told Eric Shawn, it's been a long time, but I know this much: I've seen this man before." In answer to my question she said, "No, not from a photo in the newspaper. I've seen him in the flesh." I showed her black-and-whites of a younger Sheeran, and she said, "No, too young." An older Sheeran, "No, too old." She picked up the photo of Sheeran taken around the time of the Gallo hit and said, "This picture gives me chills."

I wanted to formally interview the eyewitness alone, show her the black-and-white photos in better lighting and play her a color video of Sheeran. The lighting at Elaine's was too dim. Because of our busy schedules, nine months would elapse before I could meet the witness at her home. I brought my photos and a video I'd made of Sheeran on September 13, 2000, when he was 79. Although he was 27 years older than he'd been at Umberto's, the footage was in color, and it was Sheeran in the flesh.

"I was 18 at the time," the eyewitness told me, "a freshman in college in Chicago. It was probably spring break, and I was with my best friend. We were visiting one of her brothers and his wife, who lived near Gracie Mansion. We'd gone to the theater and then probably drove around and did some sightseeing. None of us were drinking. We were under-age, and my friend's brother and his wife didn't drink when they were out with us. We ended up at Umberto's about 20 minutes before the shooting. No way were there only seven people there besides the Gallo party, if that's what some book says. It was pretty crowded for that time of night, with people at maybe four or five tables and a couple of people sitting at the clam bar. Maybe people left after we got there and before it happened—I don't know. We came in the front door, the one on the corner of Hester and Mulberry. There were no tables to the left, on the Hester side. They were all in front of you as you walked in, between the bar on the left and the Mulberry Street wall on the right. We sat toward the back. I was facing Hester Street, and my best friend sat to my right. Her brother and his wife were opposite us. They faced the back wall and the side door off Mulberry. I remember the Gallo party to our left because of the little girl and because I thought the girl's mother was very pretty. Besides the little girl there were two or three women and two or three men. I don't remember seeing the faces of the men.

"Our seafood had just arrived when I noticed a tall man walk through the Mulberry Street door. I could see the door easily; it was just off my left shoulder. He walked on a diagonal to the bar, right in front of me, the whole way in my direct line of vision. As he walked past I remember being struck by him. I remember thinking he was distinctive—quite tall and a handsome man. He stopped at the bar, not far at all from our table. I was looking down at my plate of food when I heard the first shot. I looked up, and that same man was standing there facing the Gallo table with his back to the bar. I can't say I remember a gun in his hand, but he was definitely the one doing the shooting. There's no doubt about that. He calmly stood there while everybody else was ducking. The Gallo party didn't know what hit them.

"It was Sheeran. That man was the same man in this photo. Even the video looks more like the way he looked that night—even though he's much older in the video. It was him, I'm positive. He looks bloated and fat in the photos you showed me from 1980 but not in the video.

"My friend's brother yelled for us to get down. Other people were screaming to get down too. Besides the gunshots the thing I remember most when I was down on the tile floor was the crashing of glass. We stayed on the floor. When the shooting stopped, my friend's brother yelled, 'Let's get out of here,' and we got up and ran out the Mulberry Street door. There were a lot of others shouting, and they ran away when we did.

"We ran up Mulberry. There was nobody on Mulberry firing at any getaway car, if that's what the bodyguard claimed. Our car was parked near the police station. On the drive home we speculated about whether we had just been in a robbery or a Mob hit. Nobody wanted to stereotype Little Italy, but we thought it was Mob-related. I don't remember if we heard it on news radio on the way home, but we saw it in the papers the next day. It was pretty horrible. I think if my girlfriend and I had been there alone we might have gone back the next day, but her brother and his wife were very protective and didn't want us involved in any way."

This Gallo witness with a journalist's memory and an eye for detail, a witness who had a chance to observe before the fear set in, told me she had not read any of the stories that had cropped up over the years. She hadn't heard about the "three Italians" until Eric Shawn mentioned them. "That's ridiculous," she said. "There's no way three Italians burst through that side door on Mulberry Street and started shooting. I'd have seen them come in. If there were three men, we'd have been too scared to get up and run away. If we did get up, we wouldn't have run out that side door."

When I closed the session by asking again how sure she was that Sheeran was the man she'd seen that night, she said, "I'm positive. He's definitely the man I saw that night."

Why did Sheeran tell me all he told me? Within weeks of Hoffa's 1975 disappearance, the FBI placed Sheeran on its short list of eight suspects. As Sheeran's daughter, Dolores, put it to me, "The FBI spent almost 30 years scrutinizing my father's every move to get him to confess." When the FBI squeezed, Sheeran took the Fifth. Hoffa's daughter, a St. Louis judge, wrote him asking that he tell what he knew "under a vow of secrecy," but he remained silent. In 1980 the FBI took him to trial for two murders and other mayhem, but he was acquitted. In 1981 he was finally convicted of labor racketeering and given a 32-year sentence.

In 1991, when Sheeran was 70, my partner and I got the high-ranking Philadelphia mobster and Teamster out of jail 10 years early based on his arthritis and need for surgery. In 1999, when he was 78, after first getting absolution from his church, Sheeran contacted me, a former homicide prosecutor, and consented to tape-recorded interviews. Sheeran had been raised a strict Catholic. His father had studied for the priesthood. Sheeran knew his lease was short, as he put it, and he wanted to prepare for the next life. What most plagued the conscience of this man who had performed 25 to 30 hits was that his godfather, Bufalino, had forced him to kill his mentor, Hoffa.

Sheeran's lawyer, former Philadelphia DA F. Emmett Fitzpatrick, cautioned him from the outset that he would be indicted for what he confessed to me. Balancing a desire to confess and a fear of dying in jail, this stand-up guy let me dig the truth out of him. I put four men on death row with less evidence than I dug from him.

"Jimmy Hoffa," Dolores said, "was one of only two people my father cared anything about. Russell Bufalino was the other. Killing Hoffa tortured my father the rest of his life."

Sheeran told me Bufalino had asked Hoffa not to retake the Teamsters presidency after Hoffa got out of jail on a pardon from President Nixon. The Mob wanted to continue to have the free hand in the Teamsters pension fund that the puppet president, Frank Fitzsimmons, afforded them. Hoffa said no. Bufalino told Sheeran to tell his friend "what it is." In Mob talk this meant Hoffa would be killed if he persisted in his quest. "They wouldn't dare," Hoffa replied to Sheeran.

Sheeran saw this as Hoffa's ego talking. Sheeran said the Mob has a saying for those whose thinking appears distorted: "When in doubt, have no doubt." He said to me, "If I ever said no to Russell, you and I wouldn't be talking now. If I said no to Russell about Jimmy, he'd have been just as dead, and I'd have gone to Australia with him."

Sheeran had been a combat infantryman in World War II. The average number of combat days was 80; Sheeran had 411. He waded ashore in three amphibious invasions. He helped liberate Dachau. He learned to kill in cold blood on orders. "When an officer would tell you to take a couple of German prisoners back behind the line and 'hurry back,' you did what you had to do," he said. The Gallo hit was more like house-to-house combat than the traditional two shots behind the ear of an unsuspecting victim by a close friend. And Sheeran was an out-of-towner, not easily recognized by the mobsters of Little Italy or known to NYPD detectives.

But why did Bufalino order Sheeran to kill Gallo? Sheeran was evasive with me on this topic. We had an understanding that he would leave things out that tended to reflect badly on others—even the dead. He never wanted anyone to call him a rat.

Though a member of the Colombo crime family, Gallo had a long-standing feud with Joe Colombo, the family's boss. Colombo had formed the Italian-American Civil Rights League, claiming Italians were a minority in need of protection. On June 28, 1971, the league held a rally at Manhattan's Columbus Circle. In front of tens of thousands of people, including Colombo's family, an assassin posing as a press photographer shot Colombo three times. The assassin was immediately shot and killed. Colombo didn't die right away. He was paralyzed and in a coma and would remain in a vegetative state for several years.

All eyes—law enforcement and Mob—were on the recently released Crazy Joey Gallo. The assassin was a black man with a long rap sheet. Only Gallo cultivated alliances among the city's black criminals. Sheeran said Bufalino and Colombo were friends. Some say the Colombo family represented Bufalino's family on the Mob's ruling commission. But clearly Bufalino was close to Colombo. Bufalino even established a chapter of Colombo's Italian-American Civil Rights League near his northeastern Pennsylvania headquarters.

April 6, 1972, was Gallo's 43rd birthday. His bride of three weeks, Sina Essary, her 10-year-old daughter, Lisa, Gallo's sister Carmella and two bodyguards—Bob "Bobby Darrow" Bongiovi and Pete "the Greek" Diapoulos—began Gallo's birthday celebration at the Copacabana nightclub. Gossip columnist Earl Wilson and his wife and secretary were there. NYPD detective Joe Coffey, author of *The Coffey Files*, was also at the Copa that night with his partner and their wives. They had seen Gallo come in. Coffey told me that if their wives hadn't been with them they would have tailed Gallo that night and "walked right into the jackpot."

When the Copa closed at four on the morning of April 7, Gallo urged Bobby Darrow to take Wilson's secretary home in a cab. Gallo, Diapoulos, his date Edith Russo, Carmella, Sina and Lisa got into Diapoulos's limo and headed downtown in search of a late dinner. Their first choice was Chinatown, but they ended up at Umberto's, which Genovese *capo* Mattie "the Horse" Ianello had recently opened.

Earlier at the Copa an incident occurred that would explain the forces that led to the Umberto's shooting. It was something I didn't know about when Sheeran was alive. I discovered it after I interviewed the *New York Times* journalist. As a result of what she said, I figured I should know more about the informant Luparelli's version and ordered all the books I could find on the subject. Many bordered on the silly, especially Luparelli's own book, but Diapoulos's 1978 book, *The Sixth Family*, was more revealing.

Sheeran had told me that the evening began when he'd gotten a call from Bufalino to go to Yonkers to meet John "the Redhead" Francis, a former IRA hit man. Francis drove Sheeran to Umberto's, dropped him off and circled the block once. If Sheeran did not come outside in a reasonable amount of time, Francis was to leave, and Sheeran would be on his own.

Sheeran described the hit, explaining he had two little brothers—guns—in his hands that night. "You wanted to do some noisy stray shooting all over the place to send the witnesses for cover," he told me. He walked in as the witness had described, stopped at the bar and first wounded Diapoulos the bodyguard in the buttocks because there was no reason to mortally wound him. Sheeran figured that Gallo, as a convicted felon, would not have a piece on him. Gallo ran from the table, either to get between Sheeran's fire and the women or simply to save himself. Sheeran followed him out the front corner door and finished him off. Francis was on the corner waiting for Sheeran.

But Sheeran never told me how he knew Gallo would be at Umberto's that night. He also hadn't told me details about Bufalino's motive. I learned the answers to both questions from one seemingly insignificant anecdote in Diapoulos's book about events at the Copa earlier that night.

"After the show we all went down to the lounge and had drinks at the round bar. The girls sat at the table talking among themselves. Champagne was still being sent over. A wiseguy named Frank sent some. He was with an old-timer, Russ Bufalino, a regular greaseball, the boss of Erie, Pennsylvania. Joey, feeling no pain with all the champagne, grinned at the button in Bufalino's lapel. It was a Colombo NUMERO UNO button with a diamond in it. 'Hey,' said Joey, 'what're you doing with that? You really believe in that bullshit league?' You saw how Bufalino's chin went, his back going very straight, turning away from us. Frank, with a very worried look, took Joey by the arm. 'Joey, that's nothing to talk about here. Let's just have a few drinks.' 'Yeah, we'll have a few drinks.' 'Joey, he's a boss.' 'So he's a boss. So am I a boss. That make him any better than me? We're all equal. We're all supposed to be brothers.'

Brothers came out like it was anything but. 'Joey,' I said, 'Let's go to the table. Let's not have a beef.'"

A boss doesn't have a beef. The real-life Donnie Brasco, undercover FBI agent Joe Pistone, wrote in *The Way of the Wiseguy,* "Insulting the boss even in passing can easily get you killed." Now that we know about the insult, no doubt Sheeran called the Redhead to drive down from Yonkers with the little brothers. Together they followed Gallo to Umberto's. Retired NYPD detective Joe Coffey told me, "The Gallo hit was my case. Sheeran's confession makes the most sense of all the versions I heard, and I was the first one to interview Luparelli."

Thirty-one years later a "wiseguy named Frank" did a final taping for me, a video to serve as the signature on the audio confessions I already had. The next day the man who shot Hoffa and the "fresh kid" Gallo because they showed disrespect to Bufalino stopped eating the food on his tray. Frank Sheeran died on December 14, 2003, at the age of 83, after giving credible and corroborated confessions that finally solved the murder mysteries of Jimmy Hoffa and Crazy Joey Gallo.

The End
of the Mob

by **JIMMY BRESLIN**

August 2005

L ate at night I am watching Bobby De Niro in some *Analyze* movie, and I feel sorry for him because these Mafia parts, at which he is so superb and which he could do for the next 30 years, soon will no longer exist. Simultaneously he could be forced into new subjects. Al Pacino, too. Which is marvelous because both are American treasures and should be remembered for great roles, not for playing cheap punks who are unworthy of getting their autographs. I would much prefer De Niro or Pacino to Sir Laurence Olivier in anything.

Now, watching the late movie, I am remembering where I saw it start for De Niro. It was on a hot summer afternoon when the producer of a movie being made from a book I wrote, *The Gang That Couldn't Shoot Straight,* asked me to meet De Niro because he was replacing Pacino in a big part. Pacino was going into some movie called *The Godfather.* De Niro was looking for his first major movie role.

We talked briefly in a bar, the old Johnny Joyce's on Second Avenue. De Niro looked like he was homeless. It was a Friday.On Sunday morning my wife came upstairs in our home in Queens and said one of the actors from the movie was downstairs. I flinched. Freak them. Downstairs, however, was De Niro. He was going to Italy on his own to catch the speech nuances of people in towns mentioned in the script. He was earning $750 a week for the movie. I remember saying when he left, "Do not stand between this guy and whatever he wants."

What he wanted first was to play Italians who were in the Mafia. The crime actors had been mostly Jewish: Edward G. Robinson, Alan King, Rod Steiger, Eli Wallach, Paul Muni, Jerry Orbach. De Niro and Pacino

357

took it over. They were the stars of an American industry of writers, editors, cameramen, directors, gofers, sighting men, soundmen, location men and casting agents who were all on the job and on the payroll because of the Mafia.

Now the whole Mafia industry is slipping on a large patch of black ice. Soon it will be totally gone.

"We had one wiseguy in the first season," Bill Clark, former executive producer of the now departed *NYPD Blue*, told me the other day. "That was all, because they just couldn't make it as characters for us. Their day was gone." Both of us remember when it wasn't. There was a hot late afternoon in July 1979 when Carmine Galante, the boss of the Bonanno Mob at the time, was shot dead at a picnic lunch in the backyard of Joe and Mary's Restaurant on Knickerbocker Avenue in Brooklyn. Bill Clark, then a homicide detective, was the first detective on the scene. He looked at Galante and grabbed the phone and called my office at the *New York Daily News*.

The great A.M., secretary, took the call. She was a Catholic schoolgirl who was a true daughter of the Mafia in the Bronx.

"Tell Jimmy that Galante is down on Knickerbocker Avenue," Clark said. Then he hung up. Inspectors were barging in to grab the phone and have it for themselves the rest of the day. There was no such thing as a cell phone.

Secretary A.M. sat on the call for one hour.

"People shouldn't know about a thing like this," she said.

Today, aside from grieving showmen, the only ones rooting for the mobsters to survive—or at least for keeping some of them around—are FBI agents assigned to the squads that chase Mafia gangsters across the hard streets of the city. Each family has a squad assigned to it. The squads are numbered, such as C-16 for the Colombo squad. Each agent is assigned to watch three soldiers and one capo in the family. The work is surveillance and interviews. Agents will interview a cabdriver or a mobster's sister. It doesn't matter. Just do the interview. Then they get to their desk and fill out FD-302 forms that get piled up in the office. They must do it in order to keep the FBI way of life in New York. They earn $70,000 or so a year, live in white suburbs and do no real heavy lifting on the job. After a five-hour day they go to a health club, then perhaps stop for a drink with other agents, and they always talk about what jobs they want when they retire. If, after interviewing, surveilling and paying stool pigeons, they do not come in with some Mafia dimwit whose arrest makes the news, they face doing true work for their country: antiterrorism detail in a wet alley in Amman, Jordan, or tent living in Afghanistan.

• • •

"What do you want?" Red Hot said. He is on First Avenue, in front of the great De Robertis espresso shop.

"We just want to talk to you," one of the two FBI agents said.

"You'll have to wait here until I get a lawyer to stop by," Red Hot said.

"We just wanted you to take a ride with us down to the office."

"The answer is no," Red Hot said.

"We just want to get fresh fingerprints. We haven't taken yours in a while."

"That's because I was in jail. And nothing happened to the prints you have. What are you trying to say, that they faded? They wore out?"

His friend Frankie "Biff" LoBritto cut in, "Red Hot, if you go with them, you won't come back. They'll make up a case in the car."

When the agents left, Red Hot said in a tired voice, "They'll be back. They're going to make up something and lock me up. Don't even worry about it."

Some nights later Red Hot was walking into De Robertis when he dropped dead on the sidewalk.

"He ruined the agents' schedules," Frankie Biff said. "They were going to put him away for sure without a case."

• • •

I will now take you into intensive care to observe the last of the Mafia.

The floor under them didn't even give a warning creak before opening up and causing everybody to tumble into the basement. This happened in March of this year when the United States Attorney in Brooklyn announced that, in the 1990s, two detectives, Louis Eppolito and Stephen Caracappa, had killed at least eight people for money paid by Anthony "Gaspipe" Casso, a demented killer and a boss of the Luchese Mob.

From out of the basement climbed Tony Cafe. Immediately the FBI visited him for the second time. It needed some help. If there were any shooters roaming around Brooklyn, Tony Cafe had to stop them. For if any bodies appeared on the streets or in the gutters of Brooklyn, perhaps the FBI agents, in absolutely desperate trouble for having Eppolito and Caracappa accused of shooting people practically in front of them, would be thrown like miscellaneous cargo onto transport planes bound for Kabul and Baghdad.

Politicians and the news media claimed the two detectives had committed the most treacherous and treasonous acts in the history of the police department. Would that it were true. Police officers serve wonderfully well and in these times do not even take a free cup of coffee. But there are isolated madmen who still pass the test and who have guns and could use money, and over the years the belief has been that many Mob shootings in Brooklyn have been done by cops.

Tony's favor to the FBI consisted of finding the only two Mob gunmen left in Brooklyn and ordering them to keep their fingers still.

There were other issues for the Mob. As ordered by the mandates of Christmas for Mafia captains, collections were taken up late in 2004 for traditional presents for the bosses of the five New York City Mafia families. The bosses now mainly were worried defendants and long-term prisoners. There was only one recognized boss, Joe Massino of the crime family named for the late big old mobster Joe Bonanno. I don't know what the other families did about Christmas collection money, for there was nobody worth a gift certificate.

The men in the Bonanno crime family raised $200,000 for Massino, the last boss. His liberty, however, was as shaky as a three-legged chair. He was in jail under the Gowanus Expressway in Brooklyn, held without bail while standing trial in federal court some blocks away. There were three murders and seven or eight prosecution witnesses of the type known as rats, including his wife's brother, "Good-Looking Sal" Vitale. Seated in the first row of the courtroom one afternoon was the wife, Josephine Massino. On the witness stand her brother was telling the court how Joe Massino's people came busting out of a closet and began firing away at three Bonanno mobsters he felt were dangerous dissidents.

Joe Massino sat at the defense table with a computer. He was good and overweight. He had a round, bland face and short white hair. The heritage of great suits ended at his plain blue suit and open-collar white shirt. Glasses were perched on his nose as his pudgy fingers touched the computer keyboard. I don't know what he was looking for. What he needed was an old movie of the battle of Dien Bien Phu, where he could identify closely with the French, who lost; the brother-in-law, Good-Looking Sal, would be shooting at him from the hillside. When Massino stopped typing, his hand went to the top of his head and, with thumb and forefinger, moved the glasses. This was the style of removing eyeglasses for all those in the underworld in Queens County.

On this day he noticed a reporter who had just had a death in the family. Massino mouthed, "I'm sorry." This was probably the last time we'd see someone in the Mafia showing the old-world class it was always reputed to have but rarely did.

Watching her brother destroy her husband, Mrs. Massino wailed softly, "This is the same as a death in my family. You don't know what I am going through."

"How could Sal do this? Joe taught him how to swim," Tony Rabito, from Massino's restaurant, the Casa Blanca, complained. Sal Vitale is on his way to prison for a whole lot of years.

Joe Massino always was a very good swimmer. He could swim from Coney Island all the way across a wide inlet to Breezy Point, on the ocean. He taught his wife's brother, Good-Looking Sal, how to swim. This is a very big thing; you teach a kid to swim so he never drowns. Joe Massino could do that. He taught all the strokes to Good-Looking Sal. A lot of good that did.

During the trial, from out of the past, from Jimmy Weston's on 54th Street and P.J. Clarke's on 55th, from Pep McGuire's on Queens Boulevard, from his *scungilli* restaurant on Second Avenue, came Tony Café, who is called that because he was always in saloons. He arrived at my building one night with a handwritten open letter from Joe Massino's daughter. She pointed out that Massino had been in prison and Good-Looking Sal Vitale had been running the Bonanno family when many of the murders were committed. While this was true, she was not able to cover all the murders. But she did try.

"I don't know why the government is so mad at Joe," Tony Café said. "He's a nice fat guy, likes food."

• • •

At this time Tony was a blessed unknown, but that would change.

Tony Café's previous experience was to make the mistake of rolling through the nights 25 years ago with the whole Mob and its new big hitter, Donnie Brasco.

"He is Joe DiMaggio!" everybody said one night at the old Pep McGuire's on Queens Boulevard.

When next seen, Brasco took the witness stand in room 103, federal court, Manhattan. Tony Café (his courtroom name Anthony Rabito) sat listening with his lawyer, Paul Rao.

Q: What is your name?
A: Joseph Pistone.
Q: What is your occupation?
A: I am a special agent for the Federal Bureau of Investigation.

Tony was sentenced to eight years. Rao told the judge that Tony had served two years in the artillery in Korea, that both his brothers had served and that he deserved something for this.

THE COURT: Mr. Rabito, is there anything you would like to add to what Mr. Rao has told us on your behalf?
DEFENDANT RABITO: Judge, I think I got a fair trial. There are a couple of things I don't like. I fought for that flag. I was in the Army. I believe in the press. I believe in you. You open up somebody's head, you find love in my head, but in some people you find the little Italian flag.

The judge took two years off the sentence, one for each year Tony spent in the service. He did six years at Otisville federal prison in upstate New York. I didn't see him when he came out and never heard about him, so I figured he wasn't up to much, which I thought was good because a second sentence would run a thousand years. In court for one thing or another over several years, I would take a look at the government's Mafia three-deep charts. The pictures of the Bonanno varsity players were mounted on cardboard. I never saw Tony's picture nor found his name in a news story, even if it was about guys at the bottom.

Bad things now happened in the courtroom. Joe Massino was convicted and faced sentences of more years than he had to give for his country.

Right away, in Washington, Attorney General John Ashcroft directed prosecutors in Brooklyn to start a capital punishment case against Massino for another murder. They find you guilty in federal court on any charge, from stealing a postage stamp to murder. If the federals said they wanted an execution case, Massino was going to die.

No, he wasn't. He called for a prosecutor and said he wanted to cooperate. He knows everybody and everything about the waning days of the Mafia. He is a traditional mobster. He eats until he can't fit at the table. He had a restaurant with the best pork *braciola* for miles. He flicks a thumb down and somebody dies. He has a wife and daughters and several girlfriends. He lives in Howard Beach, Queens, which had an overcrowding of big gangsters. His house was a few blocks from that of

John Gotti and also Vic Amuso, another boss. The first sounds of anger about Massino's turning came from Vito from Metropolitan Avenue. He had put up $1,500 for Massino's Christmas present.

"Joe is a rat. I don't give my money to rats," he said. "I want my money back."

"How are you going to get it from him? He's in jail," he was told.

"From his wife," he said.

"You go ask his wife."

When mobsters are reduced to fighting under the mistletoe, there is no reason for them to exist.

And now, in this court building at the same time, you saw the reason the Mafia must die. Four members of Local 15 of the Operating Engineers Union were in court to plead guilty to selling out workingmen. They work cranes, backhoes, bulldozers and hoists. They are proud and physical and, along with Local 40 of the Iron Workers, were about the first to walk up to the fiery mountains of the old World Trade Center, fierce, powerful, unafraid, and did all the gruesome heavy lifting for the next year. They were Irish, and their union heads admitted to being controlled by Mafia gangsters. Tom Robbins of *The Village Voice*, who seems to be the only reporter in the city who thinks labor is important, called the union the Mob's Engineers.

The government indicted 24 Mob guys in Brooklyn, including one Jackie DeRoss, who was listed as a union member but was recognized on the streets as an underboss in the shrinking Colombo family. His sons, John and Jamie, had union books and were placed on jobs where attendance might have been taken. In Manhattan another 18 mobsters in the union were indicted; one was Ernie Muscarella, a reputed boss in the Mob.

The one that bothered the most was Tom McGuire Jr., the business agent for the local. Everybody in labor knew his father, who had been business agent before him. Junior, out of Manhattan College, was unable to wail that he had to steal in order to make it in life. He was in the son game, as in "son of. . . ." If America is weaker at this time, blame the son game, the nepotism, as much as, in this case, the Mafia.

As Massino told agents stories that would end the Mafia, McGuire was in the same court building pleading guilty to a charge of selling union books. There were many other charges, including extorting $50,000 a year from a paving company and then giving an $80,000 bribe to the president of the International Union of Operating Engineers in order to become a vice president of the International. But selling the union books was the hideous crime. People beg, plead and implore for a union book. If your son can get a book, you can sleep all through the night; union jobs pay up to $45 an hour, and your son has a fine living for life. Tom McGuire Jr., now 60, pudgy and arrogant, sold union books for $12,000. He had a man running things for him, purportedly a Local 15 member, Anthony Polito. He took care of anything to do with organized crime. There were no-show jobs to be given to wiseguys or allowing work rules for health and safety to be ignored on any job where contractors had come up with money. Polito is in prison.

Reading through the government's indictment, I found that one of its legal standards for introducing evidence was based on *United States v. Brennan,* the defendant being "a former New York State Supreme Court justice who was charged with fixing four criminal cases," the indictment reads. "The government's witness, Anthony Bruno, served as a middleman."

I used to see Justice Brennan on Queens Boulevard, and we'd have a beer once in a while. He would walk across the street to the courthouse and fix narcotics cases and, I believe, a homicide for the Mafia. He was another one of those who come without a shred of shame. His was a complete character collapse that turned him into a cheap errand boy. Reading on, I found a page of testimony about the labor men pleading guilty in Brooklyn federal court to robbing their own.

Simultaneously Joe Massino sat in the jailhouse and bargained for his life, his $10 million in plunder and his two houses, one for his mother and the second, larger one for his wife and daughters. For life and possessions he would give up the entire underworld he had sworn to keep secret.

There are murders all over the place, and he must solve so many of them for the FBI. This is catastrophic for the guys on the street. Any mobsters nearing the end of their sentence will be hit with new charges and never see civilization again.

The publicity stool pigeons, "Sammy the Bull" Gravano being the latest, are illusions. Massino will end the Mafia. All the murders and dialogue that have been a large part of this nation's culture will disappear. All Mafia books and shows, *The Sopranos* foremost, will be based on nothing and therefore too unrealistic to make.

Massino put himself into a small room with desperation with the murder of one Gerlando Sciascia, who was known as George from Canada because he was from Canada. According to testimony, Sciascia and Massino killed three Bonanno family dissidents in 1984. Sciascia then thought he was as good as Massino. They found Sciascia and his ambitions in a lot in the Bronx. Entire flights of stool pigeons immediately went to the grand jury to put a gun into Massino's hand in premeditated murder. And now he talks.

Bosses must go first. There are five families, and they are supposed to have bosses, but most of them change every 48 hours. The Gambino family had John Gotti. The old man of the Gambino crew, Joe N. Gallo, told Gotti, "It took 100 years to put this together, and you're ruining it in six months."

This appears to be right. This old crime organization—which started in the narrow, wet alleys of Palermo and Lercara Friddi and other towns in Sicily, then rose out of the packed streets of the old downtown east side of New York, with names like Joe the Boss and Lucky Luciano, then with Al Capone coming out of Brooklyn and putting the Mafia into Chicago—had a murderous, larcenous hand everywhere. It weakened with time and the convictions of commission members in New York, but nothing matched the magnitude of what Gotti did to the Mafia. He had Paul Castellano hit in the midst of rush hour on the east side of Manhattan. It was brazen, and Gotti loved it. He failed to hear the sound of tank treads on Mulberry Street. They were bringing in an armored division to get him. They did.

He proudly put his son, Junior Gotti, in charge, and agents fell from the skies on him. He did six years and now is up for attempted murder, and he may not be seen for decades. The new head of the Gambino family was Nick Corozzo. He said he was exhausted from not working and needed a vacation. He flew to Miami and was on the beach for about half an hour when two men in subdued business suits walked along the beach toward him.

"So what's up, fellas?" Nick said.

"You are," they said. They displayed FBI cards. Nick the Boss went off the beach in handcuffs and then to court, where nobody wins. He is back on the street now but is a loud target.

The family named after Joe Profaci, an old-time Mafia boss, was shot up by an insurgency group, the Gallos, in the 1960s. Crazy Joe Gallo was shot dead at Umberto's Clam House on Mulberry Street. The news business loved the story. Joe Colombo took over. He believed he was a legitimate citizen. He invented the Italian-American Civil Rights League and ran a rally at Madison Square Garden during which his crowd shouted "Una, uno, uno," the old Roman cheer for Benito Mussolini. New York Post columnist Murray Kempton observed, "The entertainment was provided by Diahann Carroll and Sammy Davis Jr., two striking illustrations of pre-Norman Sicilians."

Colombo then ran an outdoor rally at Columbus Circle during which he was shot, later dying from his injuries. The killing gave the Mafia a bad name. The next boss was Carmine Persico Jr., known as Junior. He is in federal prison in Lompoc, California, for about the rest of his life. During a succession disagreement, one Vic Orena, pronounced "Vicarena," was convicted of mayhem and sentenced to two lifetimes and one 80-year sentence.

"Which one should I do first?" he asked Judge Jack Weinstein, who nodded to his clerk. "You name it," the clerk said.

"Put me down for the 80 years first," Orena said.

He went to Atlanta, and his lawyers entered a motion to throw everything out and let him come home. He was certain his motion would prevail over the whole government. He called Gina, his girl on Long Island, and told her, "Get my suits and have the tailor take them in. I've lost weight down here. Then go and get me some new shirts. I'm going to win this motion and make bail. We're going to Europe on the first day."

Orena was brought up by prison bus from Atlanta. His motion, a foot-high stack of paper, was on Weinstein's desk. The judge had studied it for some days.

Gina was in the courtroom with a suit for her now-slim love. The clerk called out "All rise," and Weinstein entered the courtroom. The door to the detention pens opened and a slim Vic Orena came in, his eyes glistening with hope.

"What is he doing here?" Weinstein asked. "He belongs in prison."

"He is here on his motion," the lawyer said.

"Motion denied," Weinstein said. "Marshal, take this man back to prison."

Vic Orena, his one and a half minutes of hope over, went through the door and onto a prison bus that would stop five or six times at dingy county jails on the way to Atlanta.

His love, Gina, with his suit folded neatly over her arms, went back to Long Island.

Vic Orena is still doing the 80-years part of his sentence; then all that remains for him to do is the two lifetimes.

There is now no real Colombo family boss whose name is worth typing.

• • •

The largest, fiercest and busiest family, the Genovese, had Vincent "the Chin" Gigante as boss—the boss in a bathrobe. Babbling in pajamas, robe and truck driver's cap, he staggered through the night on Sullivan

Street in Greenwich Village and entered the black-painted private club at number 206, where the guys played cards all night. The Chin, suddenly alert, sat down at the game. The cards were dealt. He picked up his hand and without looking at it called "Gin!" Money was pushed to him. Next he tired of picking up the cards. While they were being dealt, he called "Gin!" Always he got paid.

When in front of Judge Jack Weinstein in Brooklyn, he flopped around in his chair and mumbled for hours without stopping. My guess, and it is well educated, is that he was saying the Hail Mary, a lovely prayer that is short and can be repeated without end. Lawyers presented results of new tests they said showed the Chin had Alzheimer's. Weinstein, who reads science periodicals every morning, was greatly interested in the new test, the PET scan. "Congratulations. You are on the cutting edge of science," he told the lawyers. "But you omitted one important part of your test. In order to show that it is Alzheimer's, you need an autopsy."

Gigante shook and went to prison. The outfit was left with nothing.

Now there were five families in name and no bosses. At the start of 2005, in the midst of all the squalling over the Christmas money that went to Joe Massino's wife, federal agents came through Brooklyn like armed locusts and arrested 27 members of the Bonanno family.

It followed that one morning when Tony Café was at home in Brooklyn, where he lives with his 80-year-old sister, the last of four sisters, the first three dead of cancer, he heard knocking on the door downstairs. He looked out. He could see two agents, each holding up identification.

Tony Café sighed. "I'll be right down," he called. He threw his wallet to his sister.

When he got downstairs there were three agents, one of them a little Irish woman who did the talking.

"Are you going to lock me up?" Tony asked.

"No, but you're number one."

She made it official. A week before, an article by Jerry Capeci appeared in *New York* magazine and was first to mention that Tony Café—proper name Anthony Rabito—was suddenly an important figure. Capeci, whose *Gangland News* is on the Internet, is the authority on the Mafia to the extent that all those left in crime know that on Thursday, when Capeci's work comes out on the Net and in the afternoon's *New York Sun*, they will find out where they stand, if anybody is left to stand. Now on Tony's stoop, the FBI confirmed that Tony was number one in the Bonanno family. He was in shock as the agent, Kim something, told

THE END OF THE MOB

him, "We don't want any bodies in the street, we don't want witnesses bothered, and we don't want agents threatened."

"I live upstairs with my sister. I don't have any money or guns in the house," he said.

The agents sniffed and left.

And now Tony Café, who is allegedly the boss replacing the last boss of the Bonanno family, was sitting alone at the bar of Bamonte's Restaurant on Withers Street in Greenpoint, Brooklyn, his hair short and turning white, his voice like gravel pouring from a truck and his build entirely too wide.

Bamonte's appears to be an out-of-the-way place, but it is on Broadway in the world of New York people who know what they eat. It is a short drive across the Williamsburg Bridge. At lunchtime half the city seems to walk past the bar and into the dining room.

Here was police commissioner Ray Kelly coming in and shaking hands with everybody. At the bar Tony Café held out his hand, and Kelly grabbed it and then moved on. Later, in the gloaming, Tony Café sat in the empty restaurant and said, "The police commissioner shook my hand. How do you like it? He didn't know who I was. Nobody knows who I am. I don't know anybody else. They're all in jail. Once the top of the family turns like Joe did, nobody from the other families will talk to you."

"What was the worst thing to happen to the outfit?" he was asked.

"Gotti," he said slowly, "when he had the case against him with a woman prosecutor and he fixed the jury. That got the government mad. Nobody was safe after that. They got Gotti and then they came after everybody else. Because of him, all of a sudden I'm standing out here alone."